Hands-on Azure Functions with C#

Build Function as a Service (FaaS) Solutions

Ashirwad Satapathi
Abhishek Mishra

Apress®

Hands-on Azure Functions with C#: Build Function as a Service (FaaS) Solutions

Ashirwad Satapathi
Gajapati, Odisha, India

Abhishek Mishra
Mumbai, Maharashtra, India

ISBN-13 (pbk): 978-1-4842-7121-6
https://doi.org/10.1007/978-1-4842-7122-3

ISBN-13 (electronic): 978-1-4842-7122-3

Managing Director, Apress Media LLC: Welmoed Spahr
Acquisitions Editor: Smriti Srivastava
Development Editor: Laura Berendson
Coordinating Editor: Shrikant Vishwakarma

Cover designed by eStudioCalamar

Cover image designed by Pexels

Distributed to the book trade worldwide by Springer Science+Business Media LLC, 1 New York Plaza, Suite 4600, New York, NY 10004. Phone 1-800-SPRINGER, fax (201) 348-4505, e-mail orders-ny@springer-sbm.com, or visit www.springeronline.com. Apress Media, LLC is a California LLC and the sole member (owner) is Springer Science + Business Media Finance Inc (SSBM Finance Inc). SSBM Finance Inc is a **Delaware** corporation.

For information on translations, please e-mail booktranslations@springernature.com; for reprint, paperback, or audio rights, please e-mail bookpermissions@springernature.com, or visit www.apress.com/rights-permissions.

Apress titles may be purchased in bulk for academic, corporate, or promotional use. eBook versions and licenses are also available for most titles. For more information, reference our Print and eBook Bulk Sales web page at www.apress.com/bulk-sales.

Any source code or other supplementary material referenced by the author in this book is available to readers on GitHub via the book's product page, located at www.apress.com/978-1-4842-7121-6. For more detailed information, please visit www.apress.com/source-code.

Printed on acid-free paper

*This book is dedicated to my father, Mr. Upendra Satapathi,
and mother, Mrs. Sabita Panigrahi, for supporting me through
each and every phase of my life. Without your support I wouldn't
have been able to complete this book.*

—Ashirwad Satapathi

*This book is dedicated to my super dad, Mr. Balabhardra Mishra,
and loving mom, Mrs. Pragyan Mishra.*

—Abhishek Mishra

Table of Contents

About the Authors

Ashirwad Satapathi works as a software developer with a leading IT firm and has expertise in building scalable applications with .NET Core. He has a deep understanding of building full-stack applications using .NET Core along with Azure PaaS and serverless offerings. He is an active blogger in the C# Corner developer community. He was awarded the C# Corner MVP in September 2020 for his contributions to the developer community.

Abhishek Mishra is an architect with a leading multinational software company and has deep expertise in designing and building enterprise-grade intelligent Azure and .NET-based architectures. He is an expert in .NET full stack, Azure (PaaS, IaaS, serverless), infrastructure as code, Azure machine learning, intelligent Azure (Azure Bot Services and Cognitive Services), and robotics process automation. He has a rich 15+ years of experience working in top organizations in the industry. He loves blogging and is an active blogger in the C# Corner developer community. He was awarded the C# Corner MVP in December 2018, December 2019, and December 2020 for his contributions to the developer community.

About the Technical Reviewer

 **Carsten Thomsen** is primarily a back-end developer but works with smaller front-end bits as well. He has authored and reviewed a number of books and created numerous Microsoft Learning courses, all focused on software development. He works as a freelancer/contractor in various countries in Europe, using Azure, Visual Studio, Azure DevOps, and GitHub. He is an exceptional troubleshooter, asking the right questions in a most logical to least logical fashion; he also enjoys working in the areas of architecture, research, analysis, development, testing, and bug fixing. Carsten is a good communicator with great mentoring and team-lead skills and is skilled at researching and presenting new material.

About the Technical Reviewer

Acknowledgments

We would like to thank the Apress team for giving us the opportunity to work on this book. Also thanks to the technical reviewer and the editors for helping us deliver this manuscript.

Introduction

Azure Functions is a function as a service (FaaS) offering on the Azure Platform. In this book, you will explore Azure Functions in detail and learn how to work with Azure Functions using a practical and example-based approach that will help you grasp the subject with ease.

The book will start with the essential topics. You will learn how to set up the application development environment for Azure Functions. Then you will get example-based steps for building a serverless solution using a combination of bindings and triggers in C#. The book will then dive into areas that will help you learn how to create custom bindings, connect with various data sources, ingest telemetry data for Azure Functions into Application Insights, and learn various ways to deploy the functions to the Azure environment.

You will also explore advanced areas such as running Azure Functions in an Azure Kubernetes Service cluster using Kubernetes Event Driven Autoscaling (KEDA). You will learn the DevOps way of working with Azure Functions using Azure DevOps, as well as the best practices you should follow while using Azure Functions.

This book provides production-like scenarios and provides labs that will deliver the right set of hands-on experience. The practical approach in the book will help you gain deep proficiency in the subject.

This book is intended for experienced developers, cloud architects, and tech enthusiasts looking forward to building scalable and efficient serverless solutions using Azure Functions. Anyone having a prior experience with C# and knowing the Azure basics can use this book to start their journey in building serverless solutions with Azure Functions.

CHAPTER 1

Introduction to Azure Functions

Function as a service (FaaS) is getting more popular every day on all the major cloud platforms. With FaaS, you can build small chunks of code that run for a short time and host them on the FaaS cloud offering. You get billed for the time your function runs, and you do not need to bother about the hosting infrastructure and the scaling aspects.

Microsoft Azure provides Azure Functions as an FaaS offering. You build your function code and host it on Azure Functions, part of Azure App Service. The underlying platform takes care of all the hosting and scaling needs. Executing your code on Azure Functions is cost-effective most of the time compared to other hosting services available in the cloud.

In this chapter, you will get a basic understanding of Azure Functions that will help you grasp the next set of chapters with ease.

Structure of the Chapter

In this chapter, we will explore the following aspects of Azure Functions:

- Introduction to Azure Functions

- Introduction to serverless

- Azure WebJobs vs. Azure Functions

- Advantages and disadvantages of Azure Functions

- Hosting plan for Azure Functions

- Use cases for Azure Functions

1

© Ashirwad Satapathi and Abhishek Mishra 2021
A. Satapathi and A. Mishra, *Hands-on Azure Functions with C#*, https://doi.org/10.1007/978-1-4842-7122-3_1

Objectives

After studying this chapter, you will be able to do the following:

- Understand the fundamentals of serverless computing and Azure Functions

- Identify scenarios where you can use Azure Functions

Introduction to Azure Functions

Azure Functions is a serverless computing service on the Microsoft Azure platform and is based on the FaaS computing model. You need to build your code, spin up a function, and host your code on Azure Functions. The underlying cloud platform manages the hosting infrastructure and hosting software. You do not need to worry about the scaling aspects of your hosted code. The underlying Azure platform manages all the scaling aspects for your code running on Azure Functions. You get billed when the function is active and doing its work. You do not get billed whenever Azure Functions is idle.

Azure Functions hosts code that runs for a short time interval. However, you can increase the execution time by choosing an appropriate hosting plan for the function. A function gets invoked and starts running using triggers. Azure Functions supports a wide range of triggers. For example, a timer can trigger a function in predefined time intervals, a new message in the Queue Storage can trigger it, or a simple HTTP call can trigger a function. Azure Functions interacts with a wide range of services, such as Blob Storage, Table Storage, Queue Storage, Event Grid, Cosmos DB, Service Bus Queue, and many more, using bindings. You can declare both the triggers and the bindings declaratively without writing any code.

Azure Functions supports three runtime versions and an array of programming languages based on the runtime you select. 3.x is the newest runtime, and 1.x is the oldest runtime available. You can build your code using any of the programming languages in Table 1-1.

Table 1-1. *Azure Functions Runtimes and Supported Programming Languages*

Language	Runtime 1.*x*	Runtime 2.*x*	Runtime 3.*x*
C#	.NET 4.7	.NET Core 2.2	.NET Core 3.1
JavaScript	Node 6	Node 10 and 8	Node 12 and 10
F#	.NET 4.7	.NET Core 2.2	.NET Core 3.1
Java	Not supported	Java 8	Java 11 and 8
PowerShell	Not supported	PowerShell Core 6	PowerShell 7 and Core 6
Python	Not supported	Python 3.7 and 3.6	Python 3.8, 3.7, and 3.6
TypeScript	Not supported	Supported	Supported

A function executes whenever it gets invoked by a trigger. The function runs for a particular time interval and gets into an idle state. It wakes up whenever it gets invoked again by a trigger. The function takes some time to get warmed up and start executing whenever it gets triggered.

Introduction to Serverless

You start getting billed for cloud services as soon as you spin them up. You get billed even if you do not use the services. Also, you need to plan and configure the scaling strategy for these services. Some services give you the flexibility to set autoscaling, and for others, you need to set the scaling configuration manually. In either case, you end up providing the necessary settings so that the services can scale.

In the serverless cloud services case, you get billed when the service is running and is executing your hosted code, and you do not get billed when the service is idle and is not executing anything. You pay the cloud vendor on an actual consumption basis, which saves you money. The underlying platform manages all the scaling aspects of your application running inside the serverless service. You need not configure any scaling settings for the serverless service. The serverless services are intelligent enough to add new instances to handle incoming traffic and remove the additional instances when the incoming traffic decreases.

Serverless does not mean that the cloud services are not hosted on any server. You cannot run any code without a server. In the case of serverless services, you do not have control over the server hosting your code. You need to bring your code and host it on the serverless services without worrying about the underlying infrastructure. The cloud vendor manages the underlying infrastructure.

The following are a few of the popular serverless offerings provided by Microsoft Azure:

- Azure Functions

- Azure Logic Apps

- Azure Event Grid

- Serverless Azure Kubernetes Service

- Serverless SQL Database

Note In the case of serverless services and platform as a service (PaaS), you can get your code and host it on the service without managing the underlying infrastructure. The cloud vendor manages the infrastructure. However, you need to manage the scaling aspects in the case of PaaS. The cloud vendor manages the scaling for the serverless service. In the case of PaaS, you get billed as soon as you spin up the service. However, in a serverless service, you get billed when the service is active and executes your code.

Azure WebJobs vs. Azure Functions

You create a WebJobs job in an App Service Plan. A web job works as a background worker for your applications hosted on Azure App Service. For example, you can host an application that facilitates users to upload files in Azure Blob Storage. Usually, these files will be in a user-specific format. Before the application processes the files, the files should be transformed into a standard format that the application can understand. In such scenarios, you can create a web job in the same App Service Plan. This web job will run as a background worker, pick up the user-uploaded file, and transform it into a format that the application can understand. Web jobs can get triggered using a wide variety of triggers such as Azure Queue Storage, Cosmos DB, Azure Blob Storage, Azure Service Bus, Azure Event Hub, and many more. Azure WebJobs meets all the necessary developer needs for background processing. However, it shares the same App Service Plan as Azure App Service. Sharing the same App Service Plan means sharing the same underlying computing infrastructure. This sharing of the underlying infrastructure leads to performance bottlenecks at times.

Functions are not just meant to process background tasks. They can host business logic for applications as well. However, they are well suited to host code that runs for a short time interval. The functions are serverless offerings and scale independently. The underlying infrastructure manages all the scaling aspects for the function. Web jobs are tied to the Azure App Service instances and scale as and when the Azure App Service instance scales. You need to set scaling configurations explicitly for each web job. Functions can run as and when triggered using consumption-based plans, or they can run continuously using a Dedicated Plan. Web jobs are always tied to the App Service Plan that is a dedicated hosting plan. However, you are not charged separately for web jobs. They come with the App Service Plan. The Azure portal provides a browser-based editor that you can use to build, test, and deploy functions inside the Azure portal. This feature enhances the productivity of the developer. You can integrate Azure Functions with Azure Logic Apps with ease and build enterprise-grade solutions on Azure. Azure Functions supports various triggers such as HTTP WebHooks (GitHub/Slack) and Azure Event Grid that Azure WebJobs does not support.

Advantages and Disadvantages of Azure Functions

You build your code and host it on Azure Functions without worrying about the underlying hosting infrastructure. The cloud vendor takes care of all the hosting aspects such as the hosting server and the hosting software. As a developer, you get more time to focus on building your application code and working on its functionality. The underlying infrastructure scales your application without needing you to configure the scale settings. Also, you get billed when a function gets triggered and the code gets executed. This feature saves you money. You can use Azure Functions with Logic Apps and build truly enterprise-grade applications. In fact, you can integrate Azure Functions with a wide range of Azure services with ease. Azure Functions is well suited to execute code that runs for a short time interval. You can break down your application functionality into smaller chunks and host it on Azure Functions. This will help you bring in the single responsibility pattern at a more granular level. The single responsibility pattern states that a module or a component of a software program should perform a single functionality of the program. For example, in a calculator application, you should have a component or a module that performs an add operation, a different component that performs a subtract operation, and so on. The component of the application should be designed to perform a single functionality instead of doing everything for the application.

However, functions execute when they get triggered and move into an idle state when they do not do any work. Whenever a function is idle, it will take some time for the function to spring into action whenever triggered. This is because it will take some time for the underlying infrastructure to get warmed up and start executing the code. This phenomenon is referred to as a *cold-start* issue that you must consider while designing solutions for Azure Functions. At times, Azure Functions can cost more compared to hosting your code on Azure Web App. The underlying platform spins up new instances for Azure Functions whenever the load increases, and you do not have any control over the scaling aspect. Spinning more instances will increase the cost of your solution. You should predict the user concurrency for your application and have the right cost estimate for your solution. In addition, you should devise an appropriate strategy to control or manage the user concurrency using queues or some other techniques and control the Azure Functions' degree of scalability in your solution.

Hosting Plans for Azure Functions

The hosting plan helps you choose the underlying infrastructure specification for the function, define how the function should scale, and set up any other advanced features such as virtual network support that the function will need. You get billed based on the hosting plan you choose for Azure Functions. The following are the hosting plans supported by Azure Functions:

- Consumption Plan
- Premium Plan
- Dedicated Plan

Consumption Plan

In the Consumption Plan case, you do not have control over how the functions scale. The underlying Azure platform adds or removes instances on the fly based on the incoming traffic that the functions receive. You do not have any control over the underlying hosting infrastructure. You get billed when the function runs. This hosting plan is an ideal serverless plan, but you may encounter a cold-start phenomenon. It takes a while for the Azure Functions instances to warm up and spring into action whenever triggered. Your code does not run instantaneously when the function is triggered as it takes some time to wake up from its idle state. This phenomenon is referred to as the cold-start phenomenon. In the Consumption Plan case, the function can execute for a maximum of ten minutes and has a default value of five minutes. The default value of five minutes refers to the amount of time the function will execute before timing out without explicitly setting the timeout value for the function.

Premium Plan

In the Premium Plan case, you can have prewarmed Azure Functions instances that can spring into action and execute the code as soon the function is triggered. The prewarmed instances help you overcome the cold-start phenomenon. Like with the Consumption Plan, you do not have any control over how Azure Functions scales or over the underlying hosting infrastructure in the Premium Plan case. However, you get options to choose an SKU (EP1, EP2, or EP3) that will meet the memory and CPU requirements for your application. The underlying Azure platform manages all the scaling aspects. You get support for a virtual network. In the Premium Plan case, you can configure a function to run for a longer duration without timing out. By default, the function execution will time out after 30 minutes. Your functions can run continuously or nearly continuously.

Dedicated Plan

The Dedicated Plan in Azure Functions is the same as the App Service Plan in Azure WebApp. You get to choose from a wide range of SKUs and sizes compared to the Premium Plan that will meet the application's memory and CPU requirements. You can configure manual scaling or automatic scaling for your functions. You also get virtual network support. This hosting plan is best suited for long-running applications.

Use Cases for Azure Functions

The Azure Functions service can fit into any modern application patterns and use cases. The following are a few of the best-fit scenarios where you can use Azure Functions:

- You can build an *n*-tier application using Azure Functions. You can break the business and data access logic into smaller chunks and host each of these chunks in a function.

- You can run background processing jobs in Azure Functions.

- You can use Azure Functions and Durable Functions to build workflow-based applications where you can orchestrate each of the workflow steps using Azure Durable Functions and Azure Functions.

- You can use Azure Functions to build microservices-based applications. Each function can host a business service.

- You can use Azure Functions to build schedule-based applications that run on particular time intervals or during a particular time of day or month or year.

- You can build notification systems to trigger a function to notify an end user or a system based on conditions and events.

- You can use Azure Functions in Internet of Things (IoT) scenarios to implement functions to perform a business activity or process the ingested data and put it in storage or send it to the next set of processing.

- You can use Azure Functions and Azure Event Grid in event-driven scenarios where these functions can get triggered and perform a task.

Summary

In this chapter, you learned the basics of Azure Functions. You explored what Azure Functions is and discussed the concepts of serverless computing. You then learned about how Azure WebJobs is different from Azure Functions and then explored the advantages and disadvantages of using Azure Functions and the scenarios in which to use the service. You also learned about the different hosting plans available for Azure Functions.

The following are the key takeaways from this chapter:

- Azure Functions is a serverless computing service on the Microsoft Azure platform and is based on the FaaS computing model.

- You need to build your code, spin up a function, and host your code on Azure Functions. The underlying cloud platform manages the hosting infrastructure and hosting software.

- The underlying platform manages the scaling aspects for Azure Functions, and you need not do any scaling configurations.

- You get billed when a function executes, and you do not incur any cost when a function is idle.

- Azure Functions supports the Consumption, Premium, and Dedicated Plans.

- You can use Azure Functions in current scenarios like the Internet of Things, microservices, event-driven applications, and many more.

CHAPTER 2

Build Your First Azure Function

You can create a function for Azure Functions using a wide variety of options. If you are comfortable with command-line interfaces, then you can use Azure PowerShell or the Azure command-line interface (CLI). You can use an integrated development environment (IDE) or a code editor like Visual Studio IDE or Visual Studio Code. You can also use the Azure portal to create a function.

In the previous chapter, you learned the basics of the Azure Functions service and explored some of its essential concepts. In this chapter, you will explore various options available to create a function. You will learn how to set up the development prerequisites and explore how Azure Functions works under the hood.

Structure of the Chapter

In this chapter, we will explore the following topics:

- Creating a function using the Azure portal
- Creating a function locally using the command line
- Creating a function using Visual Studio Code
- Creating a function using Visual Studio

© Ashirwad Satapathi and Abhishek Mishra 2021
A. Satapathi and A. Mishra, *Hands-on Azure Functions with C#*, https://doi.org/10.1007/978-1-4842-7122-3_2

Objectives

After studying this chapter, you will be able to do the following:

- Understand the core tools of Azure Functions

- Create a function using various tooling options

Create Functions Using the Azure Portal

In this section, you'll create a function in the Azure portal. The Azure portal provides an in-portal editor to create and customize functions. To create a function in the Azure portal, you will first have to create a *function app*. Then you can create multiple functions inside the function app.

To create a function app, visit `https://portal.azure.com` and log in to the portal using your credentials (Figure 2-1).

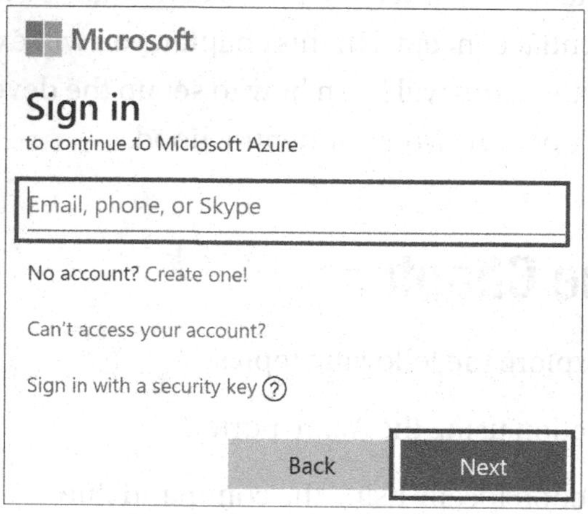

Figure 2-1. Sign in to the Azure portal

Once your login is successful, you will get redirected to the Azure portal dashboard. Type **function app** in the search bar and click the Function App option, as shown in Figure 2-2.

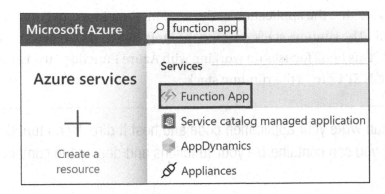

Figure 2-2. *Search for function app*

Now click the Create button, as shown in Figure 2-3, to create a new function app resource. If you have already created a function, you can see that listed in the portal.

Figure 2-3. *Create a new function app*

Now you will get redirected to a new screen, as shown in Figure 2-4, where you need to fill in the required fields for the Basics section. These details are crucial to create your function app in your subscription.

Select the subscription in which you want to get billed for this Azure function app. After you select the subscription, choose or create the resource group where you need to create the function app. Then provide a unique name for your function app. This name needs to be globally unique, and no other function app should have the same name across Azure.

You can host either the application code or a container in Azure Functions. Select the option Code. The runtime stack refers to the language in which you need to create your functions. This book focuses on working with Azure Functions using C#, so for this example select .NET Core as the runtime stack.

Note   You can write your application code and host it directly on function apps. Alternatively, you can containerize your functions and deploy the container in the function app.

Next, you need to select the version. We discussed the supported runtime stacks and supported language versions in Chapter 1; refer to Table 1-1. Finally, select the region where you need to create this function app. It is recommended that you select the nearest or same geographic region where the consuming services or applications are hosted.

Once you have filled in all the fields highlighted in Figure 2-4, click Next: Hosting to configure your function app's hosting plan–related configurations. Alternatively, you can click Review + Create to review your function configuration and then click Create to spin up the function app.

Note   An Azure function app consists of multiple functions. All functions of a function app share the same resources, configurations, language runtime, and pricing plan.

Create Function App

Select a subscription to manage deployed resources and costs. Use resource grou
all your resources.

Subscription * ⓘ

Resource Group * ⓘ   (New) HandsOnAzureFunction
                       Create new

Instance Details

Function App name *   HandsOnAzureFunction01

Publish *   ⦿ Code   ◯ Docker Container

Runtime stack *   .NET Core

Version *   3.1

Region *   East US

[Review + create]   [‹ Previous]   [Next : Hosting ›]

Figure 2-4. *Provide basic configuration details*

In the Hosting section, you need to fill in a few more details, as highlighted in Figure 2-5. You need to select an Azure storage account. You can select an existing storage account or create a new general-purpose Azure storage account. We need the storage account for monitoring and logging purposes. All the logs and metrics data gets stored in the storage account. The storage account also facilitates storing the code, as well as the binding configuration files for the functions created using the Consumption Plan or Premium Plan. So, we must have a storage account associated with a function to facilitate storing the code and the binding configuration files.

Note   If you delete the function app's storage account, configured while creating the function app, all the functions that are part of that function app will stop working.

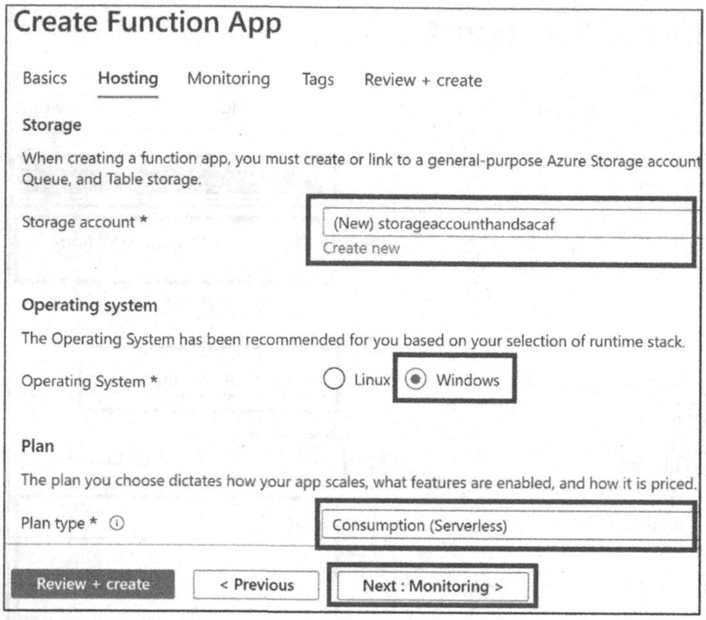

Figure 2-5. *Provide the hosting details*

After selecting the storage account, select the operating system for your function. Let's choose Windows as the operating system. Azure Functions on Linux does not support in-portal editing. We will use the in-portal editor to build the function code, so let's use Windows as the operating system. Finally, let's select the hosting plan. We can use the Consumption Plan, which is a pure serverless plan. To know more about the available hosting plans, refer to the "Hosting Plans for Azure Functions" section in Chapter 1. Once you have filled in the necessary details on this tab, click Next: Monitoring and navigate to the Monitoring tab.

It is highly recommended that you enable Application Insights for your Azure function app because it will help you to monitor and analyze Azure Functions. Click Yes to enable Application Insights and create a new insight. If you already have an insight provisioned, you can use that. Click Next: Tags, as shown in Figure 2-6.

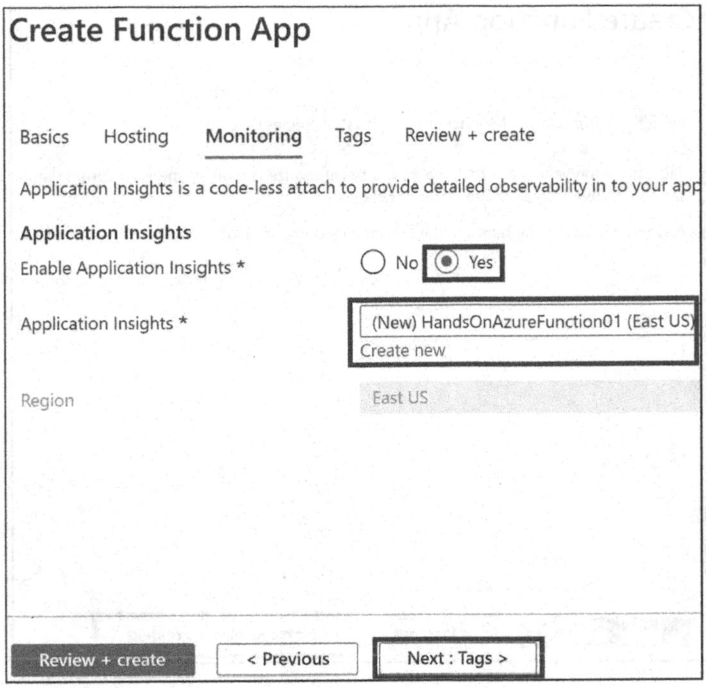

Figure 2-6. *Provide the monitoring details*

Tags help you categorize Azure resources. You can add tags along with tag values for Azure resources and use the tags to classify a group of resources. For example, you can create a tag called Production for all Azure resources running in production or a tag called Stage for all Azure resources running in the staging environment. In this case, you can consolidate the billing for all the Azure resources in the production or stage environment. Adding a tag is optional. However, it is a good practice to add a tag for your Azure resource. Now click Next: Review + create, as shown in Figure 2-7.

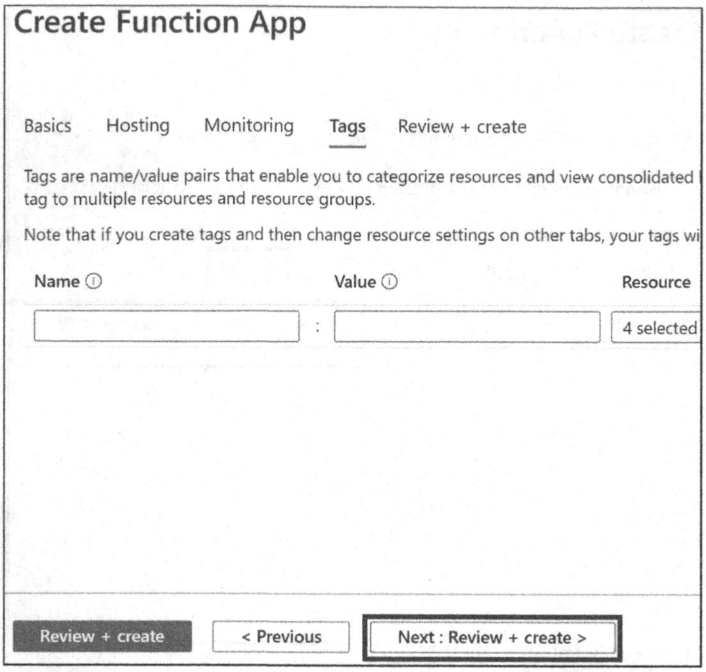

Figure 2-7. *Provide tags if you'd like*

On the Review + Create tab, you will see a summary of the configurations you have selected for the function app, as shown in Figure 2-8. To create the function app, click Create. Your configuration inputs for the function app get validated. If there are no validation issues, then the function app creation will start.

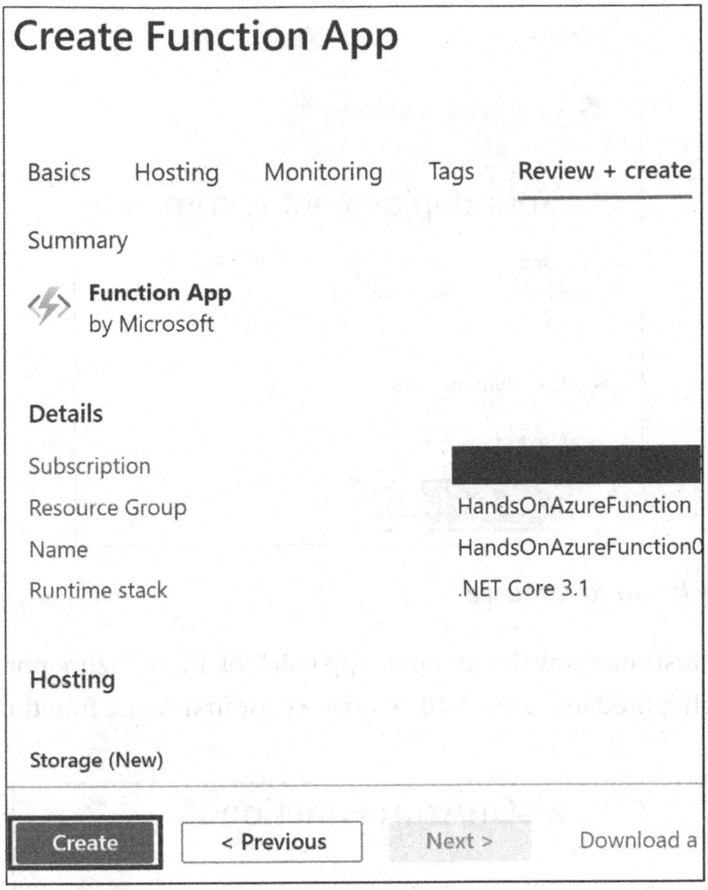

Create Function App

Basics   Hosting   Monitoring   Tags   **Review + create**

Summary

⟨⚡⟩   **Function App**
         by Microsoft

Details

Subscription

Resource Group   HandsOnAzureFunction

Name   HandsOnAzureFunction0

Runtime stack   .NET Core 3.1

Hosting

Storage (New)

| Create | < Previous | Next > | Download a |

Figure 2-8. *Click Create*

While your function app is deploying, you will be redirected to a screen like the one shown in Figure 2-9. Once the deployment of all your function app resources is completed, you will see an update. Click "Go to resource" to navigate to the function app.

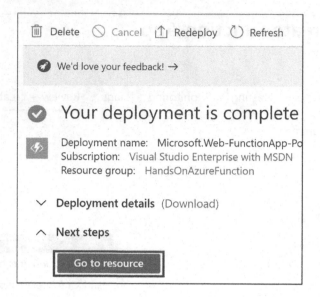

Figure 2-9. *Click "Go to resource"*

Figure 2-10 illustrates how the function app will look in the Azure portal. Click Functions, as highlighted in Figure 2-10, to create your first Azure function.

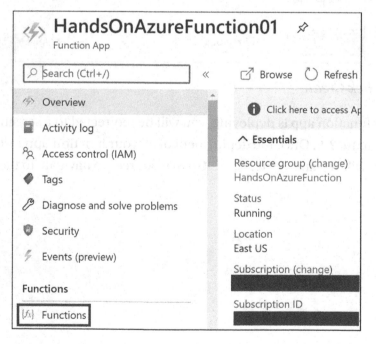

Figure 2-10. *Click Functions*

We need to add a function to the function app. Click Add, as shown in Figure 2-11.

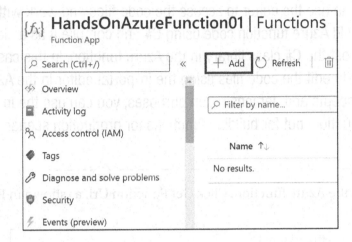

Figure 2-11. *Click Add*

Now let's select an HTTP trigger for the function and click Add, as shown in Figure 2-12.

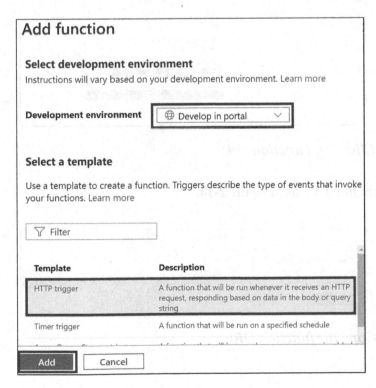

Figure 2-12. *Select "Function trigger" and click Add*

> **Note**   You can use the in-portal editor and build your Azure function code using a C# script. You can use the editor to access the code files and work with the code. You can also build Azure function code using C# and compile it as a class library. Then you can host the C# class library in the Azure function. In this case, you do not have a way to edit the code files using the in-portal editor in the Azure portal. For proof of concepts and demonstration purposes, you can use the in-portal editor to write your function, but for building functions for production scenarios, it is wise to use an IDE.

Now let's test the Azure function. Click Get Function Url, as shown in Figure 2-13.

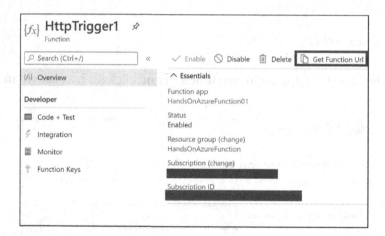

Figure 2-13. *Click Get Function Url*

Copy the function URL as in Figure 2-14.

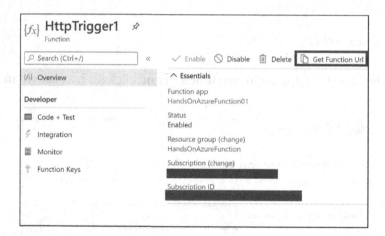

Figure 2-14. *Copy the function URL*

Open the browser, paste the URL into the address bar, add &name=ashirwad at the URL's end, and hit Enter. You should see a response like the one shown in Figure 2-15.

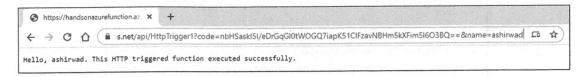

Figure 2-15. *Browse the function URL*

Create Functions Locally Using the Command Line

In the previous section, you learned how to create a function using the Azure portal. Now let's explore more interesting developer-focused ways to build a function using the command line.

To build functions in your local systems, you will need to install the Azure Functions core tool in your system and the SDKs or the language's runtime environment that you will use to develop your functions. The prerequisites for building a function using the command-line are listed here:

- Azure Function Core Tool

- .NET Core 3.1

You can install .NET Core version 3.1 from the following location: https://dotnet.microsoft.com/download/dotnet-core/3.1

To install the Azure Functions Core Tools, visit https://github.com/Azure/azure-Functions-core-tools and refer to the README.md for installation assistance. We are using the MSI installer from the repository to install it, as highlighted in Figure 2-16.

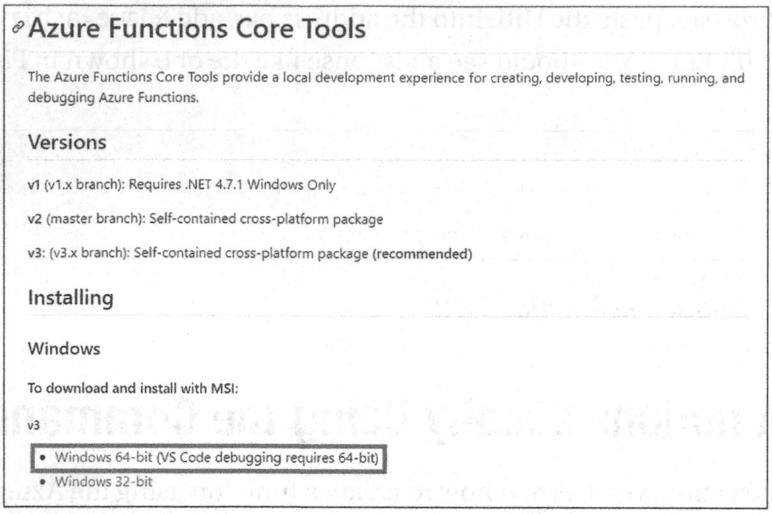

Figure 2-16. *Download the Azure Functions Core Tools*

Alternatively, you can use Node Package Manager to install the Azure Functions Core Tools. Open a command prompt and execute the command in Listing 2-1 to install the Azure Functions Core Tools using Node Package Manager.

Listing 2-1. Install the Azure Functions Core Tools Using Node Package Manager

```
npm install -g azure-Functions-core-tools
```

Note   The Azure Function Core Tools provide a set of command-line utilities and the Azure Functions runtime to build, develop, and deploy functions from the command line or a terminal.

Once you have installed the Azure Functions Core Tools, open a command prompt, and execute the command in Listing 2-2 to verify whether the Azure Functions Core Tools were successfully installed.

Listing 2-2. Verify the Azure Function Core Tools installation

```
func
```

If the installation is successful, you will see the version for the Azure Functions Core Tools, as illustrated in Figure 2-17.

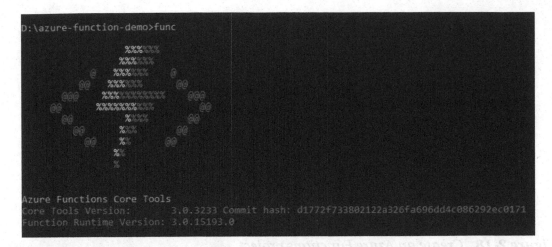

Figure 2-17. *Verify the installation for the Azure Functions Core Tools*

With the Azure Functions Core Tools installed, you are all set to build your Azure functions locally. To create a function project, execute the command in Listing 2-3 at the command prompt.

Listing 2-3. Create an Azure Functions Project

```
func init --worker-runtime dotnet
```

You can also execute the command in Listing 2-4 to create an Azure function project.

Listing 2-4. Create an Azure Function Project

```
func init
```

You will be prompted to choose the worker runtime for the function project. The worker runtime is the language you will use in this example to build your Azure functions. Provide the worker runtime and press Enter. The Azure Function Core Tools will create all essential function files for you, as illustrated in Figure 2-18. The files host. json and local.setting.json will get created for all the function projects irrespective of the worker runtime chosen.

```
D:\azure-function-demo func init --worker-runtime dotnet

Writing D:\azure-function-demo\.vscode\extensions.json

D:\azure-function-demo>dir
 Volume in drive D has no label.
 Volume Serial Number is B8EA-EAD9

 Directory of D:\azure-function-demo

01/26/2021  05:29 PM    <DIR>          .
01/26/2021  05:29 PM    <DIR>          ..
01/26/2021  05:29 PM             4,626 .gitignore
01/26/2021  05:29 PM    <DIR>          .vscode
01/26/2021  05:29 PM               692 azure-function-demo.csproj
01/26/2021  05:29 PM               231 host.json
01/26/2021  05:29 PM               163 local.settings.json
               4 File(s)          5,712 bytes
               3 Dir(s)  37,952,999,424 bytes free
```

Figure 2-18. *Create an Azure Functions project*

Let's understand the work of the host.json and local.settings.json files, which were created in the function project.

- The file host.json stores the runtime configuration values, which are later used by functions when running.

- The file local.settings.json stores the configuration values used by function apps when you are running them locally using the Azure Functions Runtime Tool.

Note   You can have functions created with multiple languages with version 1.*x* of the Azure Functions runtime. However, with versions 2.*x* and 3.*x*, all Azure functions in a function app should be written in the same language and the worker runtime selected while creating the function project.

Once you have created a function project, you need to create Azure functions inside it. To create an Azure function, you need to execute the command in Listing 2-5 in the command-line interface.

Listing 2-5. Create a Function inside the Azure Functions Project

```
func Function new --template HttpTrigger --name TestFunction
```

You provide the type of function trigger in the template parameter of the command along with the name parameter. This command creates a function named TestFunction that can be invoked using an HTTP trigger. After the command executes successfully, it will create a TestFunction.cs file, as shown in Figure 2-19. TestFunction.cs will have the same boilerplate code as in the Azure function that we created using the Azure portal.

```
D:\azure-function-demo>func function new --template HttpTrigger --name TestFunction
Use the up/down arrow keys to select a template:Function name: TestFunction

The function "TestFunction" was created successfully from the "HttpTrigger" template.

D:\azure-function-demo>dir
 Volume in drive D has no label.
 Volume Serial Number is B8EA-EAD9

 Directory of D:\azure-function-demo

01/26/2021  05:56 PM    <DIR>          .
01/26/2021  05:56 PM    <DIR>          ..
01/26/2021  05:29 PM             4,626 .gitignore
01/26/2021  05:29 PM    <DIR>          .vscode
01/26/2021  05:29 PM               692 azure-function-demo.csproj
01/26/2021  05:29 PM               231 host.json
01/26/2021  05:29 PM               163 local.settings.json
01/26/2021  05:56 PM             1,309 TestFunction.cs
               5 File(s)          7,021 bytes
               3 Dir(s)  37,952,978,944 bytes free
```

Figure 2-19. *Create a function inside an Azure Functions project*

Now let's run the Azure function using the Azure Functions Core Tools. To do so, execute the command in Listing 2-6.

Listing 2-6. Execute the Azure Function

```
func host start
```

This command restores all the NuGet packages and then builds the function project. Once the build finishes successfully, the Azure Functions runtime gets started and hosts all the functions in the Azure function app. It displays endpoints for all the hosted functions endpoint, as shown in Figure 2-20. If there is any build error, it will get displayed in the console.

```
D:\azure-function-demo>func host start
Microsoft (R) Build Engine version 16.8.3+39993bd9d for .NET
Copyright (C) Microsoft Corporation. All rights reserved.

  Determining projects to restore...
  Restored D:\azure-function-demo\azure-function-demo.csproj (in 31.22 sec).
  azure-function-demo -> D:\azure-function-demo\bin\output\azure-function-demo.dll

Build succeeded.
    0 Warning(s)
    0 Error(s)

Time Elapsed 00:01:09.06


Azure Functions Core Tools
Core Tools Version:       3.0.3233 Commit hash: d1772f733802122a326fa696dd4c086292ec0171
Function Runtime Version: 3.0.15193.0

[2021-01-26T12:29:59.072Z] Found D:\azure-function-demo\azure-function-demo.csproj. Using for user secrets file configuration.

Functions:

        TestFunction: [GET,POST] http://localhost:7071/api/TestFunction

For detailed output, run func with --verbose flag.
```

Figure 2-20. *Execute an Azure function*

Let's copy the endpoint/URL for the TestFunction, append the query string
?name=ashirwad to the URL, and then send a GET request to the function using the
command in Listing 2-7.

Listing 2-7. Send a GET Request to the Azure Function

```
curl –get http://localhost:7071/api/TestFunction?name=ashirwad
```

Figure 2-21 shows the response, and you can see that it is the same as what we got for
the function that we created earlier using the Azure portal.

```
D:\test>curl --get http://localhost:7071/api/TestFunction?name=ashirwad
Hello, ashirwad. This HTTP triggered function executed successfully.
```

Figure 2-21. *Response to CURL request*

Create Functions Using Visual Studio Code

In the previous sections, we discussed ways to develop Azure functions locally using a
command line with the Azure Function Core Tools.

In this section, we will look at ways to leverage the power of Visual Studio Code to build Azure functions and run them. To follow along with this section, here are the prerequisites:

- .NET Core 3.0 SDK

- VS Code

- Azure Functions Core Tools

Go to `https://code.visualstudio.com/download` to download the latest version of VS Code. You can visit `https://dotnet.microsoft.com/download/dotnet-core/3.1` to install .NET core version 3.1.

If you have not installed the Azure Functions Core Tools yet, you can refer to the section "Create Functions Locally Using the Command Line." After installing all the prerequisites mentioned, open Visual Studio Code and click Extensions to go to the extension marketplace and search for the C# extension for IntelliSense and debugging support. Type **C#** in the search bar and install Microsoft's extension, as shown in Figure 2-22. You are free to select any other extension for C# based on your preference.

Figure 2-22. *Install the C# extension*

After this, you need to install the Azure Functions extension from the extension marketplace to create a function project and deploy it to the Azure infrastructure. To install it, search for *azure function* in the search bar, select Azure Functions, and install it, as shown in Figure 2-23.

Figure 2-23. *Install the Azure Functions extension*

Now that you have installed the required dependencies, you are all set to build a function using Visual Studio Code. Click the Azure extension icon or press Ctrl+Alt+A to go to the Azure Functions extension to create your function project. Now click Create New Project or click the icon, as shown in Figure 2-24. You will be prompted to select the location. Then you will be required to select the language in which you will create all the functions of this function app. Since the objective of the book is to create functions using C#, let's select C# as the worker runtime of your function app.

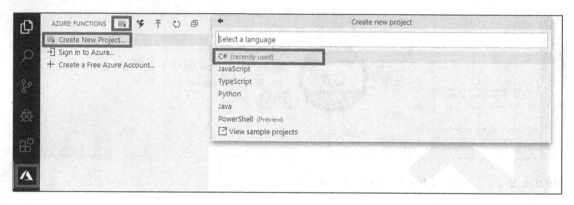

Figure 2-24. *Create a new function app project*

Then you will get prompted to select the template for the function. For this section's purpose, let's select the HttpTrigger template, as shown in Figure 2-25.

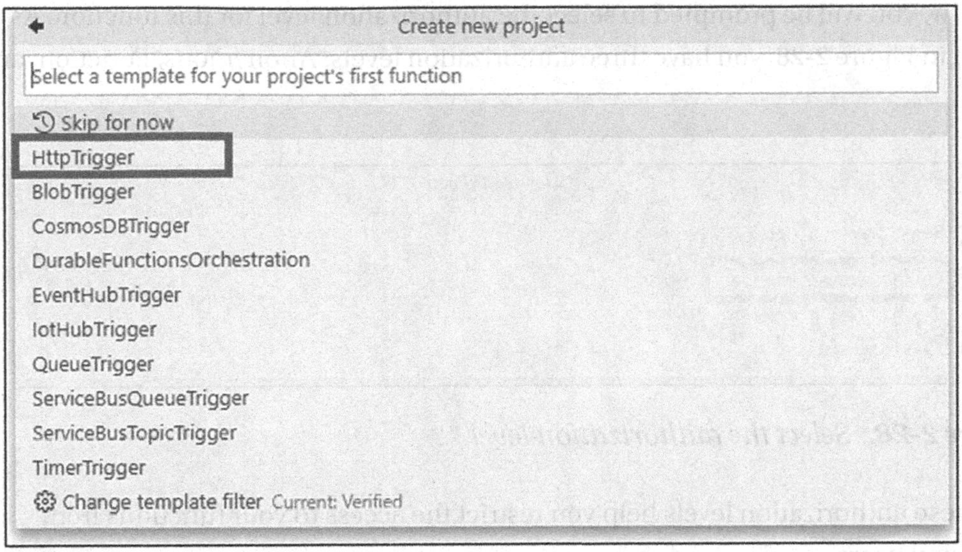

Figure 2-25. *Select HttpTrigger*

Next, you will be prompted to give your Azure function a name. Let's name it TestHttpFunction, as shown in Figure 2-26.

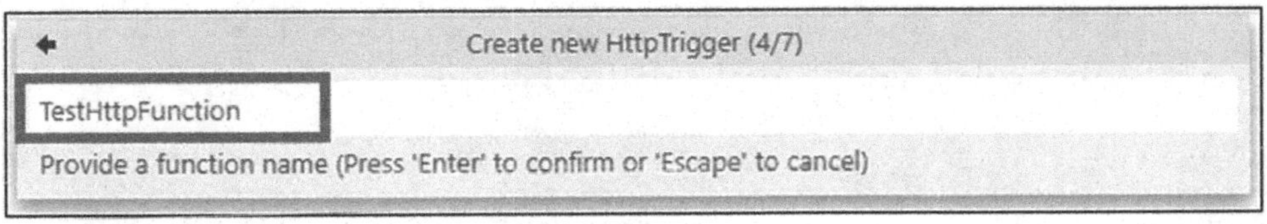

Figure 2-26. *Provide a name for the function*

Then you will be prompted to provide a namespace. Name the namespace of the function HandsOnAzureFunction.FunctionDemo, as shown in Figure 2-27.

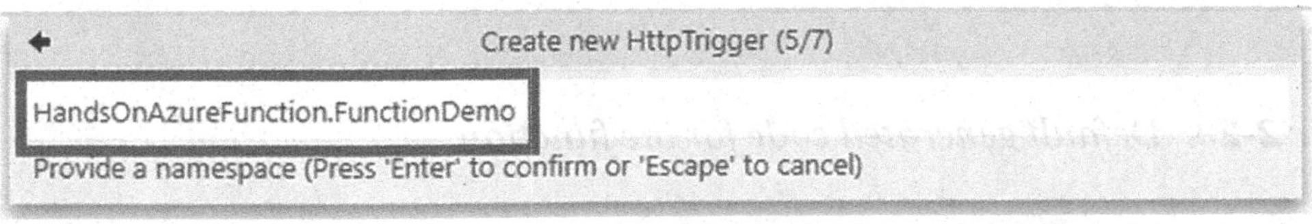

Figure 2-27. *Provide a namespace*

Now, you will be prompted to select the authorization level for this function. As shown in Figure 2-28, you have three authorization levels: Anonymous, Function, and Admin.

Figure 2-28. *Select the authorization level*

These authorization levels help you restrict the access to your functions from unwanted users.

Now Visual Studio Code has generated some boilerplate code for the HttpTriggered Azure function TestHttpFunction to display the value passed to it as a query string, as shown in Figure 2-29.

```
14    {
15        [FunctionName("TestHttpFunction")]
          0 references
16        public static async Task<IActionResult> Run(
17            [HttpTrigger(AuthorizationLevel.Anonymous, "get", "post", Route = null)] HttpRequest req
18            ILogger log)
19        {
20            log.LogInformation("C# HTTP trigger function processed a request.");
21
22            string name = req.Query["name"];
23
24            string requestBody = await new StreamReader(req.Body).ReadToEndAsync();
25            dynamic data = JsonConvert.DeserializeObject(requestBody);
26            name = name ?? data?.name;
27
28            string responseMessage = string.IsNullOrEmpty(name)
29                ? "This HTTP triggered function executed successfully. Pass a name in the query str
30                : $"Hello, {name}. This HTTP triggered function executed successfully.";
31
32            return new OkObjectResult(responseMessage);
33        }
34    }
35 }
```

Figure 2-29. *Default generated code for the function*

As you have created a function, let's run it and see what response you get. To run the function, press F5. This action will start the function runtime, host the function, and list all the functions present in the function project. This action internally runs the `func host start` command.

Once the function app is running, you will be able to see the URL to access the HttpTriggered function along with a few buttons to restart, disconnect, and other debugging options at the top, as shown in Figure 2-30.

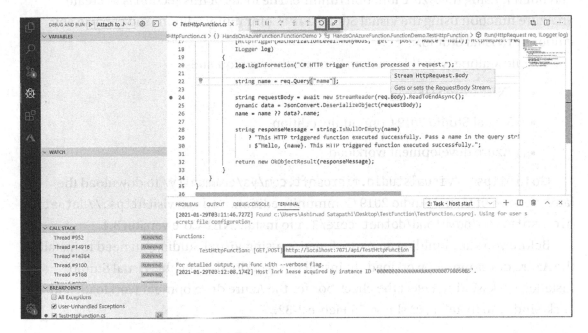

Figure 2-30. *Run the function app*

Copy the URL and append it with the query string ?name=ashirwad. Then send a request to the function by pasting the URL and the query string in the browser's address bar and press Enter. As shown in Figure 2-31, we get a similar response from our function previously obtained from the other sections.

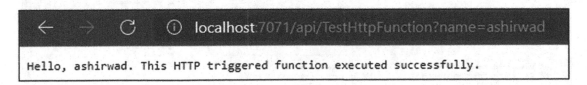

Figure 2-31. *Function output in the browser*

Create Functions Using Visual Studio

In the previous section, we discussed ways to create an Azure function using VS code and build it using the Azure function runtime. The focus of this section is to create an Azure function using the Visual Studio 2019 Community edition. You can use any editions of Visual Studio.

To follow along with this section, here are the prerequisites:

- .NET Core SDK

- Visual Studio 2019 Community edition

- Azure development workload

Go to `https://visualstudio.microsoft.com/vs/community/` to download the latest version of Visual Studio 2019 Community edition. You can visit `https://dotnet.microsoft.com/download/dotnet-core/3.1` to install .NET Core version 3.1.

Before you start building an Azure function using Visual Studio, you need to install the Azure development workload. To install this workload, open the Visual Studio installer, click Modify, select the check box for the Azure development workload, and click Modify to install it, as shown in Figure 2-32.

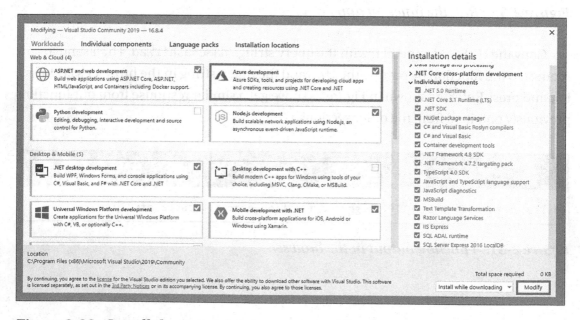

Figure 2-32. *Install the Azure development workload*

Once the installation of the workload is completed, open the Visual Studio 2019 Community edition and click "Create a new project," as shown in Figure 2-33.

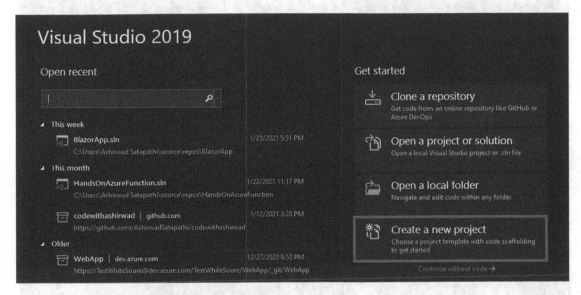

Figure 2-33. *Create a new project*

Now you can see all the available project templates in the window. Select the Azure Functions project template as shown in Figure 2-34 and click Next.

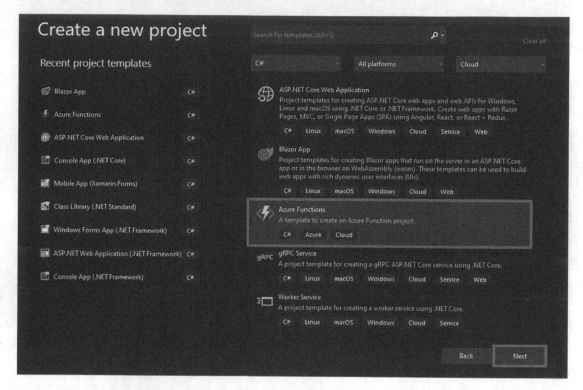

Figure 2-34. *Select the Azure Functions template*

You need to fill in the project details such as the project name, solution name, and source location. All of these are required fields. Once you fill in all of those fields, click Create, as shown in Figure 2-35.

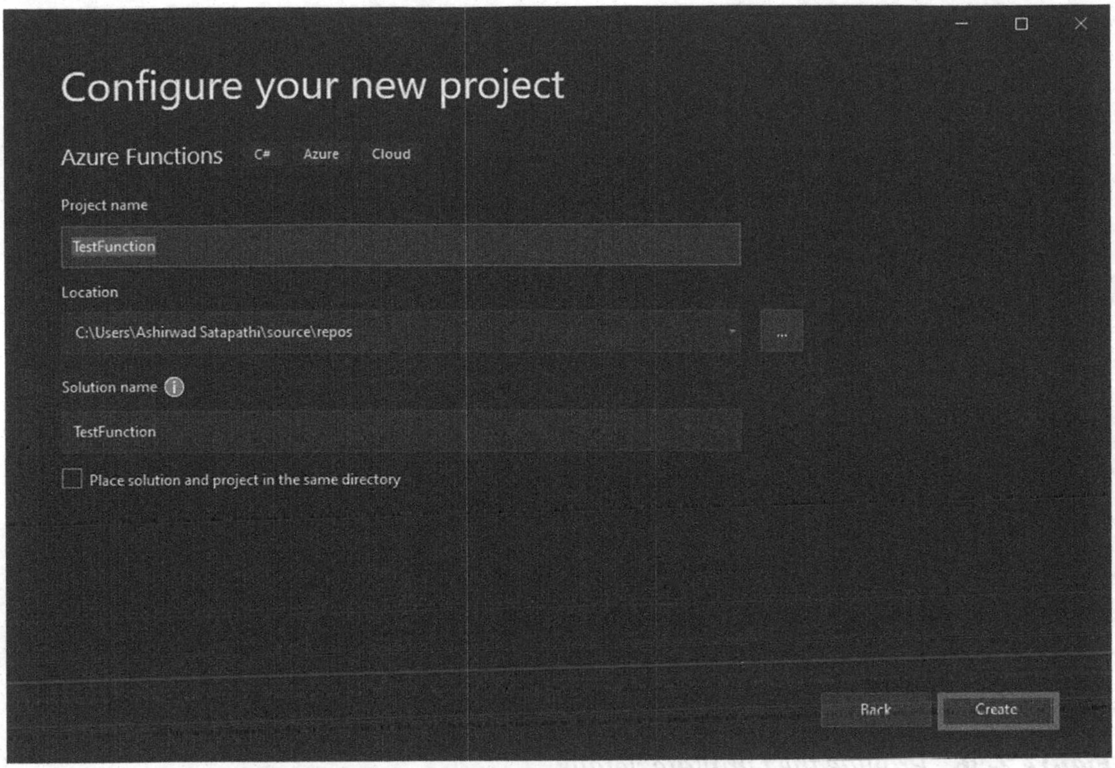

Figure 2-35. *Click Create*

Now select the runtime version, trigger type, storage account, and authorization level for your Azure function, as shown in Figure 2-36. You need to set the runtime version to Azure Function v3, the trigger type of the function to "Http trigger," the storage account to "Storage emulator," and the authentication level as Anonymous; then click Create.

Note   You can connect to your existing storage account in your Azure subscription instead of the storage emulator.

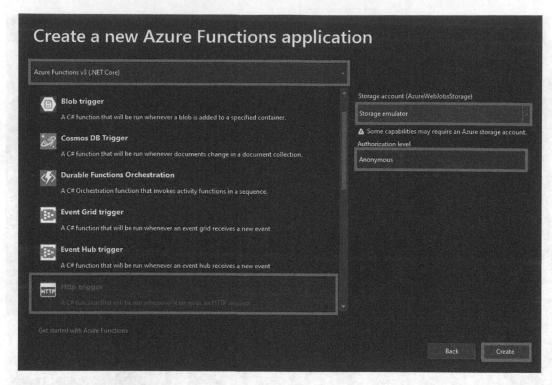

Figure 2-36. Provide the template details

Now Visual Studio will generate a function named **Function1** with some boilerplate code as in the case with functions created in other sections. To start the function app, click TestFunction, as highlighted in Figure 2-37.

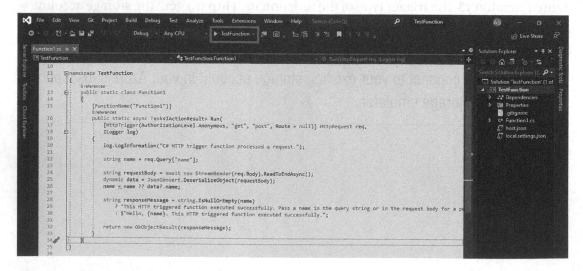

Figure 2-37. Execute the function

Note   By default, the first function in the function project gets named as Function1 in Visual Studio. But after the project gets created, you can change the function name by changing the `FunctionName` attribute's value.

Once you click TestFunction, it starts the storage emulator, starts the function runtime, and hosts all the functions present inside the function app.

This activity is similar to using the `func host start` utility of the Azure Functions Core Tools. Now you should be able to see the Azure Functions Runtime Tool.

Copy the URL route of the Azure function to send it a request. Paste the URL in the browser's address bar, append the query string `?name=ashirwad`, and then press Enter to send a request to the Azure function (Figure 2-38).

```
Azure Functions Core Tools
Core Tools Version:       3.0.3233 Commit hash: d1772f733802122a326fa696dd4c086292ec0171
Function Runtime Version: 3.0.15193.0

[2021-01-30T07:17:14.605Z] Found C:\Users\Ashirwad Satapathi\source\repos\TestFunction\TestFunction\TestFunction.csproj.
 Using for user secrets file configuration.

Functions:

        Function1: [GET,POST] http://localhost:7071/api/Function1

For detailed output, run func with --verbose flag.
[2021-01-30T07:17:39.268Z] Host lock lease acquired by instance ID '000000000000000000000000798050B5'.
```

Figure 2-38. *Copy the function endpoint*

Figure 2-39 shows the response from the Azure function. If you notice, the response will be the same as the functions we have created in other sections of this chapter.

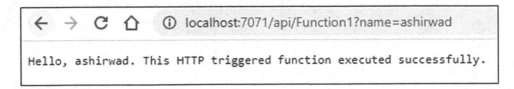

```
←  →  C  ⌂     ⓘ localhost:7071/api/Function1?name=ashirwad

Hello, ashirwad. This HTTP triggered function executed successfully.
```

Figure 2-39. *Function execution output*

Summary

In this chapter, you explored different ways to create Azure functions. We learned how to create Azure functions using the Azure portal. Then you learned how to create a function using a command-line tool like the Azure Functions Core Tools and code editors and integrated development environments like Visual Studio Code and Visual Studio.

The following are the key takeaways from this chapter:

- You can create a function using the Azure portal. You get an in-portal editor to write and work on the function code with ease.

- You can install the Azure Functions Core Tools and create Azure functions using a command-line interface. This option helps you automate the creation of Azure functions.

- You can install C# and the Azure Functions extension in Visual Studio Code and create functions using Visual Studio Code.

- You can install an Azure functions workload in Visual Studio and build Azure functions.

CHAPTER 3

What Are Triggers and Bindings?

Azure functions are serverless components. They remain in an idle state whenever they are not doing any work. You need to invoke Azure functions so that they can wake up and execute the hosted code. Triggers define how the functions run. You can invoke Azure functions using triggers, and they provide all the necessary input data or the input payload for the function. Your Azure functions need to send or receive data from other resources, such as the Queue Storage, Blob Storage, RabbitMQ, and many more, to Azure Functions. Bindings enable functions to interact with other services declaratively without needing to write any code.

In the previous chapter, you explored how to create functions using the various options available. In this chapter, you will explore what triggers and bindings are and how to configure them for functions.

Structure of the Chapter

In this chapter, you will explore the following aspects of triggers and bindings:

- Introduction to triggers and bindings
- Supported triggers and bindings
- Triggers and bindings use cases
- Implementing triggers and bindings for functions

© Ashirwad Satapathi and Abhishek Mishra 2021
A. Satapathi and A. Mishra, *Hands-on Azure Functions with C#*, https://doi.org/10.1007/978-1-4842-7122-3_3

Objectives

After studying this chapter, you will be able to do the following:

- Understand what triggers and bindings are and where to use them

- Create and use them with functions

Introduction to Triggers and Bindings

Triggers define how the functions execute. They wake up functions from their idle state and make them execute. Functions can be invoked from a wide range of services. These services invoke functions using triggers and pass on the input data as a payload to the functions. You can configure a single trigger for an Azure function.

Azure functions need to interact with other services such as Blob Storage, Cosmos DB, Kafka, and more to achieve business functionality. You can use bindings to facilitate data exchange between these services and Azure Functions. Functions can send data to these services or get data from these services as needed.

You do not need to write any code to implement triggers and bindings. You need to build declarative configurations to enable triggers and bindings and facilitate interaction with Azure Functions and other services. This functionality saves much programming effort for you. Otherwise, you would have to write a lot of code and handle complexities to facilitate these interactions. If you are creating a C# class library for an Azure function using the Visual Studio IDE or Visual Studio Code, you can decorate your function method with attributes to enable triggers and bindings. If you are using the Azure portal to create functions, you can modify the `function.json` file and add all the necessary configurations to enable triggers and bindings.

The following is an example of `function.json` that adds a Blob trigger to the Azure function created using the Azure portal. This configuration enables a Blob trigger for the function. The Azure function can accept binary data as input from the Azure Blob.

```
{
    "dataType": "binary",
    "type": "blobTrigger",
    "name": "blob",
    "direction": "in"
}
```

Triggers are unidirectional. Azure functions can receive data from triggers but cannot send back any data to the triggering service. Bindings are bidirectional. Functions can send data to a configured service or receive data from a configured service. The following are the available directions that you define for the bindings:

- in

- out

- inout

Figure 3-1 illustrates triggers and bindings with an Azure function. The function gets triggered whenever a message gets added in the Azure Service Bus Queue. Alternatively, you can use a Storage Account Queue instead of the Service Bus Queue. The message in the Service Bus Queue is passed to the Azure function as a trigger payload. Azure Queue Storage and Azure Cosmos DB are configured as bindings. Azure Cosmos DB supports bindings in both directions. Functions can send and receive data from Azure Cosmos DB. The Azure Service Bus Queue supports output binding. Azure Functions can send data to functions. Azure Functions processes the payload message and passes on the processed output to Azure Queue Storage and Azure Cosmos DB. It can also get data from Azure Cosmos DB if needed.

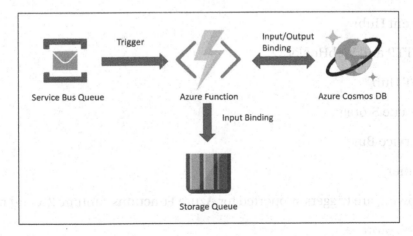

Figure 3-1. *Triggers and bindings with Azure Functions*

> **Note**   You can have a single trigger configured for an Azure function. Triggers support the input direction. You can have multiple bindings for an Azure function. In the case of bindings, you can have either input, output, or both directions.

Supported Triggers and Bindings

Triggers and bindings are crucial for Azure Functions. Actual business scenarios will need an Azure function to exchange data with other services. Azure Functions supports a wide range of triggers and bindings. The supported triggers and bindings depend on the runtime version of Azure Functions. If none of the supported bindings matches your requirements, you can create your custom binding using .NET and use it anywhere per your needs.

The following are triggers supported for Azure Functions runtime 1.*x*:

- Blob Storage

- Azure Cosmos DB

- Event Grid

- Event Hubs

- HTTP and WebHooks

- IoT Hub

- Queue Storage

- Service Bus

- Timer

The following are triggers supported for Azure Functions runtime 2.*x* and newer:

- Blob Storage

- Azure Cosmos DB

- Dapr

- Event Grid

- Event Hubs

- HTTP and WebHooks

- IoT Hub

- Kafka

- Queue Storage

- RabbitMQ

- Service Bus

- Timer

The following are the bindings supported along with the input and output directions supported for Azure Functions runtime 1.*x*:

- Blob Storage (input, output)

- Azure Cosmos DB (input, output)

- Event Grid (output)

- Event Hubs (output)

- HTTP and WebHooks (output)

- IoT Hub (output)

- Mobile Apps (input, output)

- Notification Hubs (output)

- Queue Storage (output)

- SendGrid (output)

- Service Bus (output)

- Table Storage (input, output)

- Twilio (output)

The following are the bindings supported along with the input and output directions supported for Azure Functions runtime 2.*x* and newer:

- Blob Storage (input, output)

- Azure Cosmos DB (input, output)

- Event Grid (output)

- Event Hubs (output)

- HTTP and WebHooks (output)

- IoT Hub (output)

- Queue Storage (output)

- SendGrid (output)

- Service Bus (output)

- Table Storage (input, output)

- Twilio (output)

- Dapr (input, output)

- Kafka (output)

- RabbitMQ (output)

- SignalR (input, output)

Note   You cannot create Kafka and RabbitMQ triggers using the Consumption Plan. Dapper triggers are applicable for the Azure Kubernetes Service.

Trigger and Binding Use Cases

Let's discuss some of the use cases for triggers and bindings. These use cases will give you a further understanding of how to use triggers and bindings in real-time production scenarios. The following are a few of the use cases:

- An Azure function gets triggered when a message arrives in a queue, and the processed message is put into another queue.

- A scheduled job picks up images for Blob Storage.

- An HTTP call invokes an Azure function to execute some business logic.

- An event grid can invoke an Azure function to send an email with event data.

- RabbitMQ triggers an Azure function that processes the message sent by RabbitMQ and puts the processed message in Azure Cosmos DB.

Use Case: An Azure function gets triggered when a message arrives in a queue, and the processed message is put into another queue

You can configure a Queue Storage trigger for an Azure function. Whenever a message arrives in the queue, it invokes the Azure function. Azure Functions starts executing the hosted code as soon as it gets invoked. The message in the queue is passed on to the Azure function as the input payload. The Azure function code processes the message and passes on the processed message to another Queue Storage. Figure 3-2 illustrates the use case.

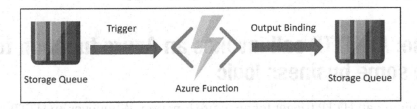

Figure 3-2. *Azure function triggered by a Queue Storage*

This use case will best fit in an e-commerce application scenario. Whenever a customer places an order, the order gets added to the Queue Storage as a message. As soon as an order message gets added in the Queue Storage, the function gets invoked. Azure Functions processes the order message and sends the processed message to another Queue Storage. Some other service can pick up this message for further processing.

Use Case: A scheduled job picks up images for Blob Storage at a particular time interval and then processes and stores them back in the Blob Storage

You can configure a timer-based trigger for your Azure function. You can set up particular time intervals when the timer should invoke the Azure function. Once the Azure function gets triggered by the timer, it can pick up a Blob from the Blob Storage, process the Blob, and put the processed Blob back in Azure Blob Storage. Figure 3-3 illustrates the use case.

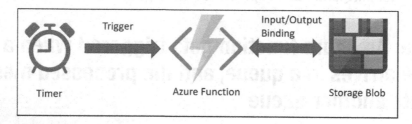

Figure 3-3. *Azure function triggered by a timer*

This use case is best when you need to perform a couple of background activities. For example, you can use this strategy for image processing systems where a user will upload an image to process in Blob Storage using a user interface. At particular time intervals in the day, the Azure function will run. It will pick up the image from Blob Storage, process it, and put the processed image back in Azure Blob Storage.

Use Case: An HTTP call invokes an Azure function to execute some business logic

You can configure an HTTP trigger for an Azure function. Whenever an HTTP request such as GET, PUT, POST, or DELETE invokes an Azure function, the Azure function executes the hosted code. The input payload for the HTTP trigger will consist of the data to process. Azure Functions processes the data and inserts the data into Azure Cosmos DB. Figure 3-4 illustrates the use case.

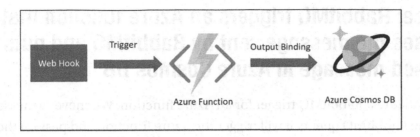

Figure 3-4. *Azure function triggered by an HTTP trigger*

This scenario best fits where you need to build a data access layer on top of the database. This data access layer will expose the data from the underlying database using REST APIs.

Use Case: An event grid can invoke an Azure function to send an email with event data

You can configure an event grid that can trigger an Azure function. An event subscriber such as Azure Service Bus Queue can subscribe to the event grid. Whenever a message arrives in the Azure Service Bus Queue, it will raise an event and send the message as event data to an Azure event grid topic. The event grid will invoke the function and send the message data as input payload. Azure Functions processes the message data and sends the message data to the concerned back-end team for further processing using an email sent by Send Grid. Figure 3-5 illustrates the use case.

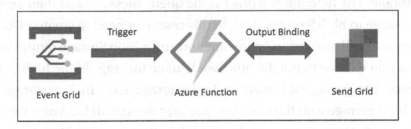

Figure 3-5. *Azure function triggered by event grid*

Use Case: RabbitMQ triggers an Azure function that processes the message sent by RabbitMQ and puts the processed message in Azure Cosmos DB

You can configure a RabbitMQ trigger for an Azure function. Whenever a message gets added to the RabbitMQ queue, it will trigger the Azure function and pass on the message as input payload to the Azure function. Azure Functions processes the message and puts the processed message in Azure Cosmos DB. Figure 3-6 illustrates the use case. You can build microservices-based applications using Azure Functions and RabbitMQ with ease.

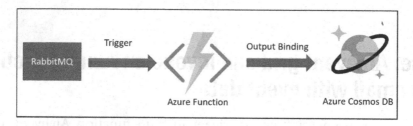

Figure 3-6. Azure function triggered by RabbitMQ

Implement Triggers and Bindings for Azure Functions

Let's create an Azure function that is invoked whenever a message is inserted into the Queue Storage. The function will process the queue message and then insert the processed message to Blob Storage. Here, in this case, you need to create a Queue Storage trigger that will invoke the Azure function and a Blob Storage output binding that the Azure function will use to put the processed queue message in the Blob Storage.

As a prerequisite, you should create an Azure storage account. The storage account should have Blob Storage with the container name `processeddata`. Azure Functions processes the queue message and puts it as a Blob in the `processeddata` container. The storage account should have a queue named `rawdata`. Whenever you put a message in the `rawdata` queue, it will invoke the Azure function.

Figure 3-7 illustrates the Blob Storage container created as a prerequisite.

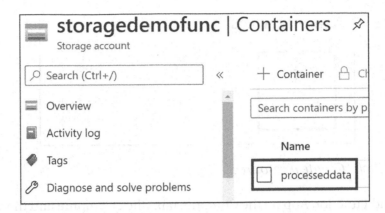

Figure 3-7. *Blob Storage Container for function output binding*

Figure 3-8 illustrates the Queue Storage that we should create as a prerequisite.

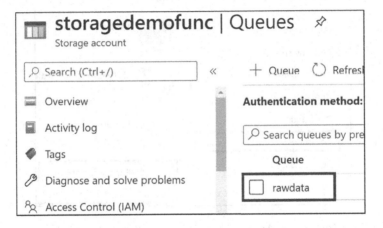

Figure 3-8. *Queue Storage for function trigger*

Now let's create an Azure function. Go to the Azure portal in your browser. Click "Create a resource," as shown in Figure 3-9.

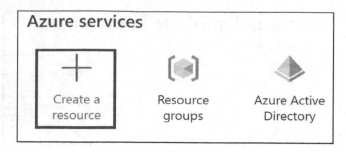

Figure 3-9. *Click "Create a resource"*

You will find Function App on the Compute tab. Click Compute and then click Function App, as in Figure 3-10.

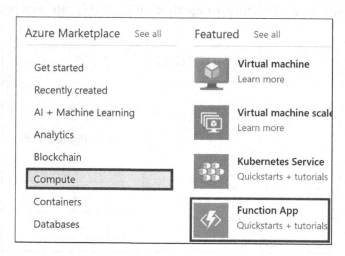

Figure 3-10. *Click Function App*

Provide the subscription, resource group, function app name, runtime stack, version, and region. Click "Review + create," as shown in Figure 3-11.

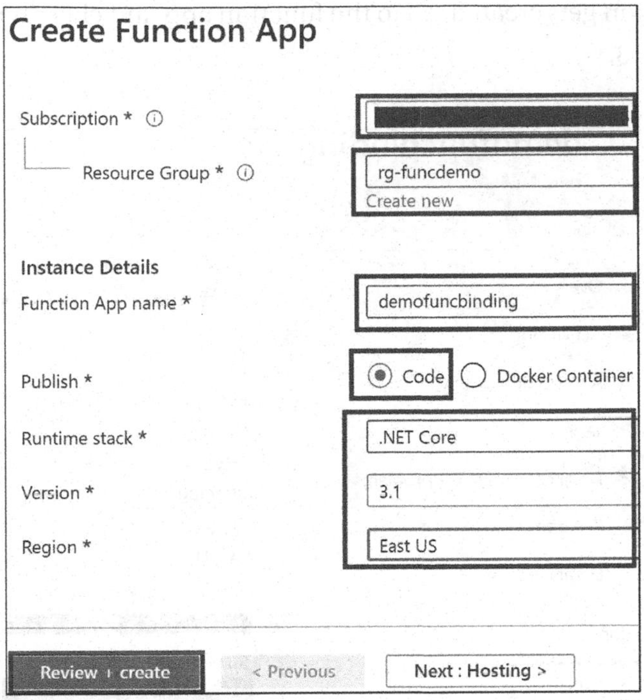

Create Function App

Subscription * ⓘ

└─── Resource Group * ⓘ
rg-funcdemo
Create new

Instance Details

Function App name *
demofuncbinding

Publish *
◉ Code   ○ Docker Container

Runtime stack *
.NET Core

Version *
3.1

Region *
East US

[Review + create]   [< Previous]   [Next : Hosting >]

Figure 3-11. *Click "Review + create"*

Click Create (see Figure 3-12). This action will spin up the Azure function.

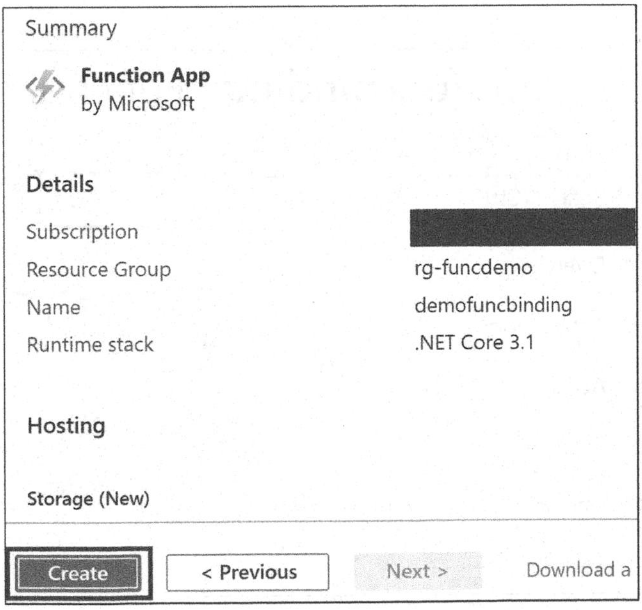

Summary

⚡ **Function App**
by Microsoft

Details

Subscription

Resource Group   rg-funcdemo
Name   demofuncbinding
Runtime stack   .NET Core 3.1

Hosting

Storage (New)

[Create]   [< Previous]   [Next >]   Download a

Figure 3-12. *Click Create*

Once the function gets created, go to the function app and click the Functions tab, as shown in Figure 3-13.

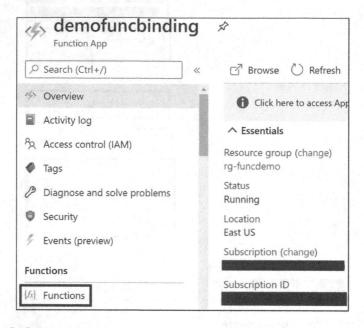

Figure 3-13. *Click Functions*

Now let's add a function. Click Add, as in Figure 3-14.

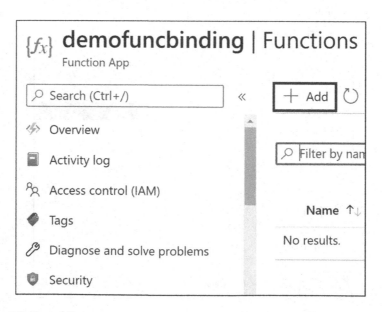

Figure 3-14. *Click Add*

Select "Azure Queue Storage trigger," as shown in Figure 3-15. You need to invoke the function whenever a message gets added to the queue.

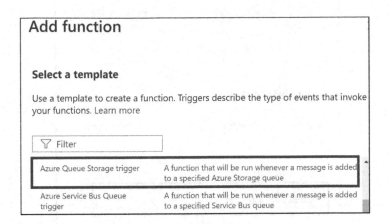

Figure 3-15. *Select "Azure Queue Storage trigger"*

Scroll down and provide a name for the trigger and the storage account queue name where you will add the messages to trigger the function, as in Figure 3-16. Click New and provide the storage account where you have created the queue.

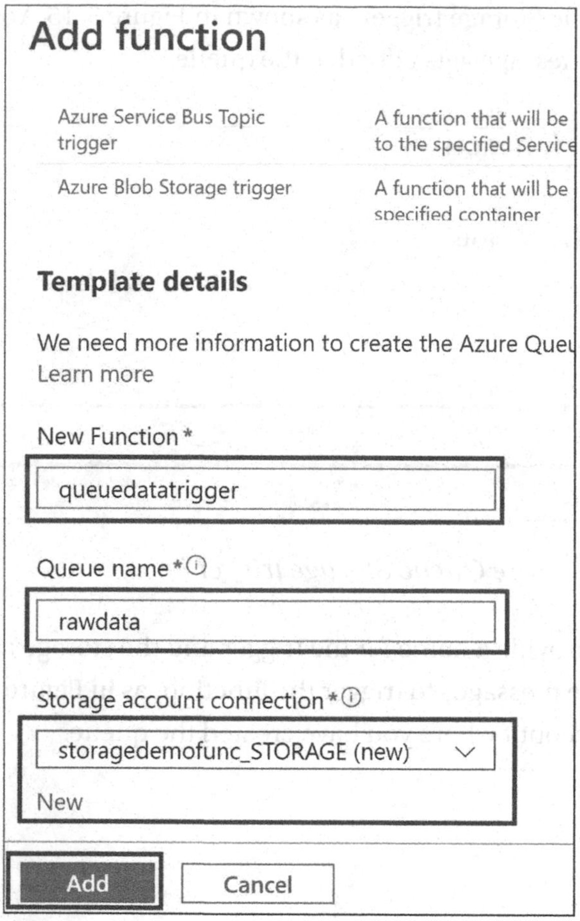

Add function

Azure Service Bus Topic trigger	A function that will be to the specified Service
Azure Blob Storage trigger	A function that will be specified container

Template details

We need more information to create the Azure Queu
Learn more

New Function *

> queuedatatrigger

Queue name * ⓘ

> rawdata

Storage account connection * ⓘ

> storagedemofunc_STORAGE (new)   ∨
> New

Add	Cancel

Figure 3-16. *Click Add*

Once the function gets created, click Integration, as shown in Figure 3-17. Here we can add the output binding for the Blob Storage.

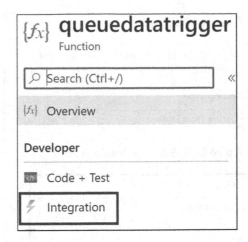

Figure 3-17. *Click Integration*

Click "Add output," as in Figure 3-18. Here you will add the output binding.

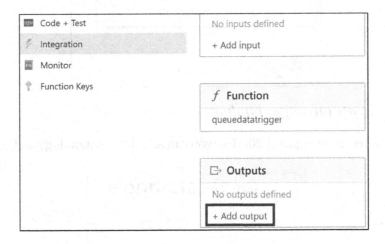

Figure 3-18. *Click "Add output"*

Provide a name for the output parameter used in the function code to access the Blob Storage. The parameter name specified here should match exactly with the out parameter in the Run method in the run.csx file. Provide a path for the Blob container. Here name the Blob file as a randomly generated GUID. The {rand-guid} expression helps you generate a random GUID for the Blob filename. Provide a storage account connection name. Click OK as in Figure 3-19.

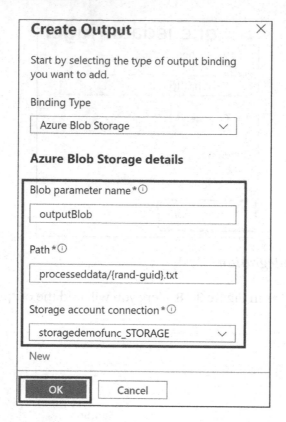

Figure 3-19. *Create an output binding*

Click Code + Test as in Figure 3-20. Here you can add the function logic in the run.csx file.

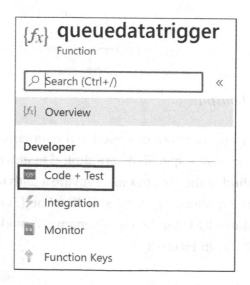

Figure 3-20. *Click Code + Test*

Add the logic shown in Listing 3-1 to the `run.csx` file. You can see that the `out` parameter named `outputBlob` matches precisely the name of the output Blob parameter name specified while creating the output binding, as shown earlier in Figure 3-19.

Listing 3-1. Function Code

```
using System;

public static void Run(string myQueueItem, out string outputBlob, ILogger log)
{
    log.LogInformation($"C# Queue trigger function processed:
    {myQueueItem}");

    //Process Message. We are just adding a "Processed Text" to the message
    myQueueItem = myQueueItem + "-Processed !!!!";

    //Storing Queue Message to Blob Storage
    outputBlob = myQueueItem;
}
```

Make sure you are adding this code to the `run.csx` file as in Figure 3-21 and save the file.

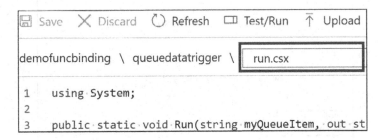

Figure 3-21. *Add the function logic to Code + Test*

Now let's test the Azure function. Navigate to the queue in the storage account and click "Add message," as shown in Figure 3-22.

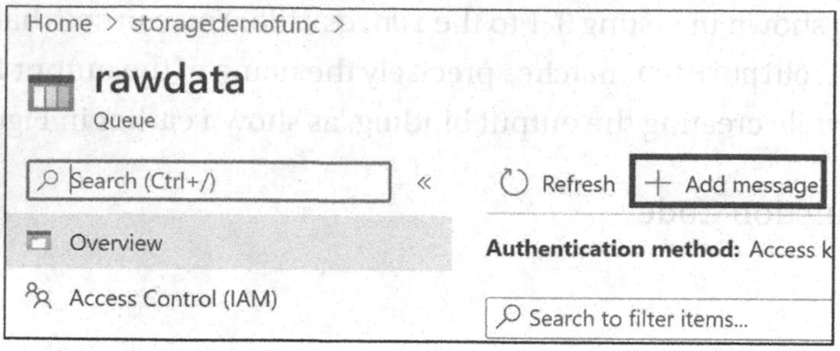

Figure 3-22. *Click "Add message" in the queue storage*

Add a message in the queue, as in Figure 3-23.

Figure 3-23. *Provide the message text and click OK*

Go to the Azure Blob container in the storage account. You can find the processed message here, as shown in Figure 3-24. You can download the file and verify the text in the file.

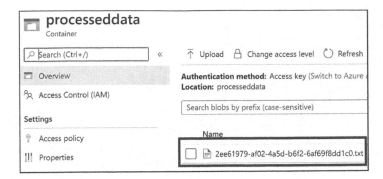

Figure 3-24. *Blob added in the Blob container*

Summary

In this chapter, you learned the basics of triggers and bindings. You explored the different triggers and bindings supported by functions. We then discussed a few of the use cases for triggers and bindings. You learned how to create and enable triggers and bindings for an Azure function using the Azure portal.

The following are the key takeaways from this chapter:

- Triggers define how the functions execute. They wake up functions from their idle state and make them execute.

- You can configure a single trigger for an Azure function.

- You can use bindings to facilitate data exchange between these services and functions.

- You can have multiple bindings configured for an Azure function.

- You do not need to write any code explicitly to implement triggers and bindings. You need to write declarative configurations to enable triggers and bindings and facilitate interaction with functions and other services.

- The supported triggers and bindings depend on the runtime version of functions. If none of the supported bindings matches your requirements, you can create your own custom binding using .NET and use it anywhere per your needs.

CHAPTER 4

OTP Mailer with Queue Storage Trigger and SendGrid Binding

You may encounter scenarios where you need to invoke Azure Functions whenever a Queue Storage gets a message. Azure Functions will pick the message from the Queue Storage and process it. You may also have scenarios where you have to execute an Azure function's business logic and then send an email from an Azure function. You can use a Queue Storage trigger to invoke an Azure function and a SendGrid output binding to send an email from Azure Functions. You can also use the Microsoft Graph API instead of SendGrid to send mails using Azure Functions.

In the previous chapter, you learned all about the essential concepts of triggers and bindings. You explored different types of triggers and bindings available for Azure Functions. Let's now explore how to implement a Queue Storage trigger and a SendGrid binding for Azure Functions and build a one-time password (OTP) mailer using SendGrid.

Structure of the Chapter

In this chapter, you will explore the following aspects of Queue Storage triggers and SendGrid bindings:

- Getting started with Queue Storage triggers and use cases

- Building a sample application using a Queue Storage trigger

- Getting started with a SendGrid output binding and use cases

© Ashirwad Satapathi and Abhishek Mishra 2021
A. Satapathi and A. Mishra, *Hands-on Azure Functions with C#*, https://doi.org/10.1007/978-1-4842-7122-3_4

- Building a sample application using a SendGrid output binding

- Creating an OTP mailer using a Queue Storage trigger and a SendGrid output binding

Objectives

After studying this chapter, you will be able to do the following:

- Implement a Queue Storage trigger for Azure Functions

- Implement a SendGrid output binding for Azure Functions

Getting Started with a Queue Storage Trigger and Use Cases

Queue Storage provides an excellent mechanism to decouple different application components and make your application architecture loosely coupled. Each decoupled application component can exchange data by sending messages to Queue Storage and receiving messages from Queue Storage. You can break your application code into smaller chunks and host them in functions, and each of these smaller chunks of code running inside a function performs a specific task. These functions can communicate among themselves using Queue Storage. An Azure function can process data and send it to Queue Storage. Queue Storage can then invoke another Azure function that can pick up the Queue Storage data and process it. The Queue Storage trigger can invoke an Azure function whenever it gets a message and passes on the Azure function message.

The following are a few of the example scenarios where you can use a Queue Storage trigger:

- The customer can place an order for a purchase using the user interface. The user interface invokes a business service that places the order as a Queue Storage message. The Queue Storage trigger invokes an Azure function that picks the order and validates the stock availability for the item that the customer has ordered.

- A customer can provide feedback for the service used in a user interface. The user interface invokes a service that puts the feedback in Queue Storage. An Azure function gets triggered by Queue Storage, analyzes the customer feedback, and responds to customers with corrective actions if needed.

- An Internet of Things (IoT) application can monitor a factory floor's temperature and ingest the temperature into Queue Storage in an event the temperature rises beyond a prescribed limit. Queue Storage will then invoke an Azure function to analyze the temperature data and invoke automation or take corrective action to cool down the factory floor.

Build a Sample Application Using a Queue Storage Trigger

Let's implement a Queue Storage trigger for an Azure function. As a prerequisite, let's create a storage account and a Queue Storage to add a message. As soon as a message gets added to the queue, it will trigger the function.

Go to the Azure portal and click "Create a resource," as shown in Figure 4-1.

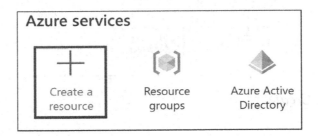

Figure 4-1. *Create a resource*

Search for *storage account* and click the search result "Storage account," as shown in Figure 4-2.

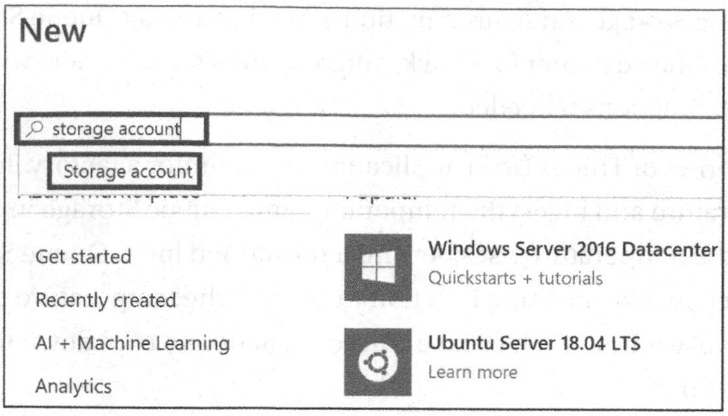

Figure 4-2. *Select "Storage account"*

Click Create, as shown in Figure 4-3.

Figure 4-3. *Click Create*

Select your Azure subscription, the resource group, and the location where you need to create the storage account. Provide a name for the storage account. Click "Review + create," as shown in Figure 4-4.

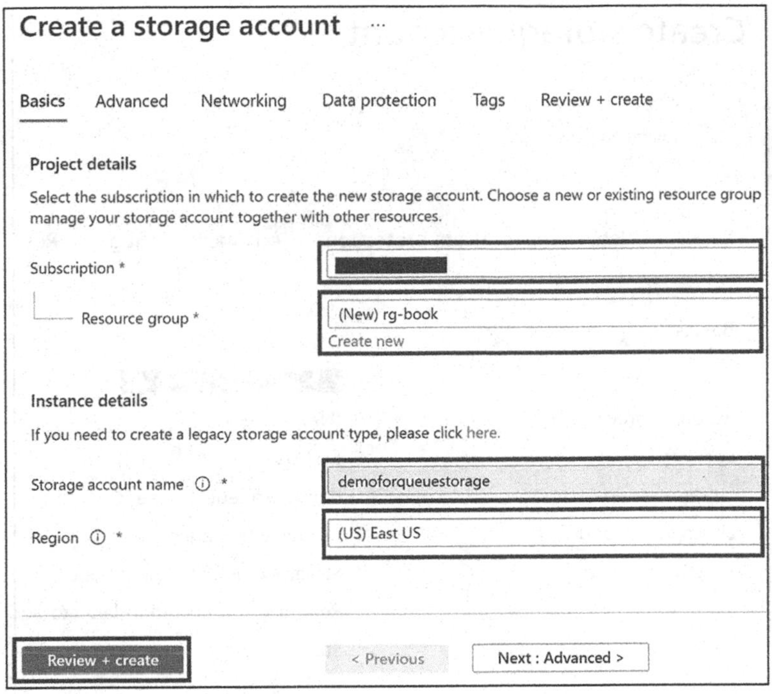

Figure 4-4. *Click "Review + create"*

A validation check will be done for the configuration values provided for the storage account, and if the check succeeds, you will get a message on the screen that the validation passed. Once the validation passes, click Create, as shown in Figure 4-5. This action will create the storage account.

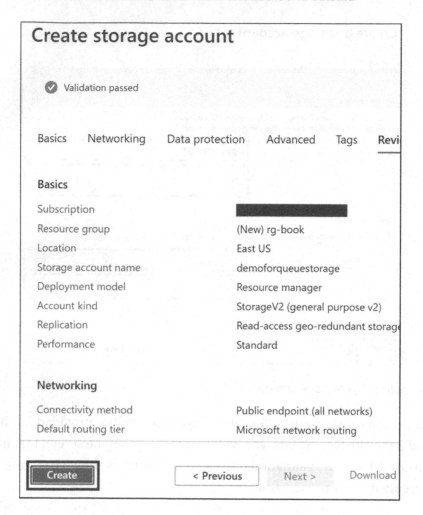

Figure 4-5. Click Create

Go to the storage account once it gets created and then search for *Queue* in the search box. Click Queues, as shown in Figure 4-6.

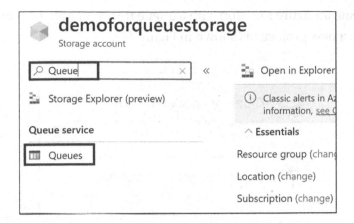

Figure 4-6. *Click Queues*

To create a queue in the storage account, click + Queue, as shown in Figure 4-7.

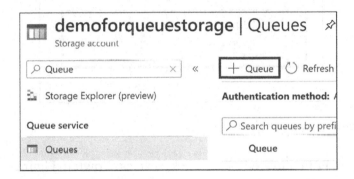

Figure 4-7. *Add a queue*

Provide a name for the queue and click OK, as shown in Figure 4-8.

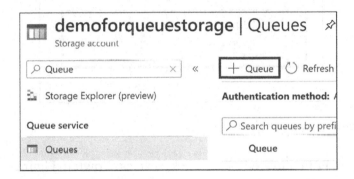

Figure 4-8. *Click OK*

Now let's create an Azure function with a queue trigger enabled. Open Visual Studio and click "Create a new project," as shown in Figure 4-9.

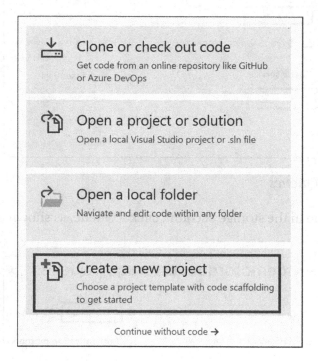

Figure 4-9. *Create a new project*

Select the Azure Functions template. Click Next, as shown in Figure 4-10.

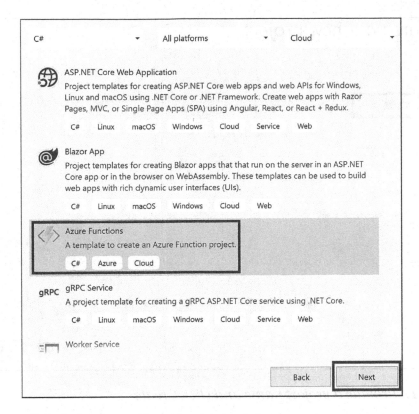

Figure 4-10. *Select the Azure Functions template*

Provide a name for the project and click Create, as shown in Figure 4-11.

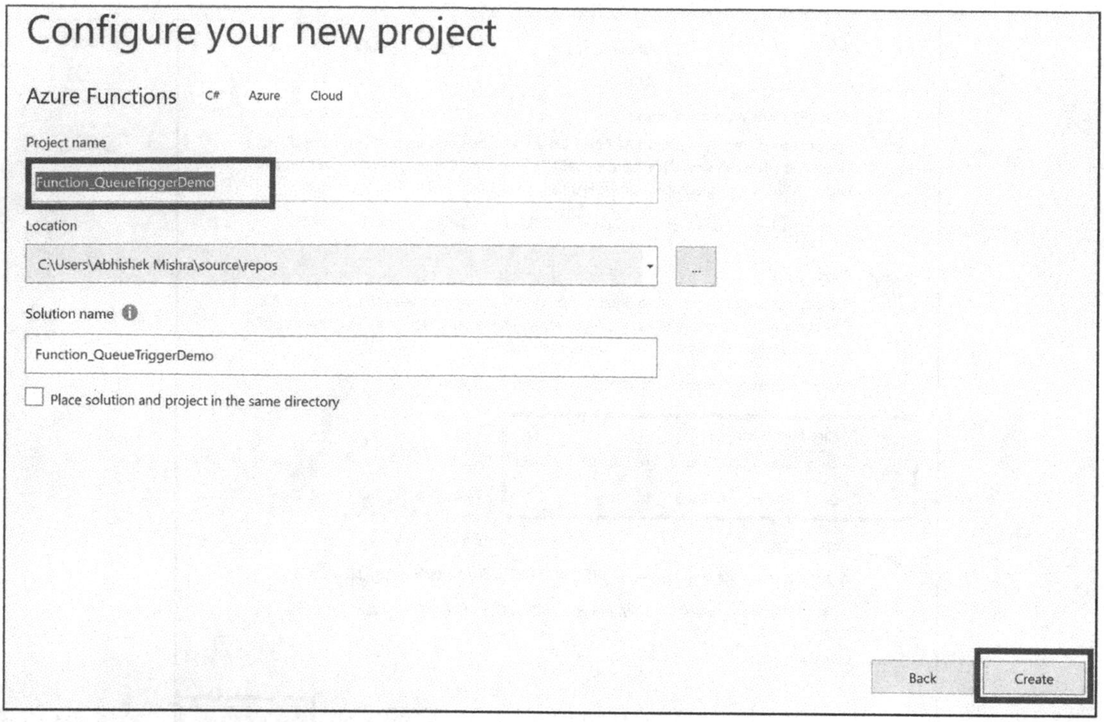

Figure 4-11. *Provide a project name and click Create*

Select "Queue trigger" and provide the connection string name for the queue and the queue's name that will trigger the function. Provide **demoforqueuestorage** for the name of the queue that you created earlier in this chapter. You need to add a key for this connection string in the `local.settings.json` file in the solution and provide the connection string for the key in the `local.settings.json` file. Click Create. A solution with the queue-triggered function gets created. See Figure 4-12.

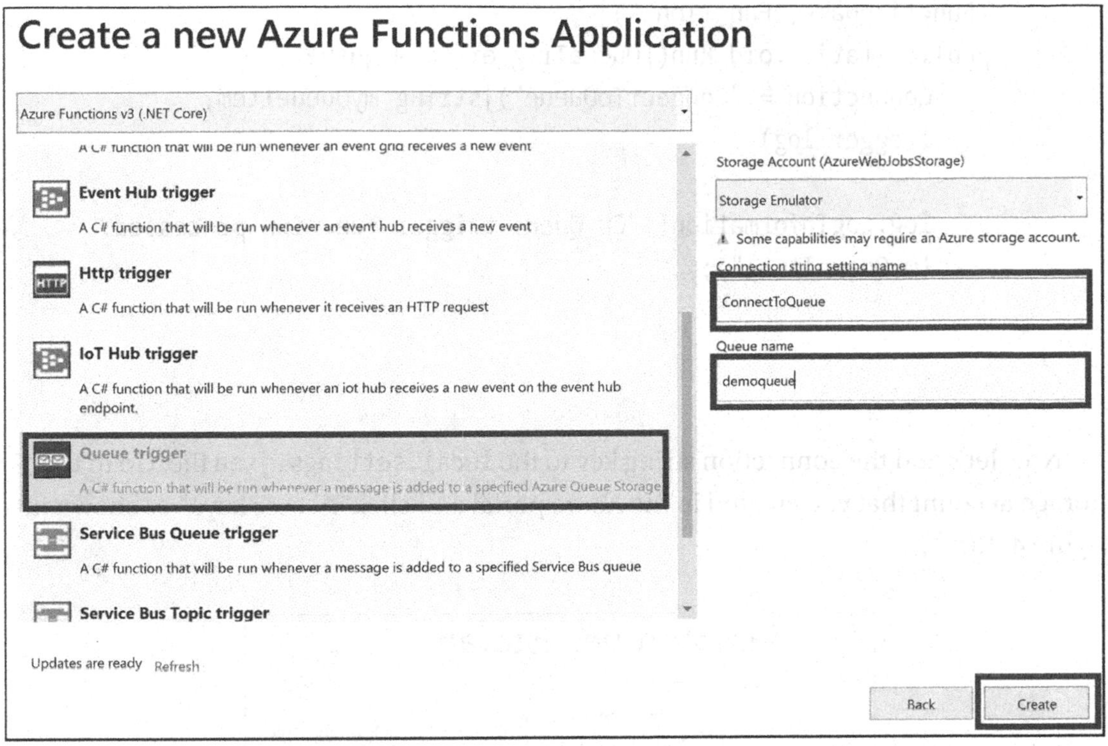

Figure 4-12. *Select "Queue trigger"*

Listing 4-1 shows the code for the Function1.cs file. In the Run method, a method parameter called myQueueItem gets created. The myQueueItem parameter is decorated with the QueueTrigger attribute. The QueueTrigger attribute takes the storage account's queue name that can trigger this function and the connection string's name that is in the local.settings.json file.

Listing 4-1. Function1.cs Code

```
using System;
using Microsoft.Azure.WebJobs;
using Microsoft.Azure.WebJobs.Host;
using Microsoft.Extensions.Logging;

namespace Function_QueueTriggerDemo
{
    public static class Function1
    {
```

```
[FunctionName("Function1")]
public static void Run([QueueTrigger("demoqueue",
    Connection = "ConnectToQueue")]string myQueueItem,
    ILogger log)
{
    log.LogInformation($"C# Queue trigger function processed:
    {myQueueItem}");
}
}
}
```

Now let's add the connection string key to the local.settings.json file. Go to the storage account that you created in the Azure portal and click "Access keys," as shown in Figure 4-13.

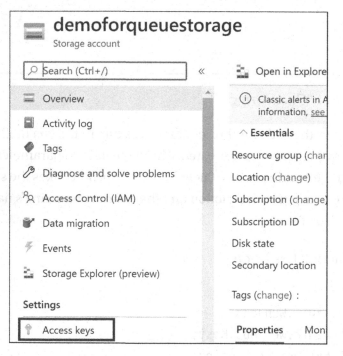

Figure 4-13. *Click "Access keys"*

Click "Show keys." Copy the connection string, as shown in Figure 4-14.

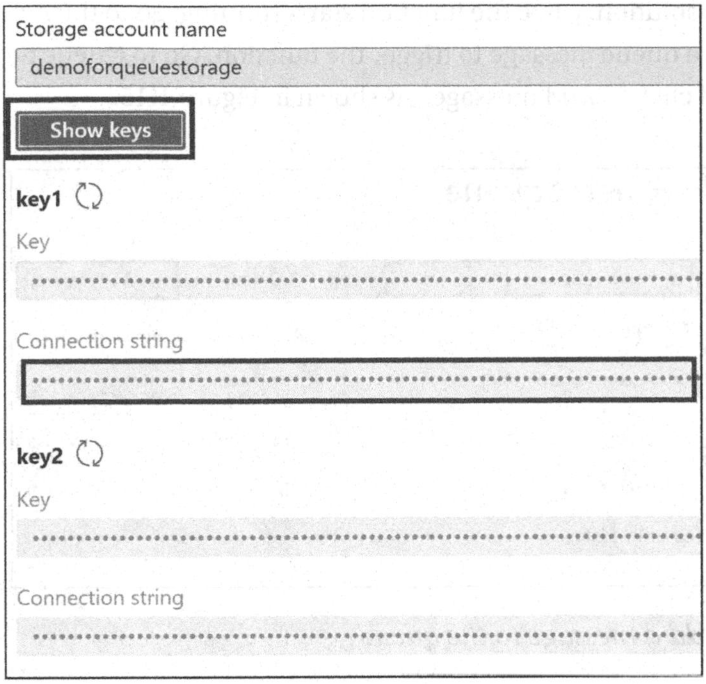

Figure 4-14. *Copy the connection string*

Go back to the Azure function solution in Visual Studio and open the `local.settings.json` file, as shown in Listing 4-2. Add the key for the connection string. Replace the placeholder `[value]` with the connection string value that you copied from the Azure portal.

Listing 4-2. Local.settings.json Code

```
{
  "IsEncrypted": false,
  "Values": {
    "AzureWebJobsStorage": "UseDevelopmentStorage=true",
    "FUNCTIONS_WORKER_RUNTIME": "dotnet",
    "ConnectToQueue": "[value]"
  }
}
```

Now run the solution. Once the function starts running, go to the Azure Queue Storage and add a queue message to trigger the function. Go to Queue Storage in the Azure portal and click "+ Add message," as shown in Figure 4-15.

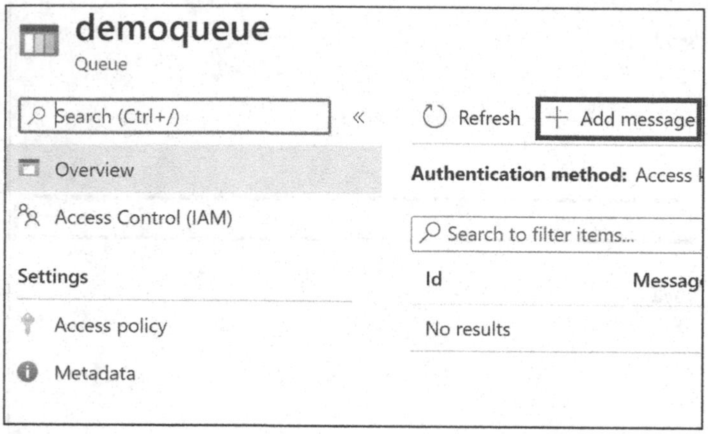

Figure 4-15. *Add a message to the queue*

Provide some message and click OK. You can configure when the message expires in the queue. In this case, the message will expire in seven days. You can set the "Expires in" value to configure the message expiration, as shown in Figure 4-16.

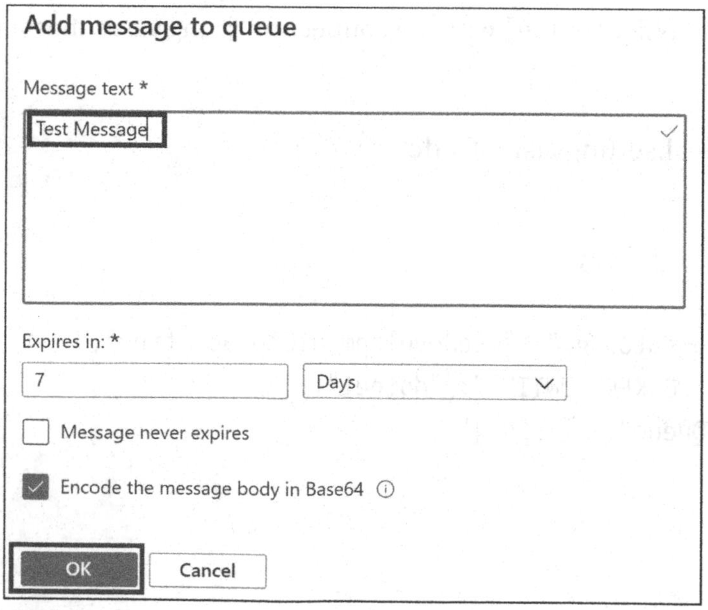

Figure 4-16. *Click OK*

The Azure function gets triggered, and you can see that the message gets logged in the debug console of Visual Studio, as shown in Figure 4-17.

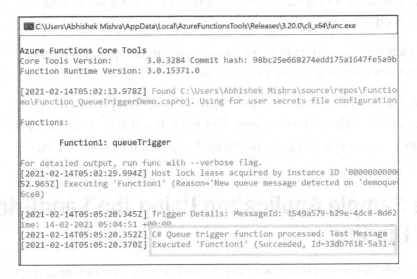

Figure 4-17. *Function execution output*

Getting Started with a SendGrid Output Binding and Use Cases

You may have a scenario where the function will process the business logic and then send the processing output in an email to the intended recipients. To address this requirement, you can use SendGrid as an output binding. You do not need to implement much code to send an email from an Azure function. You just need to declaratively configure SendGrid as an output binding and send emails from the Azure Functions service. SendGrid is a third-party email delivery service that is available as an Azure service. You can spin up a SendGrid account in the Azure portal with a few clicks and start using it.

The following are a few of the example scenarios where you can use SendGrid:

- In the case of an e-commerce website, an Azure function can send an email to the customer once it processes the order.

- In the case of an IoT application monitoring the factory floor's temperature, an Azure function can check for an abnormal temperature and send an email to the concerned team to take corrective action.

- In a reporting application, an Azure function can process a report and send the report data in an email.

- In the case of a customer feedback management system, the Azure function analyzes the customer feedback. It sends an email with the necessary corrective steps to the back-end team to take action.

Build a Sample Application Using the SendGrid Output Binding

Let's add a SendGrid output binding to the Azure function you developed earlier. You have already created a Queue Storage that will trigger the Azure function. Now let's create a SendGrid service in the Azure portal. Go to the Azure portal and click "Create a resource," as shown in Figure 4-18.

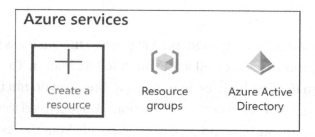

Figure 4-18. *Create a resource*

Search for *sendgrid* and click the search result for SendGrid, as shown in Figure 4-19.

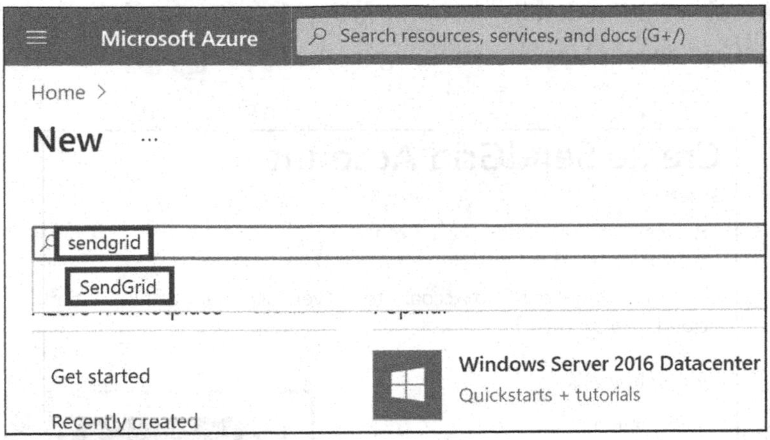

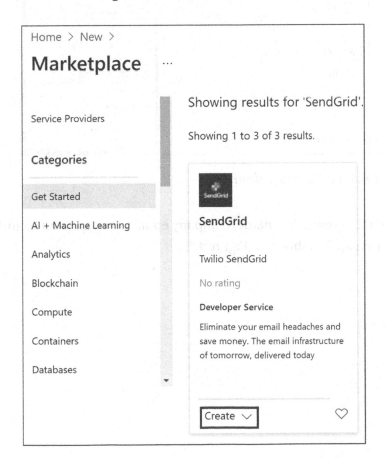

Figure 4-19. *Select SendGrid*

Click Create, as shown in Figure 4-20.

Figure 4-20. *Click Create*

Provide the subscription details, resource group, location, and account details to access the SendGrid account, as shown in Figure 4-21.

Create SendGrid Account

SendGrid

Basics   Tags   Review + Create

Configure your SendGrid Account to deliver customer communication cloud. Learn more ⧉

Project details

Subscription *

Resource group * ⓘ   (New) rg-sendgrid
                           Create new

Location *   (US) East US

Account details

Name *   abhisekmisra

Password * ⓘ   ••••••••

Confirm password *   ••••••••

Figure 4-21. *Provide the basic details*

Provide your first name, last name, company email, company name, and website. Click "Review + create," as shown in Figure 4-22.

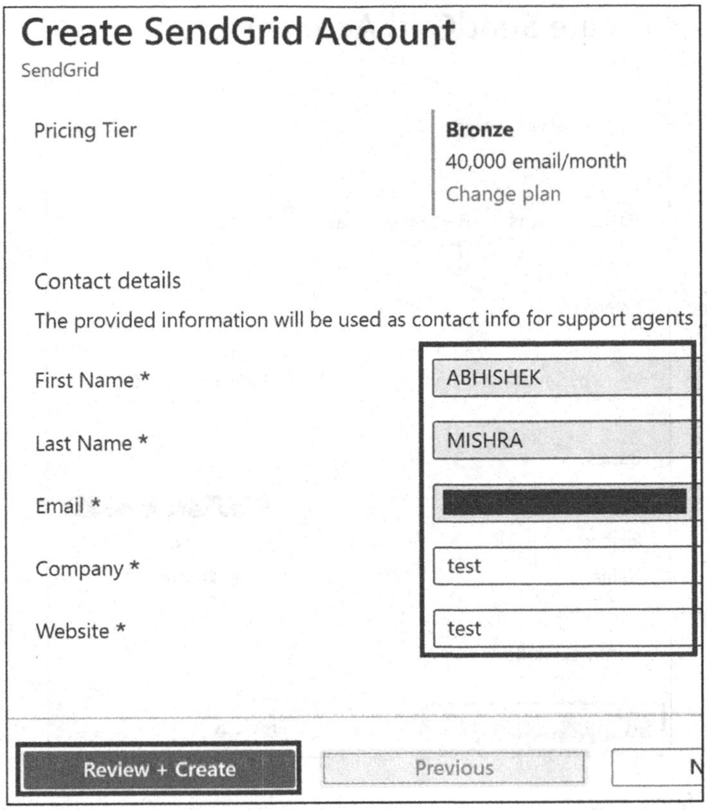

Create SendGrid Account
SendGrid

Pricing Tier | **Bronze**
40,000 email/month
Change plan

Contact details
The provided information will be used as contact info for support agents

First Name *   ABHISHEK

Last Name *   MISHRA

Email *   ▌▌▌▌▌▌▌▌

Company *   test

Website *   test

Review + Create   Previous   N

Figure 4-22. *Provide the contact details*

Click Create, as shown in Figure 4-23.

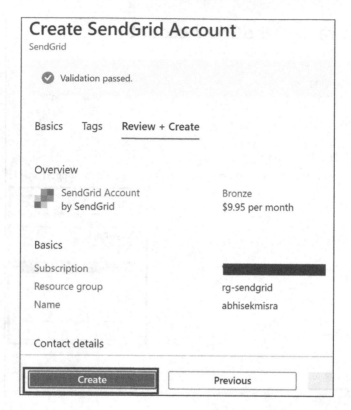

Figure 4-23. *Click Create*

Once the SendGrid service gets created, navigate to the service in the Azure portal. You need to create a sender identity that you can send emails from using the SendGrid account. Click Sender Identity, as shown in Figure 4-24. You will be navigated to the SendGrid portal.

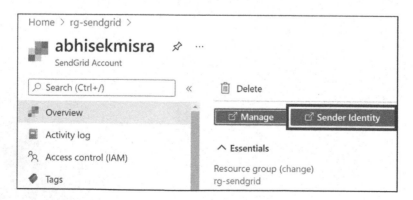

Figure 4-24. *Click Sender Identity*

Click Create a Single Sender, as shown in Figure 4-25.

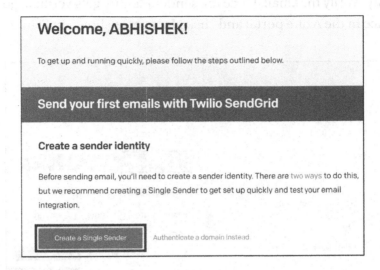

Figure 4-25. *Create a sender*

Provide your information for the email details. SendGrid uses these details to send emails. Click Create, as shown in Figure 4-26.

Figure 4-26. *Provide the sender details*

You will get an email for verification in the email address you specified while creating a sender identity. Verify the email. Once the sender identity gets verified, go to the SendGrid service in the Azure portal and click Manage, as shown in Figure 4-27.

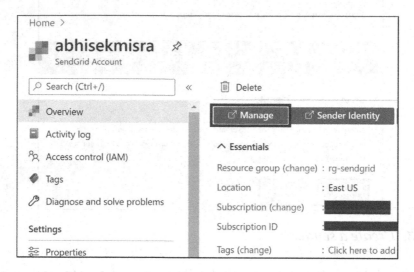

Figure 4-27. *Click Manage*

You will get navigated to the SendGrid portal. Click API Keys, as shown in Figure 4-28.

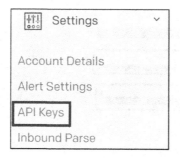

Figure 4-28. *Click API Keys*

Create an API key. Copy the API key that you created. You will use this in your Azure function code. Make sure you select Full Access for API Key Permission, as shown in Figure 4-29. This will help you perform all the necessary HTTP actions such as GET, PATCH, PUT, DELETE, and POST for the SendGrid endpoint.

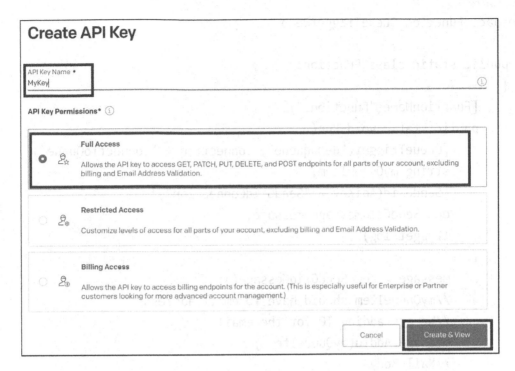

Figure 4-29. *Create an API key*

Now let's open Visual Studio and the Azure function project you created earlier. Add the following NuGet package to the function project:

- `Microsoft.Azure.WebJobs.Extensions.SendGrid`

Modify the `Function1.cs` code as illustrated in Listing 4-3. You are adding an output binding for SendGrid using the `SendGrid` attribute for the method parameter. The `SendGrid` attribute takes the name of the API key settings in the `local.settings.json` file.

Listing 4-3. Function1.cs Code

```
using System;
using Microsoft.Azure.WebJobs;
using Microsoft.Azure.WebJobs.Host;
using Microsoft.Extensions.Logging;
using SendGrid.Helpers.Mail;
```

```csharp
namespace Function_QueueTriggerDemo
{
    public static class Function1
    {
        [FunctionName("Function1")]
        public static void Run(
            [QueueTrigger("demoqueue", Connection = "ConnectToQueue")]
            string myQueueItem,
            [SendGrid(ApiKey = "SendGridConnection")]
            out SendGridMessage message,
            ILogger log)
        {
            message = new SendGridMessage();
            //myQueueItem should have TO email address
            //We are adding TO for the email
            message.AddTo(myQueueItem);
            //Mail Body
            message.AddContent("text/html", "This is Demo Mail");
            //From Mail ID. Shuld be exactly same as
            //that in Sender Identity of Send Grid
            message.SetFrom(new EmailAddress("abc@mycompany.com"));
            //Subject for the mail
            message.SetSubject("Demo Mail");
            log.LogInformation($"Email Triggered to : {myQueueItem}");
        }
    }
}
```

Modify the `local.settings.json` file as shown in Listing 4-4. You need to add the key name for `SendGrid`. Replace [`KeyValue`] with the API key that you created in the SendGrid portal earlier. Replace [`Value`] with a Queue Storage connection string.

Listing 4-4. Local.settings.json Code

```json
{
  "IsEncrypted": false,
  "Values": {
```

```
    "AzureWebJobsStorage": "UseDevelopmentStorage=true",
    "FUNCTIONS_WORKER_RUNTIME": "dotnet",
    "ConnectToQueue": "[Value]",
    "SendGridConnection": "[KeyValue]"
  }
}
```

Now run the Azure function in Visual Studio. Whenever you add any message to the Queue Storage, the Azure function gets triggered, and a message is sent to the email address specified in the queue message. Make sure you add an email address in the message to the queue, as shown in Figure 4-30.

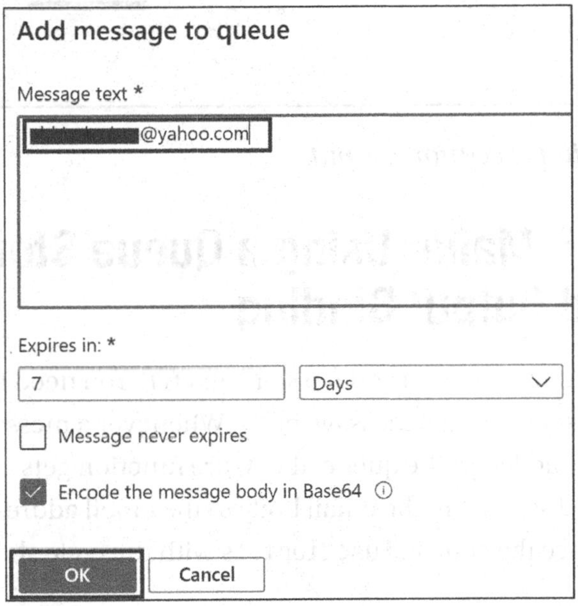

Figure 4-30. *Add a message to the queue*

The Azure function gets triggered, and an email gets delivered to the email address specified in the queue message, as shown in Figure 4-31.

```
C:\Users\Abhishek Mishra\AppData\Local\AzureFunctionsTools\Releases\3.20.0\cli_x64\func.exe

Azure Functions Core Tools
Core Tools Version:      3.0.3284 Commit hash: 98bc25e668274edd175a1647
Function Runtime Version: 3.0.15371.0

[2021-02-23T17:50:18.533Z] Found C:\Users\Abhishek Mishra\source\repos\F
mo\Function_QueueTriggerDemo.csproj. Using for user secrets file configu

Functions:

        Function1: queueTrigger

For detailed output, run func with --verbose flag.
[2021-02-23T17:50:29.626Z] Host lock lease acquired by instance ID '0000
[2021-02-23T17:51:09.220Z] Executing 'Function1' (Reason='New queue mess
45b4-abf8-29e347ebf64c)
[2021-02-23T17:51:09.223Z] Trigger Details: MessageId: adc6bbb5-9a6f-477
ime: 23-02-2021 17:51:07 +00:00
[2021-02-23T17:51:09.231Z] Email Triggered to : ████████@yahoo.com
[2021-02-23T17:51:10.702Z] Executed 'Function1' (Succeeded, Id=bd711f33-
```

Figure 4-31. Function execution output

Create an OTP Mailer Using a Queue Storage Trigger and SendGrid Output Binding

Now let's modify the Azure function code to send an OTP. You need to generate a random number and send it in the message body. Whenever a message with an email address as a value gets added in the queue, the Azure function gets triggered, generates a random number, and sends it in the email body to the email address specified in the queue message. Replace the code in Function1.cs with the code shown in Listing 4-5.

Listing 4-5. Function1.cs Code

```
using System;
using Microsoft.Azure.WebJobs;
using Microsoft.Azure.WebJobs.Host;
using Microsoft.Extensions.Logging;
using SendGrid.Helpers.Mail;
```

```csharp
namespace Function_QueueTriggerDemo
{
    public static class Function1
    {
        [FunctionName("Function1")]
        public static void Run(
            [QueueTrigger("demoqueue", Connection = "ConnectToQueue")]
            string myQueueItem,
            [SendGrid(ApiKey = "SendGridConnection")]
            out SendGridMessage message,
            ILogger log)
        {
            //Generate OTP
            Random random = new Random();
            int num = random.Next(10000);
            message = new SendGridMessage();
            //myQueueItem should have TO email address
            //We are adding TO for the mail
            message.AddTo(myQueueItem);
            //Mail Body with random One Time Password (OTP) generated
            message.AddContent("text/html", "One Time Password for your
            transaction : " + num.ToString());
            //From Mail ID. Shuld be exactly same as that in
            //Sender Identity of Send Grid
            message.SetFrom(new  EmailAddress("abc.mycompany.com"));
            //Subject for the mail
            message.SetSubject("OTP Mail - Valid for 10 minutes");
            log.LogInformation($"Email Triggered to : {myQueueItem}");
        }
    }
}
```

Summary

In this chapter, you learned how to work with a Queue Storage trigger and SendGrid output binding using Visual Studio. You then used these concepts to build an OTP mailer Azure function that gets triggered whenever you add a message to the Queue Storage and send an email using the SendGrid output binding.

The following are the key takeaways from this chapter:

- You can trigger an Azure function using a Queue Storage trigger. The function gets triggered whenever a message gets added to the Queue Storage.

- You can send an email from an Azure function using the SendGrid output binding.

- You can declaratively configure a Queue Storage trigger and the SendGrid output binding without having to write much code.

- Visual Studio provides a template to work with a Queue Storage trigger.

- You can enable only one SendGrid account per Azure subscription. You need to enable Azure SendGrid using only a company email address. A personal mail address will not work when creating a SendGrid service in the Azure environment and integrating it as a binding in Azure function.

- The free tier for SendGrid is not available in Azure, so you must use a pay-as-you-go subscription instead of a trial subscription or a subscription that offers free monthly credits.

CHAPTER 5

Build a Report Generator with a Timer Trigger and Blob Storage Bindings

You may have had to run certain services of your application at uniform time intervals for a defined frequency. Often such service executions do not take much time to complete. So, allocating dedicated resources for such applications will result in inefficient use of provisioned resources, resulting in higher costs.

Using a timer trigger, you can develop such scheduled-based tasks to trigger Azure functions to avoid providing dedicated infrastructure resources. Along with invoking such services for a particular frequency at a uniform time interval, you may also need to store the insights or data gathered by the service in persistent storage. You can achieve that with a Blob Storage binding in Azure Functions to write into Azure Blob Storage.

In the previous chapter, you learned all about the essential concepts and the use cases of a queued-triggered Azure function and SendGrid output binding by building a one-time password (OTP) mailer. Let's explore how to implement a timer trigger and Blob Storage bindings for the Azure Functions service by building a report generator.

© Ashirwad Satapathi and Abhishek Mishra 2021
A. Satapathi and A. Mishra, *Hands-on Azure Functions with C#*, https://doi.org/10.1007/978-1-4842-7122-3_5

Structure of the Chapter

This chapter will explore the following aspects of timer triggers and Blob Storage input and output bindings:

- Getting started with timer triggers and use cases

- Building a sample application using a timer trigger

- Getting started with Blob Storage bindings

- Building a sample application using a Blob Storage binding

- Creating a report generator using Blob Storage input and output bindings

Objectives

After studying this chapter, you will be able to do the following:

- Implement a timer trigger for Azure Functions

- Implement Blob Storage input and output bindings for Azure Functions

Getting Started with Timer Triggers and Use Cases

Using a timer trigger is an excellent way to build a scheduling application that executes specific tasks at uniform intervals. You can use timer triggers to build cost-effective cron jobs in Azure that execute for a short time as you pay only for your Azure function's execution time.

A word of caution here: you should not consider using Azure Functions to run long-running cron jobs while you are using a Consumption Plan because the maximum timeout duration of a function app is 10 minutes. But with a Premium Plan, you can overcome the timeout limits faced with the Consumption Plan as the default timeout is 30 minutes, and theoretically it can be configured to be unlimited. If you are hosting your function in a dedicated App Service Plan or App Service Environment, you can configure the trigger time depending on your requirements. Alternatively, if you have an existing

App Service Plan, you can write a web job that is configured as run on a schedule to execute long-running cron jobs.

Unlike other trigger types, the timer trigger comes out of the box along with an HTTP trigger in `Microsoft.Azure.WebJobs.Extensions` version 2.*x* and newer.

The following are a few use cases where you can use a timer trigger:

- The customer can use a timer-triggered function to work as a schedule-based report generator to gather data from data sources, build a report depending on the business requirements, and later save the report in persistent storage like Azure Blob Storage or an AWS S3 bucket for further use.

- The customer may want to send weekly newsletters to their end users. There can be a mailing list containing all the end users who are recipients of the newsletter. The timer-triggered function solves this business requirement well.

- The customer may have monthly or yearly membership plans for its end user and may want to revoke the membership status of all the users who didn't renew their plans at the end of each month or year. You can use a timer-triggered function to deactivate or delete all such users' records depending on the business requirements.

A timer-triggered function uses the NCrontab expression to define the schedule expression. NCrontab expressions are similar to cron expressions. The NCrontab expressions have an additional sixth field to define the seconds in the schedule expression, making them different from cron expressions.

Note   Azure Functions does not support five cron expression fields. Timespan is supported, but only while you are running your functions inside an App Service Plan.

This is the structure of a NCrontab expression:

`{seconds} {minute} {hour} {day} {month} {day-of-week}`

Each of the fields in an NCrontab expression can have one of the types shown in Table 5-1.

Table 5-1. *Different Types of NCrontab Expressions with Examples*

Type	Example	When Trigger
A specific value	0 2 * * * *	Once every hour of the day at minute 2 of each hour
All values (*)	0 * 2 * * *	At every minute in the hour beginning at hour 2
A range operator (-)	1-7 * * * * *	7 times a minute: at 1 through 7 seconds during every minute of every hour of each day
An interval value operator (/)	0 */5 * * * *	12 times an hour: at second 0 of every 5th minute of every hour of each day
A set of values operator (,)	1,5,10 * * * * *	Three times a minute: at seconds 1, 5, and 10 during every minute of every hour of each day

Build a Sample Application Using a Timer Trigger

You will be creating a timer-triggered Azure function in the Azure portal with the portal editor's help in this section.

Go to the Azure portal and search for *function app* in the search bar. Click Function App, as shown in Figure 5-1.

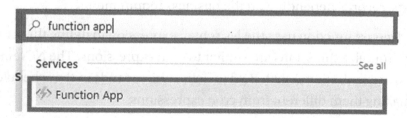

Figure 5-1. *Click Function App*

Now click Create to create a new function app, as shown in Figure 5-2.

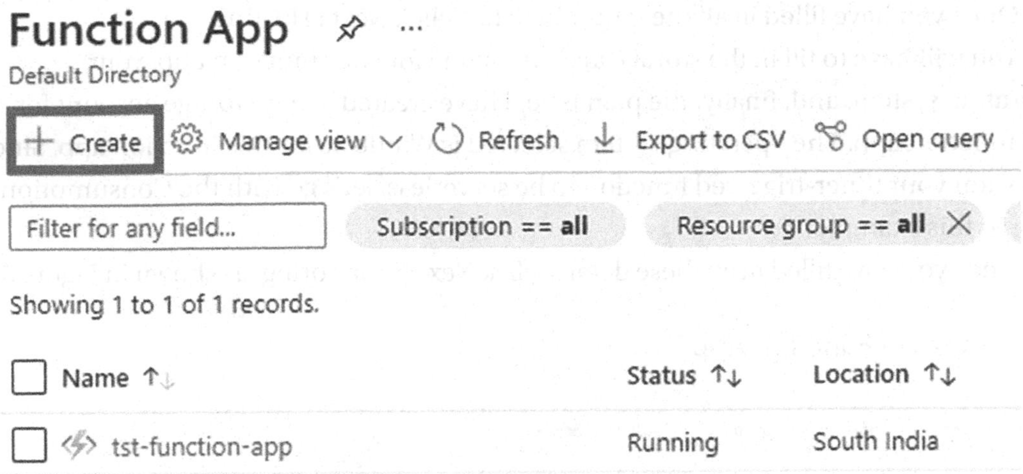

Function App

Default Directory

+ Create   ⚙ Manage view ∨   ↻ Refresh   ↓ Export to CSV   ⚬ Open query

Filter for any field...   Subscription == **all**   Resource group == **all** ✕

Showing 1 to 1 of 1 records.

Name ↑↓	Status ↑↓	Location ↑↓
⚡ tst-function-app	Running	South India

Figure 5-2. *Create a function app*

Fill in all the details required for creating your function app like the resource group, function app name, region, and runtime stack, to name a few, as shown in Figure 5-3.

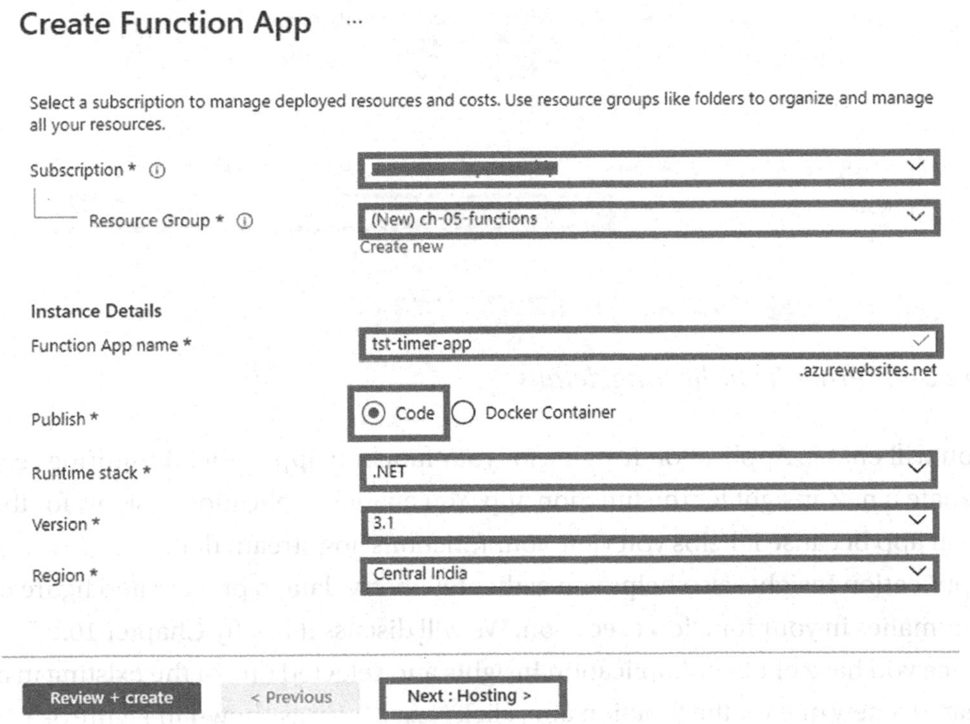

Create Function App ⋯

Select a subscription to manage deployed resources and costs. Use resource groups like folders to organize and manage all your resources.

Subscription * ⓘ   [   ] ∨

└─ Resource Group * ⓘ   [(New) ch-05-functions] ∨
                          Create new

Instance Details

Function App name *   [tst-timer-app] ✓
                                          .azurewebsites.net

Publish *   ⦿ Code   ◯ Docker Container

Runtime stack *   [.NET] ∨

Version *   [3.1] ∨

Region *   [Central India] ∨

Review + create   < Previous   Next : Hosting >

Figure 5-3. *Provide the necessary configuration details of the function app*

Once you have filled in all the required fields, click Next : Hosting.

You will have to fill in the storage account name for your function app, your operating system, and, finally, the plan type. I have created a new storage account for this function app. The operating system selected is Windows for this function app. Since you want your timer-triggered function to be serverless, let's go with the Consumption Plan in this example.

Once you have filled in all these details, click Next : Monitoring, as shown in Figure 5-4.

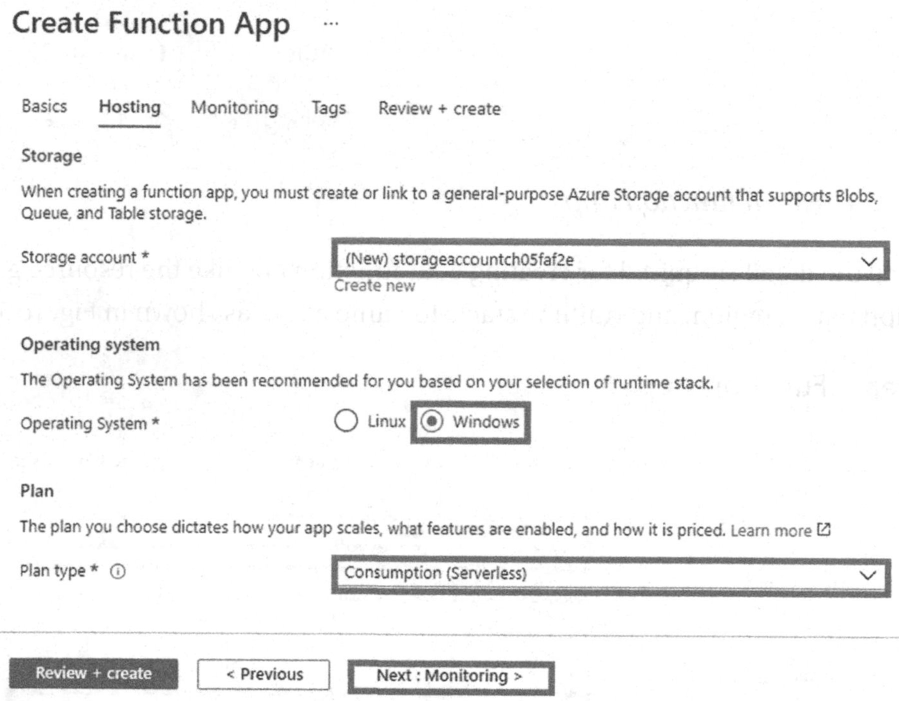

Figure 5-4. *Provide the hosting details*

You will enable Application Insights for your function app in the Monitoring section and create a new insight for the function app. You enable Application Insights for the function app because it helps you view your functions' log stream data.

Application Insights also helps you gather telemetry data to process and figure out any anomalies in your function execution. We will discuss it briefly Chapter 10.

Once you have enabled Application Insights and selected one of the existing insights or created a new one for the function app, click Next : Tags, as shown in Figure 5-5.

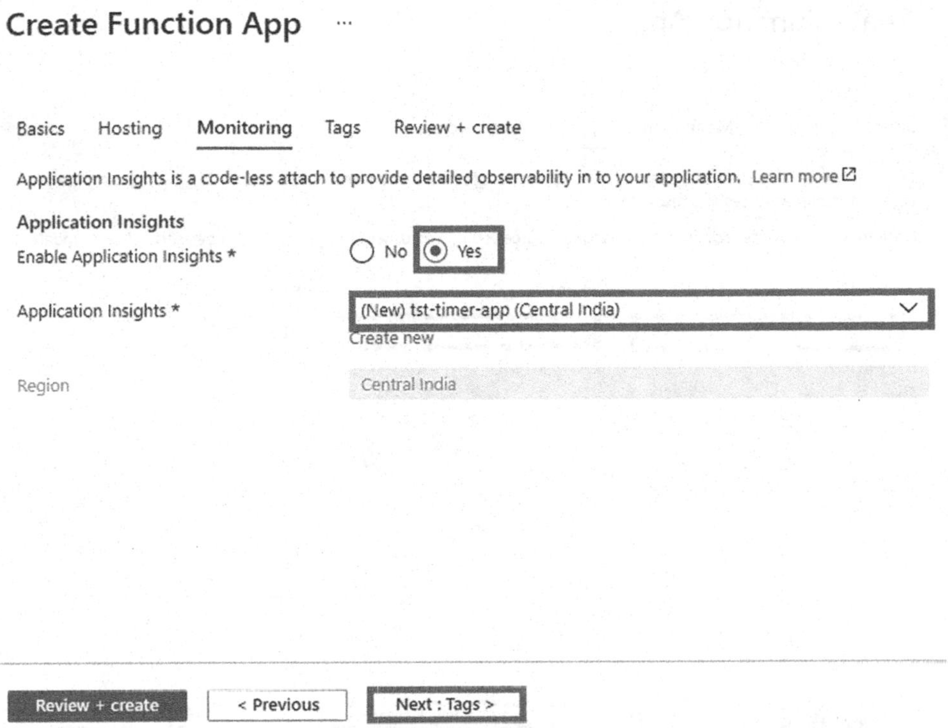

Create Function App   ···

Basics   Hosting   **Monitoring**   Tags   Review + create

Application Insights is a code-less attach to provide detailed observability in to your application. Learn more ⧉

Application Insights

Enable Application Insights *   ◯ No   ⦿ Yes

Application Insights *   (New) tst-timer-app (Central India)   ⌄
                                Create new

Region   Central India

| Review + create | < Previous | Next : Tags > |

Figure 5-5. Enable Application Insights

Now, you will be asked to assign tags for the function app. This step is optional. It is a best practice to have tags assigned for all your resources. It helps in cost management and in the logical grouping of resources. Once you have filled in the tags along with their values, click "Next : Review + create," as shown in Figure 5-6.

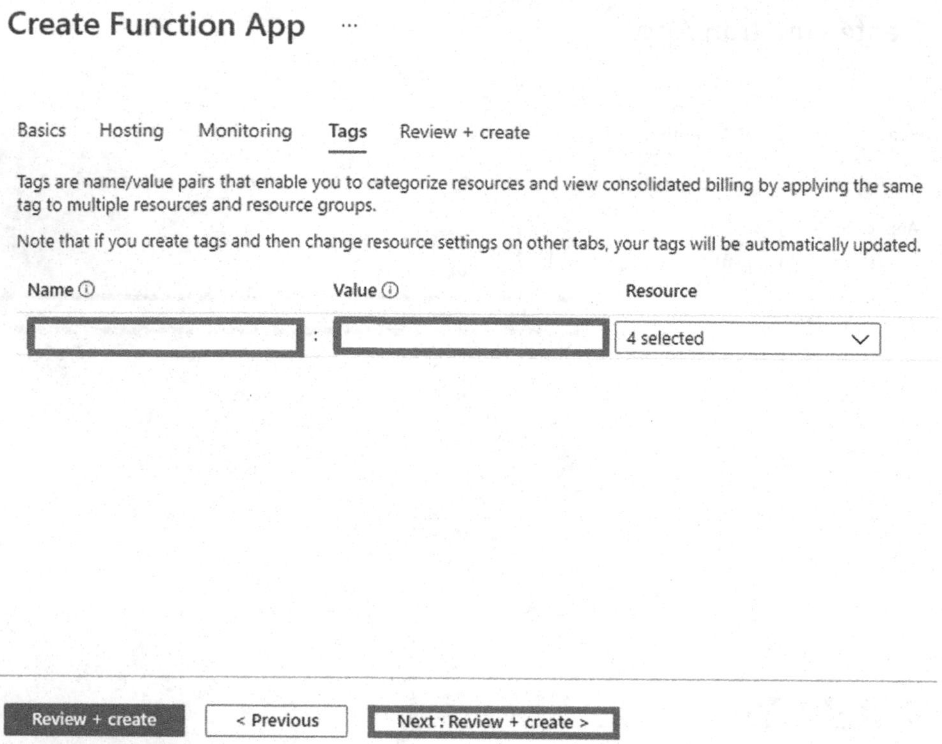

Create Function App   ⋯

Basics   Hosting   Monitoring   **Tags**   Review + create

Tags are name/value pairs that enable you to categorize resources and view consolidated billing by applying the same tag to multiple resources and resource groups.

Note that if you create tags and then change resource settings on other tabs, your tags will be automatically updated.

Name ⓘ   Value ⓘ   Resource

[   ]   :   [   ]   [4 selected   ∨]

[Review + create]   [< Previous]   [Next : Review + create >]

Figure 5-6. *Provide the tag details*

Now you will see a screen with a summary of all the details you filled in to create the function app, and validation will be done to check whether all the details are valid. Once the validation process is completed and is successful, you need to click Create, as shown in Figure 5-7.

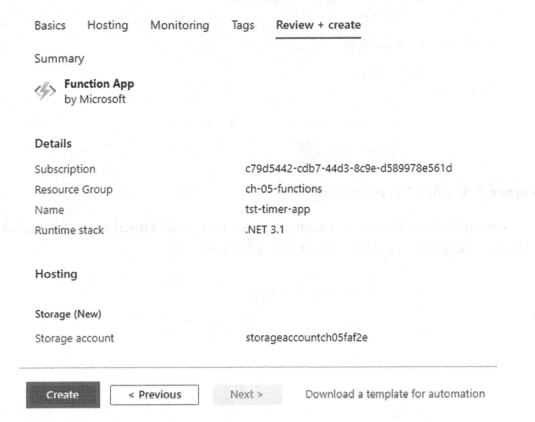

Figure 5-7. *Click Create*

While your function app is being deployed, you will be redirected to a screen like the one shown in Figure 5-8. Once the deployment of all your function app resources is completed, you will see an update, as highlighted in Figure 5-8. Click "Go to resource" to navigate to the function app.

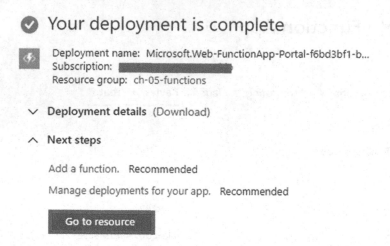

Figure 5-8. *Click "Go to resource"*

Now you will be redirected to the Functions screen. Click **Functions** and then click Add to create a new Azure function, as shown in Figure 5-9.

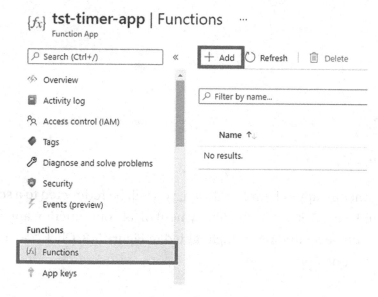

Figure 5-9. *Click Add*

Now let's select "Develop in portal" as the development environment, select "Timer trigger" as the function template, and click Add, as shown in Figure 5-10.

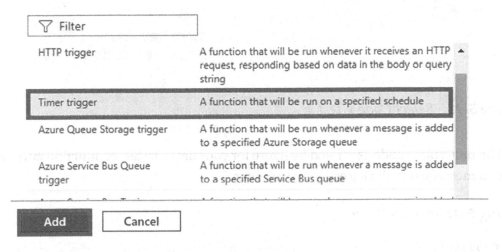

Add function   ✕

Select development environment

Instructions will vary based on your development environment. Learn more

Development environment   🌐 Develop in portal   ⌄

Select a template

Use a template to create a function. Triggers describe the type of events that invoke
your functions. Learn more

▽ Filter

HTTP trigger	A function that will be run whenever it receives an HTTP request, responding based on data in the body or query string
Timer trigger	A function that will be run on a specified schedule
Azure Queue Storage trigger	A function that will be run whenever a message is added to a specified Azure Storage queue
Azure Service Bus Queue trigger	A function that will be run whenever a message is added to a specified Service Bus queue

Add   Cancel

Figure 5-10. *Select "Timer trigger" and click Add*

Azure will generate a timer-triggered Azure function called TimerTrigger1, as shown
in Figure 5-11. By default, the function will be enabled. This function will consist of these
three files:

- `run.csx`

- `function.json`

- `readme.md`

run.csx is a C# script that contains the business logic of your Azure function, while function.json has all the configuration details of your function's trigger, binding, and other configuration settings. readme.md contains a small description about what this function does.

Now click Code + Test, as shown in Figure 5-11, to view the run.csx code; refer to Listing 5-1 for the code present in the run.csx file.

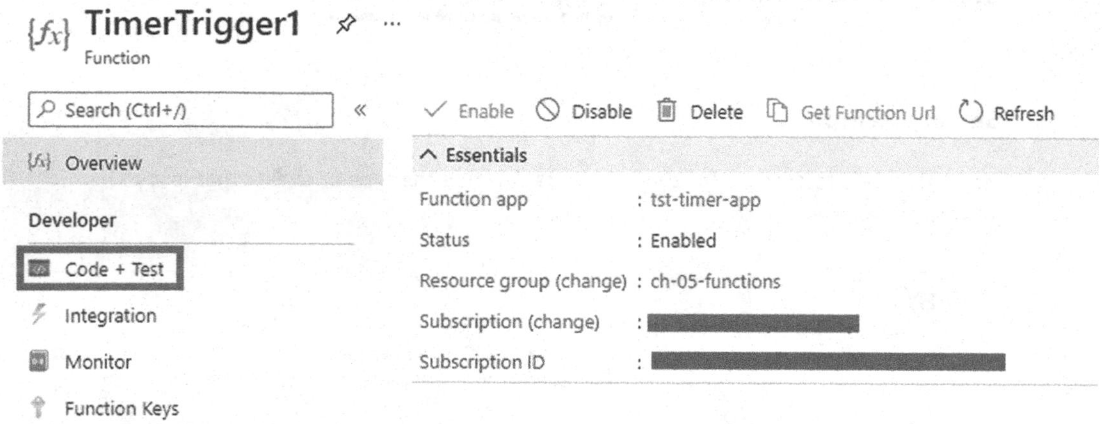

Figure 5-11. *Select Code + Test*

The boilerplate code generated by Azure for your timer-triggered function currently writes a message into the log every five minutes.

Listing 5-1. run.csx Code

```
using System;
public static void Run(TimerInfo myTimer, ILogger log)
{
    log.LogInformation($"C# Timer trigger function executed at:
    {DateTime.Now}");
}
```

The function and the trigger type's schedule expression and other details are mentioned in the function.json file. Listing 5-2 shows the content of function.json.

Listing 5-2. function.json Code

```json
{
  "bindings": [
    {
      "name": "myTimer",
      "type": "timerTrigger",
      "direction": "in",
      "schedule": "0 */5 * * * *"
    }
  ]
}
```

You can modify the function name along with the schedule expression in the function.json file. Alternatively, you can do the same by clicking Integration in the Developer section of your function screen and then clicking the trigger, as shown in Figure 5 12.

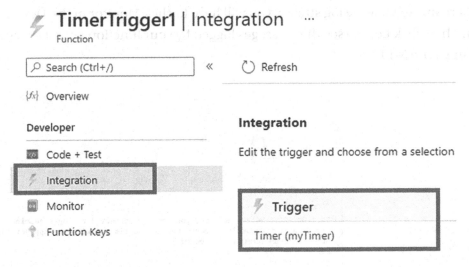

Figure 5-12. *Click Integration*

Now, you will see a screen with all the function details as mentioned in function. json. You can modify the name of your function by modifying the timestamp modifier name and do the same with the schedule expression by modifying the schedule value, as shown in Figure 5-13.

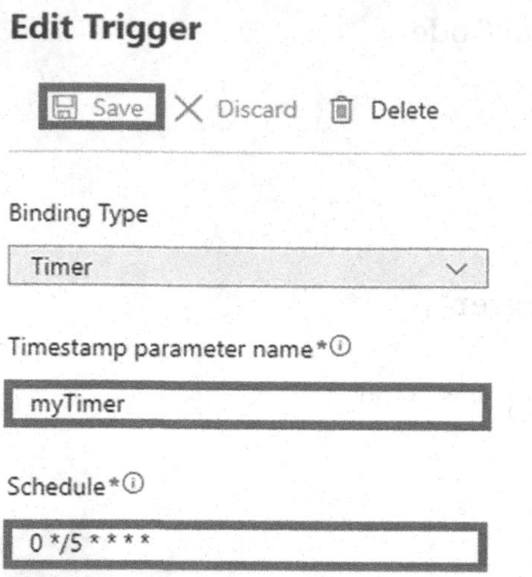

Edit Trigger

🖫 Save   ✕ Discard   🗑 Delete

Binding Type

| Timer | ⌄ |

Timestamp parameter name*ⓘ

| myTimer |

Schedule*ⓘ

| 0 */5 * * * * |

Figure 5-13. *Modifying function settings*

Now that you have created and understand your timer-triggered Azure function and looked into ways to customize it, let's see how it works. Since it works on a schedule and logs a message containing the time of execution when it executes, you will see it in the log stream. To view the log stream, you will have to click Monitor in the Developer section. Then click Logs to see the messages logged by your function after it executes, as shown in Figure 5-14.

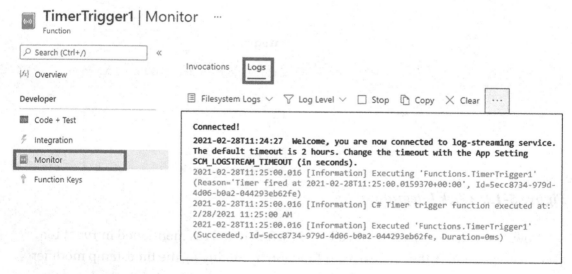

Figure 5-14. *View logs*

Note While deploying timer-triggered functions to the production environment, make sure the runOnStartup property is set to false. If set to true, your function will be invoked every time it's scaled out or whenever the function app restarts due to function changes.

You can also see the number function invocation along with their execution time and status, i.e., success or failure, in the Monitor section of your function screen. You can view these details by going to the Invocation tab instead of the Logs tab, as shown in Figure 5-15.

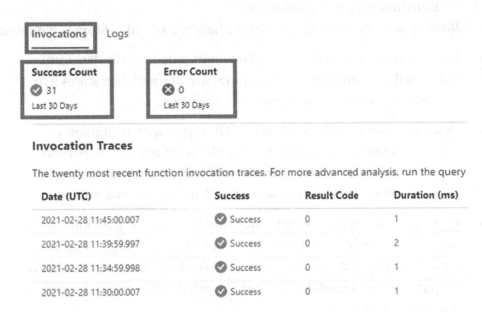

Figure 5-15. *View the function invocation details*

To learn more about timer-triggered functions, we recommend you visit https://docs.microsoft.com/en-us/azure/azure-functions/functions-bindings-timer.

Getting Started with Blob Storage Bindings and Use Cases

You may have come across scenarios where the function needs to store the processed data in a persistent storage after execution or needs some data to process a request and return a response. To address such requirements, you can use Blob Storage bindings. Blob Storage bindings provide a declarative way of connecting your functions to Azure Blob Storage and performing various operations on it. An Azure function supports both input and output bindings for Azure Blob Storage. These bindings help you focus more on solving business problems instead of focusing on configuring the boilerplate code to set up the SDKs to interact with Blob Storage.

The following are a few example scenarios where you can Blob Storage bindings:

- In a reporting application, Azure Functions processes the data from different data sources at a defined time each day and then stores it in Blob Storage for further reference by other users.

- In the case of a serverless API, an HTTP-triggered Azure function may need to return files or its content whenever required as per the business requirements. You can use a Blob Storage input binding to get a file from Blob Storage to send it back to the user as a response.

- In the case of a banking system, an Azure function can generate an account statement every month and put it in Blob Storage using the output binding and then also use a Blob Storage trigger and SendGrid output binding to send the generated account statement to the end user over email.

Note   While using the in-portal editor, you cannot use attribute-based bindings. You will have to define the properties of your triggers and bindings in the `function.json` file. Alternatively, you can also define and modify them in the Integration section of Azure Functions in the portal.

Build a Sample Function Using a Blob Storage Binding

You will be creating a timer-triggered Azure Function with a Blob Storage output binding in the Azure portal with the portal editor's help in this section. You will integrate the Blob Storage binding with the timer-triggered function that you created in the previous section. You are going to use a Blob Storage output binding to create a new file in the container every time your timer-triggered function executes, along with writing the message you used to log earlier inside this file.

Let's go to the timer-triggered function in the portal and click the Integration option available in the Developer section of the screen. You will see a screen similar to the one shown in Figure 5-16.

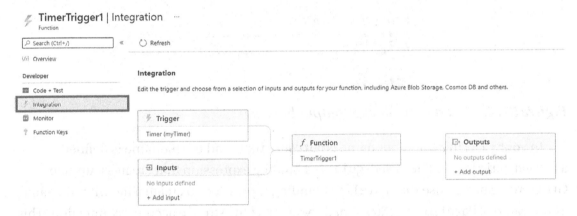

Figure 5-16. *View the Integration options for the function*

Since you have already defined the trigger type while creating the function, the trigger is updated here as Timer. As you don't have any input and output bindings configured for this function as of now, you are not able to see "No inputs defined" and "No outputs defined" on the screen.

Now you will need to click Add Output to add an output binding for this function. Once you click, you should see a screen similar to the one shown in Figure 5-17. You have to select Azure Blob Storage as the binding type, and then you will need to name the Blob parameter name. Then define the path of the container when you want to create a file every time your function executes along with the name.

Create Output   ✕

Start by selecting the type of output binding
you want to add.

Binding Type

Azure Blob Storage ⌄

Azure Blob Storage details

Blob parameter name* ⓘ

outputBlob

Path* ⓘ

outcontainer/{rand-guid}.txt

Storage account connection* ⓘ

AzureWebJobsStorage ⌄

OK		Cancel

Figure 5-17. Add a Blob Storage output binding

In your case, the container name is `outcontainer`, and the filename is defined as `{rand-guid}.txt`. The `{rand-guid}` is a binding expression that creates a unique GUID. You can also use the `{DateTime}` binding expression to create a file with the name as the value of `DateTime.UtcNow`. Finally, you select the storage account connection. This is the name of the app setting that contains the storage connection string to use for this binding. By default, it points to the storage account that you created while creating the function app. Alternatively, you can map it to a different storage account too, depending on your requirements. But you need to make sure that you configure the connection string of a general-purpose storage account and not a Blob Storage account.

By default, you have only two containers inside the storage account that you created while creating the function app, as shown in Figure 5-18. You can see these containers inside the storage account by going to the Storage Explorer and then by clicking the Blob containers.

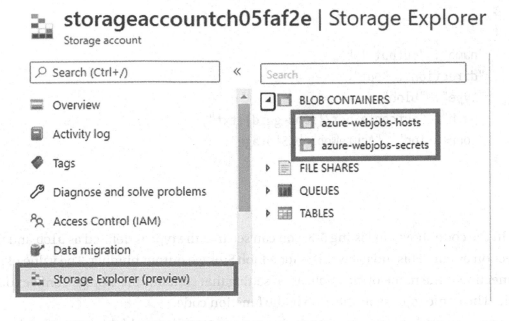

Figure 5-18. *View the existing Blob containers*

As you can see from Figure 5-18, you don't have any container called `outcontainer` that you have passed in the path of your output binding as of now. In such cases, the function creates an `outcontainer` on the fly in the storage account while executing to store the file.

Now that you have configured the output binding for your timer-triggered function app in the Integration window, let's take a look at your `function.json` file. You will see that a new code snippet has been added to your `function.json` file, as shown in Listing 5-3. Now it contains all the attributes required to add a Blob Storage output binding to your function. Any changes made in the Integration window will be reflected in the `function.json` file of your timer-triggered function.

Listing 5-3. Updated function.json Code

```
{
  "bindings": [
    {
      "name": "myTimer",
      "type": "timerTrigger",
      "direction": "in",
      "schedule": "0 */5 * * * *"
```

```
    },
    {
      "name": "outputBlob",
      "direction": "out",
      "type": "blob",
      "path": "outcontainer/{rand-guid}.txt",
      "connection": "AzureWebJobsStorage"
    }
  ]
}
```

In the code shown in Listing 5-3, you can see that the type is defined as blob and the direction as out. This indicates this is for a Blob Storage output binding. The value of the connection is the name of the application setting that contains the storage connection value. The name represents the Blob in the function code.

Now you need make some changes in your run.csx file to add this output binding in your timer-triggered function, as shown in Listing 5-4.

Listing 5-4. Modified run.csx

```
public static void Run(TimerInfo myTimer, ILogger log, TextWriter
outputBlob)
{
    string message= $"C# Timer trigger function executed at:
    {DateTime.Now}";
    try{
        outputBlob.Write(message);
        log.LogInformation("Blob created successfully");
    }
    catch(Exception ex){
        log.LogInformation("Blob creation failed");
        }
}
```

In Listing 5-4, you add a parameter of the TextWriter type with the name defined in the function.json file of the timer-triggered function. You can bind it to different types such as string, Byte[], stream, and a few more. After that, you define a variable called message that has a string value along with the date and time when the function execution takes place. Next, you use the write method to write the value of the message variable inside a new text file stored in your outcontainer, as shown in Figure 5-19.

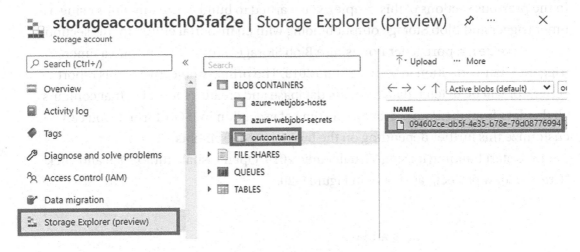

Figure 5-19. *View the newly created file in the outcontainer*

You wrap the code snippet within a try-catch block to handle any errors. If everything works well, you will see "Blob created successfully" in the log stream; if not, the logged message will be "Blob creation failed." Now this function will create a unique text file with the value of the message variable every five minutes until the function is stopped or disabled.

You can also log additional information as well as store the logs in persistent storage to investigate any issues that result in failed function execution, but this is currently out of the scope of this chapter. We will discuss the exception handling mechanism for your function in Chapter 10.

To learn more about Blob Storage input and output bindings, we recommend you look at https://docs.microsoft.com/en-us/azure/azure-functions/functions-bindings-storage-blob.

Create a Report Generator Using a Blob Storage Binding and Timer Trigger

In the previous sections of this chapter, you learned to build Azure functions using a timer trigger and Blob Storage output binding with an in-portal editor. In this section, you will create a report generator using a Blob Storage output binding and a timer-triggered Azure function in Visual Studio 2019. The primary objective of this report generator will be to fetch data from the database and create a report file that contains all the data from the data present at the time of execution in JSON format. You can customize this further depending on the business requirements.

Let's start building it using Visual Studio 2019. Open Visual Studio 2019 and click "Create a new project," as shown in Figure 5-20.

Figure 5-20. *Create a new project*

Now, you need to select the Azure Functions template for your project, as shown in Figure 5-21. You won't be able to see the Azure Functions template if you haven't installed the Azure development workload. You can find the instructions to install the Azure development workload using the Visual Studio installer in Chapter 2.

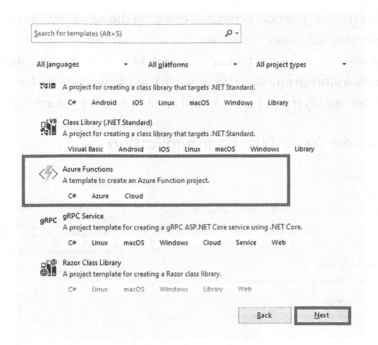

Figure 5-21. *Select the Azure Functions template*

Provide a name for the project and select the source location for the project, as shown in Figure 5-22.

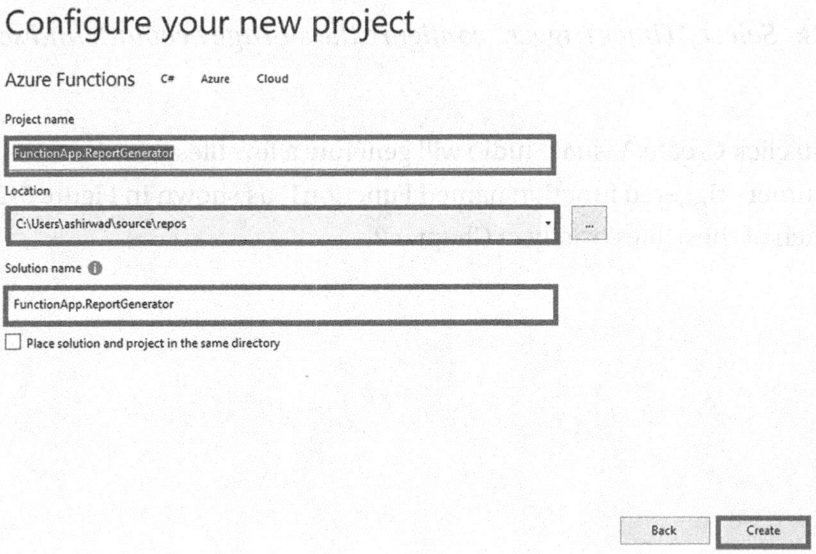

Figure 5-22. *Provide a project name and click Create*

Select "Timer trigger," provide a cron expression in the schedule, and finally select the storage account as the storage emulator. The cron expression defined in this step will be the schedule expression for your timer-triggered Azure function. We have selected the storage account as a storage emulator because we want to work in the local environment, but you can always modify the storage account connection. See Figure 5-23.

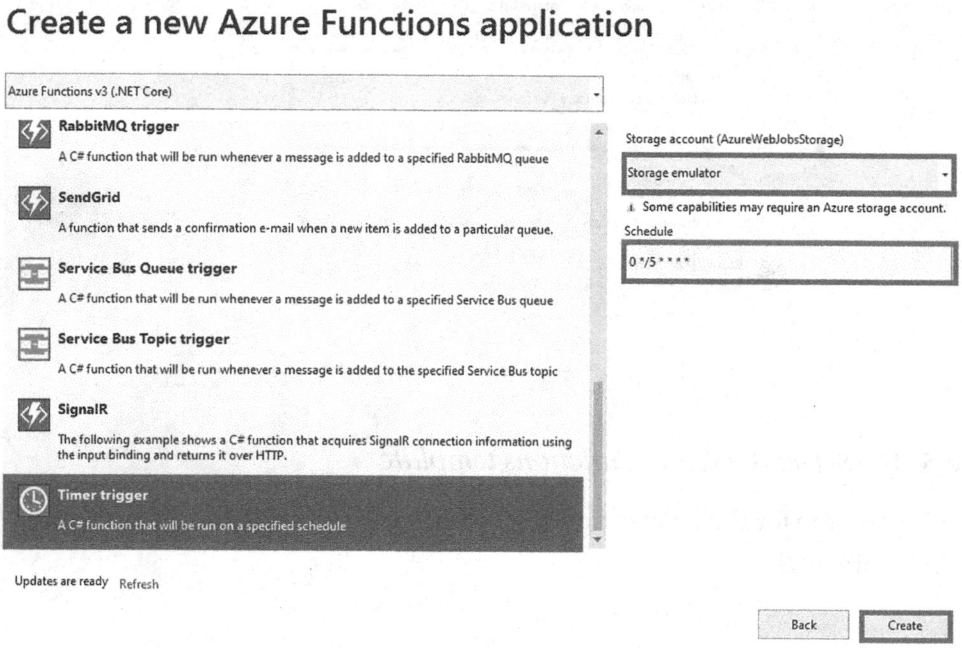

Figure 5-23. *Select "Timer trigger," configure the storage account, and schedule the expression*

Once you click Create, Visual Studio will generate a few files with some boilerplate code with a timer-triggered function named Function1, as shown in Figure 5-24. We discussed each of these files briefly in Chapter 2.

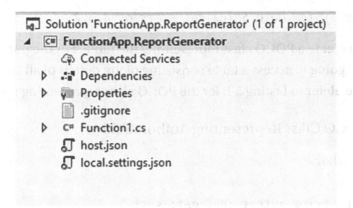

Figure 5-24. *Files generated by Visual Studio for your function*

By default, the function will have code similar to Listing 5-5. The functionality of this function is to run every five minutes and log a message with the date and time of execution.

Listing 5-5. Boilerplate Timer-Triggered Code Generated by Visual Studio

```
public static class Function1
    {
        [FunctionName("Function1")]
        public static void Run([TimerTrigger("0 */5 * * * *")]TimerInfo
        myTimer, ILogger log)
        {
            log.LogInformation($"C# Timer trigger function executed at:
            {DateTime.Now}");
        }
    }
```

You are using an attribute-based declaration of triggers and bindings in this function. While using the in-portal editor, you define it in the function.json file; otherwise, you have to use the Integration pane to define or modify the triggers and bindings of your functions. Here, the TimerTrigger attribute's constructor takes a cron expression.

To enable your function to access a SQL Server database, you need to install the System.Data.SqlClient NuGet package in your function project. You can do this using the NuGet package manager in Visual Studio as well as by typing the following command in the Package Manager Console:

```
Install-Package System.Data.SqlClient -Version 4.8.2
```

Now you will create a POCO class representing the table. For the purpose of this example, you are going to access a table consisting of the details of all the authors of a publishing house. Refer to Listing 5-6 for the POCO class representing the authors table.

Listing 5-6. POCO Class Representing Authors Table

```
public class Author
{
        public string author_id { get; set; }
        public string first_name { get; set; }
        public string last_name { get; set; }
        public string phone { get; set; }
}
```

Once you have created the `Author` class, you will use ADO.NET code to get the data from the database and store it in a list of authors, as shown in Listing 5-7. You can also use Entity Framework Core or any other ORMs like Dapper to interact with the database. But before you jump into the code to get the data from the authors table, you need to know where to store the connection string of your database. You can keep the connection string inside the `local.settings.json` file as a key-value pair and later fetch it in your function; or, you can hard-code the connection string in the function code itself while creating the connection object. The latter is not the recommended way to do it. You will learn how to manage secrets in function apps in Chapter 10.

Listing 5-7. Store the Connection String Inside local.settings.json

```
{
  "IsEncrypted": false,
  "Values": {
    "AzureWebJobsStorage": "UseDevelopmentStorage=true",
    "FUNCTIONS_WORKER_RUNTIME": "dotnet",
    "DBCon": "your-connectionString"
  }
}
```

In Listing 5-7, you created a key-value pair of DBCon inside the values of your local. settings.json file. The value of DBCon is to be replaced by the connection string of your database. Once you have added the connection string value in the local.settings.json file, you can now fetch it using the GetEnvironmentVariable method, as shown in Listing 5-8.

Listing 5-8. Get the Data from the Authors Table and Store It in a List of Authors

```
List<Author> authors = new List<Author>();
string connectionString = Environment.GetEnvironmentVariable("BookStoresDB");
using (SqlConnection myConnection = new SqlConnection(connectionString))
{
        string oString = "Select * from author";
        SqlCommand oCmd = new SqlCommand(oString, myConnection);
        myConnection.Open();
        using (SqlDataReader oReader = oCmd.ExecuteReader())
        {
                while (oReader.Read())
                {
                        Author author = new Author();
                        author.author_id = oReader["author_id"].ToString();
                        author.first_name = oReader["first_name"].ToString();
                        author.last_name = oReader["last_name"].ToString();
                        author.phone = oReader["phone"].ToString();
                        authors.Add(author);
                }

                myConnection.Close();
        }
}
```

In the code snippet in Listing 5-8, you create a list of authors called authors. Then you fetch the connection string from local.setting.json and store it in the connectionString variable using the GetEnvironment method class. Then you use a short piece of ADO.NET code to get the value of all the authors present in the table and then store all the records fetched from the authors table in your Authors list. You need to add the code snippet to the Run method of your function.

Now that we covered the code to fetch and store data from the authors table in the database to a list of authors, let's convert the `authors` list into a JSON string by using the `Serialize` method of the `JsonSerializer` class, as shown in Listing 5-9. Once you add the code snippet shown in Listing 5-9 to serialize the `authors` list object into a JSON string, pass this JSON string inside the `LogInformation` method and run your function to check whether you are able to get the data and serialize the list object into a JSON string.

Listing 5-9. Display the Serialized Authors List As a JSON String in the Azure Functions Core Tools Logs Window

```
var jsonData = JsonSerializer.Serialize<List<Author>>(authors);
log.LogInformation($"{jsonData}");
```

You should see the JSON string in the logs of your Azure Functions Runtime Tools window, as shown in Figure 5-25. This is an optional step. You can use the code snippet in Listing 5-9 to check whether your function is working as expected. (The log message will be different depending on the data you have in your tables.)

Figure 5-25. *Serialized JSON string displayed as a log message*

Now that you have checked that your function is working as expected, let's install the NuGet package required for Blob Storage bindings. You can install the required package by typing the following command in the package manager console of Visual Studio:

Install-Package Microsoft.Azure.WebJobs.Extensions.Storage

Once you have installed the NuGet package, you will have to modify the parameters of your run method. You need to add a `blob` attribute and a TextWriter type parameter called `outblob`. You will be passing the Blob path and file access rights and will define the connection property by assigning the connection string of your storage account to the attributes constructor.

You will be passing the Blob path as `report/{rand-guid}.json`, file access as `FileAccess.Write`, and the storage account connection as `AzureWebJobsStorage`. When you define the storage connection as `AzureWebJobsStorage`, your function looks at the value of `AzureWebJobsStorage` key present in your `local.settings.json` file. You need to make sure that the value is defined as `UseDevelopmentStorage=true` for the `AzureWebJobsStorage` key.

After you have configured the attribute of the `run` method of your function by adding the `blob` attribute and have added the TextWriter Type parameter as `outBlob,` which is the variable that represents the Blob in the function code, you will use `outBlob` to write the `jsonData` in a JSON file whose name will be a random GUID that will be generated with the help of the `{rand-guid}` binding expression. You will store this file inside the report container. You can see the final function code in Listing 5-10.

Listing 5-10. Code for the Schedule-Based Report Generator

```
using System;
using System.Collections.Generic;
using System.Data.SqlClient;
using System.Text.Json;
using Microsoft.Azure.WebJobs;
using Microsoft.Azure.WebJobs.Host;
using Microsoft.Extensions.Configuration;
using Microsoft.Extensions.Logging;
using Microsoft.Azure.WebJobs.Extensions.Storage;
using System.IO;
using System.Text;
namespace FunctionApp.ReportGenerator
{
    public static class Function1
```

```
{
    [FunctionName("Function1")]
    public static void Run([TimerTrigger("0 */5 * * * *")] TimerInfo
    myTimer, ILogger log,
        [Blob("report/{rand-guid}.json", FileAccess.Write, Connection
        ="AzureWebJobsStorage")]TextWriter outBlob)
    {
        log.LogInformation($"C# Timer trigger function executed at:
        {DateTime.Now}");
        List<Author> authors = new List<Author>();
        string connectionString = Environment.GetEnvironmentVariable
        ("BookStoresDB");
        using (SqlConnection myConnection = new SqlConnection
        (connectionString))
        {
            string oString = "Select * from author";
            SqlCommand oCmd = new SqlCommand(oString, myConnection);
            myConnection.Open();
            using (SqlDataReader oReader = oCmd.ExecuteReader())
            {
                while (oReader.Read())
                {
                    Author author = new Author();
                    author.author_id =oReader["author_id"].ToString();
                    author.first_name = oReader["first_name"].ToString();
                    author.last_name = oReader["last_name"].ToString();
                    author.phone = oReader["phone"].ToString();
                    authors.Add(author);
                }
                myConnection.Close();
            }
            var jsonData = JsonSerializer.Serialize<List<Author>>(authors);
            log.LogInformation($"{jsonData}");
            outBlob.Write(jsonData);
```

```
            }
        }
    }
}
```

Listing 5-10 consists of the function code that runs every five minutes and generates a report consisting of all the author records stored in the JSON format. Since you have written the code for your timer-triggered report generator function, let's test it by running the Azure Functions Runtime Tool. If your function executed successfully, then you should see a Blob container named Report and a JSON file with its name being a random GUID in your local storage account. You can view this in Visual Studio with the help of the Cloud Explorer. Alternatively, you can use the Storage Explorer to view the Blob containers.

You can open the Cloud Explorer by clicking the view in Visual Studio and then clicking Cloud Explorer. You will be able to see the Cloud Explorer in the Visual Studio screen, as shown in Figure 5-26.

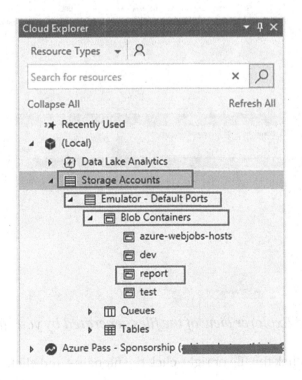

Figure 5-26. *Cloud Explorer view*

The Cloud Explorer allows you to manage your Azure resources and manage the storage accounts present in your local storage emulator. You need to install the Azure workload in Visual Studio to use the Cloud Explorer, provided you are using Visual Studio 2017 or newer.

You can see from Figure 5-26 that you have a Blob container named `report` in your local storage account. As mentioned earlier, if you do not have a Blob container named `report` in your Blob containers, your function will create a Blob container named `report` first and then create a file with a random GUID along with the serialized data from the authors table. You can click the `report` Blob container to view the file created by your function. You should see a screen similar to the one shown in Figure 5-27 after you click the report container.

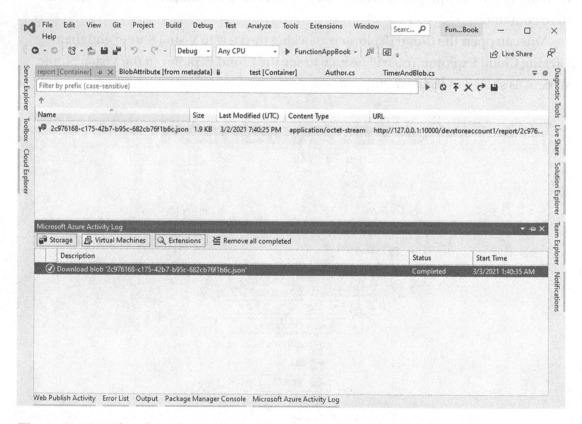

Figure 5-27. *Cloud Explorer view of the files generated by your function*

You can double-click the file or right-click the filename and click Save to download the file.

Summary

In this chapter, you learned how to work with timer triggers and Blob Storage output bindings using Visual Studio and the in-portal editor of the Azure portal. You then used these concepts to build a report generator that gets triggered every five minutes, fetches data from a database table, and creates a JSON file by serializing the fetched data from the database table using a Blob Storage output binding.

The following are the key takeaways from this chapter:

- You can trigger an Azure function using a timer trigger. The function gets triggered depending on the configured schedule.

- You can create a file inside a Blob container from Azure Functions using a Blob Storage output binding.

- You can declaratively configure a timer trigger and Blob Storage output binding without having to write much code.

- Visual Studio provides a template to work with timer triggers.

- You can work with a storage emulator to build and test functions locally that use Blob Storage bindings.

CHAPTER 6

To-Do API with an HTTP Trigger and a Table Storage Binding

At some point you may need to invoke an Azure function using HTTP calls. This will come in handy when you invoke an Azure function from your application code and pass the data to the function to process. The application code can use HTTP triggers to invoke Azure functions and pass the data to the function as the trigger payload. You may also encounter scenarios where the function will process the business logic and save the processed data in Table Storage. You can use a Table Storage binding to achieve this functionality.

In the previous chapter, you learned all about the essential concepts of timer triggers and Blob Storage bindings. You built a report generator application using a timer trigger and Blob Storage binding. In this chapter, you will explore how to implement an HTTP trigger and Table Storage binding for the Azure Functions service and build a to-do API that will populate your to-do list for the day.

Structure of the Chapter

In this chapter, you will explore the following aspects of HTTP triggers and Table Storage bindings:

- Getting started with HTTP triggers and use cases

- Building a sample application using an HTTP trigger

- Routing HTTP-triggered Azure functions

© Ashirwad Satapathi and Abhishek Mishra 2021
A. Satapathi and A. Mishra, *Hands-on Azure Functions with C#*, https://doi.org/10.1007/978-1-4842-7122-3_6

- Getting started with Table Storage bindings and use cases

- Building a sample application using a Table Storage binding

- Creating a to-do API with HTTP triggers and Table Storage bindings

Objectives

After studying this chapter, you will be able to do the following:

- Implement HTTP triggers for Azure Functions

- Implement Table Storage bindings for Azure Functions

Getting Started with HTTP Triggers and Use Cases

An HTTP trigger helps you execute an Azure function using HTTP verbs or methods. You can add your business logic or data access logic to the Azure function and enable an HTTP trigger for the Azure function. Then from your application code or user interface, you can invoke the Azure function using an HTTP trigger. As a best practice, you need to break the business logic or the data access logic into short-running code pieces so that your Azure function does not time out and you adhere to the serverless principles. HTTP triggers help you build serverless APIs and let you expose the Azure function as a web hook. You can pass data to the Azure function as the trigger payload using a query string or POST parameter value.

The following are a few example scenarios where you can use HTTP triggers:

- You can host common utility logic in an Azure function that can be used across all the application modules. The Azure function can have an HTTP trigger enabled and can be called using an HTTP GET or POST method.

- You can host code on the Azure function that performs a business functionality such as report generation or data update or any other such activity on demand. You can invoke the Azure function using an HTTP trigger whenever needed.

- You can build a data access layer to fetch data from the underlying database and give it to you. Your application can invoke the Azure function using HTTP calls to perform CRUD operations on the database.

Build a Sample Application Using an HTTP Trigger

Now let's build an Azure function using Visual Studio and enable an HTTP trigger for the Azure function. Open Visual Studio and click "Create a new project." See Figure 6-1.

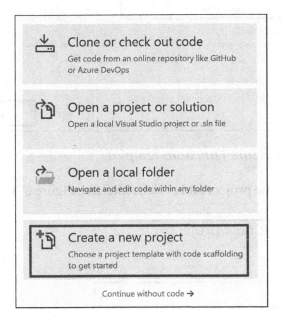

Figure 6-1. *Create a new project*

Select the Azure Functions template. Click Next. See Figure 6-2.

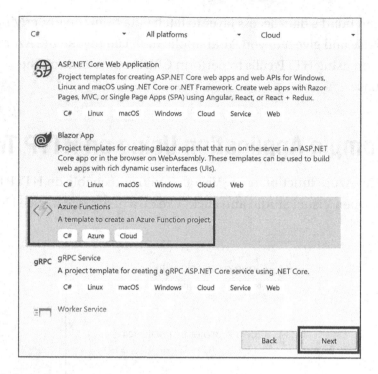

Figure 6-2. *Select the Azure Functions template*

Provide a name for the project and click Create. See Figure 6-3.

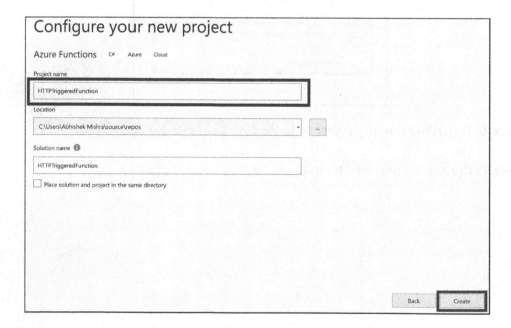

Figure 6-3. *Provide the project details*

Select the "Http trigger" template and set the authentication method to Anonymous. This action will help you invoke the function without using any access keys. However, you should choose the Anonymous authentication type only in development and testing scenarios. In other environments such as staging and production, you should use Function as the access level. See Figure 6-4.

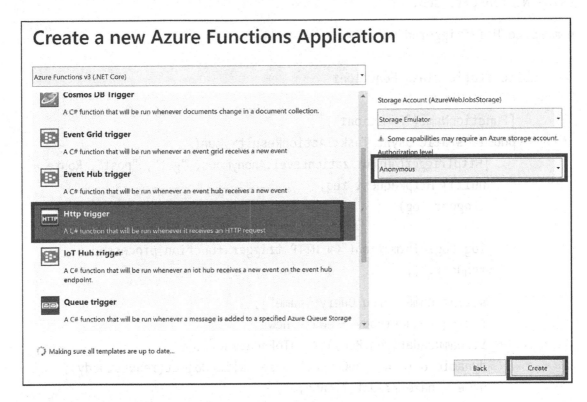

Figure 6-4. *Select an HTTP trigger template*

The Visual Studio solution with an HTTP-triggered Azure function gets created. Listing 6-1 shows the code for Function1.cs. The code gets the name parameter value passed either in the HTTP request query string or in the body, appends it to a Hello message, and returns the message to the caller.

Listing 6-1. Function1.cs Code

```
using System;
using System.IO;
using System.Threading.Tasks;
```

```csharp
using Microsoft.AspNetCore.Mvc;
using Microsoft.Azure.WebJobs;
using Microsoft.Azure.WebJobs.Extensions.Http;
using Microsoft.AspNetCore.Http;
using Microsoft.Extensions.Logging;
using Newtonsoft.Json;

namespace HTTPTriggeredFunction
{
    public static class Function1
    {
        [FunctionName("Function1")]
        public static async Task<IActionResult> Run(
            [HttpTrigger(AuthorizationLevel.Anonymous, "get", "post", Route =
            null)] HttpRequest req,
            ILogger log)
        {
            log.LogInformation("C# HTTP trigger function processed a
            request.");

            string name = req.Query["name"];
            string requestBody = await new
            StreamReader(req.Body).ReadToEndAsync();
            dynamic data = JsonConvert.DeserializeObject(requestBody);
            name = name ?? data?.name;

            string responseMessage = string.IsNullOrEmpty(name)
                ? "This HTTP triggered function executed successfully.
                  Pass a name in the query string or in the request body
                  for a personalized response."
                : $"Hello, {name}. This HTTP triggered function executed
                  successfully.";

            return new OkObjectResult(responseMessage);
        }
    }
}
```

Now run the solution. Wait until the console displays the function URL in the execution console. See Figure 6-5.

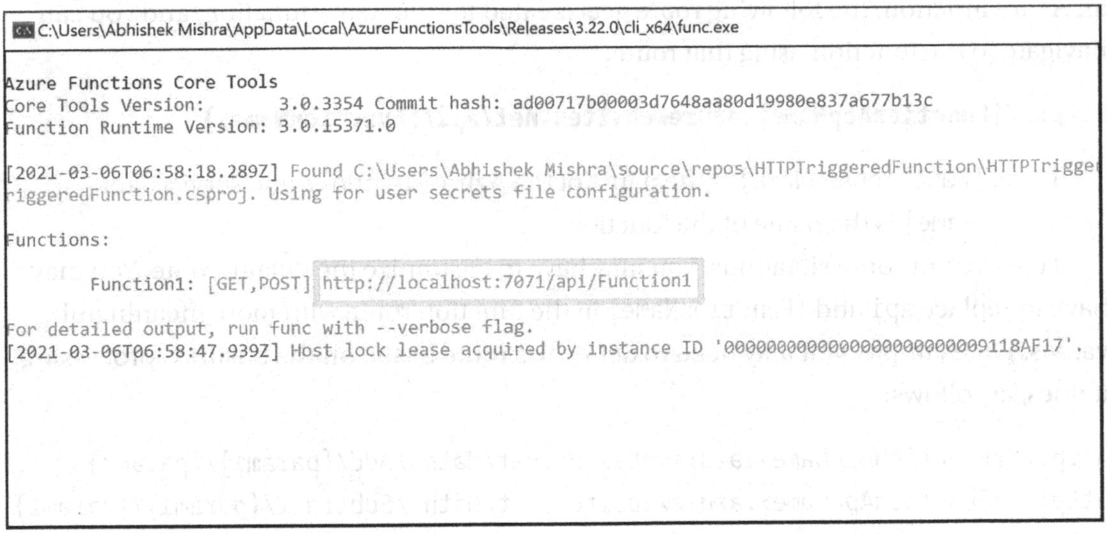

```
C:\Users\Abhishek Mishra\AppData\Local\AzureFunctionsTools\Releases\3.22.0\cli_x64\func.exe

Azure Functions Core Tools
Core Tools Version:       3.0.3354 Commit hash: ad00717b00003d7648aa80d19980e837a677b13c
Function Runtime Version: 3.0.15371.0

[2021-03-06T06:58:18.289Z] Found C:\Users\Abhishek Mishra\source\repos\HTTPTriggeredFunction\HTTPTrigge
riggeredFunction.csproj. Using for user secrets file configuration.

Functions:

        Function1: [GET,POST] http://localhost:7071/api/Function1

For detailed output, run func with --verbose flag.
[2021-03-06T06:58:47.939Z] Host lock lease acquired by instance ID '000000000000000000000009118AF17'.
```

Figure 6-5. *Function execution*

Copy the URL from the console window. Append the URL with the query string ?name=Abhishek and then browse to the URL. See Figure 6-6.

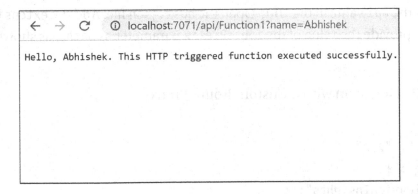

```
← → C    ① localhost:7071/api/Function1?name=Abhishek

Hello, Abhishek. This HTTP triggered function executed successfully.
```

Figure 6-6. *Browse to the function URL along with the query string*

Routing in HTTP-Triggered Azure Functions

You can define a route for an Azure function with ease. By default, whenever you create an Azure function, the following route gets created for the Azure function, and you can navigate to the function using that route:

http://{FunctionAppName}.azurewebsites.net/api/{FunctionName>}

Here, {FunctionAppName} is the name of the Azure Functions app service, and {FunctionName} is the name of the function.

However, in some situations, you may have to customize the default route. You may have to replace api and {FunctionName} in the function route with more meaningful values. For example, you may need to define the route based on the business processing it does, as follows:

```
http://<FunctionAppName>.azurewebsites.net/Maths/Add/{param1}/{param2}
http://<FunctionAppName>.azurewebsites.net/Maths/Subtract/{param1}/{param2}
http://<FunctionAppName>.azurewebsites.net/StringOps/Concat/{param1}/{param2}
http://<FunctionAppName>.azurewebsites.net/StringOps/Replace/{param1}/{param2}
```

Here, {param1} and {param2} are input parameters for the Azure function.

Let's modify the Azure function solution you developed earlier to enable a custom route. Open the Azure function solution that you built earlier using Visual Studio. Let's first modify the api value in the URL. Open the host.json file. Add the extensions section and provide the value of the routePrefix parameter as Maths, as shown in Listing 6-2.

Listing 6-2. Host.json with a Custom Route Prefix

```json
{
  "version": "2.0",
  "logging": {
    "applicationInsights": {
      "samplingExcludedTypes": "Request",
      "samplingSettings": {
        "isEnabled": true
```

```
      }
    }
  },
  "extensions": {
    "http": {
      "routePrefix": "Maths"
    }
  }
}
```

Now let's modify the Function1.cs code to add a custom route for the Azure function (see Listing 6-3). Add the route value as Maths/{param1}/{param2} in the Route parameter of the HttpTrigger attribute and add two input parameters, param1 and param2, matching the route parameters defined.

Listing 6-3. Function1.cs with a Custom Route

```
using System;
using System.IO;
using System.Threading.Tasks;
using Microsoft.AspNetCore.Mvc;
using Microsoft.Azure.WebJobs;
using Microsoft.Azure.WebJobs.Extensions.Http;
using Microsoft.AspNetCore.Http;
using Microsoft.Extensions.Logging;
using Newtonsoft.Json;

namespace HTTPTriggeredFunction
{
    public static class Function1
    {
        [FunctionName("Function1")]
        public static async Task<IActionResult> Run(
            [HttpTrigger(AuthorizationLevel.Anonymous, "get", "post",
            Route = "Add/{param1}/{param2}")] HttpRequest req,
            int param1, int param2,
            ILogger log)
```

```
    {
        log.LogInformation("C# HTTP trigger function processed a
        request.");

        string responseMessage = "The computed addtition value
        is"+(param1  + param2).ToString();
        return new OkObjectResult(responseMessage);
    }
  }
}
```

Now let's execute the Azure function in Visual Studio. You can see the Azure function with a custom route. See Figure 6-7.

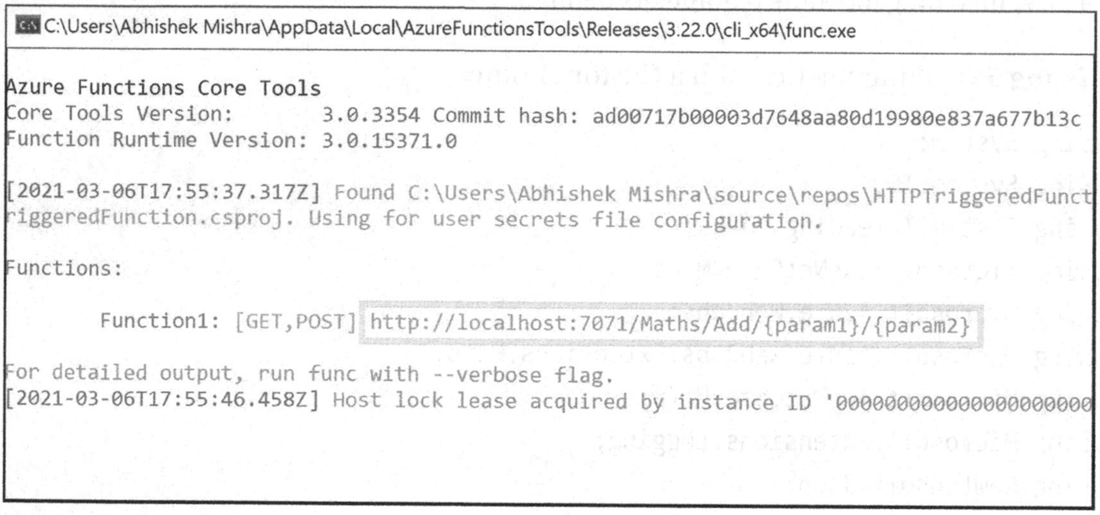

```
C:\Users\Abhishek Mishra\AppData\Local\AzureFunctionsTools\Releases\3.22.0\cli_x64\func.exe

Azure Functions Core Tools
Core Tools Version:        3.0.3354 Commit hash: ad00717b00003d7648aa80d19980e837a677b13c
Function Runtime Version: 3.0.15371.0

[2021-03-06T17:55:37.317Z] Found C:\Users\Abhishek Mishra\source\repos\HTTPTriggeredFunct
riggeredFunction.csproj. Using for user secrets file configuration.

Functions:

      Function1: [GET,POST] http://localhost:7071/Maths/Add/{param1}/{param2}

For detailed output, run func with --verbose flag.
[2021-03-06T17:55:46.458Z] Host lock lease acquired by instance ID '00000000000000000000000
```

Figure 6-7. Function execution

Now let's browse to the Azure function using the following URL (see Figure 6-8):

```
http://localhost:7071/Maths/Add/22/23
```

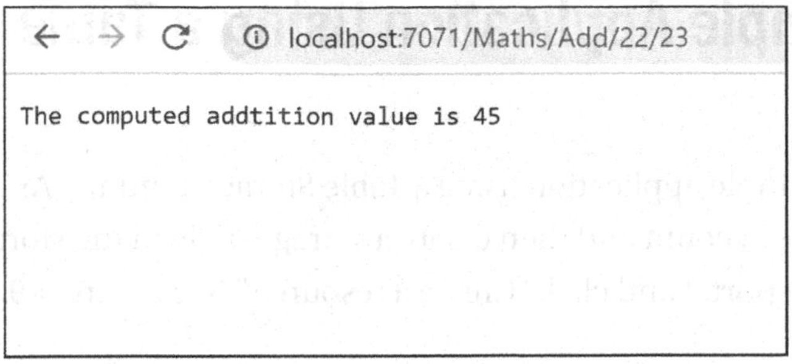

Figure 6-8. *Browse to the function URL*

Getting Started with Table Storage Bindings and Use Cases

Sometimes the Azure function will process the business logic and save the output data in Azure Table Storage. You may also have scenarios where the Azure function will read the data from Table Storage and process it. You can use a Table Storage input binding or Table Storage output binding and achieve this functionality with ease. You need to add a declarative configuration to add a Table Storage binding to the Azure function, and you can interact with the Azure Table Storage data using a few lines of code.

The following are few of the use cases where you can use an Azure Table Storage binding:

- For the applications storing data in Azure Table Storage, you can write CRUD operations using Azure functions and access the data using Table Storage input or output bindings.

- You can build a to-do list application to use an Azure function to store your daily task list in Azure Table Storage. You need to enable an Azure Table Storage binding for the Azure function.

- You may choose to persist your application logs or audit data in Table Storage. You can use an Azure function to store the errors, exceptions, logs, and audit details in Azure Table Storage. You need to enable an Azure Table Storage binding for the Azure function.

135

Build a Sample Application Using a Table Storage Binding

Now let's build a sample application using a Table Storage binding. As a prerequisite, let's create a storage account and then create a storage table in the storage account.

Go to the Azure portal and click "Create a resource." See Figure 6-9.

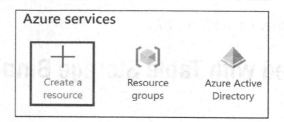

Figure 6-9. *Create a resource*

Search for *storage account* and click the search result "Storage account." See Figure 6-10.

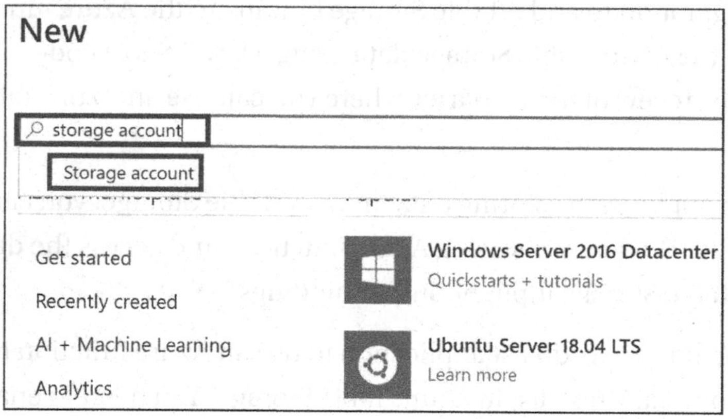

Figure 6-10. *Select "Storage account"*

Click Create. See Figure 6-11.

Figure 6-11. *Click Create*

Select your Azure subscription, your resource group, and the location where you need to create the storage account. Provide a name for the storage account. Click "Review + create." See Figure 6-12.

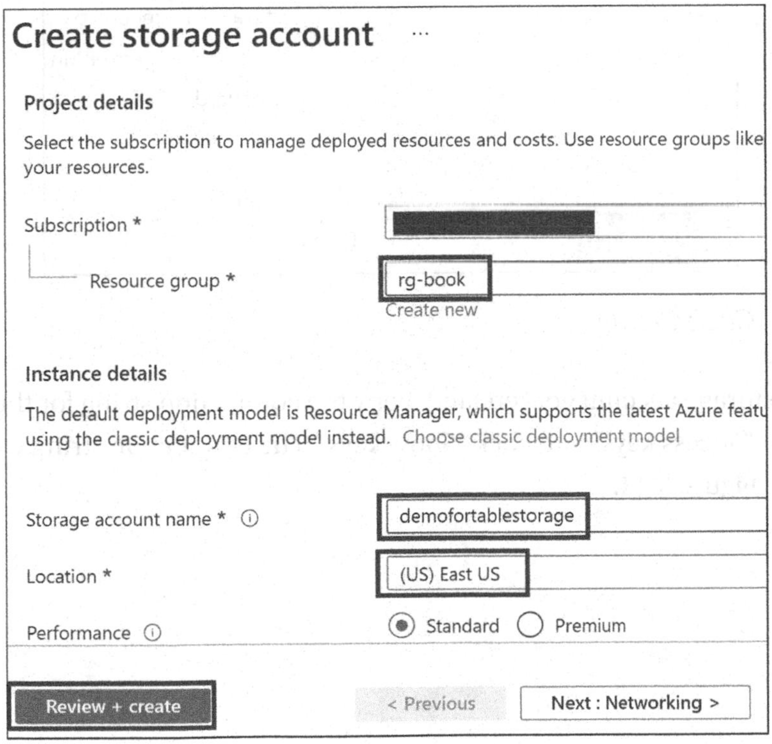

Create storage account ...

Project details

Select the subscription to manage deployed resources and costs. Use resource groups like your resources.

Subscription *

Resource group *   rg-book
                          Create new

Instance details

The default deployment model is Resource Manager, which supports the latest Azure featu using the classic deployment model instead. Choose classic deployment model

Storage account name * ⓘ   demofortablestorage

Location *   (US) East US

Performance ⓘ   ⦿ Standard   ◯ Premium

| Review + create | | < Previous | Next : Networking > |

Figure 6-12. *Click "Review + create"*

Click Create. This action will create the storage account. See Figure 6-13.

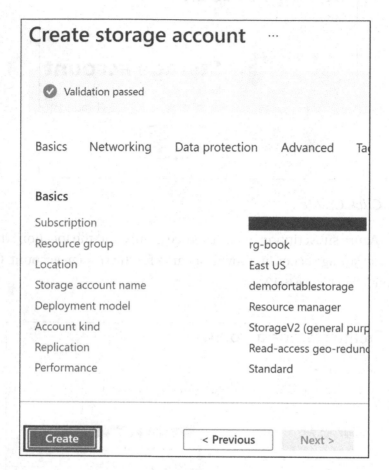

Figure 6-13. *Click Create*

Once the storage account gets created, copy the connection string for the storage account. Go to "Access keys" and click "Show keys." The connection string will be displayed. See Figure 6-14.

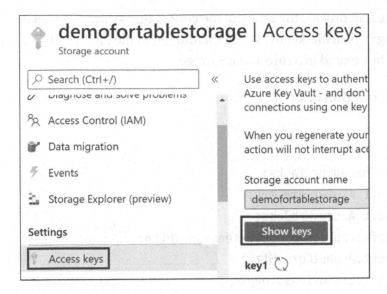

Figure 6-14. Copy the connection string

Now let's go back to the Azure function solution that you created earlier and open local.settings.json (see Listing 6-4). Add a key for the connection string named ConnectToTable and provide the Azure storage account connection string that you copied from the Azure portal earlier.

Listing 6-4. local.settings.json

```
{
    "IsEncrypted": false,
  "Values": {
    "AzureWebJobsStorage": "UseDevelopmentStorage=true",
    "FUNCTIONS_WORKER_RUNTIME": "dotnet",
    "ConnectToTable": "[Replace with connection string copied from Azure
    Portal]"
  }
}
```

Now let's add the NuGet package Microsoft.Azure.WebJobs.Extensions.Storage for the project. This action will help the Azure function interact with the Azure storage. Open Function1.cs and replace the contents with Listing 6-5. The properties in the MathResult class refer to the columns in Azure Table Storage. Specify the return:

Table attribute and provide the name of the connection string you specified in the `local.settings.json` file. ResultTable mentioned in the attribute is the name of the table that will be created in Azure Table Storage.

Listing 6-5. Function1.cs

```
using System;
using System.IO;
using System.Threading.Tasks;
using Microsoft.AspNetCore.Mvc;
using Microsoft.Azure.WebJobs;
using Microsoft.Azure.WebJobs.Extensions.Http;
using Microsoft.AspNetCore.Http;
using Microsoft.Extensions.Logging;
using Newtonsoft.Json;

namespace HTTPTriggeredFunction
{
    public static class Function1
    {
        [FunctionName("Function1")]
        [return: Table("ResultTable", Connection = "ConnectToTable")]
        public static MathResult Run(
            [HttpTrigger(AuthorizationLevel.Anonymous, "get", "post",
            Route = "Add/{param1}/{param2}")] HttpRequest req,
            int param1, int param2,
            ILogger log)
        {
            log.LogInformation("C# HTTP trigger function processed a
            request.");

            int result = param1 + param2;
            return new MathResult { PartitionKey = "Math",
                RowKey = Guid.NewGuid().ToString(),
                Operation="Add", Result = result };
        }
    }
```

```
public class MathResult
{
    public string PartitionKey { get; set; }
    public string RowKey { get; set; }
    public string Operation { get; set; }
    public int Result { get; set; }
}
}
```

Execute the Azure function and browse to the following function URL:

```
http://localhost:7071/Maths/Add/2/3
```

Go to the Storage Explorer for the storage account in the Azure portal, and you can find the table with fields as in the MathResult class. See Figure 6-15.

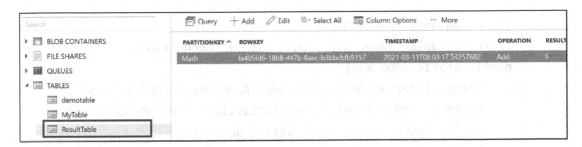

Figure 6-15. *ResultTable in Azure Storage Explorer*

Create a To-Do API with an HTTP Trigger and a Table Storage Binding

Now let's build a to-do API. Modify the Function1.cs file as shown in Listing 6-6. In the function's Route parameter, you send the date, time, and to-do activity to the Azure function. The properties in the ToDo class refer to the columns in Azure Table Storage. Specify the return: Table attribute and provide the name of the connection string you have specified in the local.settings.json file. ToDoList mentioned in the attribute is the name of the table that will get created in Azure Table Storage.

Listing 6-6. Function1.cs

```csharp
using System;
using System.IO;
using System.Threading.Tasks;
using Microsoft.AspNetCore.Mvc;
using Microsoft.Azure.WebJobs;
using Microsoft.Azure.WebJobs.Extensions.Http;
using Microsoft.AspNetCore.Http;
using Microsoft.Extensions.Logging;
using Newtonsoft.Json;

namespace HTTPTriggeredFunction
{
    public static class Function1
    {
        [FunctionName("Function1")]
        [return: Table("ToDoList", Connection = "ConnectToTable")]
        public static ToDo Run(
            [HttpTrigger(AuthorizationLevel.Anonymous, "get", "post",
            Route = "ToDo/{date}/{time}/{activity}")] HttpRequest req,
            string date, string time, string activity,
            ILogger log)
        {

        log.LogInformation("C# HTTP trigger function processed a
        request.");

            return new ToDo { PartitionKey = date,
                RowKey = Guid.NewGuid().ToString(),
                Time=time,
                Activity=activity };
        }
    }
    public class ToDo
    {
        public string PartitionKey { get; set; }
        public string RowKey { get; set; }
```

```
    public string Time { get; set; }
    public string Activity { get; set; }
    }
}
```

Execute the Azure function and browse to the following function URL:

```
http://localhost:7071/Maths/ToDo/10-Feb-2021/4 20PM/Get vegetables from
market
```

Go to the Storage Explorer for the storage account in the Azure portal, and you can find the table ToDoList with fields as in the ToDo class.

Now let's create another Azure function that you can use to read from the to-do list in Azure Table Storage. Right-click the Azure function project and add a new Azure function named Function2.cs. Make sure you use the HTTP trigger template for the function. See Figure 6-16.

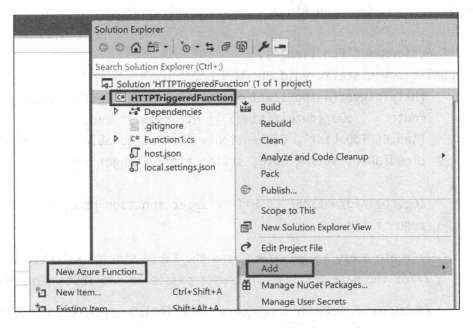

Figure 6-16. *Add a new function*

Add the ToDoRead class to the Azure function (see Listing 6-7). It should inherit from the TableEntity class. You are using CloudTable to get the results from Table Storage, and you are using TableQuery to query the records in Table Storage. You need to get the records for the date and time passed as a query string by the user.

Listing 6-7. ToDoRead Class

```
using System;
using System.IO;
using System.Linq;
using System.Threading.Tasks;
using Microsoft.AspNetCore.Http;
using Microsoft.AspNetCore.Mvc;
using Microsoft.Azure.Cosmos.Table;
using Microsoft.Azure.WebJobs;
using Microsoft.Azure.WebJobs.Extensions.Http;
using Microsoft.Extensions.Logging;
using Newtonsoft.Json;

namespace HTTPTriggeredFunction
{
    public static class Function2
    {
        [FunctionName("Function2")]
        public async static void Run(
            [HttpTrigger(AuthorizationLevel.Anonymous, "get", "post",
            Route = "ToDo/{date}/{time}")] HttpRequest req,
            [Table("ToDoList", Connection = "ConnectToTable")] CloudTable
            cloudTable, string date, string time, ILogger log)
        {

            log.LogInformation("C# HTTP trigger function processed a
            request.");

            //Create query to get items from the Table Storage selectively only
            //for the date and time that user passes in the route parameter.

            TableQuery<ToDoRead> rangeQuery = new TableQuery<ToDoRead>().Where(
                TableQuery.CombineFilters(
                    TableQuery.GenerateFilterCondition("PartitionKey",
                    QueryComparisons.Equal, date),
                    TableOperators.And,
                    TableQuery.GenerateFilterCondition("Time",
```

```
                QueryComparisons.Equal, time)));
           foreach (ToDoRead entity in
               await cloudTable.ExecuteQuerySegmentedAsync(rangeQuery, null))
           {
                log.LogInformation(
                    "Your TO DO : "+entity.Activity);
           }
       }
   }
   public class ToDoRead:TableEntity
   {
       public string Time { get; set; }
       public string Activity { get; set; }
   }
}
```

Run the Azure function project and browse to the following URL. Pass the date and time. The function will fetch the activity that you added for that date and time. See Figure 6-17.

```
http://localhost:7071/Maths/ToDo/10-Feb-2021/4 20PM
```

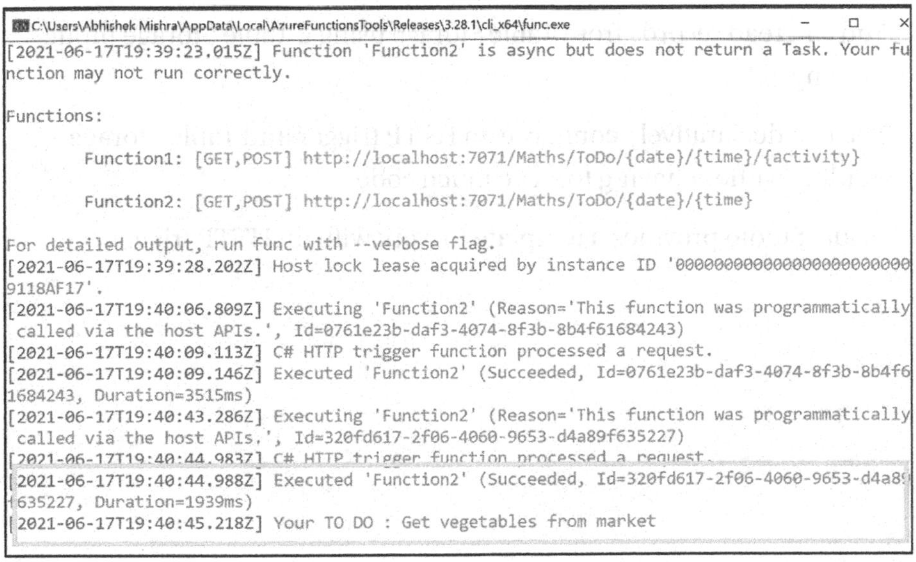

Figure 6-17. *Triggered function result*

Note   To keep the illustration simple, the date and time fields are handled as strings in Table Storage. In the actual production scenario, these fields should be corresponding date and time types.

Summary

In this chapter, you learned how to work with HTTP triggers and Storage Table input and output bindings using Visual Studio. You then used these concepts to build a to-do API that you can trigger with an HTTP GET request. You can pass the date, time, and activity you are planning to do during that time. The to-do API will add the activity to the to-do list and fetch the to-do list activity.

The following are the key takeaways from this chapter.

- You can trigger an Azure function using an HTTP trigger. The function gets invoked using HTTP verbs like GET, POST, PUT, and others.

- You can add records to Table Storage using a Table Storage output binding.

- You can read records from Table Storage using a Table Storage input binding.

- You can declaratively configure an HTTP trigger and Table Storage binding without having to write much code.

- Visual Studio provides a template to work with an HTTP trigger.

CHAPTER 7

Creating Custom Bindings for Azure Functions

Bindings help the Azure Functions service exchange data with other Azure services and external services with ease. You need to add a declarative configuration to enable bindings for functions. Azure provides a wide range of bindings out of the box. In most scenarios, the bindings provided by Azure should be good enough to achieve the intended application functionality such as reading from Blob Storage, putting some data in Queue Storage, triggering a binding from RabbitMQ, and much more. However, there will be scenarios or use cases where the standard bindings provided by Azure may not fit into your business scenarios or you need to interact with a new service for which Azure Functions does not have readily available binding support. For such scenarios, you can build a custom binding based on your needs.

In the previous chapter, you learned how to implement a to-do API using HTTP triggers and Table Storage bindings. In this chapter, you will explore the concept of custom bindings and learn how to implement a custom binding for a .NET Core–based Azure function.

Structure of the Chapter

In this chapter, you will explore the following aspects of Azure Functions custom bindings:

- Introduction to custom bindings
- Use cases for custom bindings
- Building a custom binding for Azure Functions

© Ashirwad Satapathi and Abhishek Mishra 2021
A. Satapathi and A. Mishra, *Hands-on Azure Functions with C#*, https://doi.org/10.1007/978-1-4842-7122-3_7

Objectives

After studying this chapter, you will be able to do the following:

- Understand custom bindings for Azure Functions

- Create a custom binding for Azure Functions

Introduction to Custom Bindings

Bindings require less coding on your part and simplify your code. You need to add declarative configurations in the Azure Functions code to interact with an external service or an Azure service. Azure provides an array of input and output bindings out of the box. However, there are scenarios where the standard function bindings may not meet your business requirements. In these cases, you can build a custom input or output binding to meet your business needs. Creating a custom binding is an easy and one-time activity, and the binding can be reused across functions.

You can build a custom binding using .NET by following a couple of easy steps. You can create custom input and output bindings using the Azure Functions SDK based on the WebJobs extension libraries. You just focus on building the business functionality for the custom binding, and most of the heavy lifting is done by the underlying .NET libraries. Once the custom binding is ready, you can consume it in your functions just like the standard bindings.

Use Cases for Custom Bindings

Before creating a custom binding, you should first determine whether an existing binding suffices based on your requirements. Azure offers a wide range of function bindings, and you should be able to manage most of the scenarios with those bindings. You may need to build a custom binding for the following scenarios:

- The existing bindings do not meet the requirements, and you need more functionality to be addressed. For example, you need to update some entities in Azure Table Storage. This scenario is not supported by any existing Azure Table Storage binding.

- Azure Functions does not have a binding for an Azure service. For example, say you need to interact with Azure Cache for Redis and work on cache data. There is currently no binding for Azure Cache for Redis.

- You need to connect with an external non-Azure service or component and exchange data with it. For example, you need to pull some data from Twitter. There is currently no binding available for Azure Functions to interact with Twitter.

- You need to achieve a specific functionality with functions that need to deal with multiple services and components at a time. For example, you can build a binding to fetch data from multiple storages and data sources like Azure Cosmos DB, Azure SQL, or Amazon S3 and then aggregate the data. Azure Functions can build a custom report with this data.

Build a Custom Binding for Azure Functions

Let's create a custom binding for an Azure function that will help in converting the data from one format to another. A third-party service processes the users' data and saves the data in a centralized location accessible to both the third-party service and the Azure function. The third-party service generates the data as listed in Listing 7-1.

Listing 7-1. Data Format Generated by the Third-Party Service

```
[name:Abhishek Mishra,Age:32,subject:maths]
```

The Azure function needs to further process the data generated by the third-party service. However, the Azure function does not understand the current data format being generated and can only work on the format in Listing 7-2.

Listing 7-2. Data Format That the Function Understands

```
{ "name":"Abhishek Mishra","Age":"32","subject":"maths" }
```

Before processing the data, you need to implement code that will format the data, and that code will not be reusable; it is good only for the Azure function where it is implemented. To handle this scenario, you can create a custom binding that will read the data from the central location, do the necessary conversion, and then pass on the converted data to the Azure function. You are saved from implementing code at the function level and can use the binding in multiple functions if needed. See Figure 7-1.

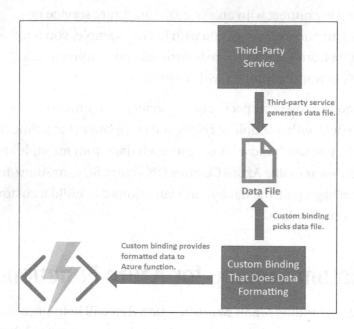

Figure 7-1. *Custom binding scenario*

You can create a custom binding using the following steps. In this chapter, you will use Visual Studio 2019 to build the custom binding.

1. Create an Azure function.

2. Implement the binding attribute class.

3. Implement the binding logic class.

4. Implement the binding extension class.

5. Implement the binding startup class.

6. Incorporate the binding in the Azure function.

Now let's implement each of these steps.

Create an Azure Function

Open Visual Studio and click "Create a new project." See Figure 7-2.

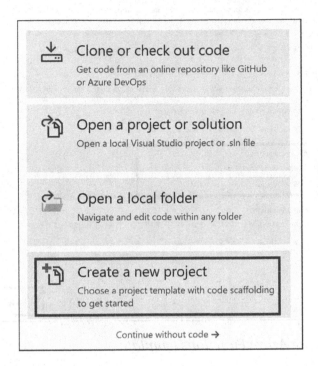

Figure 7-2. *Create a function project*

Select the Azure Functions template. Click Next. See Figure 7-3.

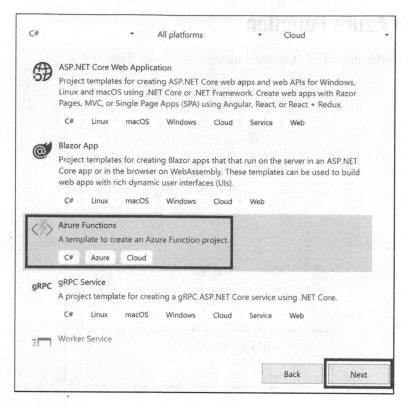

Figure 7-3. *Select the Azure Functions template*

Provide the project name and click Create. See Figure 7-4.

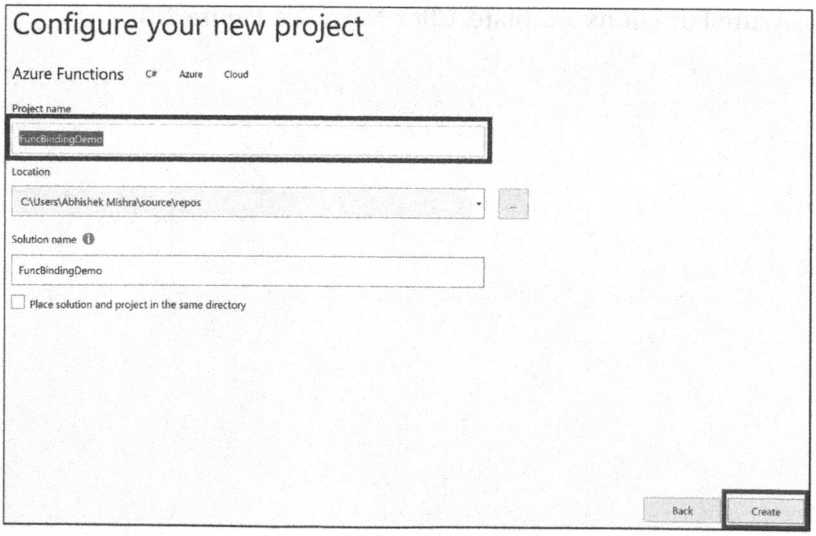

Figure 7-4. *Provide the function project details*

Select "Http trigger" and click Create. See Figure 7-5.

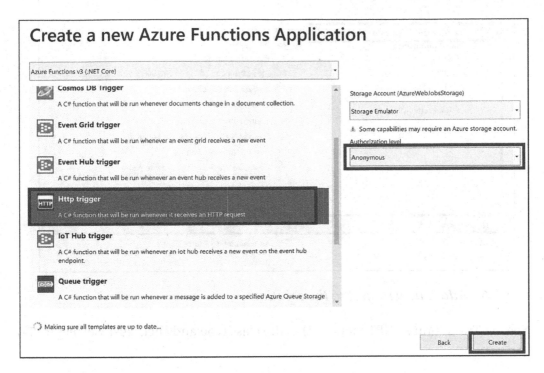

Figure 7-5. *Select "Http trigger"*

The Azure function gets created. You will modify the Azure function code once you have the custom binding ready.

Implement the Binding Attribute Class

In this section, you'll add a new project of type .NET Standard Class Library to the solution called Custom Binding. To add a new project to the solution, right-click the solution, click Add, and then click New Project. See Figure 7-6.

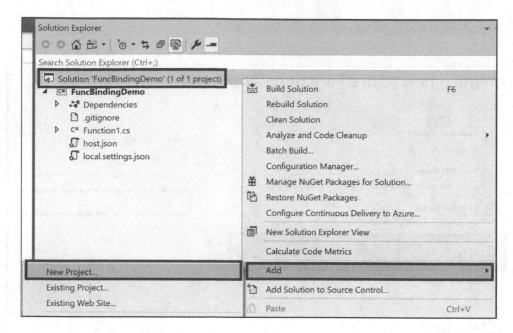

Figure 7-6. *Add a new project to the solution*

Select Class Library (.NET Standard) as the class type and click Next. See Figure 7-7.

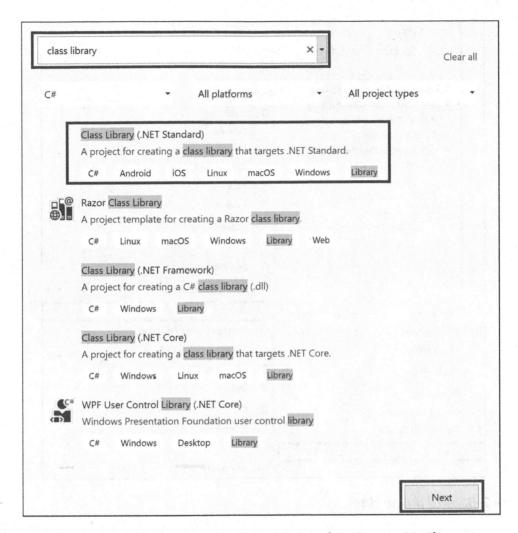

Figure 7-7. *Set the type of project as Class Library (.NET Standard)*

Provide the name of the project as **CustomFormatBinding**.

Once the project gets created, add the following packages from NuGet:

- `Microsoft.NET.Sdk.Functions`

- `Microsoft.Azure.WebJobs`

- `Microsoft.Azure.Webjobs.Core`

Now let's add a class named `FormatterBindingAttribute.cs` in the CustomFormatBinding project. Right-click the project, click Add, and then click Class. See Figure 7-8.

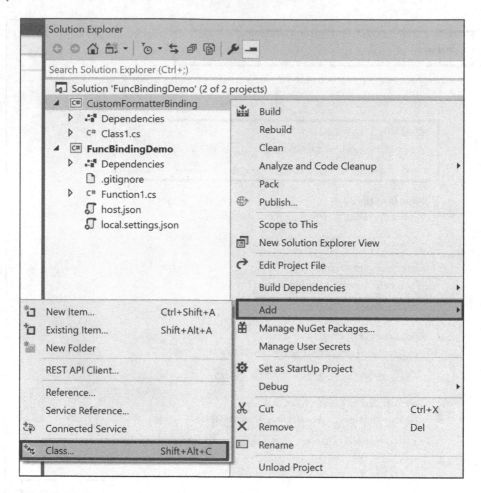

Figure 7-8. *Add a new class*

Place the code shown in Listing 7-3 in the `FormatterBindingAttribute.cs` class. You need to create a custom attribute that you can decorate as a binding for the Azure function. The attribute has a property called `DataFileLocation` that can point to the location where the file to be formatted is kept. You decorate this property with the `AutoResolve` attribute so that it will be able to resolve the path from the `local.settings.json` file.

Listing 7-3. FormatterBindingAttribute Class

```
using Microsoft.Azure.WebJobs.Description;
using System;

namespace CustomFormatBinding
```

```
{
    [Binding]
    [AttributeUsage(AttributeTargets.Parameter | AttributeTargets.
    ReturnValue)]
    public class FormatterBindingAttribute:Attribute
    {
        [AutoResolve]
        public string DataFileLocation { get; set; }
    }
}
```

Implement the Binding Logic Class

Now let's implement the binding logic class. Here you will write the logic to convert the data in the file in a format that the function will need to process the data. Before you implement the binding logic class, let's implement a model class that will hold the formatted data and will be available as an input parameter to the function. Add a class named FormatterModel.cs in the CustomFormatBinding project and replace the class code with the code shown in Listing 7-4.

Listing 7-4. FormatterModel Class

```
using System;
using System.Collections.Generic;
using System.Text;

namespace CustomFormatBinding
{
    public class FormatterModel
    {
        public string DataFilePath { get; set; }
        public string Content { get; set; }
    }
}
```

Now let's add a class for the binding logic in the CustomFormatBinding project. You will name the class `FormatterBinding.cs`. You have an `Initialize` method in this class that adds a binding rule that specifies the conversion operation's logic. The `Convert` performs the data formatting activity and must be passed as a parameter for the `BindToInput` method. Replace the code in Listing 7-5 with the code generated when you created the class.

Listing 7-5. FormatterBinding Class

```
using System.IO;
using Microsoft.Azure.WebJobs.Description;
using Microsoft.Azure.WebJobs.Host.Config;

namespace CustomFormatBinding
{
    [Extension("MyFileReaderBinding")]
    public class FormatterBinding : IExtensionConfigProvider
    {
        public void Initialize(ExtensionConfigContext context)
        {
            var rule = context.AddBindingRule<FormatterBindingAttribute>();
            rule.BindToInput<FormatterModel>(BuildItemFromAttribute);
        }

        private FormatterModel BuildItemFromAttribute(FormatterBindingAttribute
        arg)
        {
            string formattedData = string.Empty;
            if (File.Exists(arg.DataFileLocation))
            {
                formattedData = "{";
                string formattedDataAsIs =
                File.ReadAllText(arg.DataFileLocation);
                // Replace the start [ and end ]
                formattedDataAsIs= formattedDataAsIs.TrimStart(new char[] { '['
                }).TrimEnd(new char[] { ']' });
```

```csharp
            // Data formatting activity/logic
            string[] tokens = formattedDataAsIs.Split(new char[] { ',' });
            foreach (var token in tokens)
            {
                string[] subToken = token.Split(new char[] { ':' });
                formattedData = formattedData + "\"" + subToken[0] + "\" :
                " + "\"" + subToken[1] + "\" , ";
            }
            formattedData = formattedData.Trim().TrimEnd(new char[] { ','
            });
            formattedData = formattedData + "}";
        }

        return new FormatterModel
        {
            DataFilePath = arg.DataFileLocation,
            FormattedData = formattedData
        };
    }
}
```

Implement the Binding Extension Class

Now let's implement the binding extension class. Create a new class named
BindingExtension.cs in the CustomFormatBinding project. Place the code in Listing 7-6
in the class. You will invoke the method AddCustomBinding in the Startup class. When this
method gets invoked, it will call the binding formatter class to do the necessary conversion
and return the converted data.

Listing 7-6. BindingExtension Class

```
using Microsoft.Azure.WebJobs;
using System;

namespace CustomFormatBinding
{
    public static class BindingExtension
    {
        public static IWebJobsBuilder AddCustomBinding(this IWebJobsBuilder
        builder)
        {
            if (builder == null)
            {
                throw new ArgumentNullException(nameof(builder));
            }

            builder.AddExtension<FormatterBinding>();
            return builder;
        }
    }
}
```

Implement the Binding Startup Class

Now let's create the startup class that will inject the binding into the runtime execution context. Add a class called BindingStartup.cs in the CustomFormatBinding project. Use the code in Listing 7-7 in the class.

Listing 7-7. BindingStartup Class

```
using CustomFormatBinding;
using Microsoft.Azure.WebJobs;
using Microsoft.Azure.WebJobs.Hosting;

[assembly: WebJobsStartup(typeof(BindingStartup))]
namespace CustomFormatBinding
{
```

```
public class BindingStartup : IWebJobsStartup
{
    public void Configure(IWebJobsBuilder builder)
    {
        builder.AddCustomBinding();
    }
}
}
```

Incorporate the Binding in the Azure Function

Now let's add the custom binding that you created in the Azure function. Make sure you add a using reference to the CustomFormatBinding project in the function project. You pass a parameter named formatterModel of type FormatterModel, and you decorate it with the attribute FormatterBinding. The formatterBinding parameter will have the formatted data. We created the FormatterBinding attribute and the FormatterModel in the CustomFormatBinding project earlier. Listing 7-8 shows the code for the Azure function.

Listing 7-8. Function Class

```
using System.IO;
using System.Threading.Tasks;
using Microsoft.AspNetCore.Http;
using Microsoft.AspNetCore.Mvc;
using Microsoft.Azure.WebJobs;
using Microsoft.Azure.WebJobs.Extensions.Http;
using Microsoft.Extensions.Logging;
using Newtonsoft.Json;
using CustomFormatBinding;

namespace FuncBindingDemo
{
    public static class Function1
    {
        [FunctionName("Function1")]
        public static IActionResult Run(
```

```
        [HttpTrigger(AuthorizationLevel.Anonymous, "get", "post", Route =
        "custombinding/{name}")]
        HttpRequest req,
        ILogger log,
        string name,
        [FormatterBinding(DataFileLocation = "%filepath%\\{name}")]
        FormatterModel formatterModel)
    {

        return (ActionResult)new
        OkObjectResult(formatterModel.FormattedData);
    }
  }
}
```

Add the filepath parameter and specify the centralized location of the file in the local.settings.json file. See Listing 7-9.

Listing 7-9. Local.settings.json File

```
{
  "IsEncrypted": false,
  "Values": {
    "AzureWebJobsStorage": "UseDevelopmentStorage=true",
    "FUNCTIONS_WORKER_RUNTIME": "dotnet",
    "filepath": "C:\\Abhishek\\Test\\"
  }
}
```

Place a file with the content in Listing 7-10 at the location you provided in the filepath in the local.settings.json file.

Listing 7-10. Content of File to Be Converted by the Binding

```
[name:Abhishek Mishra,Age:38,subject:maths]
```

Execute the function. See Figure 7-9.

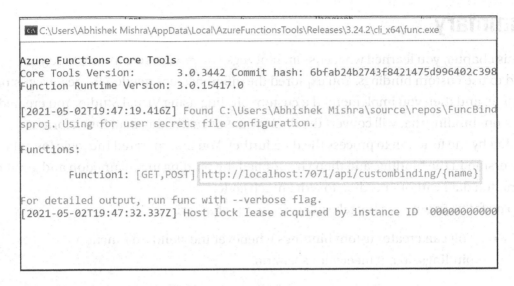

Figure 7-9. *Function execution output*

Pass the filename in the function URL route. The binding will convert the data, and the function returns the converted data in the browser. See Figure 7-10.

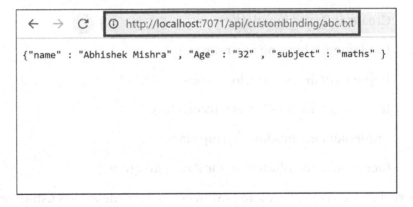

Figure 7-10. *Browse to the function*

Summary

In this chapter, you learned what custom bindings are and the scenarios where you need to use custom bindings. You explored the different steps needed to create a custom binding, and then you implemented a custom binding using Visual Studio. You created a custom binding that will convert the data format of an existing data into a format needed by the function to process the data further. You incorporated the logic for data conversion in the binding, and then you applied the binding in the function and got the formatted data without needing to write much code.

The following are the key takeaways from this chapter:

- You can create custom bindings whenever the standard function bindings do not meet your scenario.

- You need to build the custom binding using .NET.

- You can reuse the custom binding across functions.

- The following are the steps to create a custom binding and use it in an Azure function:

    1. Create an Azure function.

    2. Implement a binding attribute class.

    3. Implement the binding logic class.

    4. Implement the binding extension class.

    5. Implement the binding startup class.

    6. Incorporate the binding in the Azure function.

In the next chapter, you will explore how to create serverless APIs using Azure Functions.

CHAPTER 8

Building Serverless APIs Using Azure Functions and Azure SQL

Most applications these days have separate client-side and server-side projects. Client-side applications send a request to the server-side application to interact with the database or to perform a business operation. Server-side projects are normally a web API that takes the request from the client app, processes the request, and gives back an appropriate response that can be later used by the client application to display the data. In such scenarios, you need to deploy your client and API project in an Azure Web App, which will need an Azure App Service Plan. When you deploy your apps to an Azure Web App, you will have to pay monthly costs irrespective of the usage of your apps. This is one of the areas where Azure Functions shines.

One of the most promising and popular use cases of the Azure Functions service among developers has been to build serverless APIs. With the micro billing nature and autoscaling capability of an Azure function, it is an ideal choice to build APIs that are prone to have unexpected spikes in traffic. With the help of the Azure Functions offering, you can build highly scalable and cost-efficient solutions.

As you have already learned about HTTP-triggered Azure functions and their use cases in previous chapters, you are going to use that knowledge to build serverless APIs using HTTP-triggered functions in this chapter that will run whenever they receive a request. After being triggered, the APIs processes the request and fetches the data by interacting with Azure SQL Database and providing a response to the client.

© Ashirwad Satapathi and Abhishek Mishra 2021
A. Satapathi and A. Mishra, *Hands-on Azure Functions with C#*, https://doi.org/10.1007/978-1-4842-7122-3_8

Structure of the Chapter

This chapter will explore the following aspects of HTTP triggers and Azure SQL:

- Getting started with Azure SQL

- Building a database and table in Azure SQL

- Getting started with HTTP triggers

- Creating serverless APIs using HTTP-triggered functions and Azure SQL

Objectives

After studying this chapter, you will be able to do the following:

- Create serverless APIs using Azure Functions

- Interact with Azure SQL from your functions

Problem Statement

Let's say you are working for a large multinational company called Asgard Inc., which is a leading ecommerce firm. You have a presence across the globe and provide services to more than 180 countries with a consumer base of more than 500 million users.

Product managers need to manage the inventory and product information of all the products around the world. With the unpredictable nature of the customers' consumption patterns, your application usage can increase and decrease at any time without giving you a warning to react to a sudden traffic surge.

To handle such traffic, your team is tasked with building an API project that will be consumed by a client-side application, which can scale up and down to handle all the requests coming without letting your application crash. Your application needs to be globally available, highly scalable, and cost-effective.

Previously your team was planning to build a traditional web API for the application that will be later deployed in an Azure Web App. To make the API scalable, your team had planned to leverage the autoscale feature of the App Service Plan by defining autoscale rules for the application to scale out. Though this would have been a really good choice to make your application scalable, the cost implications were quite high. You had to pay monthly fees to your cloud vendors for the dedicated resources you used to host your application irrespective your application's usage. In other words, even if your API didn't receive a single request from the client, you had to pay the monthly fees. And every time your app scaled out to meet a surge in traffic, you had to pay for the scaled-out instance too, irrespective of resource consumption.

While your manager was elaborating on the plan for the project with the team members, it hit you that building serverless APIs for this project would be the perfect solution. By its inherent nature, a serverless API is autoscalable, which means you don't need to worry about writing conditions to enable autoscaling anymore, and they are micro billed; i.e., you pay for per-second resource consumption and execution. So, you pay only for the time your application actually runs.

Though the proposal for building serverless APIs for the application meets all the requirements of the project, your manager is a bit skeptical about using serverless APIs for production workloads yet. To check the viability of the solution, he has asked you to come up with a proof of concept on building serverless APIs for all product-related tasks that will be interacting with Azure SQL Database. See Figure 8-1.

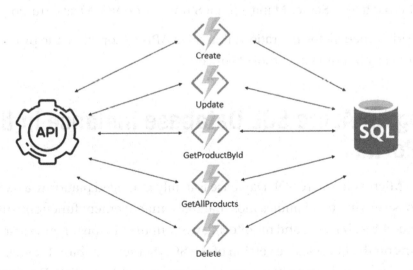

Figure 8-1. Architecture diagram of the proof of concept

So, you need to build the APIs to perform the following operations for the proof of concept:

1. Create the product.

2. Update the product.

3. Get all the products.

4. Get a product by ID.

5. Delete a product by ID.

To complete this proof of concept, you need the following resources:

- Active Azure subscription

- Azure SQL Database

- Visual Studio 2019 Community edition

- Azure development workload

- Postman

- Microsoft SQL Server Management Studio 17 or Azure Data Studio

We have identified all the operations that need APIs to complete the proof of concept. Let's start building the proof of concept.

Creating an Azure SQL Database Instance in the Azure Portal

According to Microsoft, Azure SQL Database is a fully managed platform-as-a-service (PaaS) database engine that handles most database management functions such as upgrading, patching, backup, and monitoring without user involvement. Azure SQL Database runs on the latest stable version of the SQL Server Database Engine.

In this section, you'll learn how to create an instance of Azure SQL Database to store data for your proof of concept. To create an instance of Azure SQL Database, go to the Azure portal. Type **Azure SQL** in the search bar and click the result. See Figure 8-2.

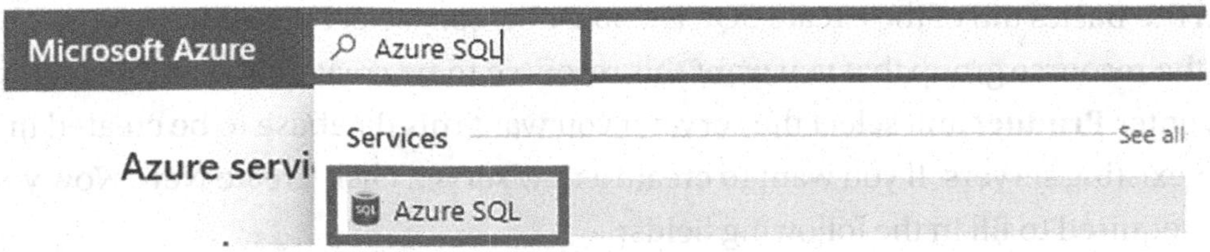

Figure 8-2. *Click Azure SQL*

Now click Create to create an instance of Azure SQL Database. See Figure 8-3.

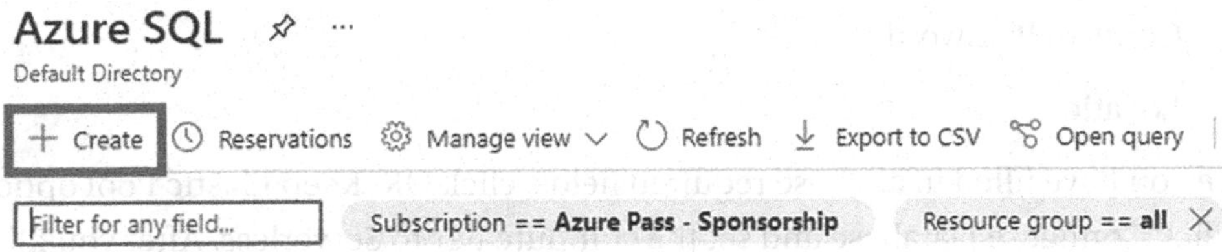

Figure 8-3. *Create an instance of Azure SQL Database*

You will need to select a deployment option in this window. Let's select "SQL databases" and leave the resource type as "Single database." Click Create. See Figure 8-4.

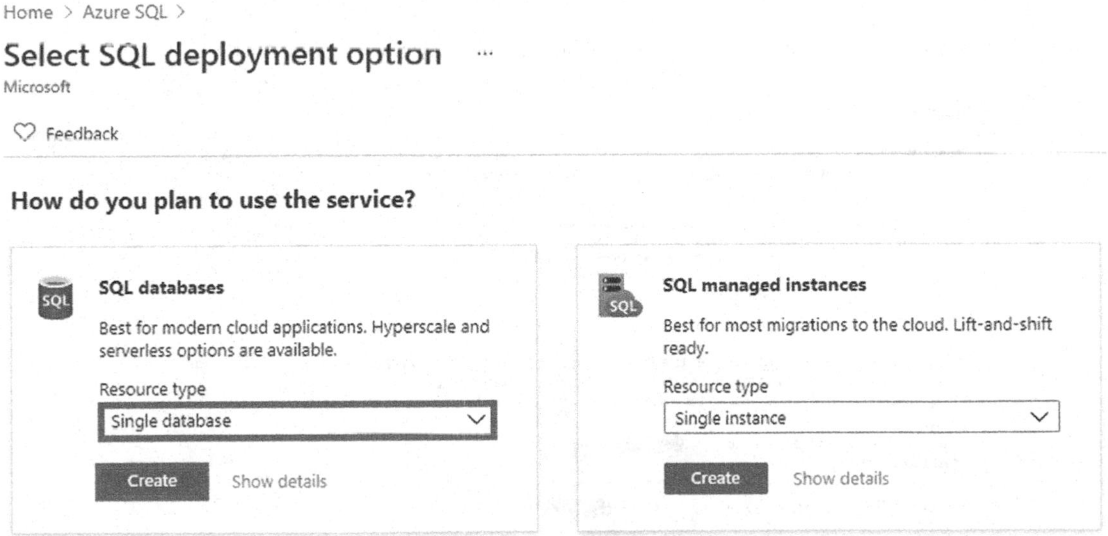

Figure 8-4. *SQL deployment options*

On the Basics tab of the Create SQL Database screen, select the subscription. Then select the resource group that you want this resource to be created in. For the database name, enter **Product** and select the server if you want this database to be created in one of your existing servers. If you want to create a new server, click Create New. Now you will be required to fill in the following fields:

- Server Name

- Server Admin Login

- Password

- Confirm Password

- Location

Once you have filled in all these required fields, click OK. Keep Elastic Pool option as No. Click Configure Database and set the compute tier to Serverless. After you fill in all the required fields for the Basic tab section, click Next : Networking.

On the Networking tab, select the Public endpoint as the connectivity method and select Yes for Add Current Client IP Address, as shown in Figure 8-5. Now click "Review + create."

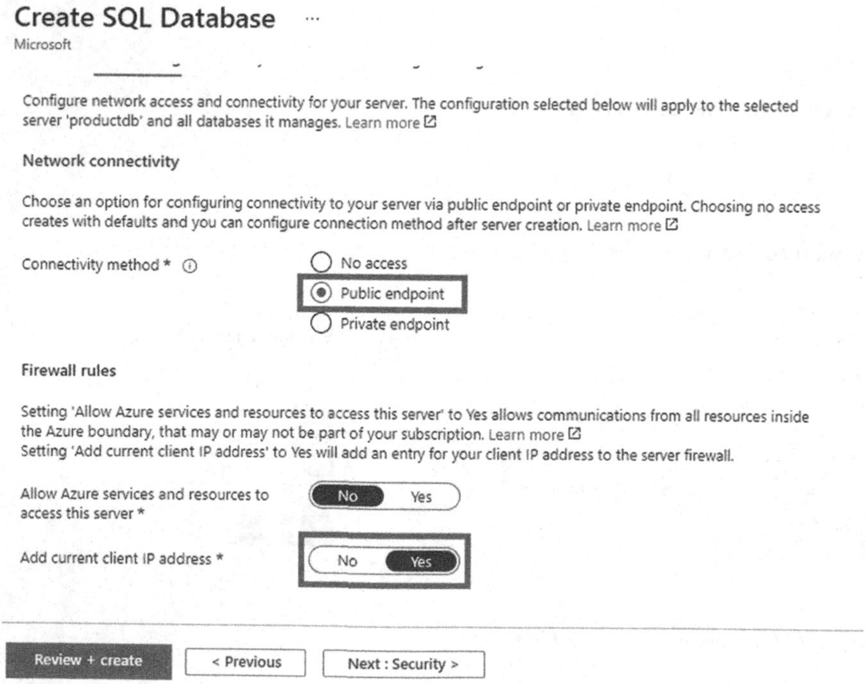

Create SQL Database
Microsoft

Configure network access and connectivity for your server. The configuration selected below will apply to the selected server 'productdb' and all databases it manages. Learn more

Network connectivity

Choose an option for configuring connectivity to your server via public endpoint or private endpoint. Choosing no access creates with defaults and you can configure connection method after server creation. Learn more

Connectivity method * ⓘ   ○ No access
                                   ● Public endpoint
                                   ○ Private endpoint

Firewall rules

Setting 'Allow Azure services and resources to access this server' to Yes allows communications from all resources inside the Azure boundary, that may or may not be part of your subscription. Learn more
Setting 'Add current client IP address' to Yes will add an entry for your client IP address to the server firewall.

Allow Azure services and resources to   No   Yes
access this server *

Add current client IP address *   No   Yes

[Review + create]   [< Previous]   [Next : Security >]

Figure 8-5. *Networking tab*

On the "Review + create" tab, you will see a summary of all the configuration and options you have selected to create this resource along with a monthly estimated cost for this resource. Click Create to provision this resource in Azure.

Once the resource has been provisioned, go to the resource. Get the server name and connection string from the Overview section of your resource, as shown in Figure 8-6.

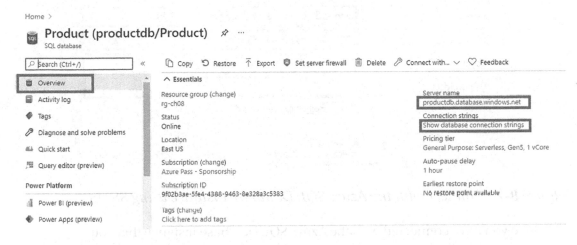

Figure 8-6. *Overview of your resource*

To get the connection string, you will need to click the "Show database connection strings" link to get the connection string depending on the SQL Server driver. You are going to copy the connection string value from the ADO.NET tab. Note that you will have to replace *{your_password}* with your server password.

Let's open SSMS to create the ProductInformation table in your product database, which will be used by your serverless APIs to perform various operations. Enter the server name of your Azure SQL Database instance. You can find it in the Overview section of the resource in the Azure portal, as shown in Figure 8-6. Then set the authentication type to SQL Server Authentication, provide your server admin login name and the password that you entered while creating the server, and click Connect, as shown in Figure 8-7, to connect with your Azure SQL Database resource via SSMS.

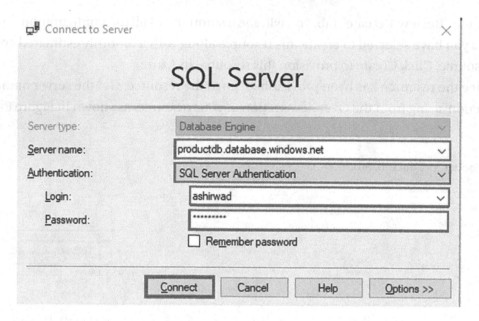

Figure 8-7. *Connect with the Azure SQL Database instance using SSMS*

Once you have connected with the Azure SQL Database instance that you have created in the Azure portal, execute the query shown in Listing 8-1 to create a ProductInformation table to store product information.

Listing 8-1. Create the ProductInformation Table

```
CREATE TABLE [dbo].[ProductInformation](
      [Product_ID] [int] IDENTITY(1,1) NOT NULL,
      [Product_Name] [varchar](40) NOT NULL,
      [Product_Description] [varchar](40) NOT NULL,
      [Product_Price] [int] NOT NULL,
      [Product_Quantity] [int] NOT NULL,
      [Category_Name] [varchar](40) NOT NULL
)
GO
```

After creating the ProductInformation table in your product database, you are all set to build your serverless APIs for the proof of concept.

Building Serverless APIs for the Proof of Concept

An Azure function can be used to build event-driven serverless solutions; in addition, you can build serverless APIs with the help of HTTP-triggered functions. In the previous chapter, we covered the different concepts of HTTP-triggered functions such as routing while building a to-do API, which interacts with table storage using bindings.

While building the proof of concept, you will learn how to interact with an instance of Azure SQL Database using ADO.NET from Azure Functions. You'll build five APIs for the purpose of this proof of concept, for the following tasks:

1. **CreateProduct function**: This HTTP-triggered function will let the product managers create new products in your ProductInformation table.

   URL endpoint: https://{functionapp-url}/api/product

   Request method: POST

2. **UpdateProduct function**: This HTTP-triggered Azure function will let the client-side app update any product information such as product price, description, category, etc., of the existing products present in your ProductInformation table.

   URL endpoint: https://{functionapp-url}/api/product

   Request method: PUT

3. **GetProduct function**: This HTTP-triggered Azure function will let the client-side app get the details like product name, description, price, etc., of all the products present inside of your ProductInformation table.

   URL endpoint: https://{functionapp-url}/api/product

   Request method: GET

4. **GetProductById function**: This HTTP-triggered Azure function will let the client-side app get the details such as product name, description, price, etc., of specific products in your ProductInformation table depending on the product ID specified in the URL route.

URL endpoint: https://{functionapp-url}/api/product/{id}

Request method: GET

5. **DeleteProduct function**: This HTTP-triggered Azure function will let the client-side app delete a specific product present in your ProductInformation table depending on the product ID specified in the URL route.

URL endpoint: https://{functionapp-url}/api/product/{id}

Request method: DELETE

As we have discussed the work of all the HTTP-triggered functions that you need for the proof concept along with their URL endpoints and request method, let's start building them.

Open Visual Studio 2019 in your workstation and click "Create a new project." See Figure 8-8.

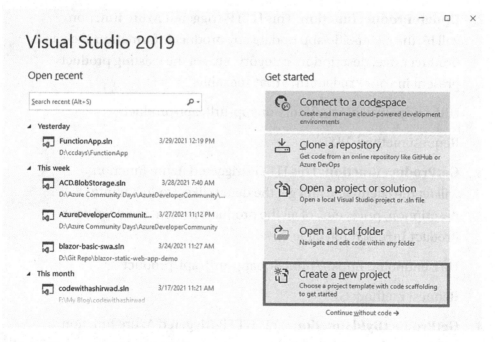

Figure 8-8. *Create a new project*

Now select Azure Functions as the project template for the project and click Next. See Figure 8-9.

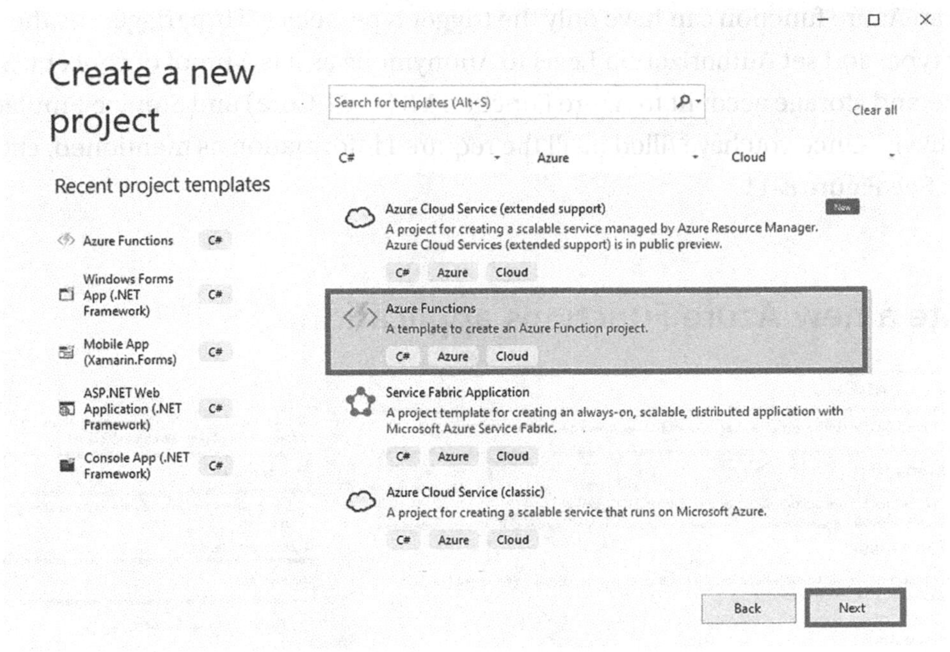

Figure 8-9. *Select Azure Functions as the project template*

You will be required to fill in the project name, project location, and solution name on this screen. Once you have filled in all of these details, click Next. See Figure 8-10.

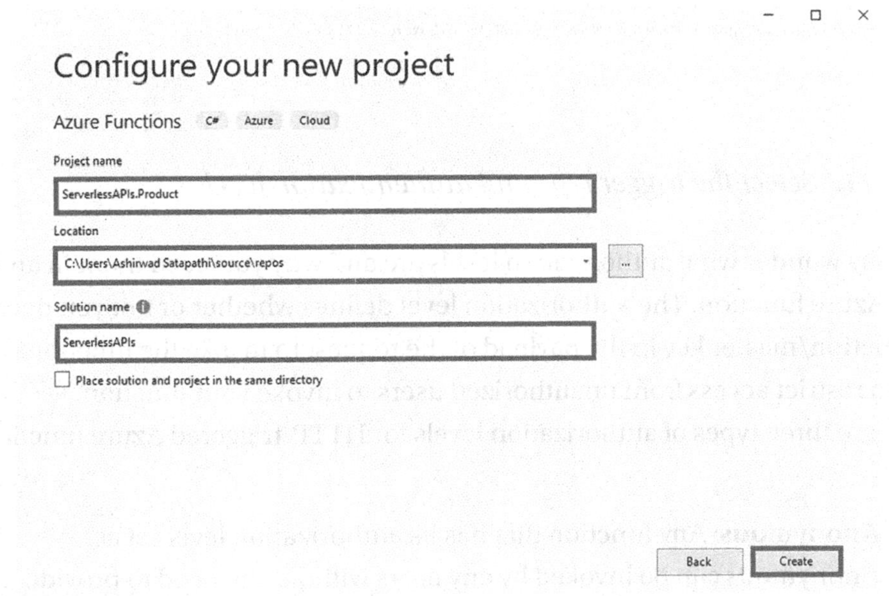

Figure 8-10. *Enter the project information*

As an Azure function can have only the trigger type, select "Http trigger" as the trigger type, and set Authorization Level to Anonymous as it is a proof of concept. Set the runtime and storage account to Azure Function V3 (.NET Core) and Storage Emulator, respectively. Once you have filled in all the required information as mentioned, click Create. See Figure 8-11.

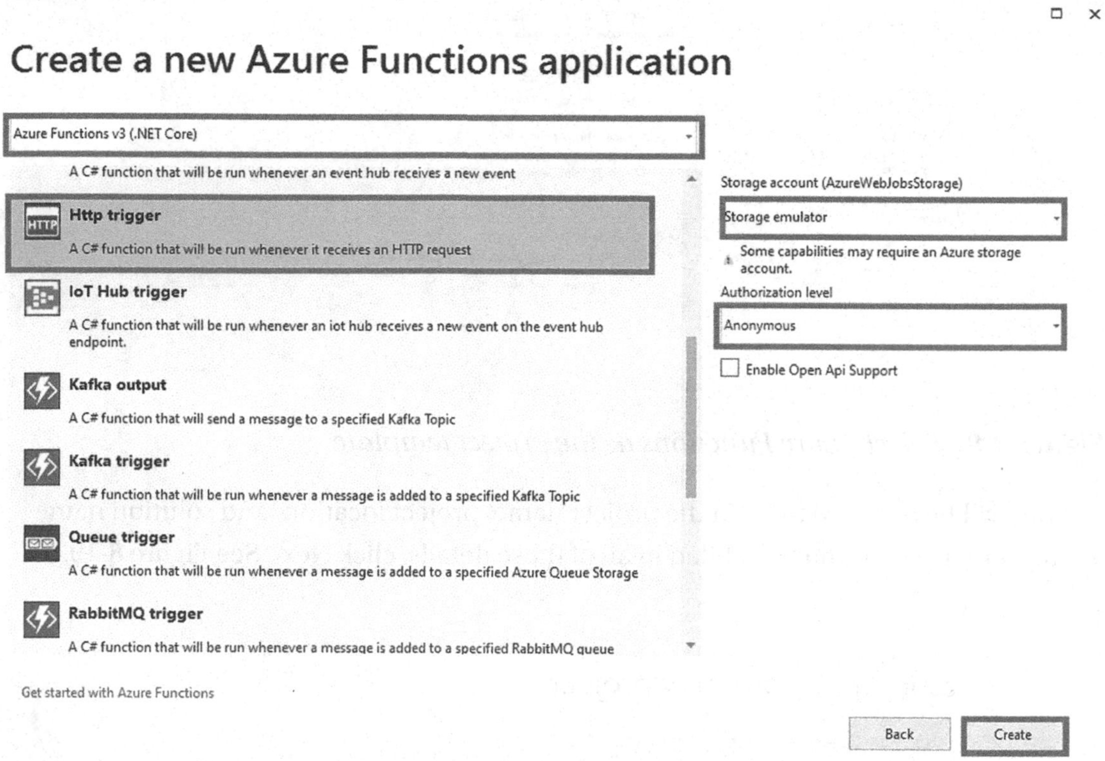

Figure 8-11. *Select the trigger type and authentication level*

You may wonder what authorization levels are and why you need them in an HTTP-triggered Azure function. The authorization level defines whether or not you need to send a function/master key in the payload of the request to invoke the function. This helps us to restrict access from unauthorized users to invoke your function.

There are three types of authorization levels for HTTP-triggered Azure functions as follows:

- **Anonymous**: Any function that has its authorization level set as Anonymous can be invoked by any users without the need to provide an API key in the request payload.

- **Function**: By defining the authentication level of your HTTP-triggered Azure function as a function, you require a function-specific key to be provided in the request payload to invoke it.

- **Admin**: With the authentication level set as Admin, you need to send the master key of your function app in the request payload to invoke the function.

Note   Due to increased permissions granted in your function app by the master key, you should not share this key with any third parties or distribute the master key in client applications. Use it with caution as master keys provide administrative access and allow you to invoke all other HTTP-triggered functions present in your function app without requiring the function key. They also have the power to manually invoke Azure functions with other trigger types like timer-triggered functions.

Visual Studio will create a function project out of the box along with an HTTP-triggered function named Function1, which has the logic to return a response of "Hello" along with the name passed in the query string or the request body.

Let's delete this function as you don't want this function as part of your proof of concept. Now, open the `local.settings.json` file and add your database's connection string here as a key-value pair, as shown in Listing 8-2. As mentioned earlier, you can find the connection string in the Overview section of your resource. Alternatively, you can use the Connection Strings menu item in the sidebar of your resource's window in the Azure portal. In this example, we will be using the connection string to connect with the instance of Azure SQL Database from the Azure functions to perform necessary operations.

Listing 8-2. local.settings.json

```
{
    "IsEncrypted": false,
    "Values": {
        "AzureWebJobsStorage": "UseDevelopmentStorage=true",
        "FUNCTIONS_WORKER_RUNTIME": "dotnet",
        "DBConnectionString": "[Enter your connection string here]"
    }
}
```

As you have added the connection string in the local.setting.json file to your project, you need to install the System.Data.SqlClient NuGet package to interact with your Azure SQL Database instance. Use the command shown in Listing 8-3 to install it using the Package Manager Console.

Listing 8-3. Install the System.Data.SqlClient Package

```
Install-Package System.Data.SqlClient -Version 4.8.2
```

After installing the NuGet package, right-click the solution and click Add ➤ Class to create a Product class representing the records of your ProductInformation table, as shown in Listing 8-4. We will use this class to perform various operations in your functions.

Listing 8-4. Product Class

```
public class Product
    {
        public int Product_ID { get; set; }
        public string Product_Name { get; set; }
        public string Product_Description { get; set; }
        public int Product_Price { get; set; }
        public int Product_Quantity { get; set; }
        public string Category_Name { get; set; }
    }
```

After creating the Product class, right-click the solution and click Add ➤ New Azure Function to create your Azure function. Azure Functions will be selected as the type. Enter the name of the function as **CreateProduct** and click Add. See Figure 8-12.

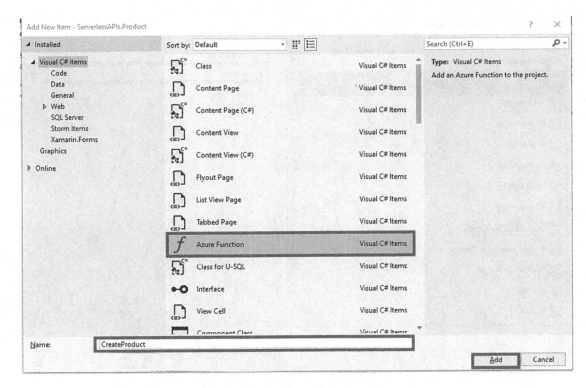

Figure 8-12. *Create a new Azure function*

You will be prompted to select the trigger type and authorization level of your CreateProduct function. Select "Http trigger" as the trigger type and Anonymous as the authorization level. Once you have selected the trigger type and authorization level, click Add to configure the function. See Figure 8-13.

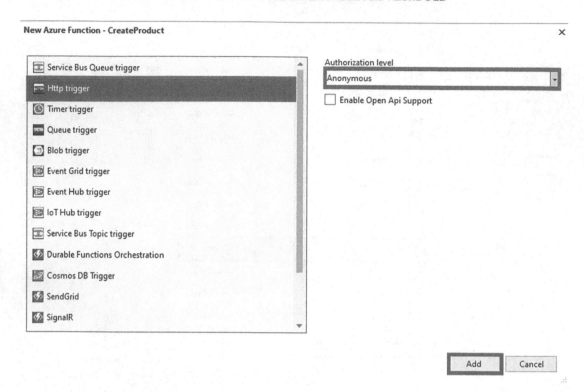

Figure 8-13. *Configure the CreateProduct function*

Visual Studio will generate a default Azure function out of the box that does the same task as described for function1 earlier. You will configure the route of this function by overriding the route parameter of the HttpTrigger attribute's value as product and pass POST as the only request method, as you will be using the function as your serverless API to create a new resource. By mentioning only POST as the request method in the HttpTriggerAttribute constructor, you are restricting this function to be invoked only by POST requests.

Now you will read the JSON payload present in the request body and deserialize it to an object called productData with a Product type. Now you will use the GetEnvironmentVariable method of the Environment class to get the value of your connection string from the local.settings.json file and then use it to create a SQL connection instance called connection. Now you will create a cmd object of the SqlCommand type and pass queryString as the parameter. queryString is a variable containing the T-SQL query to insert the record into the ProductInformation table of your database. You pass the values to the SqlParameterCollection by using the productData object, which contains the product data sent in the request body of

the request payload. After you add the values of the parameters, you will call the
ExecuteNonQuery method to execute the T-SQL statement and finally use the close
method of the connection object to close the connection.

You add the whole business logic of your CreateProduct function inside a try-catch
block. This will ensure that your function handles exceptions in a graceful manner. If
everything goes well, you will return a 200 response code along with the productData
object to the user. If you get an exception, you will return a 400 response code along
with the error message to the user. Refer to Listing 8-5 for the entire code for the
CreateProduct function.

Listing 8-5. CreateProduct Function Code

```
using System;
using System.Data.SqlClient;
using System.IO;
using System.Threading.Tasks;
using Microsoft.AspNetCore.Http;
using Microsoft.AspNetCore.Mvc;
using Microsoft.Azure.WebJobs;
using Microsoft.Azure.WebJobs.Extensions.Http;
using Microsoft.Extensions.Logging;
using Newtonsoft.Json;

namespace ServerlessAPIs.Product
{
    public static class CreateProduct
    {
        [FunctionName("CreateProduct")]
        public static async Task<IActionResult> Run(
            [HttpTrigger(AuthorizationLevel.Anonymous, "post", Route =
            "product")] HttpRequest req,
            ILogger log)
        {
            log.LogInformation("C# HTTP trigger function processed a request.");
```

```
try
{
    string requestBody = await new StreamReader(req.Body).
    ReadToEndAsync();

    Product productData = JsonConvert.DeserializeObject<Product>
    (requestBody);

    using (SqlConnection connection = new SqlConnection
    (Environment.GetEnvironmentVariable("DBConnectionString")))
    {
        string queryString = @"INSERT INTO [ProductInformation]
        (Product_Name,Product_Description,Product_Price,
        Product_Quantity,Category_Name)
        VALUES(@Product_Name,@Product_Description,
        @Product_Price,@Product_Quantity,
        @Category_Name)";

        using (SqlCommand cmd = new SqlCommand(queryString))
        {
            cmd.Parameters.AddWithValue("@Product_Name",
            productData.Product_Name);
            cmd.Parameters.AddWithValue("@Product_Description",
            productData.Product_Description);
            cmd.Parameters.AddWithValue("@Product_Price",
            productData.Product_Price);
            cmd.Parameters.AddWithValue("@Product_Quantity",
            productData.Product_Quantity);
            cmd.Parameters.AddWithValue("@Category_Name",
            productData.Category_Name);
            cmd.Connection = connection;
            connection.Open();
            cmd.ExecuteNonQuery();
            connection.Close();
        }
    }
    return new OkObjectResult(productData);
```

```
        }
        catch (Exception ex) {
            return new BadRequestObjectResult(ex.Message);
        }
    }
  }
}
```

Note   While building serverless APIs using HTTP-triggered functions, avoid long-running processes as you will get a request timeout response if your HTTP-triggered function does not respond to the request in 230 seconds. Irrespective of the function timeout setting, the timeout for an HTTP-triggered function to give a response is 230 seconds. If you want to build a function to execute long-running processes, try using a durable functions async pattern or return an immediate response to the client by passing the request payload to a queue for further processing.

As you have created the `CreateProduct` function, let's create your next function, called `UpdateProduct`, that you will use to update the product details of an existing product in your `ProductInformation` table. The process is the same as creating the `CreateProduct` function. After you have created the `UpdateProduct` function, override the `route` parameter of the `HttpTrigger` attribute as `product` and pass PUT as the only request method for this function, as you are going to modify all the values of existing resources by using the values specified in the request body of the request payload.

As you did with the `CreateProduct` function, let's read the data from the request body of the request payload and deserialize it into a object called `productData` of the Product type. Then use a block of ADO.NET code similar to the one used in the `CreateProduct` function. The few differences here are the query string and the addition of a new parameter to the `SqlParameterCollection` called `Product_ID`. You will modify the query string with a T-SQL statement to update all the records of a product depending on the value `Product_ID`. Similar to the `CreateProduct` function, you place your business logic of the function in a `try-catch` block to handle exceptions. If your function runs successfully without getting any error or exception, it will return a 200 response code along with the updated product data. Refer to Listing 8-6 for the entire code for the `UpdateProduct` function.

Listing 8-6. UpdateProduct Function Code

```
using System;
using System.Data.SqlClient;
using System.IO;
using System.Threading.Tasks;
using Microsoft.AspNetCore.Http;
using Microsoft.AspNetCore.Mvc;
using Microsoft.Azure.WebJobs;
using Microsoft.Azure.WebJobs.Extensions.Http;
using Microsoft.Extensions.Logging;
using Newtonsoft.Json;

namespace ServerlessAPIs.Product
{
    public static class UpdateProduct
    {
        [FunctionName("UpdateProduct")]
        public static async Task<IActionResult> Run(
            [HttpTrigger(AuthorizationLevel.Anonymous, "put", Route =
            "product")] HttpRequest req,
            ILogger log)
        {
            log.LogInformation("C# HTTP trigger function processed a
            request.");

            try
            {
                string requestBody = await new StreamReader(req.Body).
                ReadToEndAsync();

                Product productData = JsonConvert.DeserializeObject<Product>
                (requestBody);

                using (SqlConnection connection = new SqlConnection
                (Environment.GetEnvironmentVariable("DBConnectionString")))
                {
```

```
string queryString = @"UPDATE [dbo].[ProductInformation]
SET [Product_Name] = @Product_Name,[Product_
Description] = @Product_Description,[Product_Price]
= @Product_Price,[Product_Quantity] = @Product_
Quantity,[Category_Name] = @Category_Name WHERE
[Product_ID] = @Product_ID";

using (SqlCommand cmd = new SqlCommand(queryString))
{
    cmd.Parameters.AddWithValue("@Product_Name",
    productData.Product_Name);
    cmd.Parameters.AddWithValue("@Product_Description",
    productData.Product_Description);
    cmd.Parameters.AddWithValue("@Product_Price",
    productData.Product_Price);
    cmd.Parameters.AddWithValue("@Product_Quantity",
    productData.Product_Quantity);
    cmd.Parameters.AddWithValue("@Category_Name",
    productData.Category_Name);
    cmd.Parameters.AddWithValue("@Product_ID",
    productData.Product_ID);
    cmd.Connection = connection;
    connection.Open();
    cmd.ExecuteNonQuery();
    connection.Close();
}
}
return new OkObjectResult(productData);

}
catch (Exception ex)
{
    return new BadRequestObjectResult(ex.Message);
}
}
}
}
```

Now that you have created the CreateProduct and UpdateProduct functions, let's create the DeleteProduct function in a similar way. Since the work of this function is to delete records depending on the value of the ID passed in the route, you will need to override the route parameter of the HttpTrigger attribute as product/{id:int} and pass DELETE as the only request method for this function. After you implement these changes, you need to add a new parameter called id of the Integer type in your run method. The value passed in the function route will be stored in this id variable. Let's go into the method body of your function. Unlike the previous functions, you don't use the data from the request payload here. You will be deleting the record of the product from your ProductInformation table depending on the id value passed in the function route using ADO.NET.

Most of the ADO.NET code for the DeleteProduct function to interact with the database will be similar with the other functions. The notable difference is the queryString that you will pass to the cmd object of the SqlCommand type along with the number of parameters used. You define a simple delete statement in the queryString variable to delete a record whose Product_ID is equal to the value of id passed in the function route. Like the previous two functions, you wrap the business logic in a try-catch block to handle exceptions graciously. If your function is able to delete the records without getting any exception, then it will return a 200 response code with a message stating Product records were deleted successfully; if there is an exception, then it will give a 400 response code along with the error. Refer to Listing 8-7 for the entire code of the DeleteProduct function.

Listing 8-7. DeleteProduct Function Code

```
using System;
using System.Data.SqlClient;
using System.IO;
using System.Threading.Tasks;
using Microsoft.AspNetCore.Http;
using Microsoft.AspNetCore.Mvc;
using Microsoft.Azure.WebJobs;
using Microsoft.Azure.WebJobs.Extensions.Http;
using Microsoft.Extensions.Logging;
using Newtonsoft.Json;
```

```csharp
namespace ServerlessAPIs.Product
{
    public static class DeleteProduct
    {
        [FunctionName("DeleteProduct")]
        public static async Task<IActionResult> Run(
            [HttpTrigger(AuthorizationLevel.Anonymous, "delete", Route =
            "product/{id:int}")] HttpRequest req,int id, ILogger log)
        {
            log.LogInformation("C# HTTP trigger function processed a request.");

            try
            {
                using (SqlConnection connection = new SqlConnection
                    (Environment.GetEnvironmentVariable("DBConnectionString")))
                {
                    string queryString = @"DELETE FROM [dbo].
                    [ProductInformation] WHERE [Product_ID] = @Product_ID";

                    using (SqlCommand cmd = new SqlCommand(queryString))
                    {
                        cmd.Parameters.AddWithValue("@Product_ID", id);
                        cmd.Connection = connection;
                        connection.Open();
                        cmd.ExecuteNonQuery();
                        connection.Close();
                    }
                }
                return new OkObjectResult("Product record were deleted
                successfully ");

            }
```

```
        catch (Exception ex)
        {
            return new BadRequestObjectResult(ex.Message);
        }
    }
  }
}
```

Now that you have created the CreateProduct, UpdateProduct, and DeleteProduct functions, you are left with two more functions to build, i.e., GetProducts and GetProductById. Both these functions share the common objective of getting the product data from the ProductInformation table. The difference is that GetProducts needs to fetch all the records present in the ProductInformation table, while GetProductById only needs the records for a particular product ID from the ProductInformation table.

Let's create the GetProducts function now like you created the previous functions in Visual Studio 2019. Because you want the URL endpoint for this function to be api/product, you need to override the route parameter of the HttpTrigger attribute as product and pass GET as the only request method since you want to fetch the details of an existing resource.

In this function, you don't need any data from the request payload or from the function route to run the function. You will write similar ADO.NET code as in the previous function to interact with the database with the cmd object of the SqlCommand type but use a different queryString that contains a T-SQL query to fetch all the records present in the ProductInformation table along with using the ExecuteReader method instead of ExecuteNonQuery method this time. We will be storing the data returned after the ExecuteNonQuery method in a variable called oReader of SqlDataReader type. After this, we iterate through the data present in the oReader object and store the records present inside the oReader object in an object called productData, which is a list of products.

Like your previous functions, you have added your business logic inside a try-catch to handle exceptions graciously. If your function runs without getting any exception, then it will return a 200 response code along with a list of products, and if there is an exception, then it will give a 400 response code along with the error. Refer to Listing 8-8 for the entire code of the GetProducts function.

Listing 8-8. GetProducts Function Code

```
using System;
using System.Collections.Generic;
using System.Data.SqlClient;
using System.IO;
using System.Threading.Tasks;
using Microsoft.AspNetCore.Http;
using Microsoft.AspNetCore.Mvc;
using Microsoft.Azure.WebJobs;
using Microsoft.Azure.WebJobs.Extensions.Http;
using Microsoft.Extensions.Logging;
using Newtonsoft.Json;

namespace ServerlessAPIs.Product
{
    public static class GetProduct
    {
        [FunctionName("GetProduct")]
        public static async Task<IActionResult> Run(
            [HttpTrigger(AuthorizationLevel.Anonymous, "get",
            Route = "product")] HttpRequest req,
            ILogger log)
        {

            log.LogInformation("C# HTTP trigger function processed a
            request.");

            try
            {
                List<Product> productData = new List<Product>();
                using (SqlConnection connection = new SqlConnection
                (Environment.GetEnvironmentVariable("DBConnectionString")))
                {
                    string queryString = @"SELECT [Product_ID]
                                ,[Product_Name]
                                ,[Product_Description]
                                ,[Product_Price]
```

```
                                ,[Product_Quantity]
                                ,[Category_Name]
                            FROM [dbo].[ProductInformation]";
            SqlCommand cmd = new SqlCommand(queryString, connection);
             connection.Open();
             using (SqlDataReader oReader = cmd.ExecuteReader())
             {
                 while (oReader.Read())
                 {
                     Product productInfo = new Product();
                    productInfo.Product_ID = (int)oReader["Product_ID"];
                     productInfo.Product_Name = oReader["Product_
                     Name"].ToString();
                     productInfo.Product_Description = oReader
                     ["Product_Description"].ToString();
                     productInfo.Product_Price = (int)oReader
                     ["Product_Price"];
                     productInfo.Product_Quantity = (int)oReader
                     ["Product_Quantity"];
                     productInfo.Category_Name = oReader["Category_
                     Name"].ToString();
                     productData.Add(productInfo);
                 }
                 connection.Close();
             }
         }
         return new OkObjectResult(productData);
     }
     catch (Exception ex)
     {
         return new BadRequestObjectResult(ex.Message);
     }
   }
 }
}
```

You have created four of the five serverless APIs required to complete your proof of concept. The last one remaining is `GetProductById`. As mentioned earlier, this function will need to fetch data for a particular product from the `ProductInformation` table of your database depending on the `Product_ID` value passed in the function route.

Let's create the `GetProductById` function like you created the rest of the functions using Visual Studio. As you wanted to pass the `Product_ID` value to this function using the function route, you will have to override the `route` parameter of the `HttpTrigger` attribute as `product/{id:int}` and pass GET as the only request method. After making these changes, you need to add a parameter `id` of the Integer type to store the value of the `Product_ID` passed in the function route as was the case in the `DeleteProduct` function.

The business logic for `GetProductById` and `GetProducts` is similar, so let's copy the business logic of the `GetProducts` function and paste it inside the run method of the `GetProductById` function. You need to make a few changes in the function's business logic now to add the desired functionality in this function.

The few changes are the addition of a `where` condition in the `queryString` variable to filter the records and fetch the record whose `Product_ID` matched with the value of `id` passed in the function route and the addition of a parameter and its value to the `SqlParameterCollection` of the cmd object of the `SqlCommand` type. Here you use the `ExecuteReader` method to get the record from the Azure SQL Database instance, as was the case in the `GetProducts` function. But you are expecting a single product record here instead of multiple records as the `Product_ID` is a unique identifier for the products; thus, you can have only one product per `Product_ID`. We don't need to any other changes in the business logic. If your function runs without any exceptions, then it will return a 200 response code along with the product information of the product whose `Product_ID` matched with the value of `id` passed in the function route. Refer to Listing 8-9 for the entire code of the `GetProductById` function.

Listing 8-9. GetProductById Function Code

```
using System;
using System.Collections.Generic;
using System.Data.SqlClient;
using System.IO;
using System.Threading.Tasks;
using Microsoft.AspNetCore.Http;
```

```csharp
using Microsoft.AspNetCore.Mvc;
using Microsoft.Azure.WebJobs;
using Microsoft.Azure.WebJobs.Extensions.Http;
using Microsoft.Extensions.Logging;
using Newtonsoft.Json;

namespace ServerlessAPIs.Product
{
    public static class GetProductById
    {
        [FunctionName("GetProductById")]
        public static async Task<IActionResult> Run(
            [HttpTrigger(AuthorizationLevel.Anonymous, "get", Route =
            "product/{id:int}")] HttpRequest req, int id, ILogger log)
        {
            log.LogInformation("C# HTTP trigger function processed a
            request.");

            try
            {
                List<Product> productData = new List<Product>();
                using (SqlConnection connection = new SqlConnection
                (Environment.GetEnvironmentVariable("DBConnectionString")))
                {
                    string queryString= @"SELECT [Product_ID]
                                ,[Product_Name]
                                ,[Product_Description]
                                ,[Product_Price]
                                ,[Product_Quantity]
                                ,[Category_Name]
                            FROM [dbo].[ProductInformation] WHERE
                            [Product_ID] = @Product_ID";
                SqlCommand cmd = new SqlCommand(queryString,
                connection);
                cmd.Parameters.AddWithValue("@Product_ID", id);
```

```
        connection.Open();
        using (SqlDataReader oReader = cmd.ExecuteReader())
        {
            while (oReader.Read())
            {
                Product productInfo = new Product();
                productInfo.Product_ID = (int)oReader
                ["Product_ID"];
                productInfo.Product_Name = oReader["Product_
                Name"].ToString();
                productInfo.Product_Description = oReader
                ["Product_Description"].ToString();
                productInfo.Product_Price = (int)oReader
                ["Product_Price"];
                productInfo.Product_Quantity = (int)oReader
                ["Product_Quantity"];
                productInfo.Category_Name = oReader["Category_
                Name"].ToString();
                productData.Add(productInfo);
            }

            connection.Close();
        }
    }
    return new OkObjectResult(productData);
}
catch (Exception ex)
{
    return new BadRequestObjectResult(ex.Message);
}
    }
}
}
```

And with this you have developed all the serverless APIs required to complete the proof of concept.

Note   We can use ORM frameworks like EFCore and micro-ORMs like Dapper
to interact with the database too. Azure Functions supports the use of such ORM
frameworks in addition to supporting ADO.NET.

Testing the Serverless APIs for the Proof of Concept

Now that you have developed all the serverless APIs required for the proof of concept,
let's perform a sanity test on the functionalities of your Azure functions before
submitting them to your manager. We will be using Postman to send requests to your
serverless APIs.

Before you open Postman and start sending requests to your endpoints, you need to
run your function project. Run your function project locally in Visual Studio by clicking
the highlighted region in Figure 8-14.

Figure 8-14. *Start the function project*

Now Visual Studio will start the Azure Functions Core Tools that will host all your HTTP-triggered functions (serverless APIs) and display their endpoints along with the supported request method type for each of them and the function name, as shown in Figure 8-15.

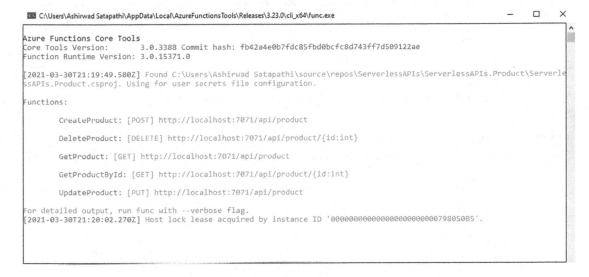

Figure 8-15. *List of functions and their endpoints*

As your function is up and running now, let's open Postman and create a collection. Inside the collection, add a request for CreateProduct. Now define the request method as POST, paste the endpoint of the CreateProduct function as shown in the Azure Functions Core Tools, and then click the Body tab to add the product information in the payload in key-value pairs. After you have configured all this information in the request, click Send to send a request to the CreateProduct API; the API will use the information shared in the request payload to create a new record in the ProductInformation table and return a 200 response code along with the product information, as shown in Figure 8-16.

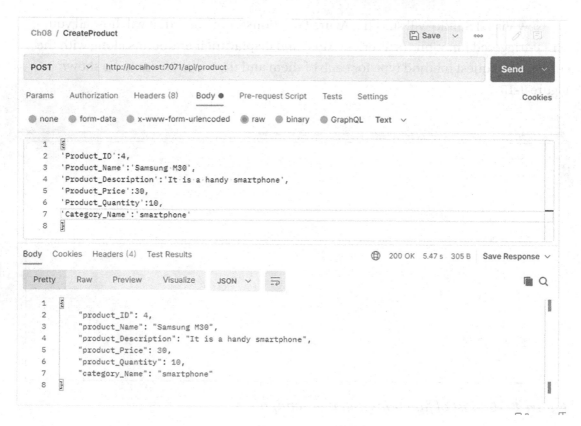

Figure 8-16. *Response from CreateProduct function*

Similarly, to send a request to the UpdateProduct function, create a new request in the requests collection. Set the request method as PUT and paste the URL endpoint of the function there by copying it from Azure Functions Core Tools. Go to the tabs and define the request payload by mentioning all the product information in key-value pairs, as shown in Figure 8-17. Once you configure all these options, click Send to send a request to your UpdateProduct function, which will use the request payload to update the records of the product in the ProductInformation table.

Note   To call these functions using their endpoints from an application, you will have to enable CORS and define your application's domain name and ports. This is to let the function know that it is OK to get requests from your application. You can configure CORS for your function project by specifying the CORS property of Host in local.settings.json, as shown in Listing 8-10. We have defined the value of the CORS property with a wildcard (*), which tells the function project that it can be called by any application irrespective of the domain it is run on. This is OK to be used in a development environment, but you should define your application's URL here, which is going to make a call to your functions while deploying it in the production environment.

Listing 8-10. Define the CORS Property in local.settings.json

```
{
    "IsEncrypted": false,
  "Values": {
    "AzureWebJobsStorage": "UseDevelopmentStorage=true",
    "FUNCTIONS_WORKER_RUNTIME": "dotnet",
   "DBConnectionString": "[Enter your connection string here]"
  },
  "Host": {"CORS": "*"}
}
```

Figure 8-17. *Response from the UpdateProduct function*

Now let's send a request to the DeleteProduct function and create a new request in the request collection. Set the request method to DELETE and paste in the endpoint of the DeleteProduct function. We need to specify the value of Product_ID in the function route. Once you define the endpoint and request method, click Send to invoke the DeleteProduct function. If the function runs without getting any exceptions, you should get a 200 response code along with a message stating the product record was deleted successfully in the response body, as shown in Figure 8-18.

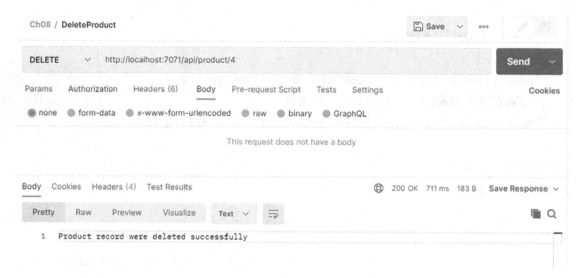

Figure 8-18. *Response from the DeleteProduct function*

Note   You can write unit tests for your Azure functions using unit test frameworks for C# like MSTest, NUnit, or XUnit. Refer to `https://microsoft.github.io/AzureTipsAndTricks/blog/tip196.html` to learn more.

Similar to the DeleteProduct request, you don't need to specify anything in the request body of the request payload for the GetProductById function, but you do need specify the Product_ID in the function route as you did in the case of the DeleteProduct request. Let's create a request in the request collection for GetProductById. Specify the request method type for this request as GET and define the function route along with the Product_ID. Once you define the request method and function route, click Send to invoke the GetProductById function. If your function works well without any exceptions, you should receive a 200 response code and the product details in the response body, as shown in Figure 8-19.

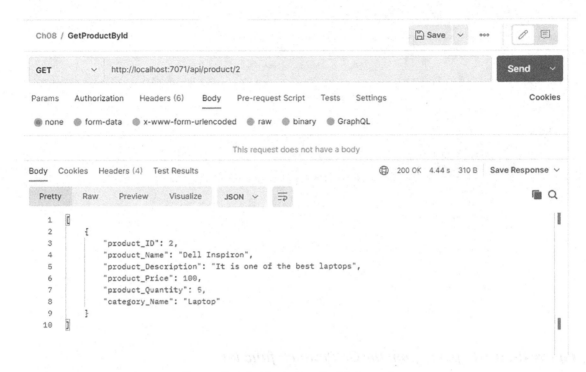

Figure 8-19. *Response from the GetProductById function*

Let's create the request in the request collection for sending a request to the GetProducts function. Unlike the previous functions, GetProducts does not take any value in the request body or in the function route. We need to set the request method type as GET and then paste the endpoint of the GetProducts function. Now click Send to invoke the GetProducts function. We will get a response code of 200 and all the records present in the ProductInformation table in the response body if your function is executed without getting any exception, as shown in Figure 8-20.

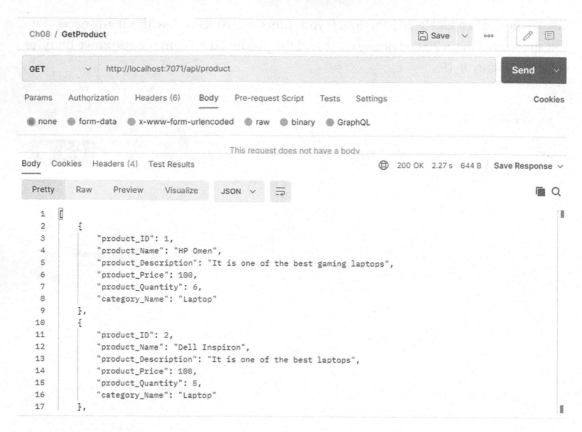

Figure 8-20. *Response from the GetProducts function*

Note   As you are using your Azure SQL Database instance to be on a serverless tier, you can get an exception while creating the first connection in your function due to the cold-start issue. This can also occur if your database was idle for a long time. However, this will be the case only for the first time you create a connection to interact with the database after it's been a long time.

As you test all your serverless APIs' functionality in Postman, you have completed your proof of concept successfully and share it with your manager.

Summary

In this chapter, you learned how to create serverless APIs with the help of HTTP-triggered Azure functions using Visual Studio 2019 by building a proof of concept to solve a use case. You developed multiple serverless APIs to perform create, read, update, and delete operations. While building the proof of concept, you learned ways to interact with an instance of Azure SQL Database from your function and learned how to test your HTTP-triggered functions using Postman.

The following are the key takeaways from this chapter:

- Azure SQL Database is a fully managed platform-as-a-service database engine.

- Azure SQL Database can be highly scalable and cost effective while running on a serverless compute tier.

- You can create serverless APIs using HTTP-triggered functions.

- You can customize the HTTP-triggered function to run on receiving requests from specific request methods.

- You can interact with an instance of Azure SQL Database from your Azure functions using ADO.NET or ORM frameworks like EF Core.

CHAPTER 9

Serverless API Using Azure Functions and Azure Cosmos DB

Azure Cosmos DB is a popular NoSQL database and is widely used in all new-generation applications. It is highly available, it scales rapidly, and the data stored can be globally distributed. You may have scenarios where an Azure function has to work on data stored in Azure Cosmos DB. You can achieve this functionality using the Azure Cosmos DB input and output bindings.

In the previous chapter, you learned all the essential concepts of the Azure SQL Database binding. You built serverless APIs using the Azure Functions binding for Azure SQL Database. In this chapter, you will explore how to implement serverless APIs using Azure Functions and Azure Cosmos DB. You will use both the Azure Cosmos DB function binding and the Azure Cosmos DB SDK approach.

Structure of the Chapter

In this chapter, you will explore the following aspects of Azure Cosmos DB and Azure Functions:

- Introduction to Azure Cosmos DB and its use cases

- Getting started with the Azure Functions Cosmos DB trigger by building a simple application

© Ashirwad Satapathi and Abhishek Mishra 2021
A. Satapathi and A. Mishra, *Hands-on Azure Functions with C#*, https://doi.org/10.1007/978-1-4842-7122-3_9

- Building an HTTP-triggered Azure function to perform CRUD operations in Azure Cosmos DB using bindings

- Leveraging the Azure Cosmos DB SDK to interact with Cosmos DB from Azure Functions

Objectives

After studying this chapter, you will be able to do the following:

- Implement Azure Cosmos DB triggers and bindings for Azure Functions

- Use the Azure Cosmos DB SDK with Azure Functions

Introduction to Azure Cosmos DB and Its Use Cases

Modern applications require databases to be constantly available, be scalable, have low latency, and be highly responsive. Azure Cosmos DB addresses all these concerns and is a perfect fit for all modern application scenarios. Azure Cosmos DB ensures business continuity with SLA-backed availability and offers security at an enterprise level. It supports replication across the globe in no time and is the best fit for mission-critical applications that always need to be available and responsive to their users.

Azure Cosmos DB is a multimodel NoSQL database and supports the following data models:

- Key-value

- Column-family

- Document

- Graph

Table 9-1 lists the APIs that can be used to work with data stored in these data models.

Table 9-1. *Azure Cosmos DB Data Models and Supported APIs*

Data Model	API
Key-value	Table API
Column-family	Casandra
Document	SQL
Graph	Gremlin

Azure Cosmos DB is a fully managed offering from Azure, and you do not need to worry about managing the underlying infrastructure hosting these databases. Any application such as web, mobile, gaming, or IoT-based applications with the following requirements can use Azure Cosmos DB as the data store:

- Massive amount of reads and writes at a global scale

- Near real-time data consistency

- Global replication

- Guaranteed high availability

- High throughput

- Low latency

Azure functions can interact with Azure Cosmos DB using triggers and bindings. You do not need to write much code or write declarative configurations to use Azure Cosmos DB.

Note   Azure Cosmos DB is a highly available and multimodel database engine. It supports the MongoDB, Gremlin, SQL Core, and Casandra APIs. It can scale rapidly and replicate data around the world quickly.

Getting Started with Azure Function Cosmos DB Triggers by Building a Simple Application

Now let's implement an Azure function that gets triggered whenever you add an item in your Cosmos DB database. Let's first provision a Cosmos DB resource using the Azure portal. Go to the Azure portal and click "Create a resource." See Figure 9-1.

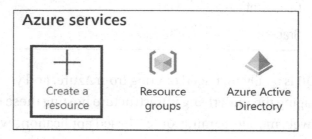

Figure 9-1. *Click "Create a resource"*

Click the Databases tab. All the database offerings will be listed here. Click Azure Cosmos DB. See Figure 9-2.

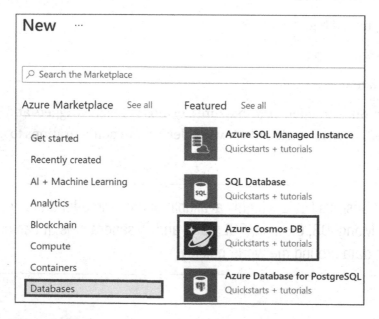

Figure 9-2. *Click Azure Cosmos DB*

Provide the subscription where you need to create the Cosmos DB resource, the name of the Cosmos DB account, and the location. Provide Core (SQL) as the API. Click "Review + create." See Figure 9-3.

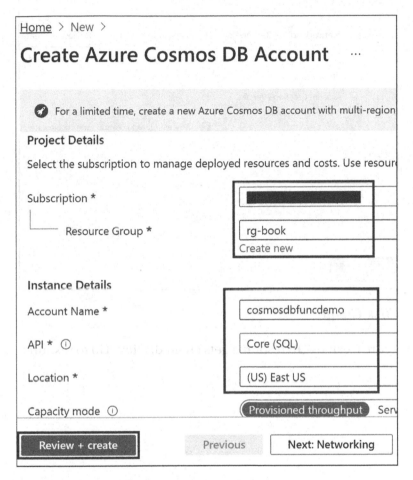

Figure 9-3. Click "Review + create"

Click Create. This action will spin up the Azure Cosmos DB resource. See Figure 9-4.

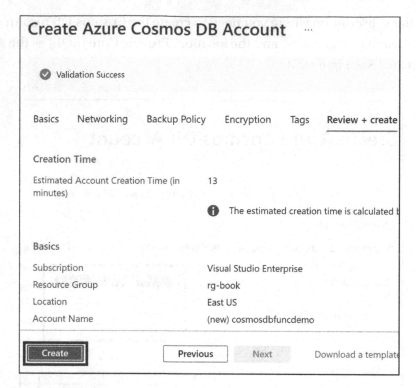

Figure 9-4. *Click Create*

Once the Azure Cosmos DB resource gets created, click "Go to resource." See Figure 9-5.

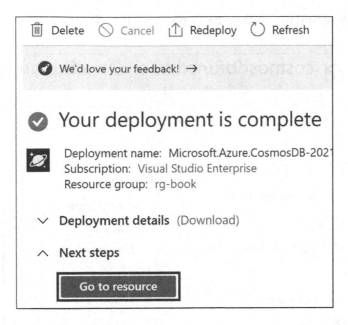

Figure 9-5. *Click "Go to resource"*

You will be navigated to the Azure Cosmos DB resource that you created. On the Overview tab, click + Add Container. See Figure 9-6.

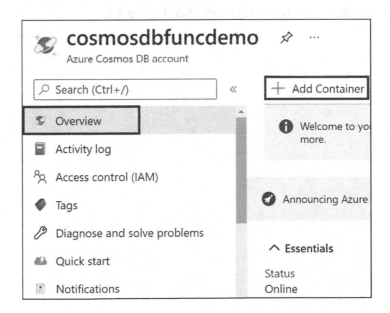

Figure 9-6. *Click + Add Container*

You will be navigated to the Data Explorer tab. Click New Container. See Figure 9-7.

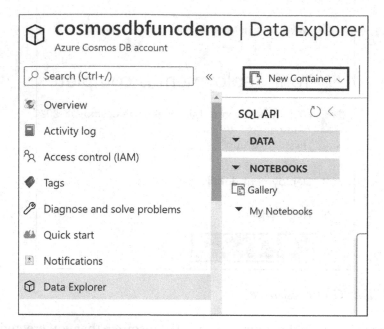

Figure 9-7. *Click New Container*

Provide the database ID and scroll down. See Figure 9-8.

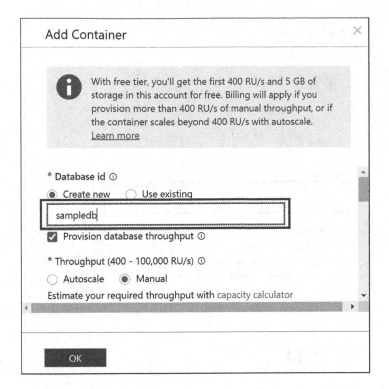

Figure 9-8. *Provide the database ID*

Provide the container ID and scroll down. See Figure 9-9.

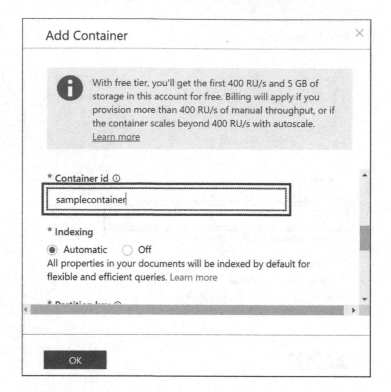

Figure 9-9. *Provide the container ID*

Provide the partition key and click OK. The container will get created. You will add an item to the container later once the Azure function is ready. See Figure 9-10.

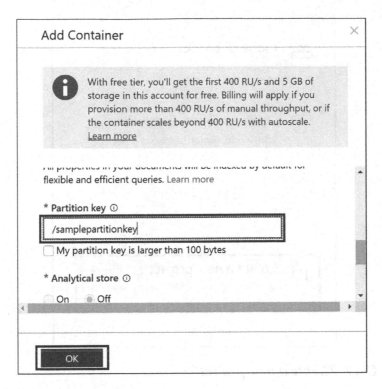

Figure 9-10. *Provide the partition key*

Now let's build the Azure function that gets triggered whenever you add an item in the Cosmos DB instance. Open Visual Studio and click "Create a new project." See Figure 9-11.

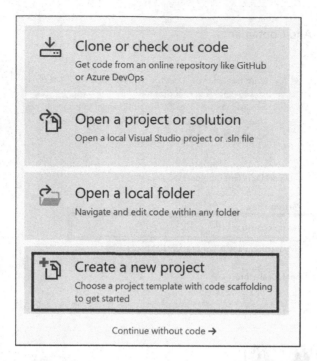

Figure 9-11. *Click "Create a new project"*

Select Azure Functions and click Next. See Figure 9-12.

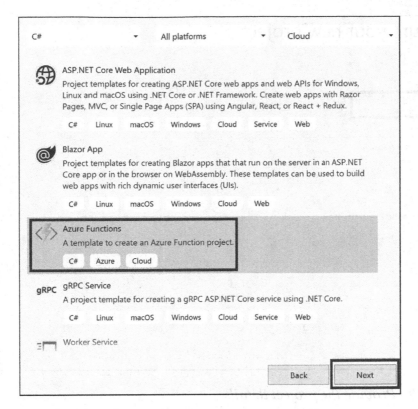

Figure 9-12. Click Next

Provide the name of the function and click Create. See Figure 9-13.

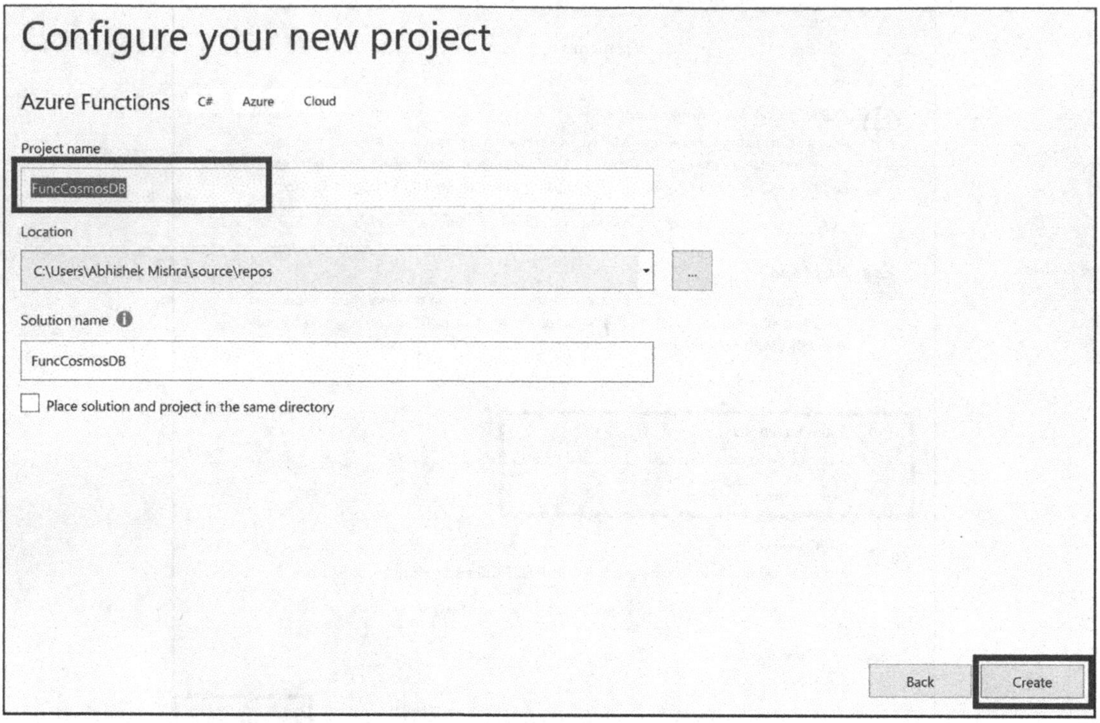

Figure 9-13. *Provide the project details*

Select Cosmos DB Trigger. Provide the name of the connection string that you will add in the `local.settings.json` file. Provide the database ID and container ID values for the Cosmos DB instance that you created earlier for the database name and container name, respectively. Click Create. See Figure 9-14. The Azure function solution will be created.

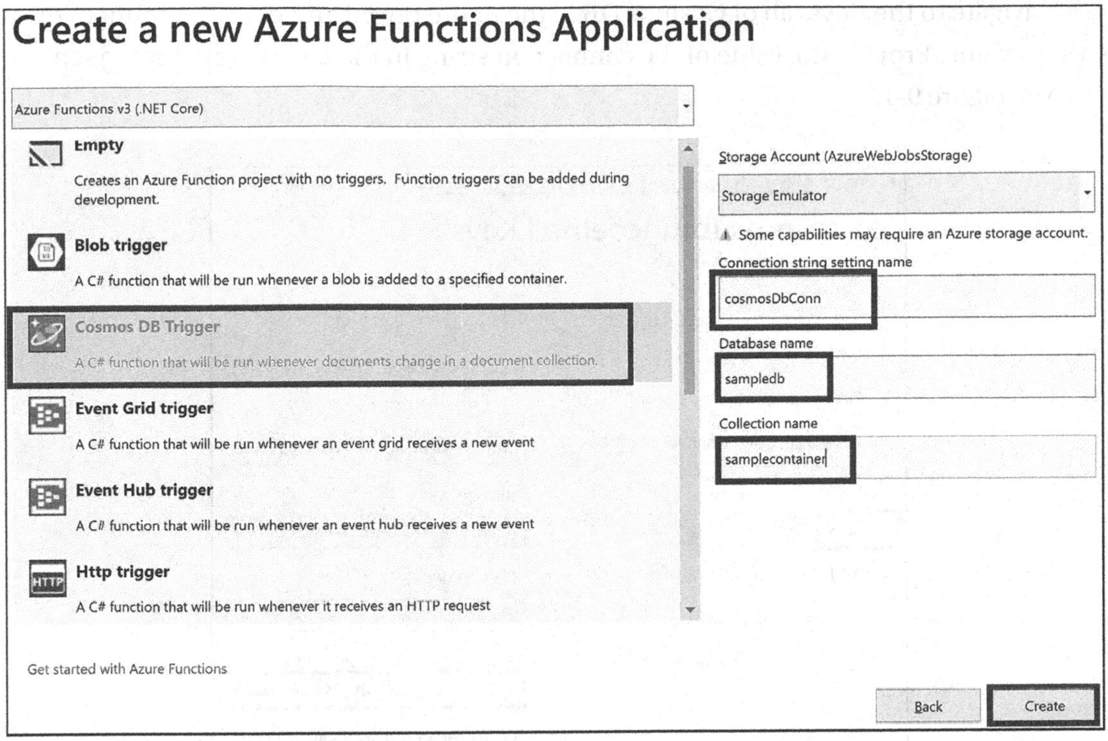

Figure 9-14. *Select the Cosmos DB trigger*

Go to the `local.settings.json` file and add the connection string, as shown in Listing 9-1. You need to provide the connection string's name the same way you did while creating the Azure function solution in Visual Studio.

Listing 9-1. local.settings.json Code

```
{
    "IsEncrypted": false,
    "Values": {
    "AzureWebJobsStorage": "UseDevelopmentStorage=true",
    "FUNCTIONS_WORKER_RUNTIME": "dotnet",
    "cosmosDbConn": "[Connection String Value from Azure portal]"
    }
}
```

Navigate to the Keys tab of Cosmos DB in the Azure portal and copy the connection string's value. Provide the value of the connection string in the `local.settings.json` file. See Figure 9-15.

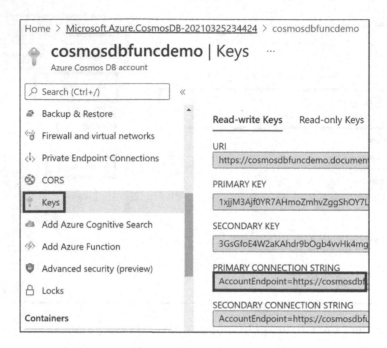

Figure 9-15. *Connection string value for Cosmos DB*

Go to `Function1.cs` and replace the contents with the code shown in Listing 9-2. The `Run` method's `input` parameter will capture the details of the items that either got added to or got modified in Azure Cosmos DB and triggered the Azure function. You add code to log the document ID and the JSON document for the item that you will add in Cosmos DB.

Listing 9-2. Function1.cs Code

```
using System;
using System.Collections.Generic;
using Microsoft.Azure.Documents;
using Microsoft.Azure.WebJobs;
using Microsoft.Azure.WebJobs.Host;
using Microsoft.Extensions.Logging;
```

```
namespace FuncCosmosDB
{
    public static class Function1
    {
        [FunctionName("Function1")]
        public static void Run([CosmosDBTrigger(
        databaseName: "sampledb",
        collectionName: "samplecontainer",
        ConnectionStringSetting = "cosmosDbConn",
        LeaseCollectionName = "leases",

        CreateLeaseCollectionIfNotExists = true)]
        IReadOnlyList<Document>  input, ILogger log)
        {
            if (input != null && input.Count > 0)
            {
                log.LogInformation("Documents modified " + input.Count);
                log.LogInformation("First document Id " + input[0].Id);
                log.LogInformation("Document " + input[0].ToString());
            }
        }
    }
}
```

Note   You need to provide a lease name for the trigger. Multiple Azure functions can get triggered by the Cosmos DB trigger. The lease for a trigger makes the invocation unique per function.

Now run the Azure function and navigate back to the Cosmos DB instance in the Azure portal. Go to the Data Explorer, expand the container that you created, and click Items. See Figure 9-16.

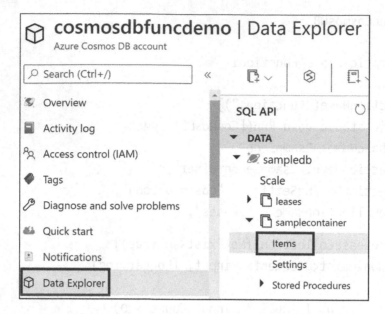

Figure 9-16. *Go to the Data Explorer*

Click New Item. See Figure 9-17.

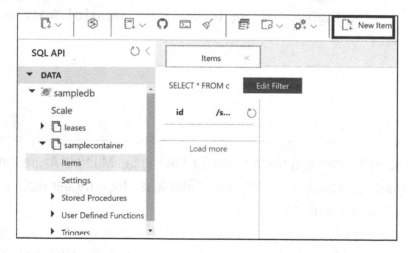

Figure 9-17. *Click New Item*

Provide the JSON document for the item and click Save. See Figure 9-18.

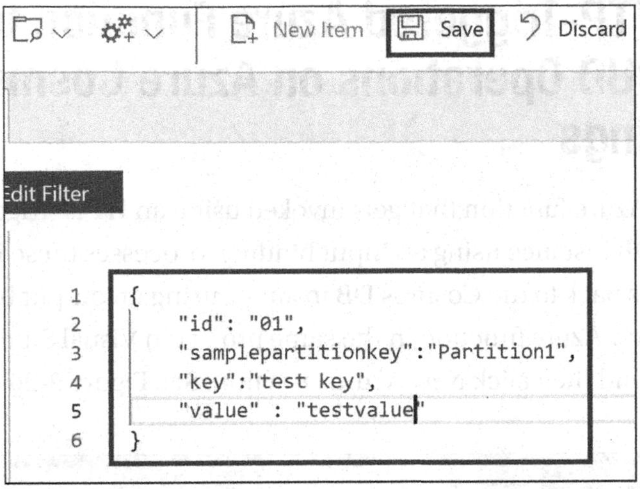

Figure 9-18. Add an item

Your Azure function gets triggered. You can see that the document ID and the document JSON get printed in the debug console. See Figure 9-19.

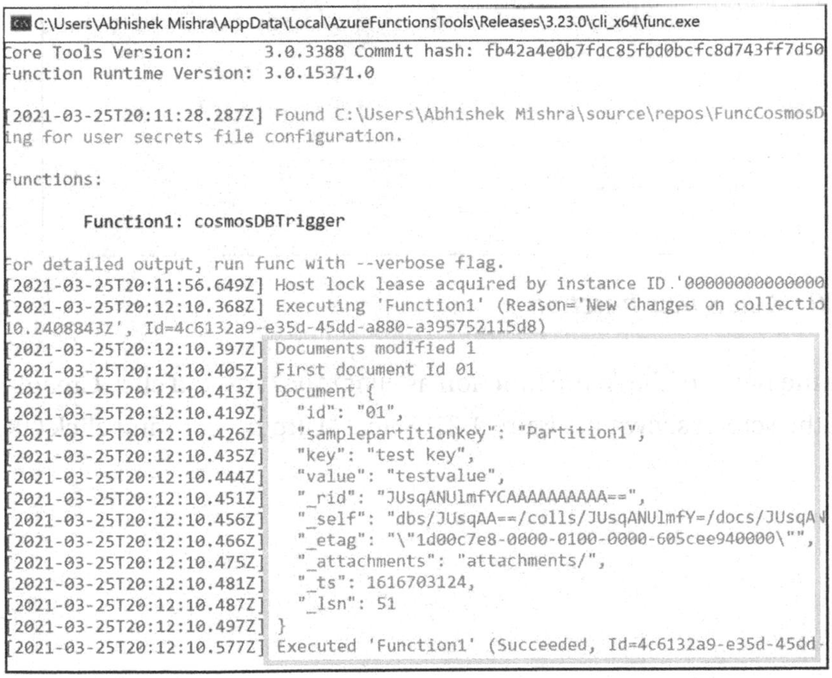

Figure 9-19. Function execution output

Build an HTTP-Triggered Azure Function to Perform CRUD Operations on Azure Cosmos DB Using Bindings

Now let's build an Azure function that gets invoked using an HTTP trigger, reads items from the Cosmos DB instance using an input binding, processes these items, and writes the processed items back to the Cosmos DB instance using an output binding.

Let's create a new Azure function in the same project in Visual Studio. Right-click the project, click Add, and then click New Azure Function. See Figure 9-20.

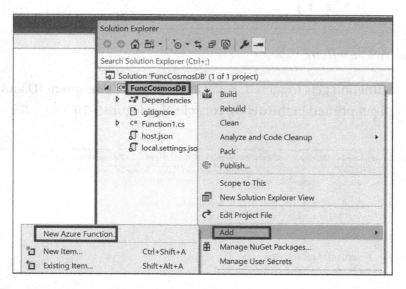

Figure 9-20. *Add a new function*

Provide the name of the Azure function as Function2.cs and click Create. Then you will get the screen shown in Figure 9-21. Select "Http trigger" and click OK. See Figure 9-21.

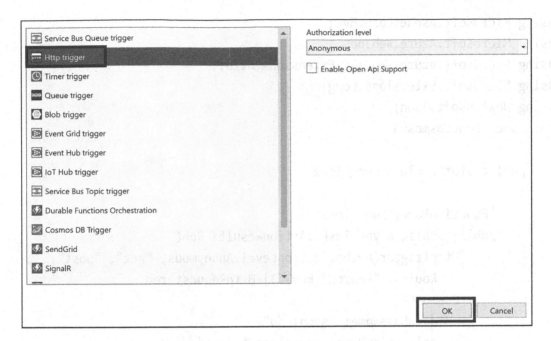

Figure 9-21. *Select "Http trigger"*

As a prerequisite, add some items in Cosmos DB in the same container that you created earlier. Let's go to the Function2.cs code and use the code shown in Listing 9-3. You add a class called SampleData that represents the items stored in Cosmos DB. The item's input parameter for the Run method is decorated with the CosmosDB attribute. This attribute takes the database name, container name, and search query. The items returned by the query get populated in the items parameter. You can populate new data of type SampleData in the outputItems input parameter for the Run method, and those items get added to the Cosmos DB instance. You invoke this function using the HTTP trigger and pass the key as the route parameter. All the items that have keys, the same as that you are passing as a route parameter, will be retrieved. You then iterate through each of these items, process them, and add a new processed item in the Cosmos DB instance.

Listing 9-3. Function2.cs Code

```
using System.Collections.Generic;
using System.IO;
using System.Threading.Tasks;
using Microsoft.AspNetCore.Http;
```

```csharp
using Microsoft.AspNetCore.Mvc;
using Microsoft.Azure.WebJobs;
using Microsoft.Azure.WebJobs.Extensions.Http;
using Microsoft.Extensions.Logging;
using Newtonsoft.Json;
namespace FuncCosmosDB
{
    public static class Function2
    {
        [FunctionName("Function2")]
        public static async Task<IActionResult> Run(
            [HttpTrigger(AuthorizationLevel.Anonymous, "get", "post",
                Route = "search/{key}")] HttpRequest req,
            [CosmosDB(
                databaseName: "sampledb",
                collectionName: "samplecontainer",
                ConnectionStringSetting = "cosmosDbConn",
                SqlQuery = "SELECT * FROM c where c.key={key} order by
                c.id")]IEnumerable<SampleData> items,
            [CosmosDB(
                databaseName: "sampledb",
                collectionName: "samplecontainer",
                ConnectionStringSetting =
                "cosmosDbConn")]IAsyncCollector<SampleData> outputItems,
            ILogger log)
        {
            log.LogInformation("C# HTTP trigger function processed a
            request.");
            // Read and process each item
            foreach (SampleData item in items)
            {
                log.LogInformation("Processing {0}-{1}-{2}-{3}",item.Id,
                item.PartitionKey, item.Key,item.Value);
                //Process the item
                string newId = item.Id + " - Processed";
```

```
            SampleData data = new SampleData() { Id = newId, PartitionKey =
            item.PartitionKey, Key = item.Key, Value = item.Value };
            //Insert a the processed Item as a new Item in the
            //Azure Cosmos DB
            await outputItems.AddAsync(data);
        }

        // Write the processed item to the database
        return new OkResult();
    }
}

public class SampleData
{
    [JsonProperty("id")]
    public string Id { get; set; }

    [JsonProperty("samplepartitionkey")]
    public string PartitionKey { get; set; }

    [JsonProperty("key")]
    public string Key { get; set; }

    [JsonProperty("value")]
    public string Value { get; set; }
}
}
```

Execute the Azure function solution and trigger the Azure function using the following link:

```
http://localhost:7071/api/search/city
```

All the items with keys as the city will get retrieved, processed, and added back to the Cosmos DB instance. See Figure 9-22.

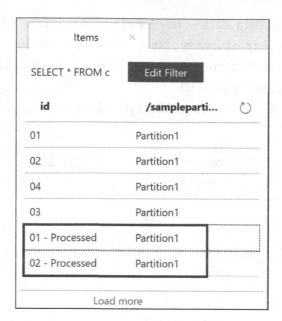

Figure 9-22. Processed items in Cosmos DB

Leverage the Azure Cosmos DB SDK to Interact with Cosmos DB from Azure Functions

You can create stored procedures, user-defined functions, and database triggers in Azure Cosmos DB. Triggers and bindings are excellent mechanisms to interact with Azure Cosmos DB data. However, they do not support invoking Azure Cosmos DB stored procedures, user-defined functions, and database triggers. You need to use the Azure Cosmos DB SDK to achieve this functionality. You can use the Azure Cosmos DB SDK to perform all the CRUD operations for the Azure Cosmos DB instance.

Let's create a stored procedure for the container that you created earlier and call that stored procedure from the Azure function. Go to the Data Explorer tab for the Azure function in the Azure portal. Hover your mouse over the container you created and click the three dots (...). See Figure 9-23.

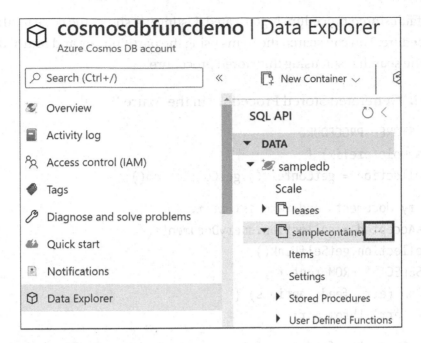

Figure 9-23. *Click the three dots*

Click New Stored Procedure. See Figure 9-24.

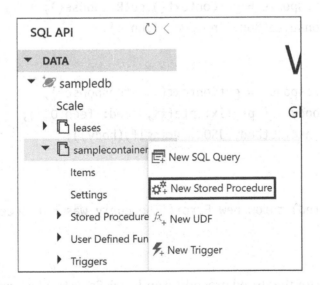

Figure 9-24. *Click New Stored Procedure*

The default stored procedure is generated. Listing 9-4 shows the code for the default stored procedure. You can search the items using the partition key and return the first item from the search result using this stored procedure.

Listing 9-4. Generated Stored Procedure in the Azure Portal

```
// SAMPLE STORED PROCEDURE
function sample(prefix) {
    var collection = getContext().getCollection();

    // Query documents and take 1st item.
    var isAccepted = collection.queryDocuments(
        collection.getSelfLink(),
        'SELECT * FROM root r',
    function (err, feed, options) {
        if (err) throw err;

        // Check the feed and if empty, set the body to 'no docs found',
        // else take 1st element from feed
        if (!feed || !feed.length) {
            var response = getContext().getResponse();
            response.setBody('no docs found');
        }
        else {
            var response = getContext().getResponse();
            var body = { prefix: prefix, feed: feed[0] };
            response.setBody(JSON.stringify(body));
        }
    });

    if (!isAccepted) throw new Error('The query was not accepted by the
    server.');
}
```

Provide a name for the stored procedure and click Save. See Figure 9-25.

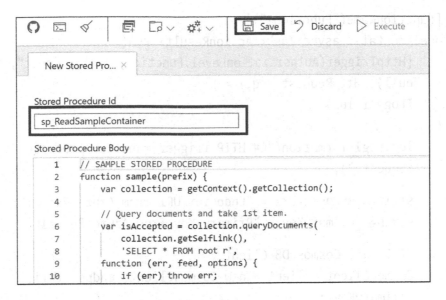

Figure 9-25. Save the stored procedure

Now let's go to the Visual Studio Azure functions project that you created earlier and add a new HTTP-triggered function named Function3. Add the NuGet package Microsoft.Azure.Cosmos to the project. Put the code shown in Listing 9-5 in Function3.cs. The ExecuteStoredProcedureAsync method invokes the stored procedure and gets the stored procedure output.

Listing 9-5. Function3.cs Code

```
using System.IO;
using System.Threading.Tasks;
using Microsoft.AspNetCore.Http;
using Microsoft.AspNetCore.Mvc;
using Microsoft.Azure.Cosmos;
using Microsoft.Azure.WebJobs;
using Microsoft.Azure.WebJobs.Extensions.Http;
using Microsoft.Extensions.Logging;
using Newtonsoft.Json;

namespace FuncCosmosDB
{
    public static class Function3
    {
```

```csharp
[FunctionName("Function3")]
public static async Task<IActionResult> Run(
    [HttpTrigger(AuthorizationLevel.Function, "get", "post", Route =
    null)] HttpRequest req,
    ILogger log)
{

    log.LogInformation("C# HTTP trigger function processed a
    request.");

    string _endpointUri = "Endpoint URI from Azure Portal";
    string _primaryKey = "Primary Key from Azure Portal";

    // Create Cosmos DB Client
    CosmosClient _client = new CosmosClient(_endpointUri,
    _primaryKey);

    // Execute Stored Procedure. Pass the Partition Key value
        that you
    // need  to query
    var result = await _client.GetContainer("sampledb",
                "samplecontainer").Scripts
        .ExecuteStoredProcedureAsync<string>
        ("sp_ReadSampleContainer",
         new PartitionKey("Partition1"),null);

    // Print the item returned by the Stored Procedure
    log.LogInformation("Returned Result : {0}",result.Resource);

    return new OkObjectResult("Success");
    }
  }
}
```

You can get the primary key and endpoint URI value from the Keys tab in the Cosmos DB instance in the Azure portal. See Figure 9-26.

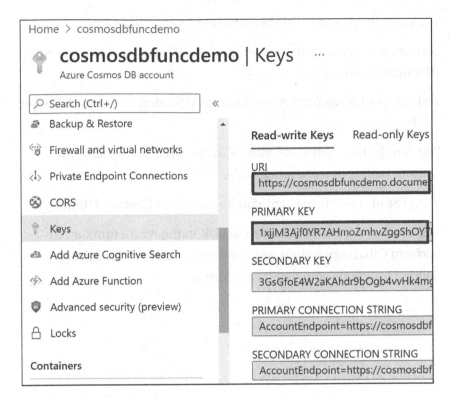

Figure 9-26. *Get the primary key and URI for the Cosmos DB instance*

When you execute the Azure function and invoke the function URL, the stored procedure result will get logged in the debug console.

Summary

In this chapter, you learned how to work with Cosmos DB triggers and Cosmos DB input and output bindings using Visual Studio. You developed Azure functions to perform CRUD operations using Azure Cosmos DB input and output bindings and the Azure Cosmos DB SDK. You can pass the date, time, and activity you are planning to do during that time.

The following are the key takeaways from this chapter:

- Azure Cosmos DB is a highly available multimodel database. It supports SQL Core, Gremlin, Mongo DB, and Casandra APIs.

- Azure Cosmos DB can scale rapidly and can replicate data across the globe quickly.

- You can trigger an Azure function using an Azure Cosmos DB trigger.

- You can add items to the Azure Cosmos DB instance using a Cosmos DB output binding.

- You can read items from Azure Cosmos DB using a Cosmos DB input binding.

- You can declaratively configure a CosmosDB trigger and binding without having to write much code.

- Visual Studio provides a template to work with Cosmos DB trigger.

- You can use the Azure Cosmos DB SDK in the Azure function to perform CRUD operations and invoke stored procedures, user-defined functions, and database triggers.

CHAPTER 10

Enabling Application Insights and Azure Monitor

Once you have developed your Azure function and have deployed it to the production environment, you must ensure that it is always ready to wake up if triggered and is doing its job as expected. In fact, you need to keep tabs on any failures and get alerts whenever the function goes down. You should have enough logs and metrics to debug issues and unexpected behavior for Azure functions in a production environment. Monitoring helps you to observe the execution behavior of an Azure function, and logs will provide you with the proper context in which you can debug Azure function failures and exceptions.

In the previous chapter, you learned how to perform CRUD operations on Azure Cosmos DB instances from Azure Functions. You explored the Azure Cosmos DB input and output bindings and the Azure Cosmos DB SDK in the context of Azure Functions. In this chapter, you'll explore how to use Application Insights and Azure Monitor with Azure Functions to gather logs and metrics.

Structure of the Chapter

In this chapter, you will explore the following aspects of Application Insights and Azure Monitor and Azure Functions:

- Enabling logging using Application Insights

- Performing diagnostics for Azure Functions

- Monitoring functions and creating alerts

- Restricting the number of scaling instances for a function app

© Ashirwad Satapathi and Abhishek Mishra 2021
A. Satapathi and A. Mishra, *Hands-on Azure Functions with C#*, https://doi.org/10.1007/978-1-4842-7122-3_10

Objectives

After studying this chapter, you will be able to do the following:

- Implement Application Insights for Azure Functions

- Use Azure Monitor for Azure Functions

Enable Logging Using Application Insights

Azure Functions provides excellent support for logging using Applications Insights. Let's create an Azure function with Application Insights enabled using the Azure portal. Then you can modify the function code to log some information, errors, and traces for the Azure function. Open the Azure portal and click "Create a new resource." See Figure 10-1.

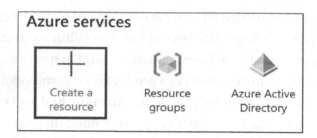

Figure 10-1. *Click "Create a resource"*

Click Compute and then click Function App. See Figure 10-2.

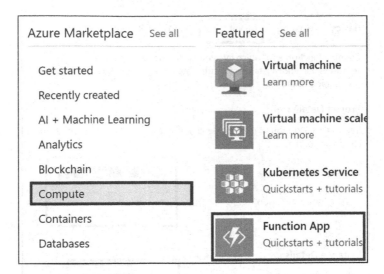

Figure 10-2. *Click Function App*

Provide the basic details for the function. Let's select .NET and 3.1 as the runtime stack and the version. Click the Monitoring tab to enable Application Insights for the Azure function app. See Figure 10-3.

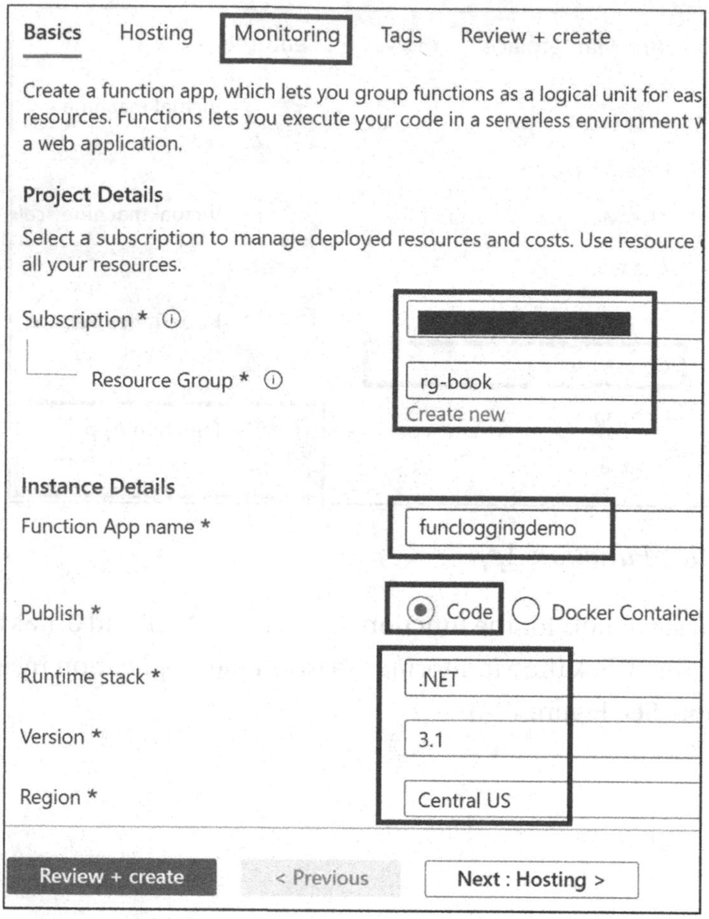

Figure 10-3. Provide basic details for the Azure function

Click Yes to enable Application Insights and provide the name for the Application Insights resource. You can also use an existing Application Insights resource. Click "Review + create." See Figure 10-4.

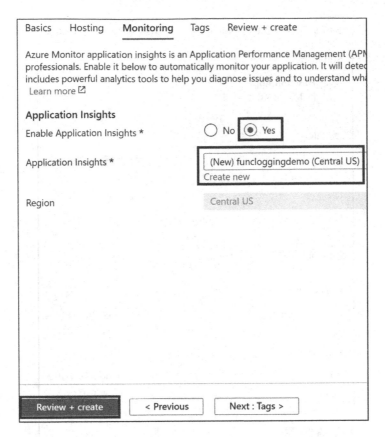

Figure 10-4. *Enable Application Insights*

Click Create. See Figure 10-5.

Figure 10-5. *Click Create*

Go to the Azure function app once it is created. Now you need to add a function to the Azure function app. Click the Functions tab and click Add. See Figure 10-6.

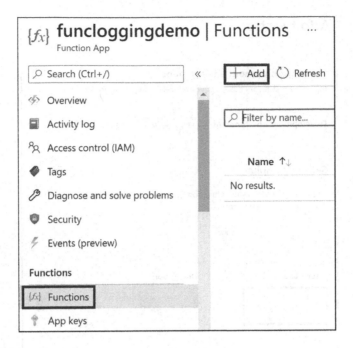

Figure 10-6. *Add a function*

Select "Http trigger" and click Add. See Figure 10-7.

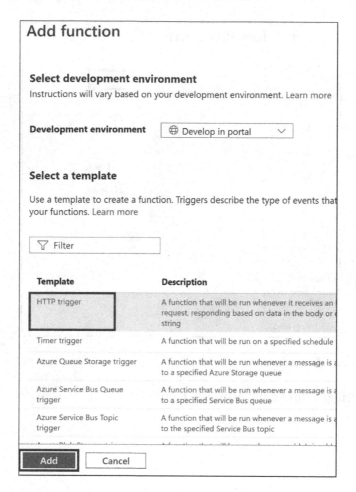

Figure 10-7. *Select "Http trigger"*

Once the function is created, go into the function and click Code + Test.
See Figure 10-8.

Figure 10-8. *Click Code + Test*

Replace the code in the `run.csx` file with the code in Listing 10-1 and save the file. Here you are using the `LogInformation` method to log information, the `LogError` method to log errors, the `LogWarning` method to log warnings, and the `LogCritical` method to log critical errors.

Listing 10-1. Function Code with Logging Enabled

```
#r "Newtonsoft.Json"

using System.Net;
using Microsoft.AspNetCore.Mvc;
using Microsoft.Extensions.Primitives;
using Newtonsoft.Json;

public static async Task<IActionResult> Run(HttpRequest req, ILogger log)
{
    // Log Information
    log.LogInformation("This is an Information.");

    // Log Trace
    log.LogError(new Exception(),"This is an Exception");

    // Log Warning
    log.LogWarning("This is a Warning");
```

```
    // Log Critical Error
    log.LogCritical("This is a Critical error");

    return new OkObjectResult("Demo Complete !!");
}
```

Click "Get function URL" and browse to the URL in the browser. Now let's go to Application Insights and verify whether these logs were added. See Figure 10-9.

```
⊟ Save   ✕ Discard   ↻ Refresh   ⊏⊐ Test/Run   ↑ Upload   [▣ Get function URL]

funcloggingdemo \ HttpTrigger1 \   run.csx                    ∨

 1    #r "Newtonsoft.Json"
 2
 3    using System.Net;
 4    using Microsoft.AspNetCore.Mvc;
 5    using Microsoft.Extensions.Primitives;
 6    using Newtonsoft.Json;
 7
 8    public static async Task<IActionResult> Run(HttpRequest req, ILogger log)
 9    {
10        //Log Information
11        log.LogInformation("This is an Information.");
12
13        //Log Trace
14        log.LogError(new Exception(),"This is an Exception");
15
16        //Log Warning
17        log.LogWarning("This is a Warning");
18
19        //Log Critical Error
20        log.LogCritical("This is a Critical error");
21
22        return new OkObjectResult("Demo Complete !!");
23    }
```

Figure 10-9. *Get the function URL*

Go back to the Azure function app and click the Application Insights tab. Click the Application Insights resource name that you are using for this function app. You will be navigated to the Application Insights resource. See Figure 10-10.

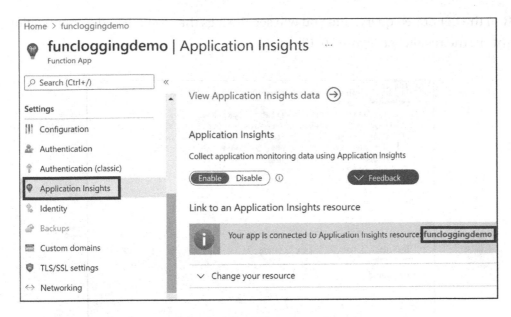

Figure 10-10. *Go to the Application Insights resource*

Click the "Transaction search" tab and then click View in Logs. This action will generate a query using the Kusto Query Language (KQL) to get the logs you have pushed to Application Insights. See Figure 10-11.

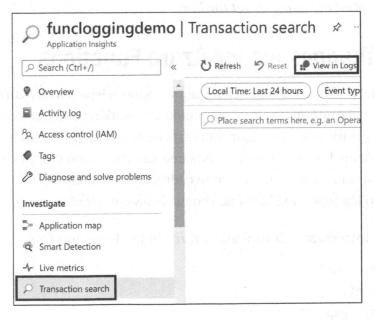

Figure 10-11. *Click View in Logs*

Run the generated query, and you will see the logs that you pushed to Application Insights in the result. See Figure 10-12.

Figure 10-12.   *Run the query to get the logs*

Perform Diagnostics for Azure Functions

The Azure portal provides a mechanism to auto-diagnose issues with Azure Functions. If you see that an Azure function is not responding or working as expected, you can diagnose the issue with ease and figure out what went wrong. Let's introduce some errors into the Azure function. Let's use the same Azure function that you created earlier for this demonstration. Modify the function code as shown in Listing 10-2. You are using a method called LogSuperCritical that should throw compilation errors.

Listing 10-2.   Introduce a Compilation Error in the Function Code

```
#r "Newtonsoft.Json"
using System.Net;
using Microsoft.AspNetCore.Mvc;
```

```
using Microsoft.Extensions.Primitives;
using Newtonsoft.Json;

public static async Task<IActionResult> Run(HttpRequest req, ILogger log)
{
    //Log Information
    log.LogInformation("This is an Information.");

    //Log Trace
    log.LogError(new Exception(),"This is an Exception");

    //Log Warning
    log.LogWarning("This is a Warning");

    //Introducing Compilation Error
    //There is no method as SuperCritical
    //Should throw compilation error
    log.LogSuperCritical("This is a Critical error")

    return new OkObjectResult("Demo Complete !!");
}
```

Now let's go to the function app's Overview tab and stop the function app.
See Figure 10-13.

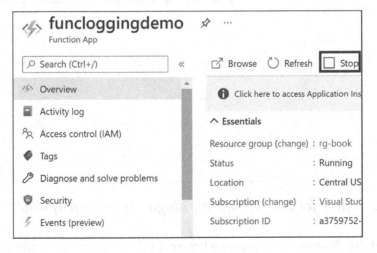

Figure 10-13. *Stop the Azure function app*

Browse to the function URL. You should get an internal 500 error or an equivalent error. Now let's diagnose these issues on the "Diagnose and solve problems" tab. You can diagnose issues in the following categories:

- Availability and Performance

- Configuration and Management

- SSL and Domains

- Risk Assessment

Let's search for *Function App Down or Reporting Errors* in the search box. See Figure 10-14.

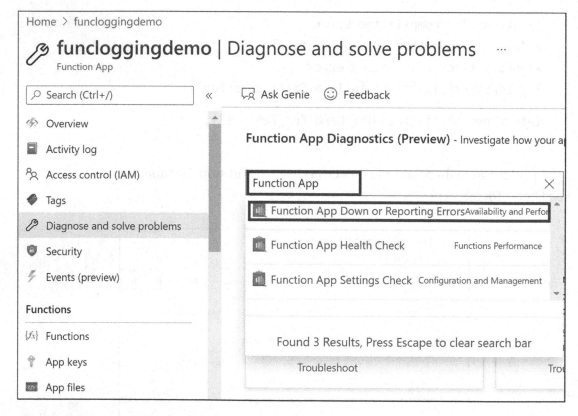

Figure 10-14. *Search for the appropriate diagnostic to be performed*

You will get the diagnostic results in a few seconds. You can see some issues being highlighted in the Function App General Information and Function App Execution and Errors sections. See Figure 10-15.

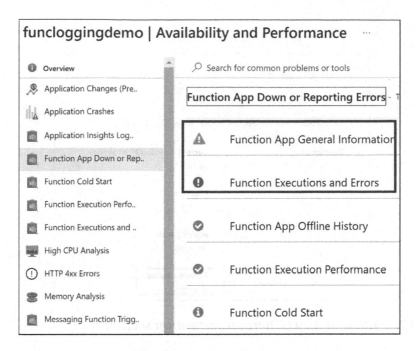

Figure 10-15. *Errors reported by the diagnostics run*

If you scroll down, you can see issues being reported as Function Compilation Error (.csx). Specifically, in Figure 10-16, you can see a red exclamation point in the Function Compilation Error (.csx) section, and when you further drill down in the subsequent steps, you can see that you have a script error highlighted as Script Compilation Error (.csx). See Figure 10-16.

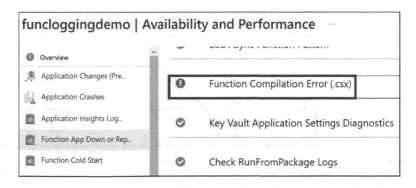

Figure 10-16. *More errors reported by the diagnostics run*

If you expand the Function App General Information section, you can see that the function app is in the Stopped state. See Figure 10-17.

Figure 10-17. *Function App General Information section*

If you expand the Function Compilation Error (.csx) section, you can see where the compilation error is in the function code. See Figure 10-18.

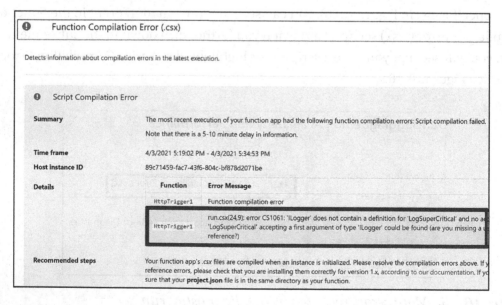

Figure 10-18. *Function compilation error*

Monitor Azure Functions and Create Alerts

You can monitor your Azure function metrics on the Metrics tab. Go to the Metrics tab.
See Figure 10-19.

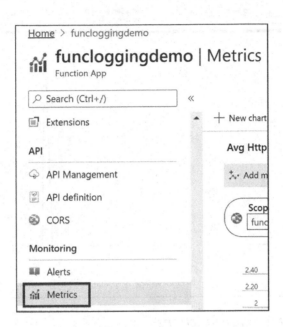

Figure 10-19. *Go to the Metrics tab*

Select a metric and an aggregation. You will get a chart for the metric that you can
use to analyze your function's performance and execution. You can toggle between a line
chart, area chart, bar chart, and scatter chart. You can also add a new chart by clicking
the "New chart" option. See Figure 10-20.

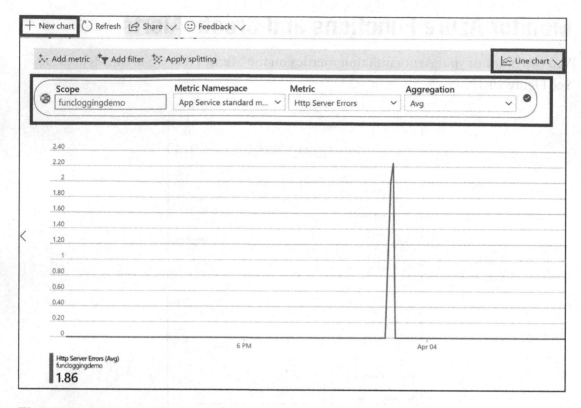

Figure 10-20. *Monitor Azure functions*

You can set alerts and be notified in case of anomalies or deviation from the normal behavior of the Azure function. To set an alert, go to the Alerts tab and click "New alert rule." See Figure 10-21.

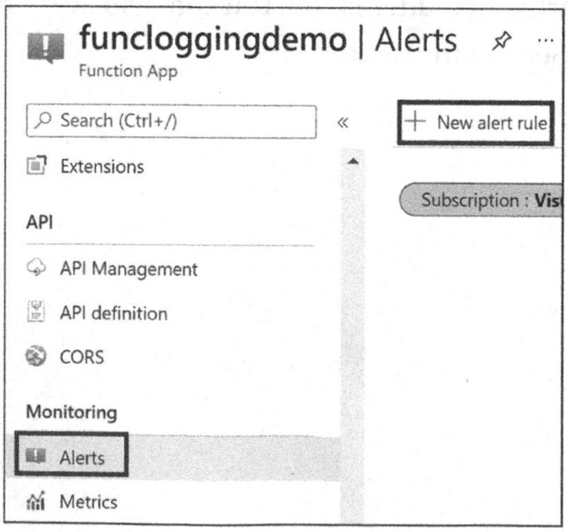

Figure 10-21. *Create a new alert rule*

Now you need to configure the scope, condition, and action for the alert. The scope specifies which Azure resource to monitor. The condition specifies what to monitor, for example, when the resource gets deleted, and the action specifies what to do when the condition is met, for example, send an email or invoke a Logic App instance. Make sure you have selected the right resource in the scope. If not, click "Edit resource" and select the right resource. Click "Add condition" to configure a condition. Let's monitor for the condition when the function app gets into a stopped state. See Figure 10-22.

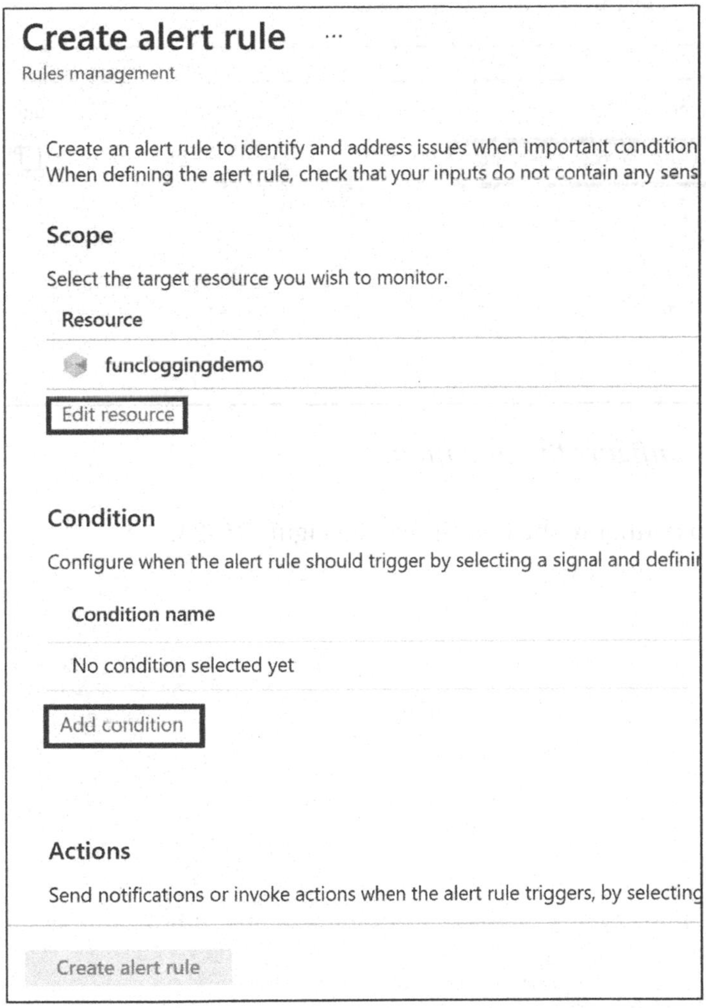

Create alert rule ···
Rules management

Create an alert rule to identify and address issues when important condition
When defining the alert rule, check that your inputs do not contain any sens

Scope

Select the target resource you wish to monitor.

Resource

funcloggingdemo

Edit resource

Condition

Configure when the alert rule should trigger by selecting a signal and defini

Condition name

No condition selected yet

Add condition

Actions

Send notifications or invoke actions when the alert rule triggers, by selecting

Create alert rule

Figure 10-22. *Add a condition*

Search for *Stop Web App* and select it. See Figure 10-23.

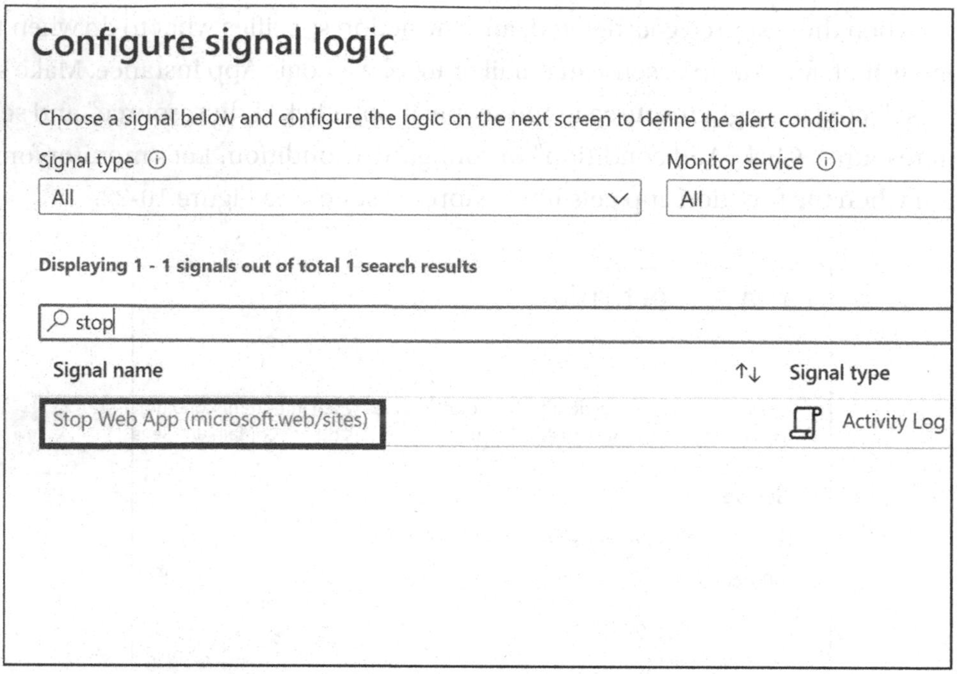

Configure signal logic

Choose a signal below and configure the logic on the next screen to define the alert condition.

Signal type ⓘ

All   ⌄

Monitor service ⓘ

All

Displaying 1 - 1 signals out of total 1 search results

🔍 stop

Signal name	↑↓	Signal type
Stop Web App (microsoft.web/sites)		📜 Activity Log

Figure 10-23. *Configure the condition*

Click Done to configure the condition. See Figure 10-24.

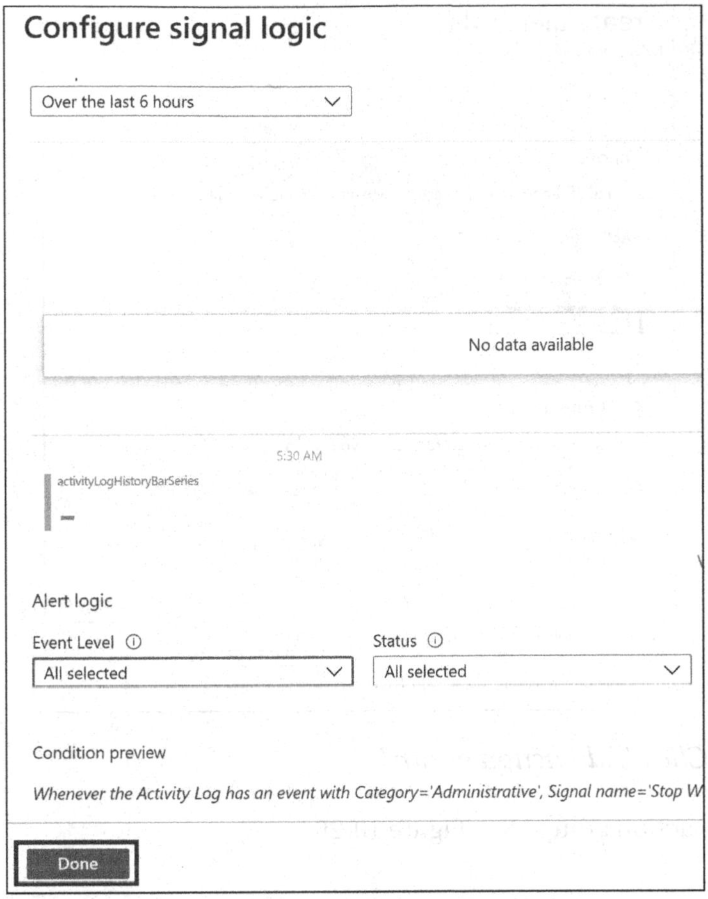

Configure signal logic

Over the last 6 hours	⌄

No data available

5:30 AM

activityLogHistoryBarSeries

—

Alert logic

Event Level ⓘ	Status ⓘ
All selected ⌄	All selected ⌄

Condition preview

Whenever the Activity Log has an event with Category='Administrative', Signal name='Stop W

Done

Figure 10-24. *Click Done to configure the condition*

Now let's add an action. Click "Add action group." See Figure 10-25.

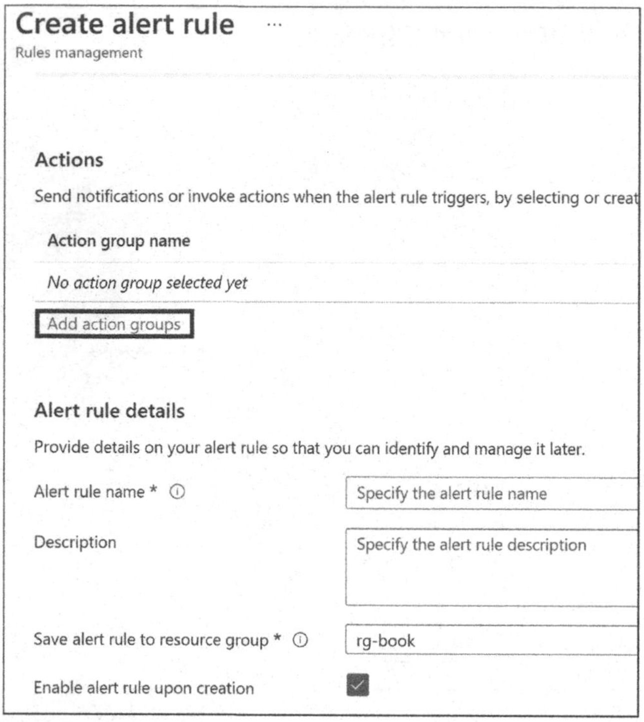

Create alert rule   ···
Rules management

Actions

Send notifications or invoke actions when the alert rule triggers, by selecting or creat

Action group name

No action group selected yet

Add action groups

Alert rule details

Provide details on your alert rule so that you can identify and manage it later.

Alert rule name * ⓘ	Specify the alert rule name
Description	Specify the alert rule description
Save alert rule to resource group * ⓘ	rg-book
Enable alert rule upon creation	☑

Figure 10-25. *Click "Add action group"*

Click "Create action group." See Figure 10-26.

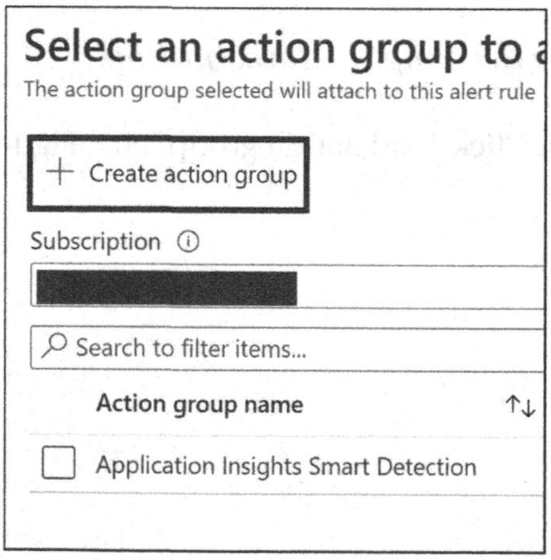

Select an action group to
The action group selected will attach to this alert rule

+ Create action group

Subscription ⓘ

▮▮▮▮▮▮▮▮▮▮▮▮▮▮▮▮

🔍 Search to filter items...

Action group name   ↑↓

☐ Application Insights Smart Detection

Figure 10-26. *Create an action group*

Provide a name for the action group and click Next: Notifications. See Figure 10-27.

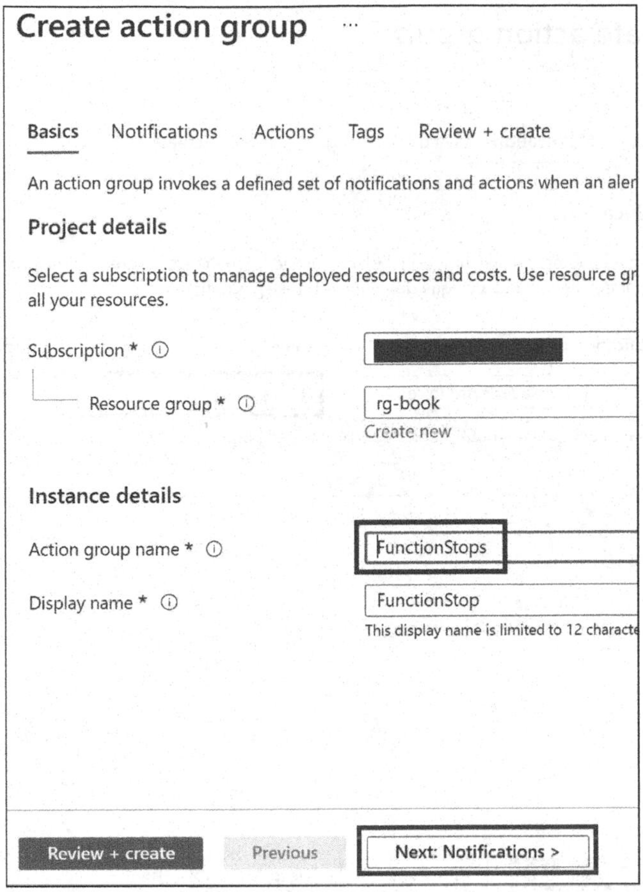

Figure 10-27. *Provide basic details for the action group*

Set the notification type to Email and provide a name for the notification.
See Figure 10-28.

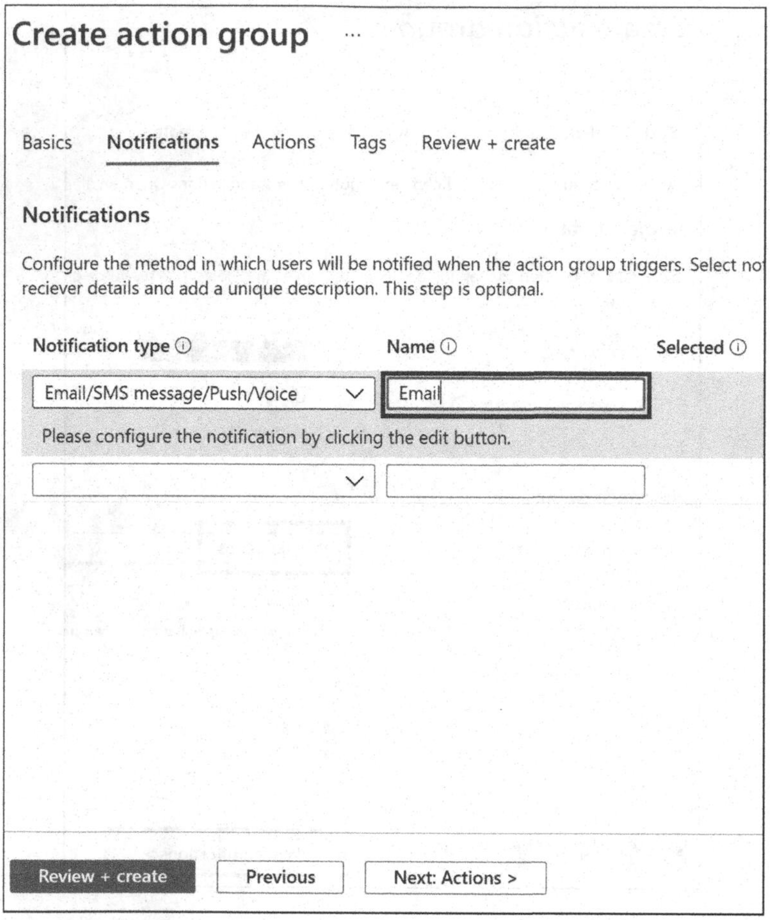

Figure 10-28. *Select Email*

You need to configure the email details. Provide email details and click OK. You can select the SMS and Voice check boxes and provide the country code and phone number. See Figure 10-29.

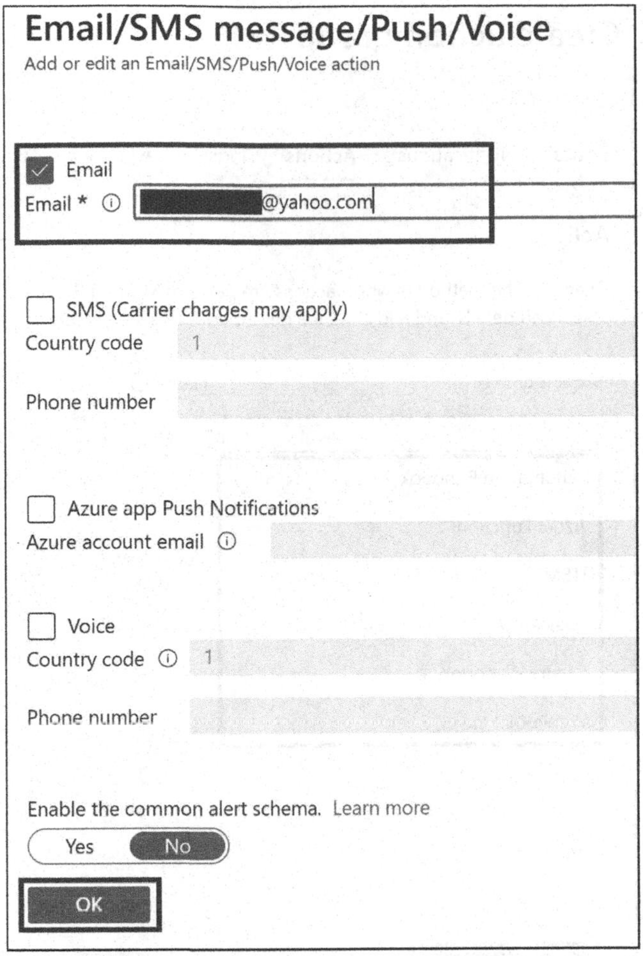

Email/SMS message/Push/Voice

Add or edit an Email/SMS/Push/Voice action

☑ Email

Email * ⓘ [████████]@yahoo.com

☐ SMS (Carrier charges may apply)

Country code   1

Phone number

☐ Azure app Push Notifications

Azure account email ⓘ

☐ Voice

Country code ⓘ   1

Phone number

Enable the common alert schema. Learn more

(Yes   No)

OK

Figure 10-29. *Provide the email details*

You can go to the Actions tab and configure an action. For example, run an Azure function when the condition meets or executes a Logic App. Configuring an action is not mandatory. You can click "Review + create" and then click Create to create the action group. See Figure 10-30.

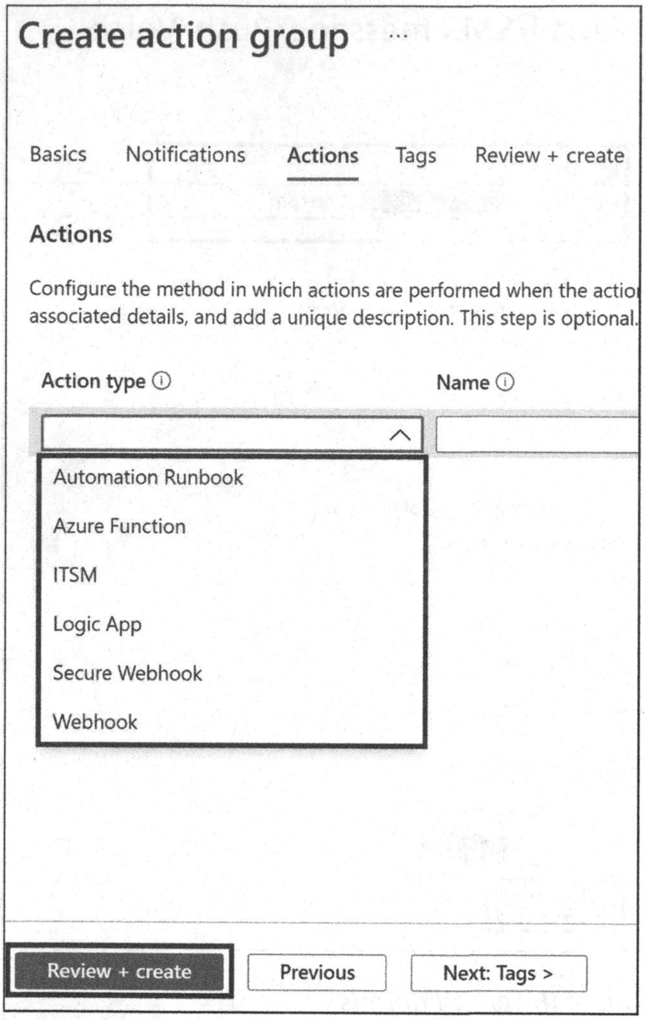

Figure 10-30. *Add an action and click "Review + create"*

Provide an alert rule name and click "Create alert rule." The alert gets created. You can stop the function app on the Overview tab to get an alert. See Figure 10-31.

Create alert rule
Rules management

Actions

Send notifications or invoke actions when the alert rule triggers, by selecting or creating a new action group. Learn more

Action group name	Contains actions
FunctionStops	1 Email ⓘ

Manage action groups

Alert rule details

Provide details on your alert rule so that you can identify and manage it later.

Alert rule name * ⓘ   Function Stop Alert

Description   Specify the alert rule description

Save alert rule to resource group * ⓘ   rg-book

Enable alert rule upon creation   ☑

Create alert rule

Figure 10-31. Click "Create alert rule"

Restrict the Number of Scaling Instances for the Azure Function App

In the Consumption Plan, the underlying Azure platform scales the Azure function. It adds new instances whenever there is a surge in load and removes additional instances whenever the incoming load decreases. You do not have explicit control of how the Azure function scales in the Consumption Plan. However, you can define a maximum limit on the number of instances that the Azure functions can scale out. This action will help you keep tabs on the infrastructure cost and efficiently plan the Azure function app infrastructure. To set a maximum scaling limit, go to the "Scale out" tab in the Azure portal. You can set the maximum scale-out limit and click Save. This setting will ensure that the Azure function will not scale out beyond the maximum limit set. See Figure 10-32.

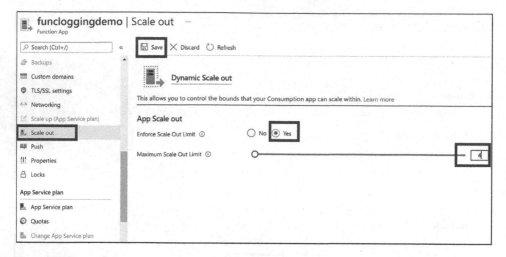

Figure 10-32. Set the maximum scale-out limit for the Azure function

Summary

In this chapter, you learned how to enable Application Insights for Azure Monitor and generate logs for your Azure function. You explored how to analyze the generated logs and troubleshoot issues from the generated logs. You learned how to diagnose issues for Azure functions with ease and troubleshoot failures. You also learned how to monitor metrics for the Azure function and set alerts. Limiting the number of scaling instances is an important aspect for Azure functions running in a Consumption Plan. You learned how to limit the number of scaling instances for the Azure function running on the Consumption Plan.

The following are the key takeaways from this chapter:

- You can use LogError, LogWarning, LogCritical, and LogInformation methods to push logs to Application Insights.

- You can go to the "Diagnose and solve problems" tab and diagnose Azure function failures. The underlying function performs the diagnostics and provides a well-articulated report for the issues.

- On the Metrics tab, you add charts based on an available metrics and then monitor an Azure function based on the metric criteria.

- You can add an alert on the Metrics tab and get alerted based on your configured anomaly condition. You can set both a notification and an action to be performed whenever the anomalous condition is met.

- On the "Scale out" tab, you can specify the maximum number of instances that your Azure function can scale out to.

In the next chapter, you will explore how to integrate Azure Key Vault for secret management with Azure Functions.

CHAPTER 11

Storing Function Secrets in Azure Key Vault

In the previous chapters, we discussed ways to build serverless solutions to solve real-world problems by using a combination of triggers and bindings in Azure Functions. In some of the cases, you used other services in the solutions such as SendGrid, Azure Blob Storage, and Azure SQL Database. To use SendGrid, you needed a valid API key, while you need the connection string to interact with Azure SQL Database, Azure Blob Storage, and Azure Queue Storage. These are confidential secrets that should not be exposed to anyone. With such information, someone could cause a lot of harm to your application and organization.

AppyMash is an Internet company that provides multiple services, ranging from ecommerce to OTT content, to its users on a subscription basis. It is currently running its applications using Azure App Service. It has been on an expansion spree and has grown from a mere startup two years ago to an Internet giant now with a huge ecosystem of services. To cope with the application development pace, the development team has integrated multiple SaaS solutions. Recently, one of the SaaS providers that provides mailing capabilities advised all its customers including AppyMash to regenerate the API keys, because of a recent security breach in its databases. Following the vendor's advice, the AppyMash team decided to regenerate the API keys. But the problem was the expected downtime to redeploy all the applications after replacing the API keys in all the applications. Almost all the applications in the app ecosystem were impacted from this mandatory modification as they were consuming the services from the SaaS vendor for sending all the required mail communications. This was a time-consuming process, which impacted all the new customers who were trying to subscribe to the services along with the existing customers who were trying to change their passwords or perform

© Ashirwad Satapathi and Abhishek Mishra 2021
A. Satapathi and A. Mishra, *Hands-on Azure Functions with C#*, https://doi.org/10.1007/978-1-4842-7122-3_11

any operations that needed mail communications. The impact of such an event can be catastrophic for the organization's business and reputation. Such a situation justifies the need for a centralized secret manager.

In this chapter, you will look at a service offered by Azure called Key Vault that helps to manage and store secrets.

Structure of the Chapter

This chapter will explore the following topics related to Azure Key Vault and Azure Functions:

- Getting started with Key Vault
- Creating vault in the Azure portal
- Creating an access policy
- Fetching secrets from Azure Key Vault using Azure Functions

Objective

After studying this chapter, you will be able to do the following:

- Create a vault and store your app secrets there
- Interact with Azure Key Vault from Azure Functions

Getting Started with Azure Key Vault

Azure Key Vault is a cloud service provided by Microsoft to store secrets and sensitive information. It provides a way to store app secrets along with certificates inside a secure container in a centralized manner. With the help of Azure Key Vault, developers no longer need to rely on configuration files or environment variables to store sensitive information. You can access the secret values using the URLs by authenticating an app with managed identities, service principals, and/or certificates.

The following are the advantages of using Azure Key Vault:

- It helps reduce deployments of your application that are caused due to a change in any of the application secrets.

- It provides a safe and secure mechanism to store and fetch sensitive information.

- It supports importing as well as generating keys, secrets, and certificates.

- It provides role-based access policy to secrets.

In this chapter, you will look at ways to store your secrets in a centralized and secure manner in Azure Key Vault.

Create an Azure Key Vault in the Azure Portal

Go to the Azure portal. Search for *key vaults* in the search box and click it. See Figure 11-1.

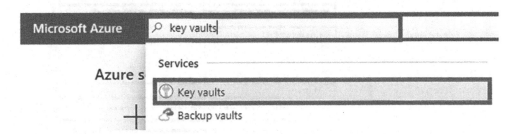

Figure 11-1. *Searching for key vaults*

Click Create to create a vault. See Figure 11-2.

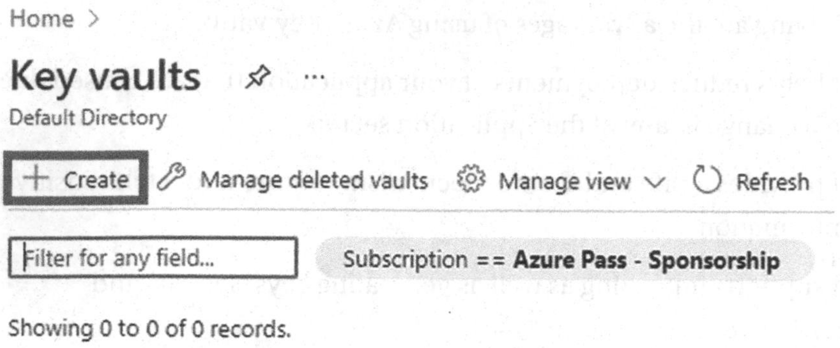

Home >

Key vaults 📌 ⋯
Default Directory

➕ Create   🔧 Manage deleted vaults   ⚙ Manage view ⌄   ↻ Refresh

Filter for any field...   Subscription == **Azure Pass - Sponsorship**

Showing 0 to 0 of 0 records.

Figure 11-2. *Create a vault*

Select the subscription you to use for billing and then enter the resource group where you want to create this resource. Enter a globally unique key vault name, select the nearest region, and then select the appropriate pricing tier. Finally, click "Next: Access policy." See Figure 11-3.

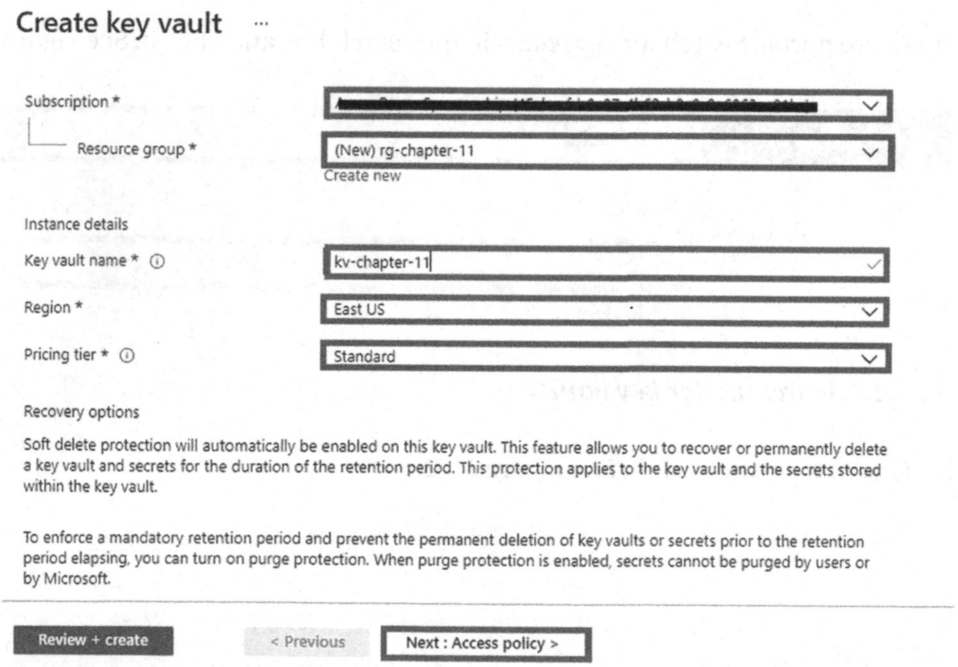

Create key vault ⋯

Subscription *   [████████████████████████████████████] ⌄

|— Resource group *   [(New) rg-chapter-11] ⌄
                            Create new

Instance details

Key vault name * ⓘ   [kv-chapter-11]   ✓

Region *   [East US]   ⌄

Pricing tier * ⓘ   [Standard]   ⌄

Recovery options

Soft delete protection will automatically be enabled on this key vault. This feature allows you to recover or permanently delete a key vault and secrets for the duration of the retention period. This protection applies to the key vault and the secrets stored within the key vault.

To enforce a mandatory retention period and prevent the permanent deletion of key vaults or secrets prior to the retention period elapsing, you can turn on purge protection. When purge protection is enabled, secrets cannot be purged by users or by Microsoft.

[Review + create]   [< Previous]   [Next : Access policy >]

Figure 11-3. *Click "Next: Access policy"*

Select an appropriate vault access model and add an access policy if you want on this screen. After you have configured all the access policy–related changes, click Next : Networking. See Figure 11-4.

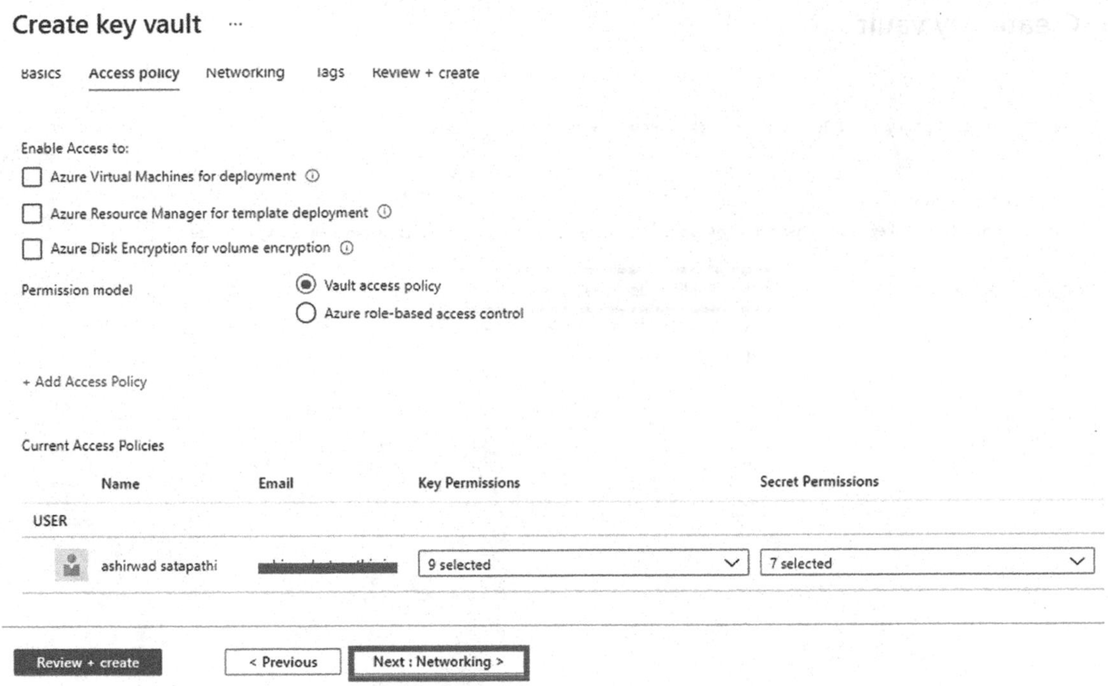

Create key vault   ...

Basics   **Access policy**   Networking   Tags   Review + create

Enable Access to:

☐ Azure Virtual Machines for deployment   ⓘ

☐ Azure Resource Manager for template deployment   ⓘ

☐ Azure Disk Encryption for volume encryption   ⓘ

Permission model   ⦿ Vault access policy
                                    ◯ Azure role-based access control

+ Add Access Policy

Current Access Policies

	Name	Email	Key Permissions		Secret Permissions	
USER						
👤	ashirwad satapathi		9 selected	⌄	7 selected	⌄

Review + create		< Previous	Next : Networking >

Figure 11-4.   *Click Next : Networking*

Select the connectivity method appropriate for your solution and click Next : Tags.
See Figure 11-5.

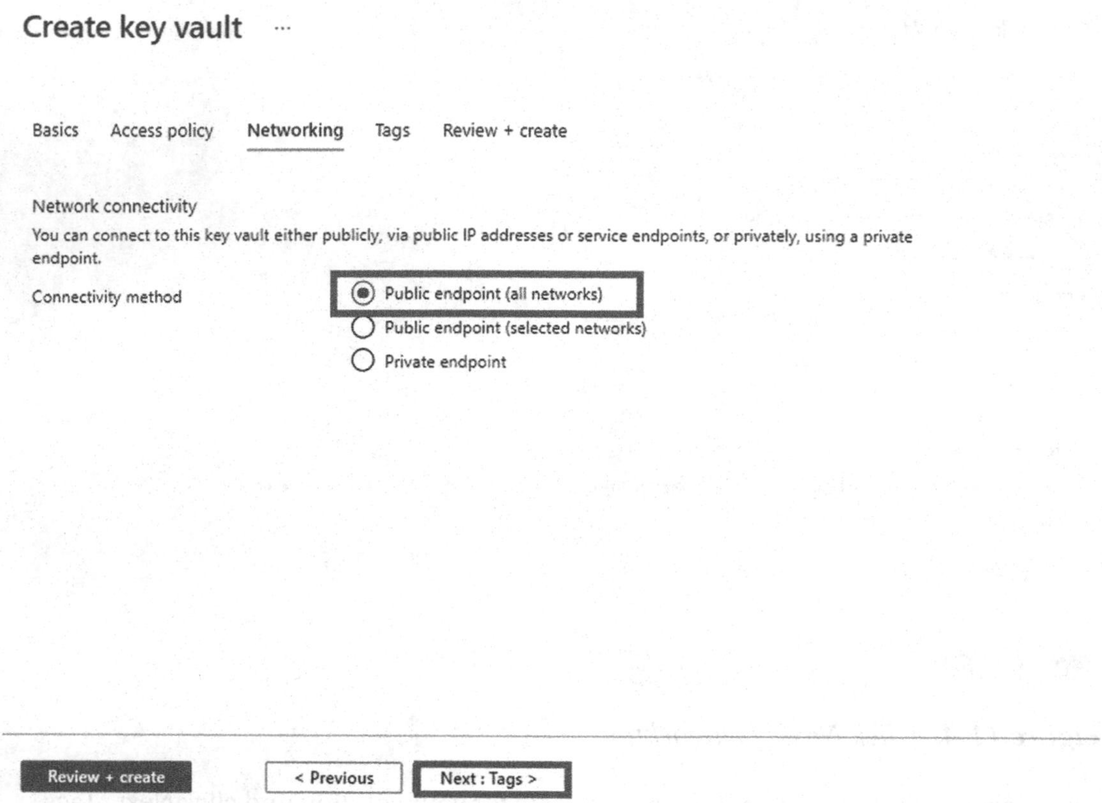

Create key vault ⋯

Basics   Access policy   **Networking**   Tags   Review + create

Network connectivity
You can connect to this key vault either publicly, via public IP addresses or service endpoints, or privately, using a private endpoint.

Connectivity method

- ⦿ Public endpoint (all networks)
- ◯ Public endpoint (selected networks)
- ◯ Private endpoint

Review + create   < Previous   Next : Tags >

Figure 11-5. *Click Next : Tags*

You can add tags for the resource, but this is optional. This helps in categorizing resources and shows the consolidated billing of all the resources having the same tag. After you fill in the name and value in the tags, click "Next : Review + create." See Figure 11-6.

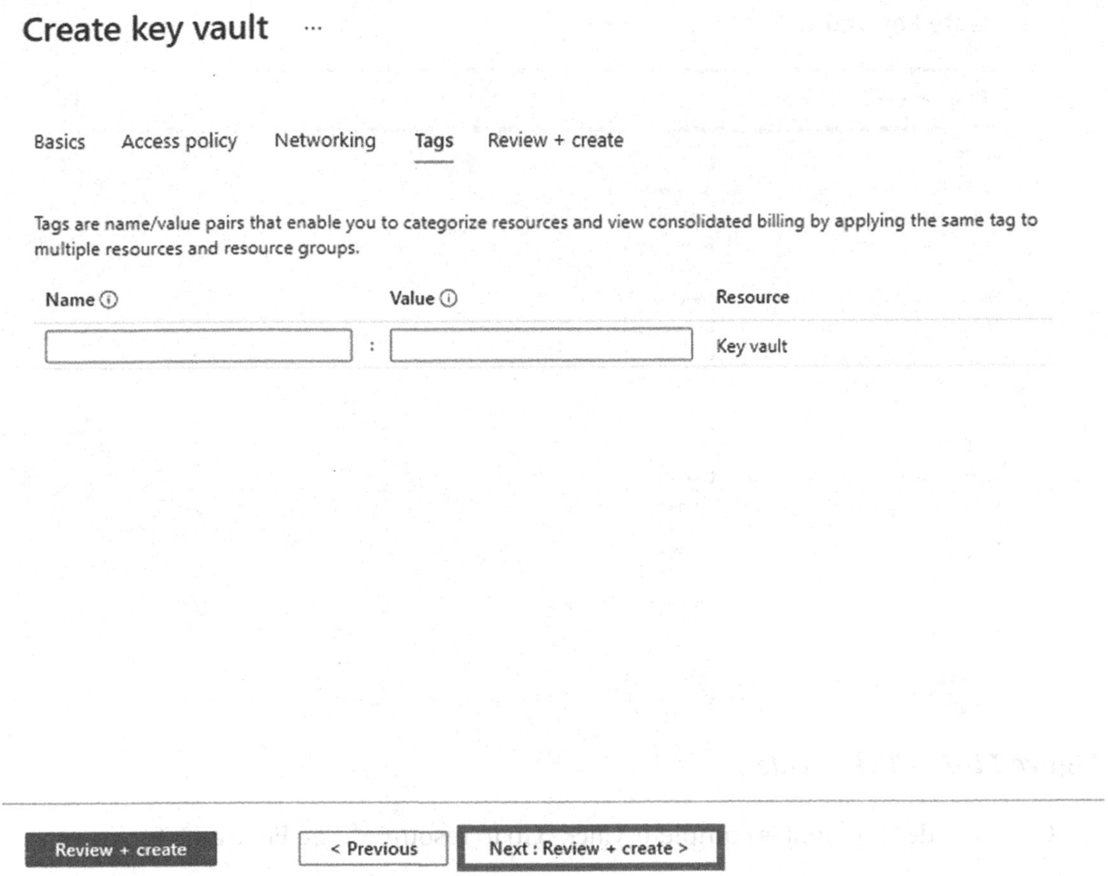

Create key vault   ...

Basics   Access policy   Networking   **Tags**   Review + create

Tags are name/value pairs that enable you to categorize resources and view consolidated billing by applying the same tag to multiple resources and resource groups.

Name ⓘ	Value ⓘ	Resource
[ ] :	[ ]	Key vault

[Review + create]   [< Previous] [Next : Review + create >]

Figure 11-6. *Click "Next : Review + create"*

On this screen, you will see a summary of all the configuration that you entered in the previous series of screens. A validation check will be performed on the entered configuration. If the validation passes, then click Create, as shown in Figure 11-7.

Create key vault ···

> ✔ Validation passed

Basics

Subscription	Azure Pass - Sponsorship
Resource group	rg-chapter-11
Key vault name	kv-chapter-11
Region	East US
Pricing tier	Standard
Soft-delete	Enabled
Purge protection during retention period	Disabled
Days to retain deleted vaults	90 days

Access policy

Azure Virtual Machines for deployment	Disabled
Azure Resource Manager for template deployment	Disabled
Azure Disk Encryption for volume encryption	Disabled
Permission model	Vault access policy
Access policies	1

Create		< Previous	Next >	Download a template for automation

Figure 11-7. *Click Create*

Once the deployment is complete, Click "Go to resource." See Figure 11-8.

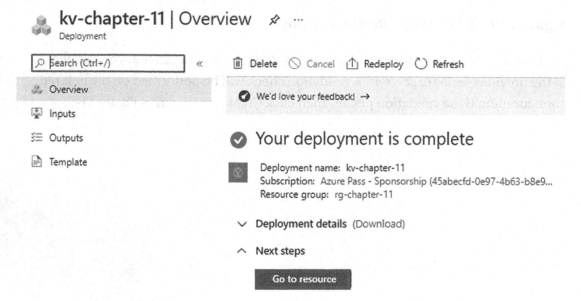

Figure 11-8. *Click "Go to resource"*

Store Secrets in Key Vault

As you have provisioned a vault, let's store your API key as a secret there. To store your secrets, search for *Secrets* in the sidebar and then click + Generate/Import, as shown in Figure 11-9.

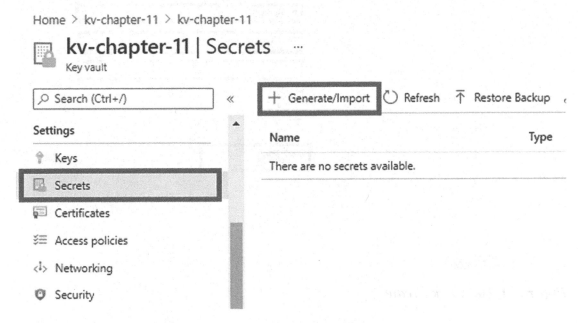

Figure 11-9. *Go to Secrets and click Generate/Import*

Here, you will be prompted to enter the required values. By default, Manual will be selected as the Upload option. Enter the name of the secret and then enter its value. In this case, I have entered **myApiKey** as the name and entered **Hello@123** as the API key in the Value field. You will fetch this value using an Azure function later in this chapter. You can also define the content type of the value. In addition, you can set the activation data and deactivation date. This enables you to define when your secret will be automatically activated or deactivated without needing any human intervention. Alternatively, you can enable the secret by selecting Yes for Enabled. After you have entered all the information in the required field, click Create. See Figure 11-10. This will redirect you to the secrets screen where you will see the name of the secret you created.

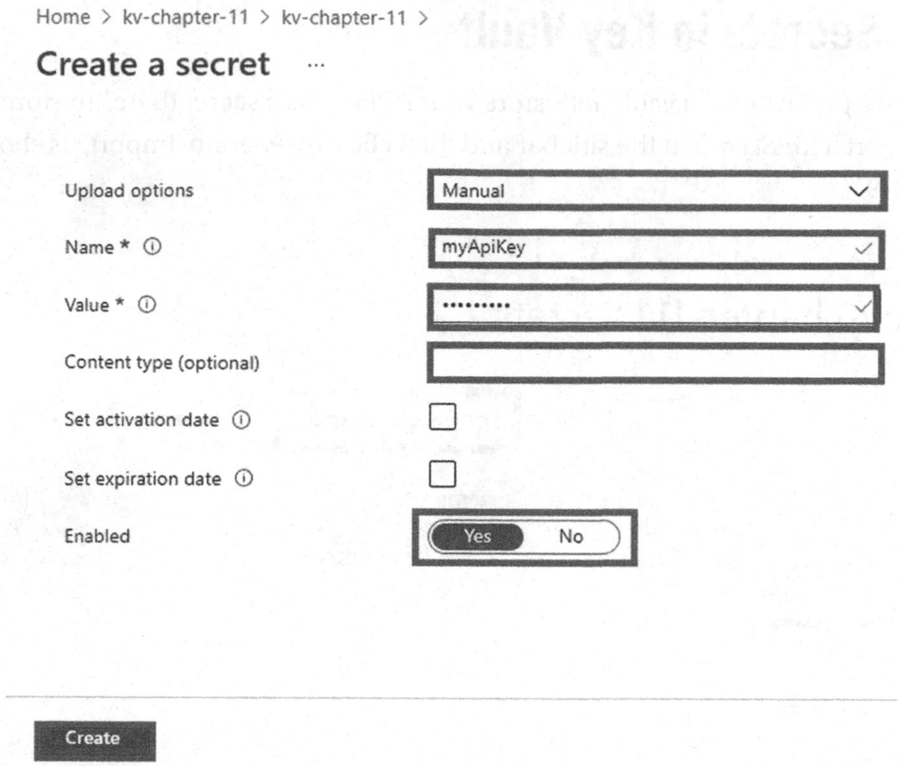

Home > kv-chapter-11 > kv-chapter-11 >

Create a secret   ...

Upload options	Manual ⌄
Name * ⓘ	myApiKey ✓
Value * ⓘ	•••••••• ✓
Content type (optional)	
Set activation date ⓘ	☐
Set expiration date ⓘ	☐
Enabled	Yes No

Create

Figure 11-10. *Click Create*

Click the row containing myApiKey to get the value of secret identity to fetch the value of your secret. See Figure 11-11.

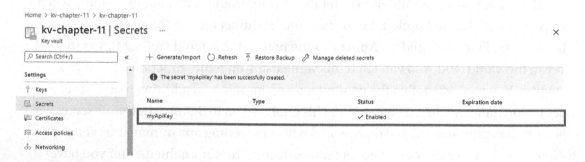

Figure 11-11. *Click myApiKey*

Now click the current version. Azure Key Vault maintains the versions of your secret. See Figure 11-12.

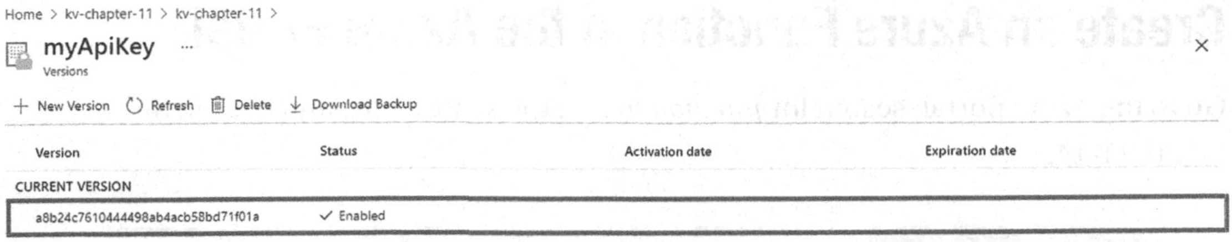

Figure 11-12. *Click Current Version*

On the current version screen, you will get all the values associated with your secret. You can also enable or disable your secret on this screen along with the option to set the activation or expiration date. You can change the value of your secrets on this screen too. Let's copy the secret identifier value from here. You will later use this value to fetch the value of the secret from your function app. See Figure 11-13.

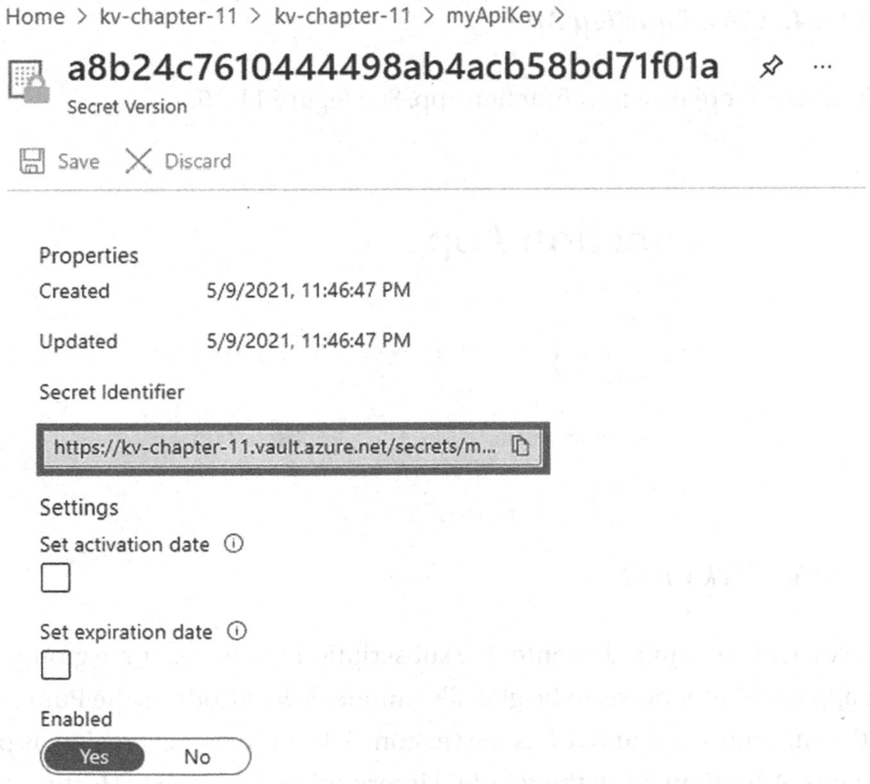

Figure 11-13. *Copy the value of the secret identifier*

Create an Azure Function in the Azure Portal

Go to the Azure portal, search for *function app* in the search box, and click it. See Figure 11-14.

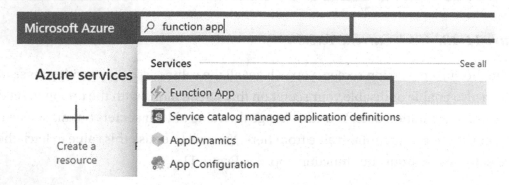

Figure 11-14. *Click Function App*

Click Create to create a new function app. See Figure 11-15.

Home >

Function App 📌 ⋯
Default Directory

╋ Create   ⚙ Manage view ⌄   ↻ Refresh

Filter for any field...   Subscription == ⁄

Showing 0 to 0 of 0 records.

Figure 11-15. *Click Create*

Now, you will be required to enter the subscription name, resource group, and function app name that needs to be globally unique. Select Code as the Publish option, .NET as the runtime stack, and 3.1 as the version. Select the nearest region as per your requirements. After filing in all the required information, click Next : Hosting. See Figure 11-16.

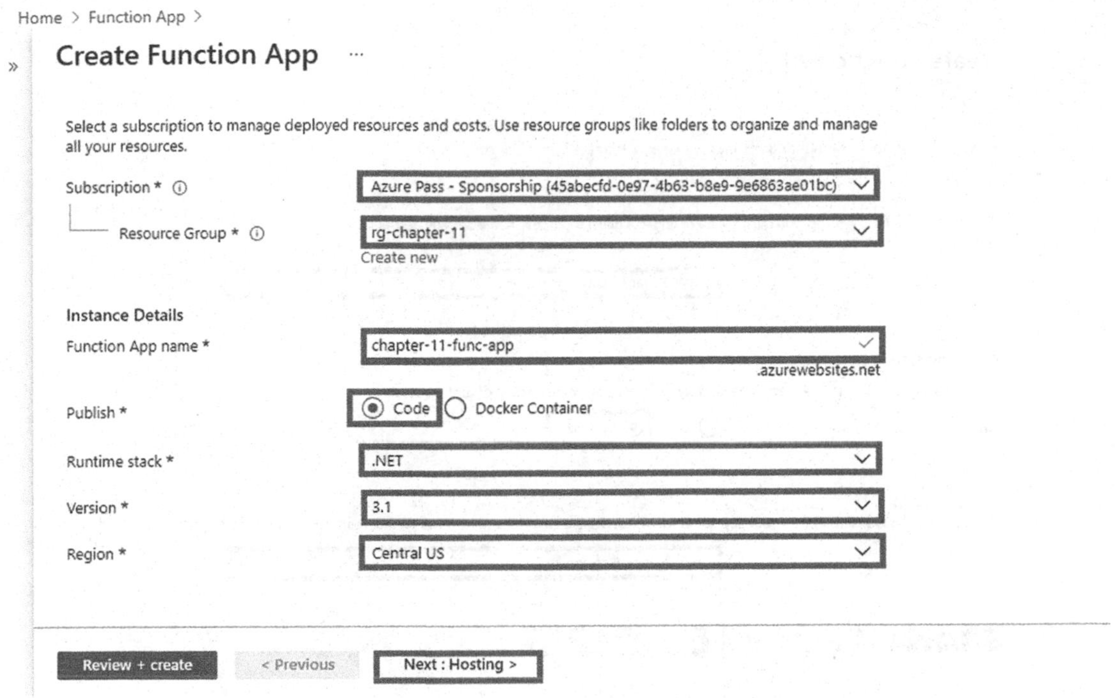

Home > Function App >

Create Function App ⋯

Select a subscription to manage deployed resources and costs. Use resource groups like folders to organize and manage all your resources.

Subscription * ⓘ   Azure Pass - Sponsorship (45abecfd-0e97-4b63-b8e9-9e6863ae01bc) ∨

    Resource Group * ⓘ   rg-chapter-11 ∨
Create new

Instance Details

Function App name *   chapter-11-func-app ✓
.azurewebsites.net

Publish *   ⦿ Code ○ Docker Container

Runtime stack *   .NET ∨

Version *   3.1 ∨

Region *   Central US ∨

[Review + create] [< Previous] [Next : Hosting >]

Figure 11-16. *Click Next : Hosting*

On the current screen, you will have to select an existing storage account or create a new one. By default, a new storage account with a random name will be filled in for you by the portal. When you click Create for this function app, it will create the storage account. Select Windows as the operating system and Consumption (Serverless) as the plan type. Now click Next : Monitoring. See Figure 11-17.

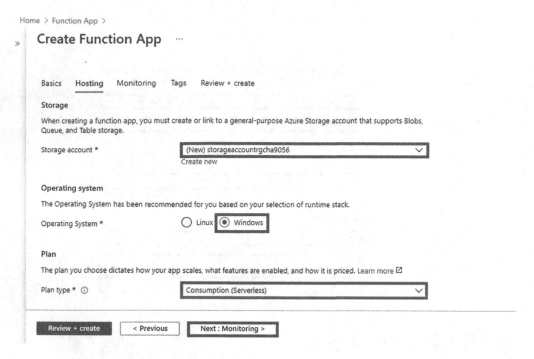

Figure 11-17. *Click Next : Monitoring*

Select Yes for Enable Application Insights and click Next : Tags. See Figure 11-18.

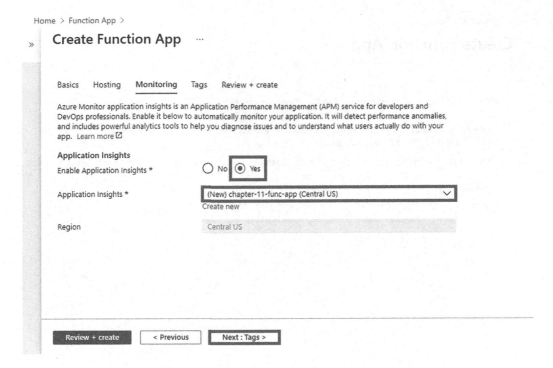

Figure 11-18. *Click Next : Tags*

You can add tags for the resource, but this is optional. After you have filled in the name and value in the tags, click "Next : Review + create." See Figure 11-19.

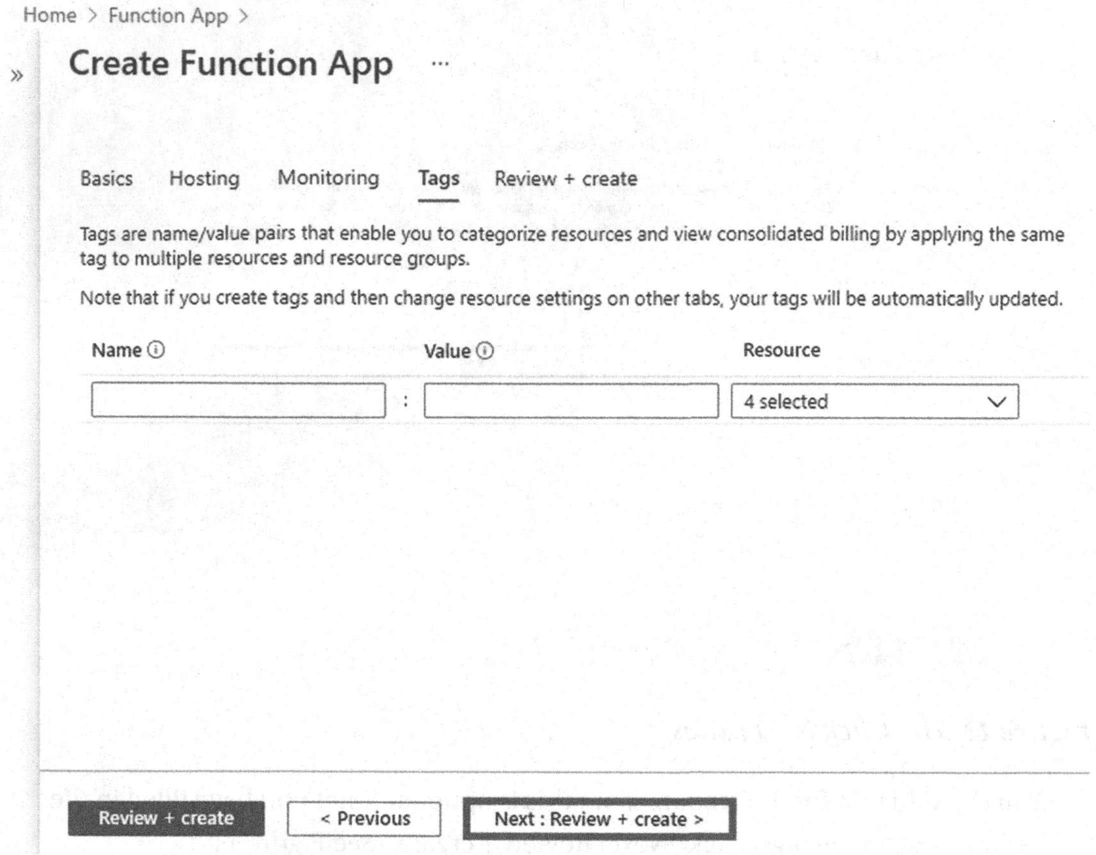

Home > Function App >

» **Create Function App** ···

Basics   Hosting   Monitoring   **Tags**   Review + create

Tags are name/value pairs that enable you to categorize resources and view consolidated billing by applying the same tag to multiple resources and resource groups.

Note that if you create tags and then change resource settings on other tabs, your tags will be automatically updated.

Name ⓘ		Value ⓘ	Resource
	:		4 selected ⌄

| Review + create | | < Previous | | Next : Review + create > |

Figure 11-19. *Click "Next : Review + create"*

On the next screen, shown in Figure 11-20, you will see a summary of all the configuration values you entered in the previous screens. A validation check will be done on the configuration values. Once the validation has passed successfully, click Create.

Figure 11-20. *Click Create*

Once the deployment is complete, click "Go to resource." See Figure 11-21.

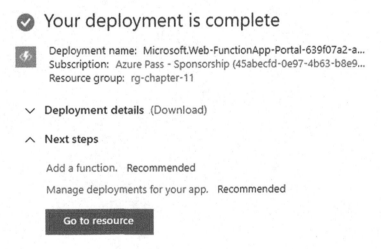

Figure 11-21. *Click "Go to resource"*

Click Functions in the side menu and then click + Add. See Figure 11-22.

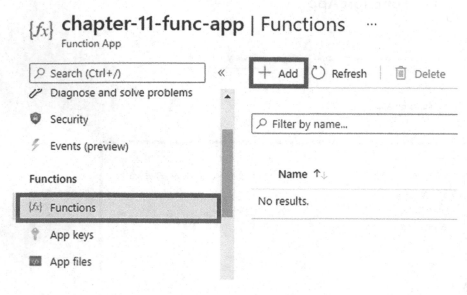

Figure 11-22. *Click + Add*

Since you are going to develop your function in the portal itself, let's select "Develop in portal" for the development environment. Select "Http trigger" as the template. Then click Add to create the Azure function. This will create an Azure function called HttpTrigger1 out of the box. See Figure 11-23.

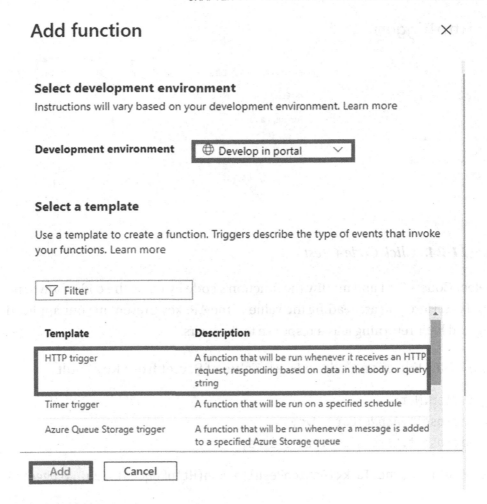

Figure 11-23. *Click Add*

The HttpTrigger1 function will have boilerplate code to return a message along with the name passed in the query string or request body payload. You can click Code + Test to view the code of the function. To send a request to this function, click Get Function Url to get the URL of this function. You can paste this URL in a browser tab to send a request. See Figure 11-24.

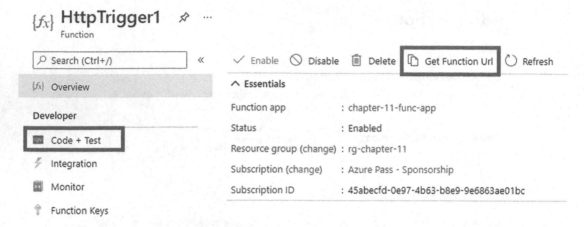

Figure 11-24. Click Code + Test

Select Code + Test and modify the function's code by using the code shown in Listing 11-1. Here you are reading the value of the API key present in your application setting and later returning it as a response to the users.

Listing 11-1. Function Code to Fetch Value of Secret from Key Vault

```
using System.Net;
using Microsoft.AspNetCore.Mvc;
using Microsoft.Extensions.Primitives;

public static async Task<IActionResult> Run(HttpRequest req, ILogger log)
{
    var apiKey = System.Environment.GetEnvironmentVariable("myApiKey");
    log.LogInformation(apiKey);
    return new OkObjectResult(apiKey);
}
```

The function will look for a key named myApiKey in the application settings and then get its value. Let's add the key-value pair of myApiKey in the application settings. Go back to the function app screen; then click Configurations in the Settings sidebar. Now click the "+ New application" setting to add a new key-value pair. See Figure 11-25.

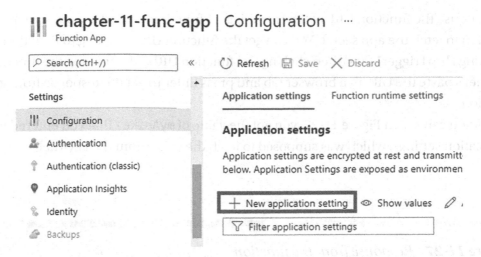

Figure 11-25. *Click "+ New application setting"*

Now enter **myApiKey** as the name and enter **@Microsoft.KeyVault(SecretUri=**{*enter the value of the secret identifier*}) as the value. This defines that the source of this value is the key vault, and it looks for the value in the key vault using the secret identifier, whenever the function wants to get the value of this key. After entering the values, click OK and then click Save on the configuration screen to save the key-value pair. See Figure 11-26.

Add/Edit application setting   ✕

Name   myApiKey   ⧉

Value   @Microsoft.KeyVault(SecretUri=https://kv-chapter-11.vault.azure.net/secrets/myApiKey/a8b24c7610444498ab4acb5...   ⧉

☐ Deployment slot setting

| OK | Cancel |

Figure 11-26. *Click OK*

Let's use the function URL of the HttpTrigger1 function to send a request to the function to fetch the app secret. You can get the function URL by going to Functions, selecting HttpTrigger1, and then clicking Get function URL. After getting the function URL, let's paste the URL in a browser tab and press Enter to get the response from your function.

As you can see in Figure 11-27, you got the value of myApiKey that you entered in the application settings, which was supposed to fetch the value from the key vault.

Figure 11-27. *Response from the function*

You may wonder why you aren't getting the value of the secret. You entered the secret identifier. Your function should have been able to fetch the value from the key vault. But because you haven't allowed this function app to access the key vault, it is unable to get the value of the secret stored in the vault. In the next section, you will learn how to configure the access policy to allow the function app to access the secrets from the key vault.

Add an Access Policy for Azure Key Vault

To allow access to your key vault from the function app, you will have to create a user-assigned identity for your function app and then add an access policy for this app in the key vault.

Go to the function app. Click Identity in the Settings section of the sidebar. Then set the status to On for the system-assigned identity and click Save. This will register your app in the Azure Active Directory. After registration, the function will get the permission to access resources protected by Azure Active Directory. Azure Key Vault authenticates with the help of the Azure Active Directory Service principals. The service principals of Azure Active Directory can be a user or application service principal or a managed identity of a resource. In this case, you create a service principal for your function app by enabling the status in the system-assigned identity. See Figure 11-28.

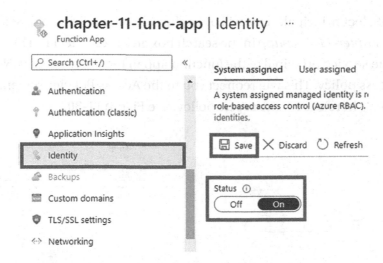

Figure 11-28. *Create a system-assigned managed identity*

Now go to the key vault. Click "Access policies" and then click Add Access Policy. See Figure 11-29.

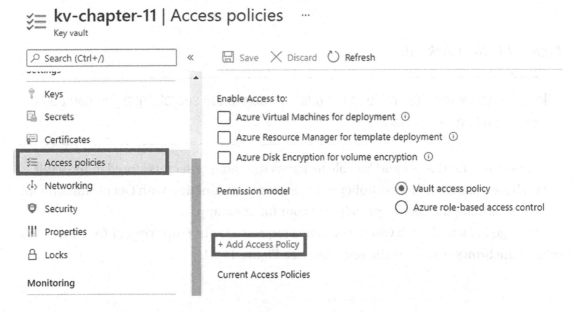

Figure 11-29. *Click + Add Access Policy*

Now, you will have to fill in all the required information in the order shown in Figure 11-30. Select Get for "Secret permissions." Following the principle of least privilege, you have granted only the Get permission in this access policy. Click "None selected" for "Select principal." This will open the side screen Principal. Search for the function app *chapter-11-func-app* in the search box and then select it. This will add a reference of the service principal of the function app in the access policy. Now click Add to add this access policy. This will redirect you to the Access Policies screen. You will have to click Save here to save the access policy. See Figure 11-30.

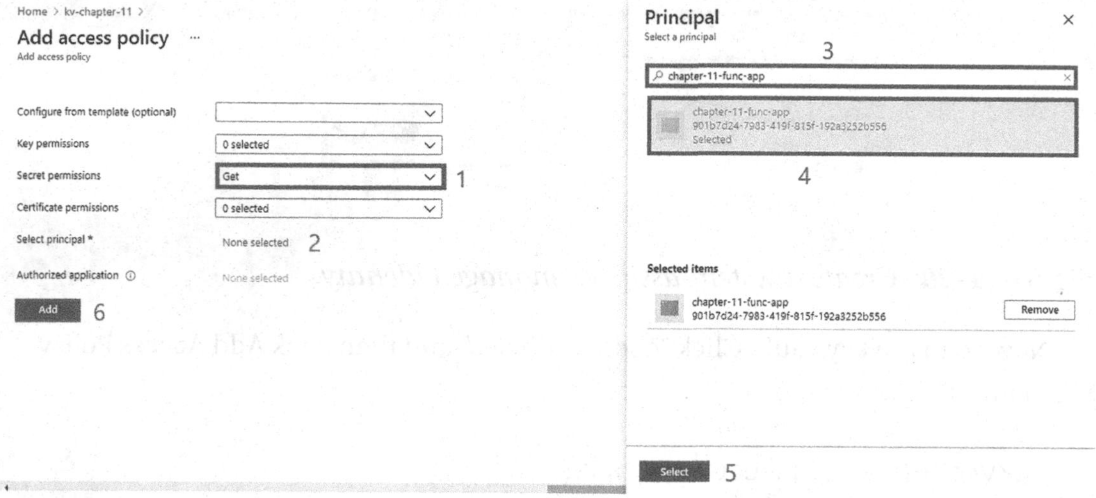

Figure 11-30. *Click Add*

Note   If you want the privilege to update or delete the secret, then you can add a permission like Set or Delete.

Now your function should be able to access the value of secrets stored in the vault as you have created an access policy empowering your function with Get permission for secrets by adding the service principal of your function app.

Let's go back to the tab where you sent a request to your HttpTrigger1 function. Let's refresh the browser and see the response. See Figure 11-31.

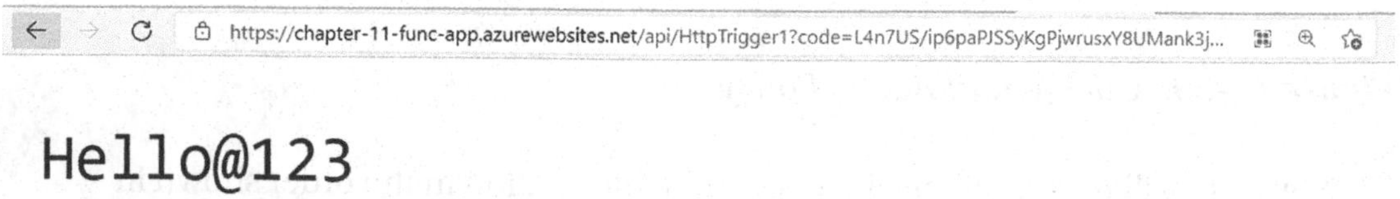

https://chapter-11-func-app.azurewebsites.net/api/HttpTrigger1?code=L4n7US/ip6paPJSSyKgPjwrusxY8UMank3j...

Hello@123

Figure 11-31. *Response from the function*

As shown in Figure 11-31, your function was able to return the value of the secret stored in the vault this time. So, you have successfully built an Azure function to fetch secrets from a vault. If you wanted to update the API key used by your function apps or other applications that are using the API key, you would have to modify the value of the secret in the key vault only, instead of modifying the value API key by going to the application settings of all those applications.

Summary

In this chapter, you learned how to create a key vault using the Azure portal, store secrets in the vault, create access policies, and fetch values of secrets stored in Azure Key Vault using your functions. While application settings offer a mechanism to reduce deployments caused by changes in application secrets, when you use common application secrets like a connection string or API key of a particular service across multiple applications, changing the values in the application settings of all the applications will be a cumbersome task. Azure Key Vault comes in handy when you need to modify the value of the secret in one place. In addition, Azure Key Vault provides a role-based access mechanism using Azure Active Directory, and it does not allow direct access to secrets to the application or to unauthorized resources/users. In the next chapter, we will discuss ways to enable authentication and authorization in your functions using Azure Active Directory.

CHAPTER 12

Authentication and Authorization Using Azure Active Directory

You can build APIs using HTTP-triggered Azure functions. These APIs can interact with databases or perform mission-critical business logic. It is highly crucial to secure these APIs. An HTTP-triggered Azure function should be available for authenticated users and perform the actions/methods the user is authorized to do. Azure Active Directory is an identity and access management solution on the Azure platform. You can integrate HTTP-triggered Azure functions with Azure Active Directory with ease and enable all of your authentication and authorization needs.

In the previous chapter, you learned how to secure the secrets and credentials used by Azure Functions in Azure Key Vault. This chapter will explore how to secure access for HTTP-triggered Azure functions using Azure Active Directory.

Structure of the Chapter

In this chapter, you will explore the following aspects of Azure Functions and Azure Active Directory:

- What Azure Active Directory is

- What authentication and authorization are

- Implementing authentication and authentication for Azure Functions using Azure Active Directory

289

© Ashirwad Satapathi and Abhishek Mishra 2021
A. Satapathi and A. Mishra, *Hands-on Azure Functions with C#*, https://doi.org/10.1007/978-1-4842-7122-3_12

Objectives

After studying this chapter, you will be able to do the following:

- Implement authentication for HTTP-triggered Azure functions using Azure Active Directory

- Implement authorization for HTTP-triggered Azure functions using Azure Active Directory

What Is Azure Active Directory?

Azure Active Directory is a multitenant identity and access management system on the Azure platform. You can build on-premises and cloud-based applications and leverage Azure Active Directory for identity management. Thousands of SaaS-based applications such as Microsoft 365, Dynamics CRM, and many more leverage Azure Active Directory as their security backbone. Azure Active Directory can be used to bring in audit and governance for users accessing Azure resources. Developers can implement single sign-on and multifactor authentication for their applications using Azure Active Directory.

Automation is an essential aspect of resource provisioning in Azure. You can use Azure PowerShell or Azure CLI or any other infrastructure-as-code solution like Terraform to interact with and use Azure Active Directory via automation. You can write automation to manage essential security aspects for an application such as user login audits, unauthorized access attempts, and more.

The following are a few of the key features of Azure Active Directory:

- Supports single sign-on and multifactor authentication.

- Manages authentication and authorization for cloud SaaS-based applications and on-premises applications.

- Rich SDK support for identity and access management to integrate with a wide range of applications built using .NET, Java, Angular, and more, such as MSAL libraries for .NET-based applications and MSAL4J libraries for Java-based applications.

- Provides an enterprise-grade identity and access management solution for business-to-business (B2B) and business-to-customer/ consumer (B2C) applications. It supports external identity providers such as Facebook, Twitter, Google, or any other identity provider that supports OAuth 1.0, OAuth 2.0, OpenID Connect, and SAML protocols.

- Manages devices for your corporation.

- Provides domain services and facilitates joining Azure virtual machines to a domain without needing a domain controller.

- Provides governance and reporting for security and access usages for your application.

- Supports role-based authentication.

- Supports invoking powerful Microsoft Graph APIs.

What Are Authentication and Authorization?

Your application should identify who is trying to access and control what the user can access. All unauthorized access to the application should be disallowed. Authentication checks who the user is. It challenges the user to provide identification, and if the challenge is successful, the application identifies the user and verifies the user's identity. Authorization dictates what an identified user can do in the application. As a good practice, you create *roles*, which define what an authenticated user can do in the application. You can assign multiple roles to the users. For example, an application has two roles: Administrator and User. All the users who are assigned the Administrator role can provide their credentials to the application and get authenticated. Then they can access and work on all the administration pages in the application. Similarly, when a user who has the User role logs in to the system, he will not have access to the administration pages and will be limited to the application's User pages. To sum up, authentication verifies who the user is, and authorization dictates what the user can do, as shown in Figure 12-1.

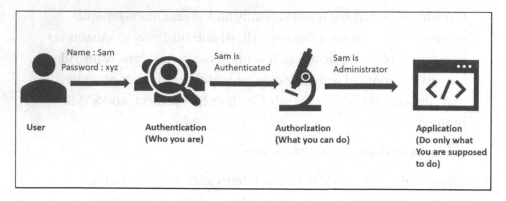

Figure 12-1. *Authentication and authorization process*

Implement Authentication and Authentication for Azure Functions Using Azure Active Directory

Azure Functions provides excellent support for logging using Application Insights. Let's create an Azure function with Application Insights enabled using the Azure portal. Then you can modify the function code to log some information, errors, and traces for the Azure function. Open the Azure portal and click "Create a resource." See Figure 12-2.

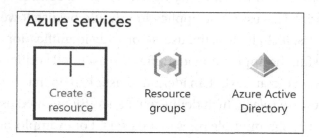

Figure 12-2. *Click "Create a resource"*

Click Compute and then click Function App. See Figure 12-3.

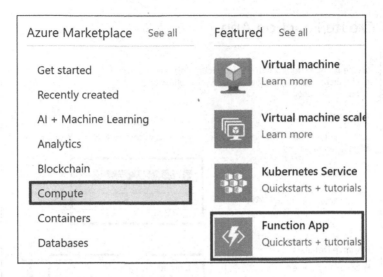

Figure 12-3. *Click Function App*

Provide the basic details for the function. Let's select .NET and 3.1 as the runtime stack and the version. Click "Review + create." See Figure 12-4.

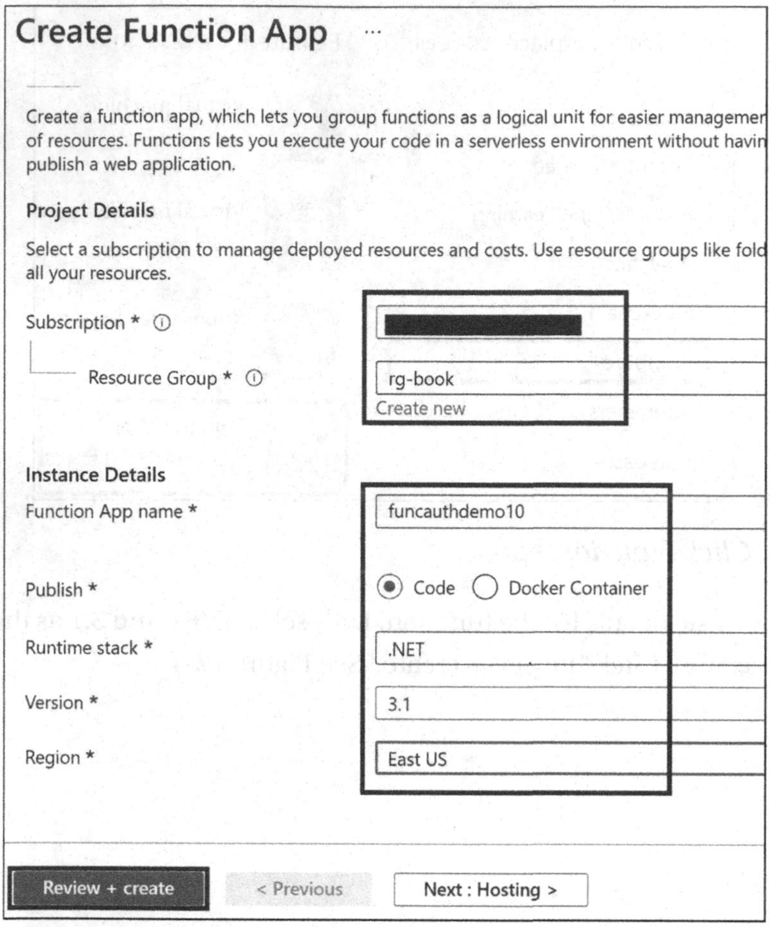

Create Function App ...

Create a function app, which lets you group functions as a logical unit for easier managemen of resources. Functions lets you execute your code in a serverless environment without havin publish a web application.

Project Details

Select a subscription to manage deployed resources and costs. Use resource groups like fold all your resources.

Subscription * ⓘ

Resource Group * ⓘ   rg-book
                        Create new

Instance Details

Function App name *   funcauthdemo10

Publish *   ◉ Code   ◯ Docker Container

Runtime stack *   .NET

Version *   3.1

Region *   East US

Review + create   < Previous   Next : Hosting >

Figure 12-4. Provide the basic details for the Azure function

Click Create. See Figure 12-5.

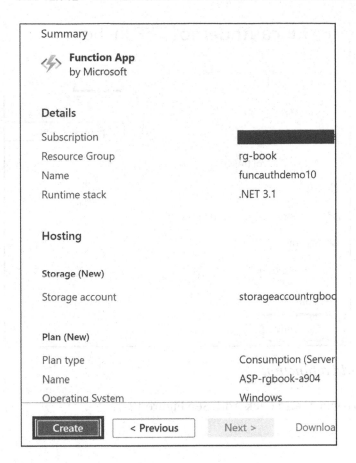

Figure 12-5. *Click Create*

Go to the Azure function app once it is created. Now you need to add a function to the Azure function app. Click the Functions tab and click Add. See Figure 12-6.

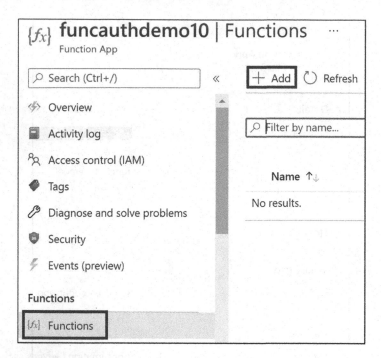

Figure 12-6. Add a function

Select "Http trigger" and click Add. See Figure 12-7.

Figure 12-7. *Select "Http trigger"*

Once the function gets created, get into the function and click Code + Test. See Figure 12-8.

Figure 12-8. *Click Code + Test*

Click Get Function Url and browse to the URL in the browser. Now let's go to Application Insights and verify whether these logs were added. See Figure 12-9.

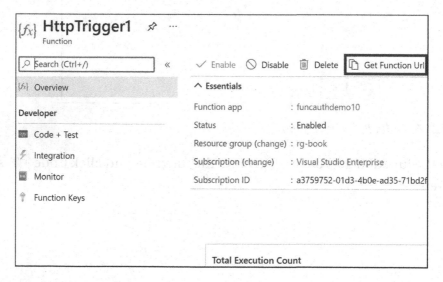

Figure 12-9. *Click Get Function Url*

Now let's enable authentication for the Azure function. Go back to the function app and click Authentication. See Figure 12-10.

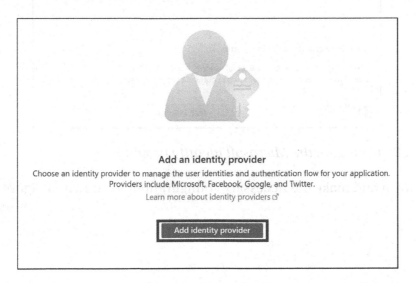

Figure 12-10. *Go to the Authentication tab*

Click "Add identity provider" to add a provider that you will use to authenticate the Azure function. See Figure 12-11.

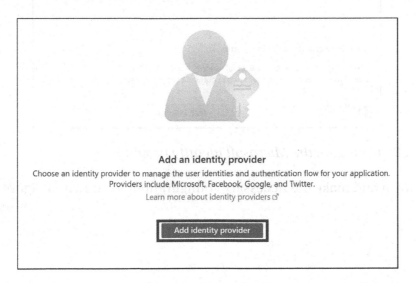

Figure 12-11. *Configure the identity provider*

Set the identity provider to Microsoft. Then select "Create new app registration" for the app registration type, and select "Current tenant – Single tenant" for the supported account types. Provide a name for the application that will get created in the Azure Active Directory tenant. See Figure 12-12.

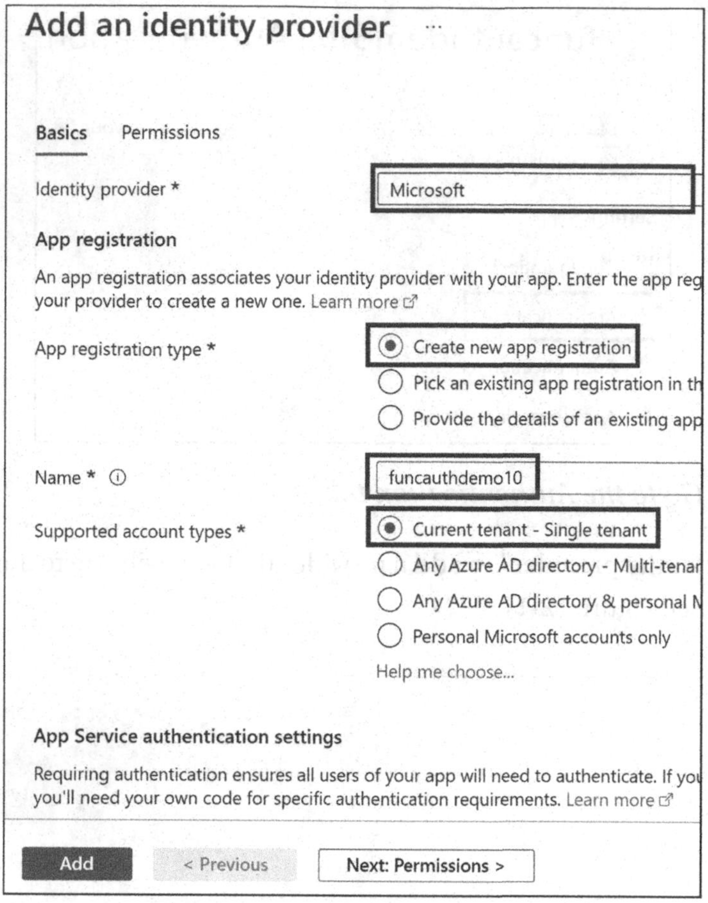

Figure 12-12.   *Configure the Microsoft identity provider*

Scroll down and make the necessary configuration, as shown in Figure 12-13.
Click Add.

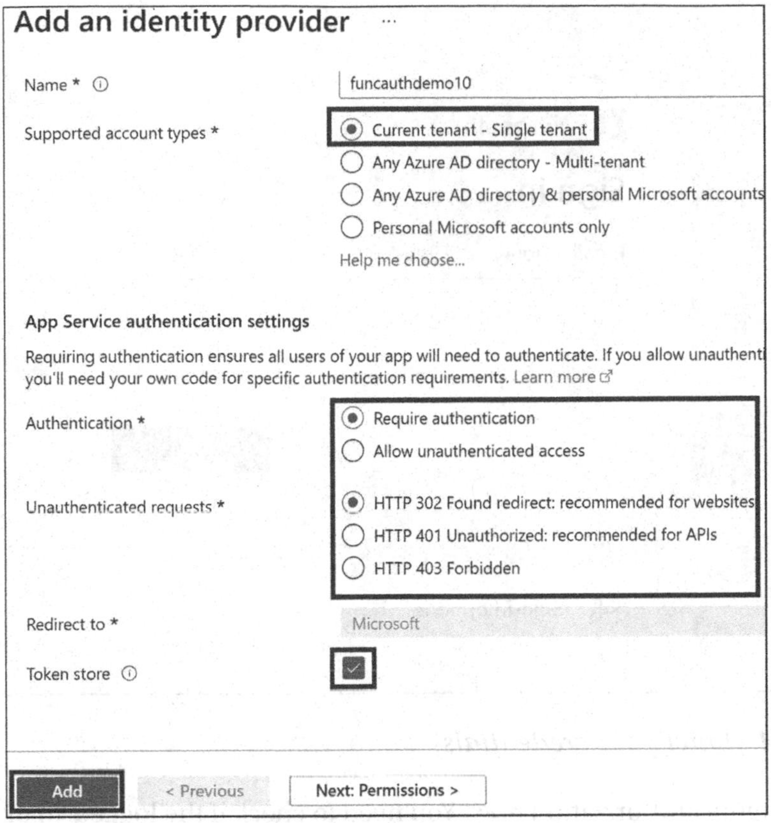

Figure 12-13. *Add a Microsoft identity provider*

Now the authentication is configured for the application. Browse the function URL that you copied earlier in an incognito or private browsing mode. It will prompt you to provide your credentials. You can use the same credentials that you used to log in to the Azure portal. See Figure 12-14.

Figure 12-14. *Enter your credentials*

Let's configure authorization now. You need to check if the logged-in user has the necessary role configured to access the page. The Microsoft Graph API can help you get the roles for the user in Azure Active Directory. Let's go to the Azure Active Directory application that you created and add the necessary permissions for Azure Active Directory. Go to the Azure portal home page and navigate to Azure Active Directory. Click "App registrations." Then click the application that you created while enabling authentication for the Azure function. See Figure 12-15.

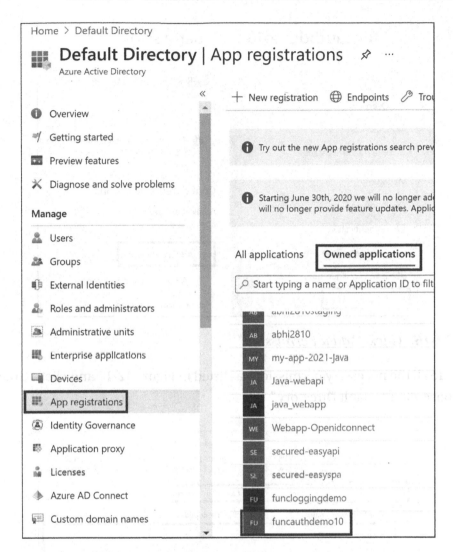

Figure 12-15. *Go to "App registrations"*

Click the "API permissions" tab and then click "Add a permission." See Figure 12-16.

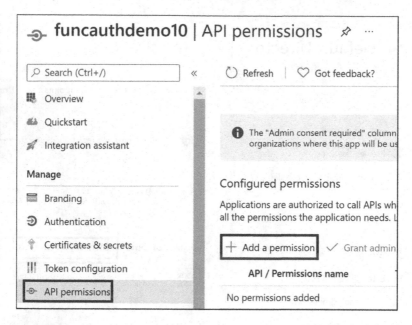

Figure 12-16. *Click "Add a permission"*

Provide all the necessary permissions as listed in Figure 12-17 and click "Grant admin consent for Default Directory."

Configured permissions

Applications are authorized to call APIs when they are granted permissions by users/admins as part of the con all the permissions the application needs. Learn more about permissions and consent

+ Add a permission | ✓ Grant admin consent for Default Directory

API / Permissions name	Type	Description
∨ Microsoft Graph (7)		
Directory.AccessAsUser.All	Delegated	Access directory as the signed in user
Directory.Read.All	Delegated	Read directory data
IdentityUserFlow.Read.All	Delegated	Read all identity user flows
RoleManagement.Read.All	Delegated	Read role management data for all RBAC providers
RoleManagement.Read.Directc	Delegated	Read directory RBAC settings
User.Read	Delegated	Sign in and read user profile
User.Read.All	Delegated	Read all users' full profiles

Figure 12-17. *Add all the permissions and grant admin consent*

You will authorize all users who have the role of application developer. Let's go to the Users tab in Azure Active Directory. See Figure 12-18.

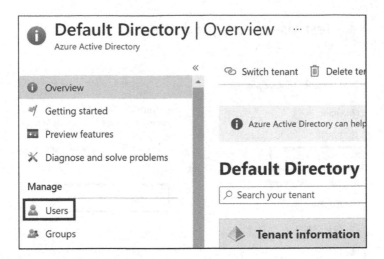

Figure 12-18. *Go to the Users tab*

Click the user you will be logging in as. You can choose to use the user you are signed in as in the Azure portal. See Figure 12-19.

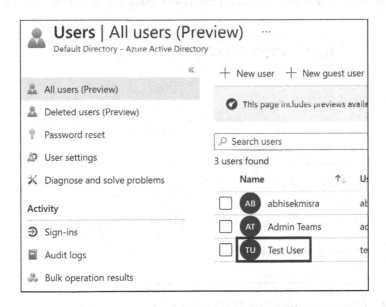

Figure 12-19. *Click the user*

Click the Assigned Roles tab. This action will list all the roles assigned to the user. Click "Add assignments" and add the "Application developer" role. Once the role gets added, click the "Application developer" role in the user's list of roles. This action will navigate you to the role details. See Figure 12-20.

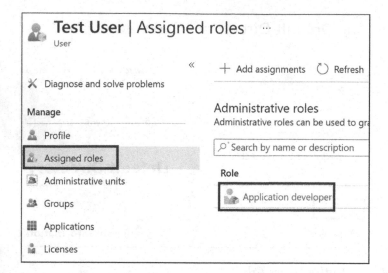

Figure 12-20. *Assign a role to the user*

Click the Description tab and copy the template ID. You will use this in the Graph API call in your function's code to pull out all the users assigned that role. See Figure 12-21.

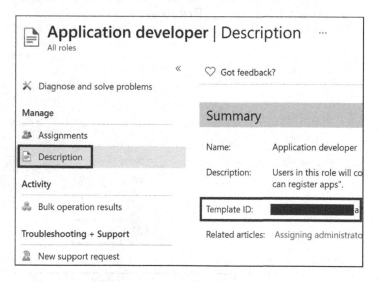

Figure 12-21. *Copy the template ID for the role*

Now let's go back to the Azure function you created earlier. You need to add the necessary code to enable authorization. You can add authorization using the NuGet package `Microsoft.IdentityModel.Clients.ActiveDirectory`. To add a NuGet package to the function script, you need to create a `function.proj` file in the root folder of the function and add the package reference for this NuGet package. You can add a new file using the App Service Editor. Click the App Service Editor tab and then click Go. See Figure 12-22.

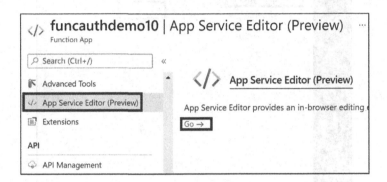

Figure 12-22. *Go to the App Service Editor*

Right-click the folder with your function name and then click New File. See Figure 12-23.

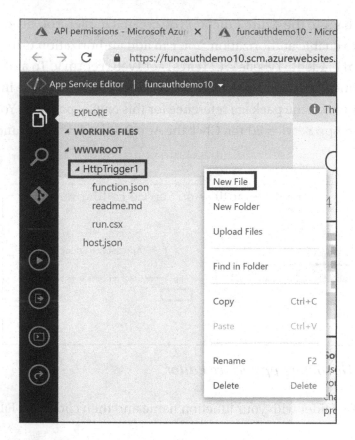

Figure 12-23. *Create the Function.proj file*

Provide the name of the file as `Function.proj`. Copy the code shown in Listing 12-1 in the `Function.proj` file, as shown in Listing 12-1. It will get autosaved.

Listing 12-1. Function.proj Code

```
<Project Sdk="Microsoft.NET.Sdk">
    <PropertyGroup>
        <TargetFramework>netstandard2.0</TargetFramework>
    </PropertyGroup>

    <ItemGroup>
        <PackageReference Include="Microsoft.IdentityModel.Clients.
        ActiveDirectory" Version="5.2.9" />
    </ItemGroup>
</Project>
```

Now let's go to the Azure function code in the `run.csx` file and replace the existing code with the code shown in Listing 12-2. Here you are getting the identity of the logged-in user. Then, from the identity, you are extracting the username for the logged-in user. You are invoking the Microsoft Graph API and fetching all the assigned users with the "Application developer" role. The Microsoft Graph API exposes a set of REST APIs that will help you work with data on Microsoft Cloud services like Microsoft 365, Azure Active Directory, and many more. You can fetch and work on data about the users in Azure Active Directory or get data from Microsoft 365 services such as OneDrive or Calendar or Outlook and many more. If the logged-in user's username is found in the list returned by the Microsoft Graph API call, you will authorize the user and return the text "Hello World." If the user is not there in the list returned by the Microsoft Graph API call, you are sending back the "Not Authorized" text. Make sure you replace {RoleTemplateId} with the template ID you copied for the "Application developer" role in the Description tab of that role earlier.

Listing 12-2. Function Code with Authorization Enabled

```
#r "Newtonsoft.Json"

using System.Net;
using System.Text;
using System.Configuration;
using System.Security.Claims;
using System.Net.Http;
using System.Net.Http.Headers;
using Newtonsoft.Json;
using Microsoft.IdentityModel.Clients.ActiveDirectory;
using Microsoft.AspNetCore.Mvc;

public static async Task<IActionResult > Run(
    HttpRequest req,
    ILogger log)
{
    // Get identity for logged in user
    var identity = req.HttpContext?.User?.Identity as ClaimsIdentity;
    var claims = identity.Claims;
    var roleClaimType = identity.RoleClaimType;
```

```
var roles = claims.Where(c => c.Type == roleClaimType).ToList();
log.LogInformation(roles.Count.ToString());
log.LogInformation("IsAuthenticated: {isAuthenticated}",identity?.
IsAuthenticated);
log.LogInformation("Identity name: {name}",identity?.Name);
log.LogInformation("AuthenticationType: {authenticationType}",
    identity?.AuthenticationType);
var userName = "";
foreach (var claim in identity?.Claims)
{
    log.LogInformation("Claim: {type} : {value}", claim.Type,
    claim.Value);
    //Get logged in user name
    if(claim.Type == "preferred_username")
    {
        userName = claim.Value;
    }
}
var accessToken = req.Headers.SingleOrDefault(h => h.Key == "X-MS-
TOKEN-AAD-ACCESS-TOKEN").Value;
log.LogInformation(accessToken);

// Call the graph API to get all the users having Role : Application
    Developer
// Provide the template id for the Role that we have copied from the
    Role Description
// in Azure Active Directory
string graphRequest = $"https://graph.microsoft.com/v1.0/
directoryRoles/roleTemplateId=cf1c38e5-3621-4004-a7cb-879624dced7c/
members";
var authHeader = "Bearer " + accessToken;
HttpClient client = new HttpClient();

client.DefaultRequestHeaders.TryAddWithoutValidation("Authorization",
authHeader);
var response = await client.GetAsync(new Uri(graphRequest));
```

```csharp
string content = await response.Content.ReadAsStringAsync();
log.LogInformation(content);

// Deserialize the JSON string into Root object
Root myDeserializedClass = JsonConvert.DeserializeObject<Root>(content);

// Loop through all the values returned by Graph API
// Verify if the logged-in username is there in the list
foreach(Value value in myDeserializedClass.Value )
{
    log.LogInformation(value.UserPrincipalName);
    //check if the user name returned matches with the logged
    //in username
    if(value.UserPrincipalName == userName)
    {
        return new OkObjectResult("Hello World");
    }
}
return new OkObjectResult("Not Authorized");
}

public class Value
    {
        [JsonProperty("@odata.type")]
        public string OdataType { get; set; }

        [JsonProperty("id")]
        public string Id { get; set; }

        [JsonProperty("businessPhones")]
        public List<object> BusinessPhones { get; set; }

        [JsonProperty("displayName")]
        public string DisplayName { get; set; }

        [JsonProperty("givenName")]
        public object GivenName { get; set; }
```

```
    [JsonProperty("jobTitle")]
    public object JobTitle { get; set; }

    [JsonProperty("mail")]
    public object Mail { get; set; }

    [JsonProperty("mobilePhone")]
    public object MobilePhone { get; set; }
    [JsonProperty("officeLocation")]
    public object OfficeLocation { get; set; }

    [JsonProperty("preferredLanguage")]
    public object PreferredLanguage { get; set; }

    [JsonProperty("surname")]
    public object Surname { get; set; }

    [JsonProperty("userPrincipalName")]
    public string UserPrincipalName { get; set; }
}
public class Root
{
    [JsonProperty("@odata.context")]
    public string OdataContext { get; set; }

    [JsonProperty("value")]
    public List<Value> Value { get; set; }
}
```

Summary

In this chapter, you learned how to enable authentication and authorization for Azure Functions using Azure Active Directory. You explored Azure Active Directory and its offerings at a very high level. You learned the basic concepts of authentication and authorization. You then registered an application in Azure Active Directory from the Authentication tab of an Azure function and then enabled authentication and authorization for the Azure function with ease.

The following are the key takeaways from this chapter:

- Azure Active Directory is a multitenant identity and access management system on the Azure platform.

- Authentication verifies who the user is, and authorization dictates what the user can do.

- You can enable authentication with just a few clicks in the Authentication tab of an Azure function.

- Enabling authentication creates an app registration in Azure Active Directory.

- We can use Graph APIs to get the logged-in roles for the user.

In the next chapter, you will explore how to integrate the API Management service with Azure Functions and build a secure and robust API service using Azure Functions.

CHAPTER 13

Securing Azure Functions with API Management

You can build APIs using HTTP-triggered Azure functions. These APIs interact with the databases and perform CRUD operations. You need to have granular control over the incoming requests and outgoing responses for the APIs developed using Azure Functions. It is highly essential to secure these APIs and control the header, body, and other necessary aspects for the API calls. You should be able to control who can consume these APIs, and only the subscribed developers should have access to them. All these requirements can be achieved by integrating the API Management service with HTTP-triggered Azure functions. All requests and responses to an HTTP-triggered Azure function should pass through the API Management service. You can control these requests and responses at a granular level using API Management.

In the previous chapter, you learned how to secure HTTP-triggered Azure functions using Azure Active Directory. In this chapter, you will learn how to gain granular control over the requests and responses for the HTTP-triggered Azure functions using the API Management service.

Structure of the Chapter

In this chapter, you will explore the following aspects of Azure Functions and Azure API Management:

- What Azure API Management is
- Advantages of using API Management
- Integrating API Management with Azure Functions

315

© Ashirwad Satapathi and Abhishek Mishra 2021
A. Satapathi and A. Mishra, *Hands-on Azure Functions with C#*, https://doi.org/10.1007/978-1-4842-7122-3_13

Objectives

After studying this chapter, you will be able to do the following:

- Understand the API Management service

- Integrate the API Management service with Azure Functions

What Is the API Management Service?

The API Management service helps you create robust API gateways that can host back-end APIs. It helps you gain granular control over the requests and responses of the back-end APIs. Developers who want to consume your API can request the APIs subscriptions, and the API Management service administrator or the owner can approve these requests. Once the request is approved, the developers can use the APIs. You can version your APIs and expose these APIs as multiple versions using the API Management service. The developers and consumers can subscribe to the version as per their requirements.

The API Management service exposes a developer portal where the developers can discover the service they need and get the API documentation. The developers can raise subscription requests for the APIs in the developer portal. The developer portal is fully customizable, and the look and feel can be modified based on your needs.

Different units or project teams can develop the APIs in your organization. You can use the API Management service to manage and expose these APIs centrally. You can modify the incoming requests and outgoing responses for the APIs. For example, modify the response body, check if the JWT security token is in the request header, or add a query string parameter to the request.

You can use Azure HTTP-triggered functions and the API Management service to build microservices-based APIs.

Advantages of Using the API Management Service

The following are a few of the advantages of using the API Management service:

- Central hosting of APIs built by different teams using different choices of technology.

- Exposing the APIs as subscriptions and versions for the developers/consumers to subscribe to and consume.

- Each of the hosted APIs can scale independently and will be warranted from failures of other APIs.

- Provides an excellent mechanism to manage the back-end services and get granular control over API requests and responses.

- Enhanced security of back-end APIs.

- It provides a developer portal that helps in the discovery, description, and subscription of APIs.

Integrate API Management with Azure Functions

Let's create an HTTP-triggered Azure function and integrate it with the API Management service. Open the Azure portal and click "Create a resource." See Figure 13-1.

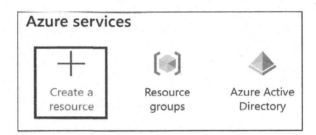

Figure 13-1. *Click "Create a resource"*

Click Compute and then click Function App. See Figure 13-2.

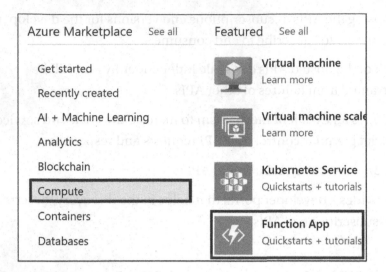

Figure 13-2. *Click Function App*

Provide the basic details for the function. Let's select .NET and 3.1 as the runtime stack and the version. Click "Review + create." See Figure 13-3.

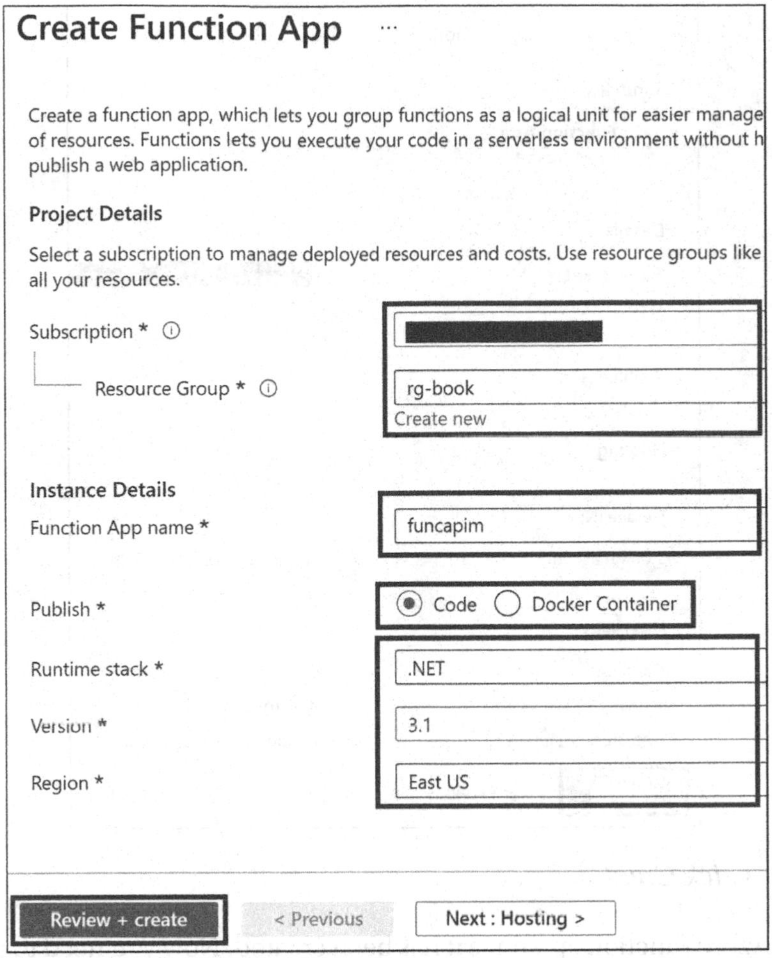

Create Function App ···

Create a function app, which lets you group functions as a logical unit for easier manage of resources. Functions lets you execute your code in a serverless environment without h publish a web application.

Project Details

Select a subscription to manage deployed resources and costs. Use resource groups like all your resources.

Subscription * ⓘ	▬▬▬▬▬▬▬
Resource Group * ⓘ	rg-book
	Create new

Instance Details

Function App name *	funcapim
Publish *	⦿ Code ◯ Docker Container
Runtime stack *	.NET
Version *	3.1
Region *	East US

[Review + create]   [< Previous]   [Next : Hosting >]

Figure 13-3. *Provide basic details for the Azure functions*

Click Create. See Figure 13-4.

Figure 13-4. *Click Create*

Go to the Azure function app once it has been created. Now you need to add a function to the Azure function app. Click the Functions tab and click Add. See Figure 13-5.

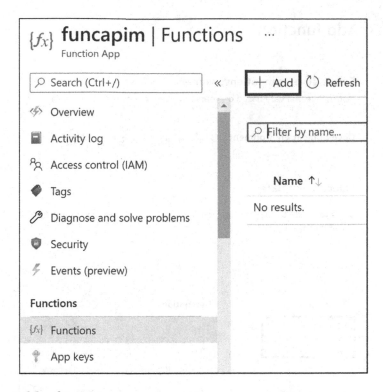

Figure 13-5. *Add a function*

Select "Http trigger" and click Add. See Figure 13-6.

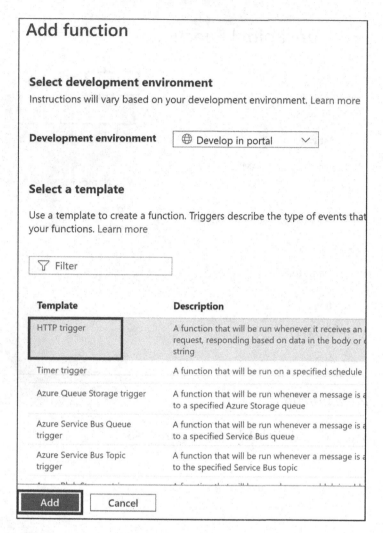

Figure 13-6. *Select "Http trigger"*

Once the function gets created, go into the function and click Code + Test. See Figure 13-7.

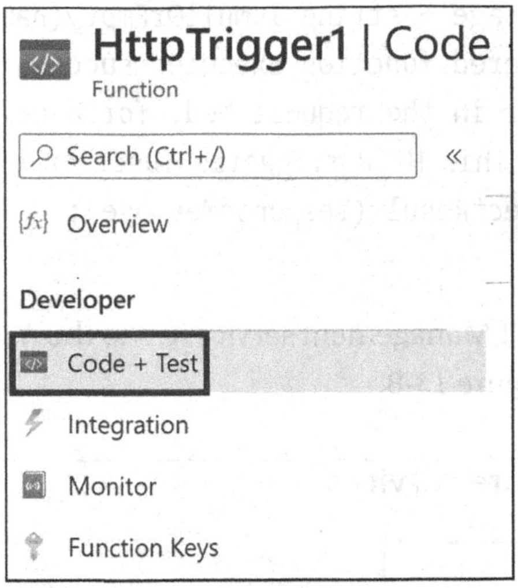

Figure 13-7. *Click Code + Test*

You can see that the code in Listing 13-1 is generated by default. You can pass the name parameter and its value in the query string, and the function will return the value you passed in the name parameter. If you do not pass the name parameter in the query string, it will return a message asking you to pass the name parameter with a value in the query string.

Listing 13-1. Function.proj Code

```
#r "Newtonsoft.Json"

using System.Net;
using Microsoft.AspNetCore.Mvc;
using Microsoft.Extensions.Primitives;
using Newtonsoft.Json;

public static async Task<IActionResult> Run(HttpRequest req, ILogger log)
{
    log.LogInformation("C# HTTP trigger function processed a request.");

    string name = req.Query["name"];

    string requestBody = await new StreamReader(req.Body).ReadToEndAsync();
    dynamic data = JsonConvert.DeserializeObject(requestBody);
    name = name ?? data?.name;
```

```
string responseMessage = string.IsNullOrEmpty(name)
? "This HTTP triggered function executed successfully. Pass a name in
the query string or in the request body for a personalized response."
: $"Hello, {name}. This HTTP triggered function executed successfully.";
    return new OkObjectResult(responseMessage);
}
```

Now let's create the API Management service. Go to the Azure portal and click "Create a resource." See Figure 13-8.

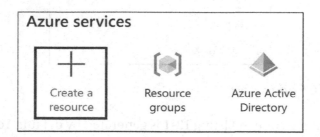

Figure 13-8. *Click "Create a resource"*

Click the Integration tab and then API Management. See Figure 13-9.

Figure 13-9. *Click API Management*

Provide the subscription details, resource group, name of the API Management service, location where you need to create the service, and other necessary details. Select "Developer (no SLA)" for "Pricing tier." Click "Review + create" and then click Create on the subsequent screen. See Figure 13-10.

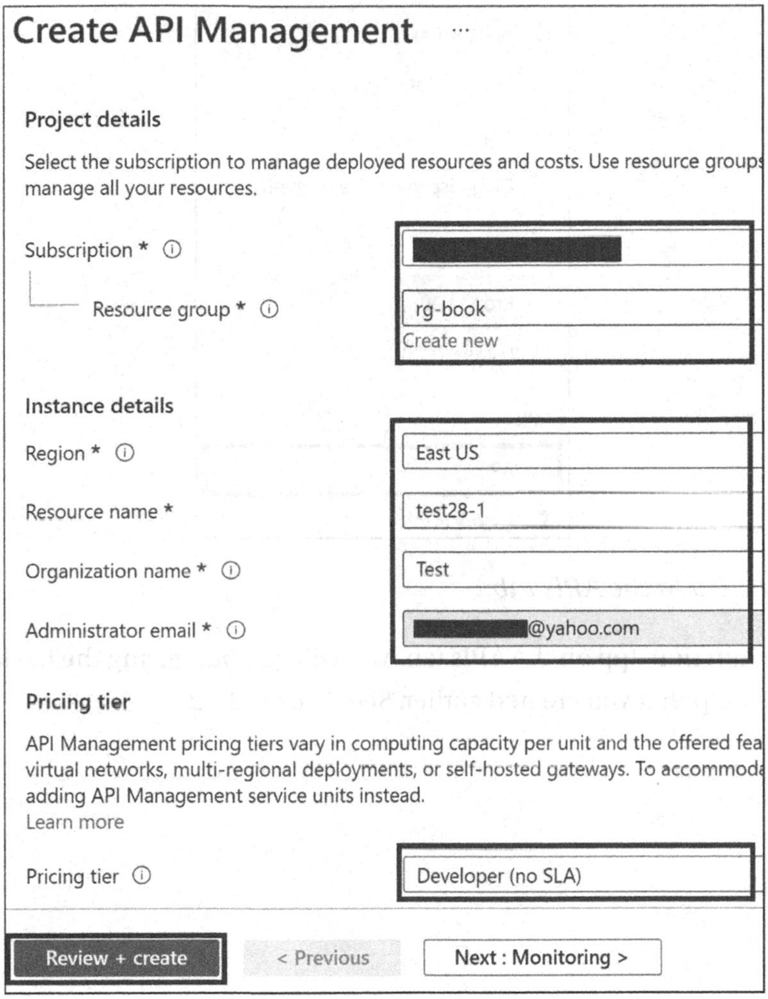

Create API Management ...

Project details

Select the subscription to manage deployed resources and costs. Use resource groups
manage all your resources.

Subscription * ⓘ

└── Resource group * ⓘ   rg-book

                             Create new

Instance details

Region * ⓘ   East US

Resource name *   test28-1

Organization name * ⓘ   Test

Administrator email * ⓘ   ▇▇▇▇▇@yahoo.com

Pricing tier

API Management pricing tiers vary in computing capacity per unit and the offered fea
virtual networks, multi-regional deployments, or self-hosted gateways. To accommoda
adding API Management service units instead.
Learn more

Pricing tier ⓘ   Developer (no SLA)

[Review + create]   [< Previous]   [Next : Monitoring >]

***Figure 13-10.**   Click Review + create*

Once the API Management service gets created, navigate to the service in the portal. Click the APIs tab. See Figure 13-11.

Figure 13-11. *Go to the APIs tab*

Select the function app on the APIs tab. You will be configuring the back-end service as the function app that you created earlier. See Figure 13-12.

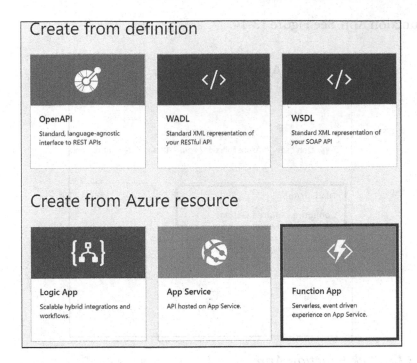

Figure 13-12. *Select Function App*

Now you need to select the function that you need to integrate with the API Management service. Click Browse. See Figure 13-13.

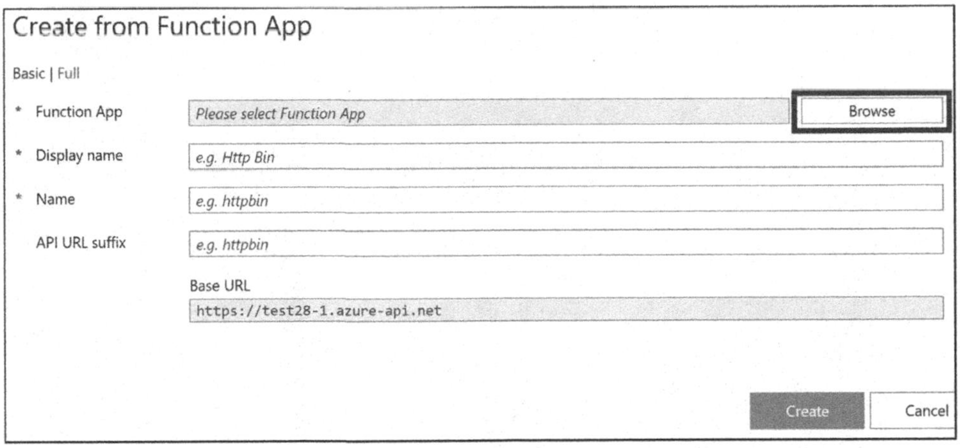

Figure 13-13. *Click Browse*

Click Function App. See Figure 13-14.

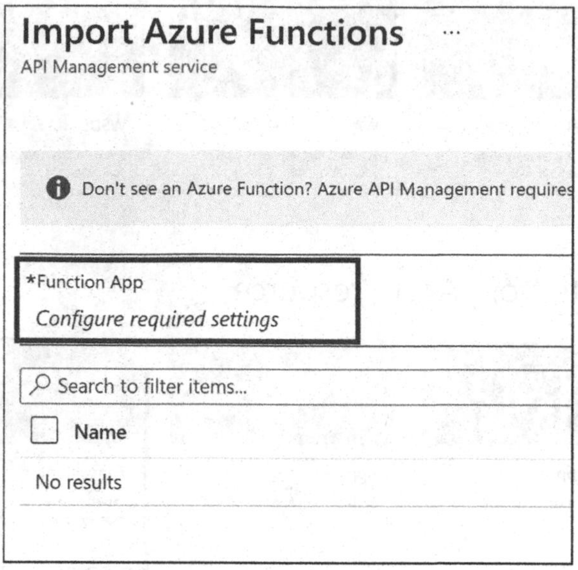

Figure 13-14. *Click Function App*

Select the function app that you need to configure as a back-end service.
See Figure 13-15.

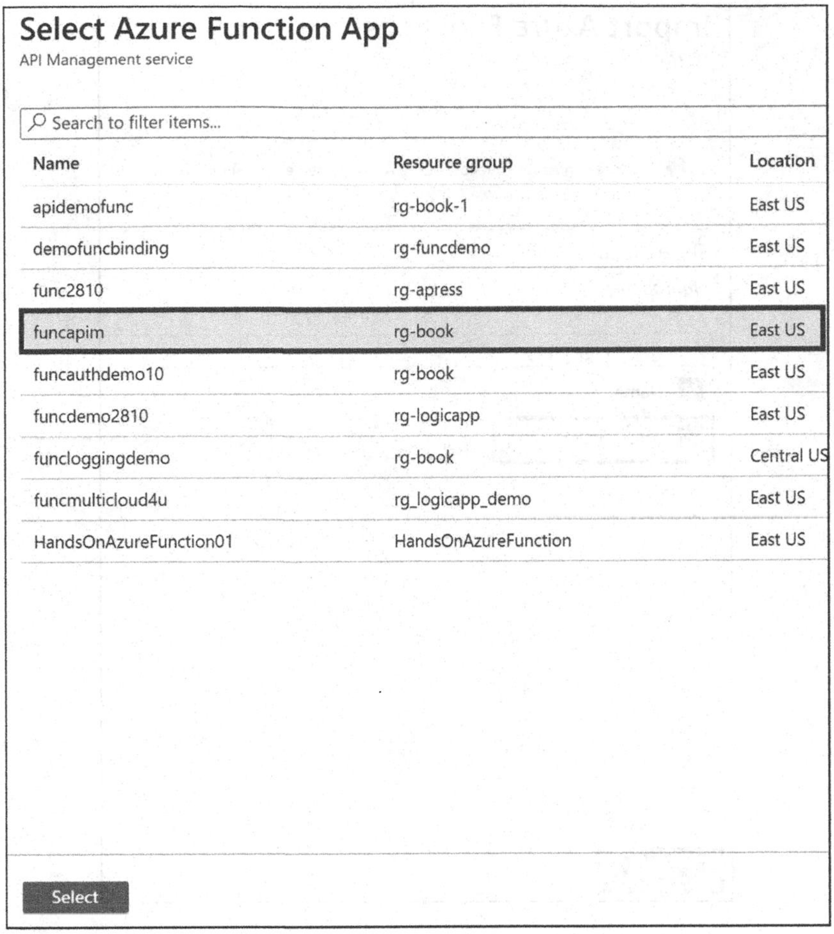
Select Azure Function App
API Management service
Search to filter items...
Name
Resource group
Location
apidemofunc
rg-book-1
East US
demofuncbinding
rg-funcdemo
East US
func2810
rg-apress
East US
funcapim
rg-book
East US
funcauthdemo10
rg-book
East US
funcdemo2810
rg-logicapp
East US
funcloggingdemo
rg-book
Central US
funcmulticloud4u
rg_logicapp_demo
East US
HandsOnAzureFunction01
HandsOnAzureFunction
East US
Select

Figure 13-15. *Select Function App*

Select the function in the selected function app that you need to expose as a back-end service. Click Select. See Figure 13-16.

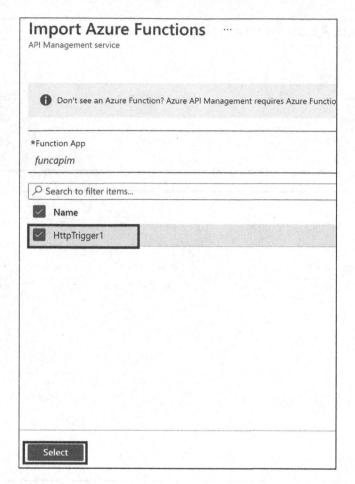

Figure 13-16. *Select the function to expose as the back-end service*

Provide the display name and name for the back-end service and then click Create. See Figure 13-17.

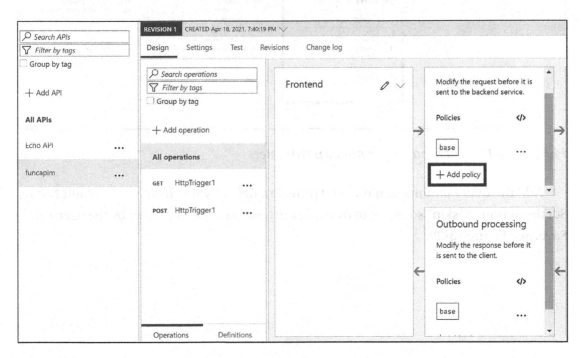

Figure 13-17. *Create the back-end service*

Go to the API back end that you created and then click "Add policy." See Figure 13-18.

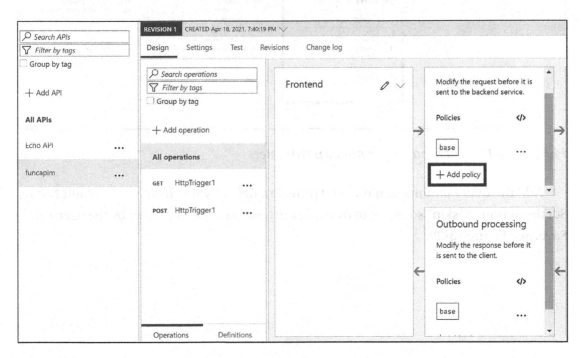

Figure 13-18. *Add a policy*

You can set a query parameter called name and provide a default value in the incoming request if the user has not provided the name parameter. If the user has provided the name parameter in the request, it will skip adding the query parameter. See Figure 13-19.

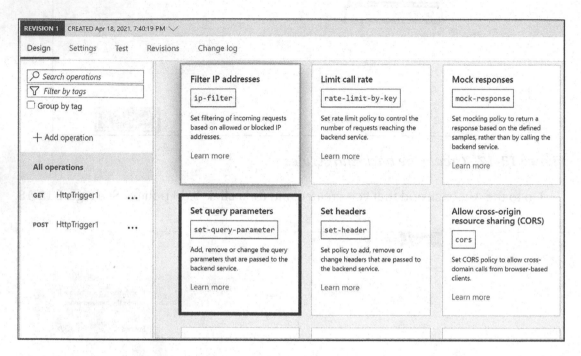

Figure 13-19. *Set a policy for query parameters*

Add the query parameter name and provide a default value instead of Default Name. Set the action to "skip" so as not to override the name parameter passed by the user. Click Save. See Figure 13-20.

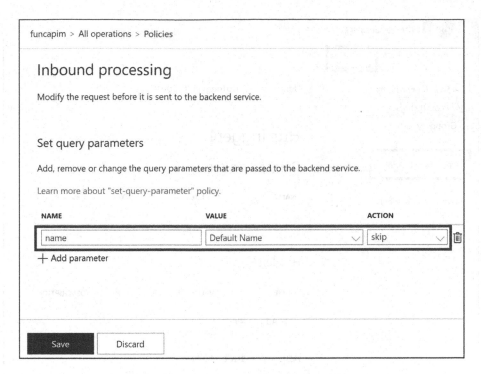

Figure 13-20. Provide the query parameter to add to the request

Now let's test the API Management service that you configured. Go to the Test tab. Select the Get method and click Send. See Figure 13-21.

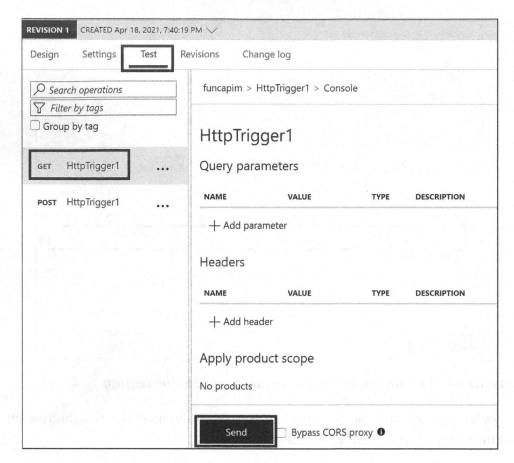

Figure 13-21. *Send a request to the API Management service without a query parameter*

You are not passing any query string parameter here. The API Management service will add the name parameter with the value Default Name in the request, and you get back the Default Name in the response. See Figure 13-22.

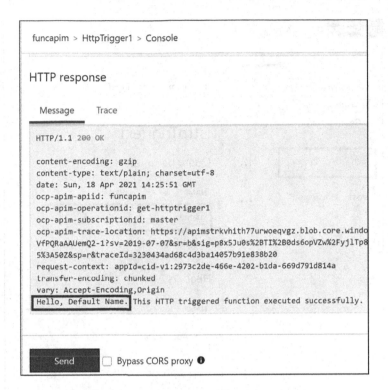

Figure 13-22. *Response from the API Management service*

Now let's add a query string name with a value. Click Send. See Figure 13-23.

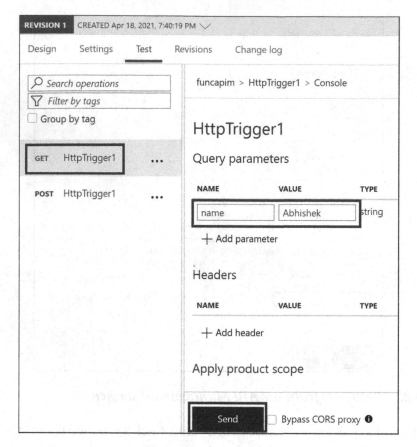

Figure 13-23. *Provide the query parameter in the request*

The value in the name parameter does not get overridden by the API Management service, and you get back the value that you sent in the parameter name. See Figure 13-24.

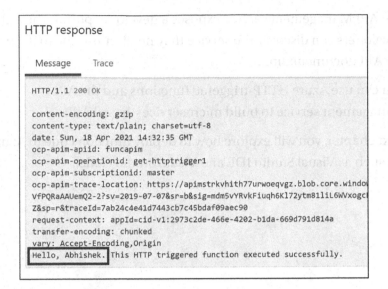

Figure 13-24. *Response from the API Management service*

Summary

In this chapter, you learned how to configure an HTTP-triggered Azure function as a back-end API for the Azure API Management service. You explored the Azure API Management service and its offerings at a very high level. You learned how to control the requests and response for an API configured as a back-end API for the API Management service. You added a policy to add a query parameter for the incoming requests in the API Management service.

The following are the key takeaways from this chapter:

- The API Management service helps you control the incoming requests and outgoing responses for HTTP-triggered Azure functions configured as the back-end APIs at a granular level.

- It enhances the security of Azure functions.

- The API Management service exposes a developer portal where the developers can discover the service they need, subscribe to it, and get the API documentation.

- You can use Azure HTTP-triggered functions and the API Management service to build microservices-based APIs.

In the next chapter, you will explore how to deploy function code to Azure functions using editors such as Visual Studio IDE and Visual Studio Code.

CHAPTER 14

Deploying Your Azure Functions Using IDEs

In the previous chapters, we discussed ways to build serverless solutions using various triggers and bindings to solve real-world problems. You studied how to store application secrets and configurations using Azure Key Vault and ways to monitor your functions using Application Insights and Azure Monitor. All these things are quite essential to building great solutions, but we have not covered an essential part yet, which is how to deploy these solutions in Azure.

As the name of the chapter suggests, the focus of this chapter will be to deploy your Azure functions using an integrated development environment (IDE). As mentioned, you can develop Azure functions using IDEs such as Visual Studio and VS Code, and you will be leveraging them to deploy the functions to Azure. Later in this book you will look at ways to deploy functions in containers and use Azure DevOps to deliver automated deployments of your Azure functions.

Structure of the Chapter

This chapter will explore the following aspects of HTTP triggers and Azure SQL:

- Deploying an Azure function to Azure using Visual Studio 2019

- Deploying an Azure function to a deployment slot using Visual Studio 2019

- Deploying an Azure function using VS Code

© Ashirwad Satapathi and Abhishek Mishra 2021
A. Satapathi and A. Mishra, *Hands-on Azure Functions with C#*, https://doi.org/10.1007/978-1-4842-7122-3_14

Objective

After studying this chapter, you will be able to do the following:

- Deploy Azure functions using IDEs

- Work with deployment slots

Deploy an Azure Function to Azure Using Visual Studio 2019

Open Visual Studio 2019, and click "Create a new project." See Figure 14-1.

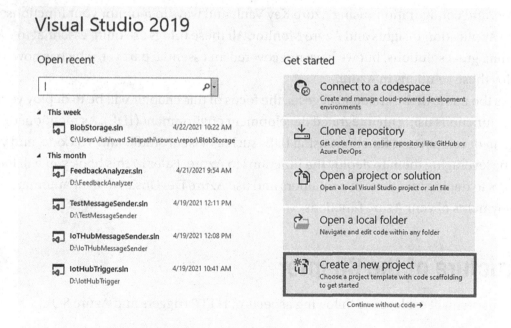

Figure 14-1. *Create a new project*

Select Azure Functions as the project template and click Next. See Figure 14-2.

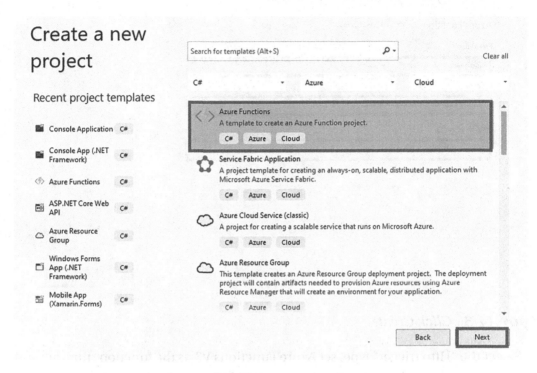

Figure 14-2. *Select the project template*

Enter the project name, location, and solution name. After you fill them in, click Create. See Figure 14-3.

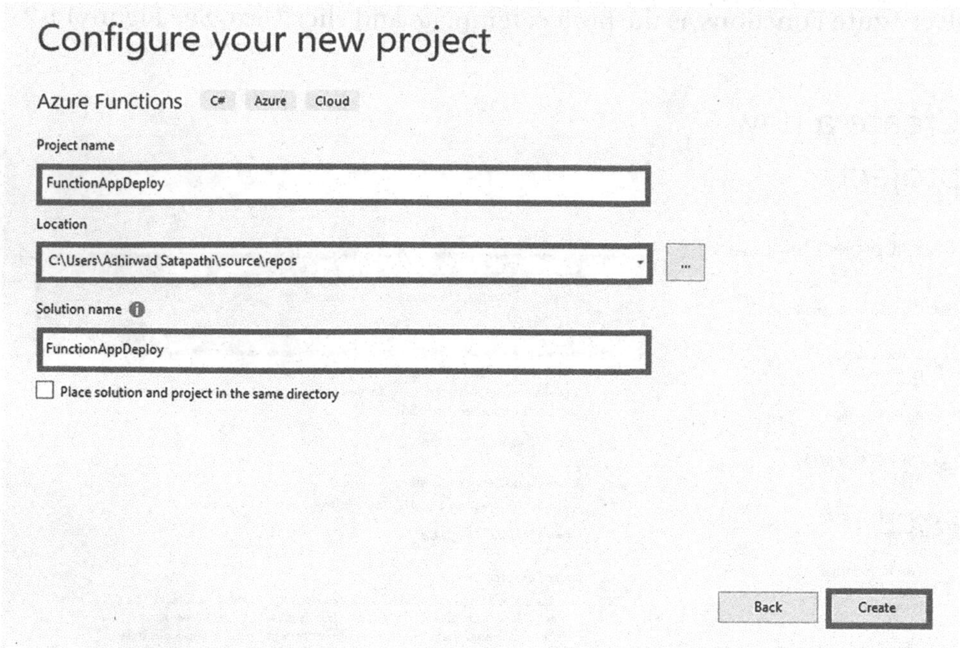

Configure your new project

Azure Functions   C#   Azure   Cloud

Project name

FunctionAppDeploy

Location

C:\Users\Ashirwad Satapathi\source\repos

Solution name ⓘ

FunctionAppDeploy

☐ Place solution and project in the same directory

Back   Create

Figure 14-3. *Click Create*

Select the "Http trigger" type, set Azure Functions V3 as the function runtime, and select Anonymous as the authentication level. Click Create. See Figure 14-4.

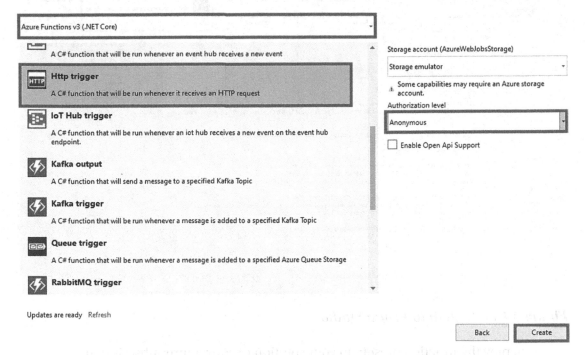

Figure 14-4. *Provide the template details*

Visual Studio will generate an Azure function named Function1 with some
boilerplate code to return a message as the response. Since you want to deploy your
function project to Azure, click the "Sign in" button in case you haven't signed into
Visual Studio with an account that has a valid Azure subscription. As you can see from
Figure 14-5, we have already logged into Visual Studio.

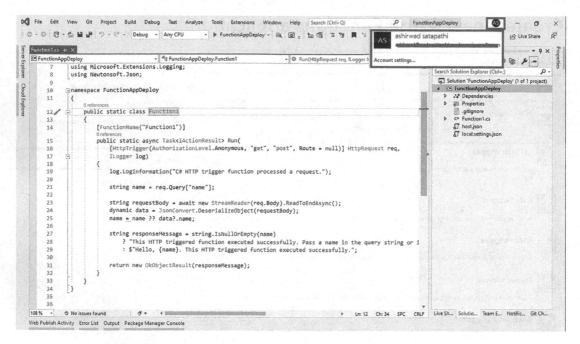

Figure 14-5. *Sign in to Visual Studio*

To deploy the function present in your solution to your Azure subscription, right-click FunctionAppDeploy Project and click Publish. See Figure 14-6.

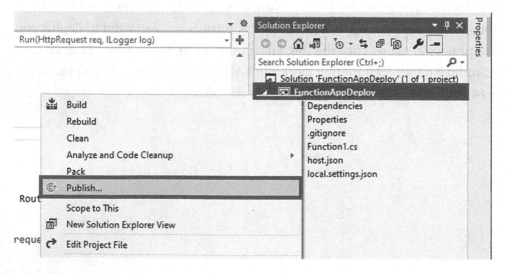

Figure 14-6. *Click Publish*

You will see a pop-up screen with various target options to deploy your function project. Select Azure as the target and click Next. See Figure 14-7.

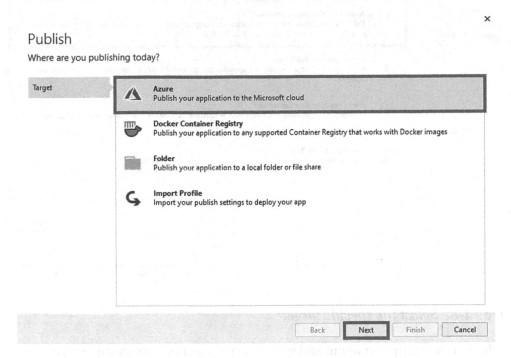

Figure 14-7. *Select Azure as the target*

Select Azure Function App (Windows) as the specific target and click Next. See Figure 14-8.

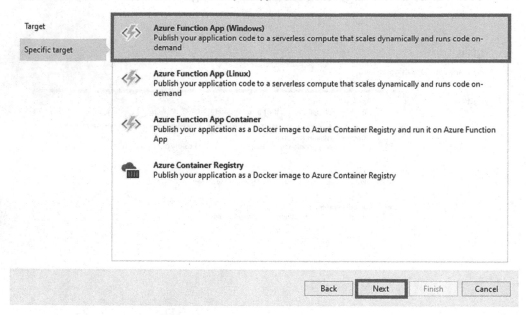

Figure 14-8.   Select the specific target

Select the subscription name and select the view as resource group. Since you don't have any existing function app in your subscription, let's click + as highlighted in Figure 14-9 to create a function app.

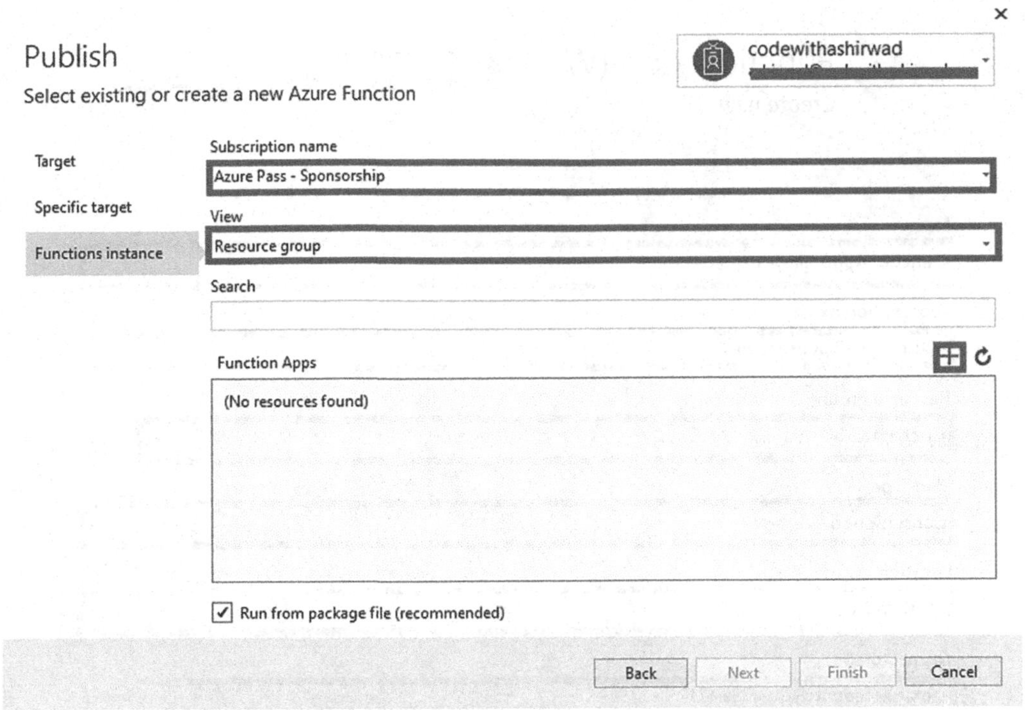

Publish

Select existing or create a new Azure Function

Target

Subscription name

Azure Pass - Sponsorship

Specific target

View

Functions instance

Resource group

Search

Function Apps

(No resources found)

☑ Run from package file (recommended)

Back   Next   Finish   Cancel

Figure 14-9. *Select the subscription and view*

Enter the name of the function app, select the subscription where you want to create this function app, choose the resource group, select Consumption as the plan type, select the location where you want to create this function app, and select a storage account or create a new one for the function app by clicking New. Once you have entered all the required fields, click Create. Then Visual Studio will create a function app running on a Consumption Plan inside the selected resource group and subscription in the background. It is similar to creating a function app through the Azure portal. It usually takes some minutes to provision all the resources. See Figure 14-10.

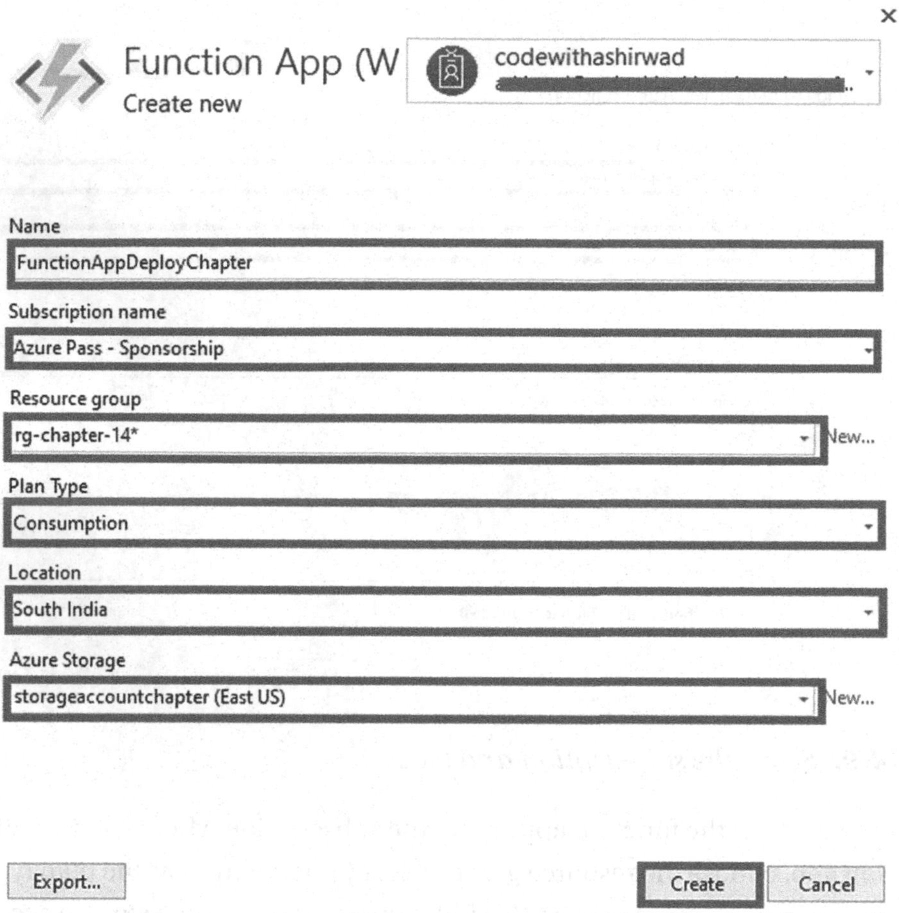

Figure 14-10. *Create a new function app*

Visual Studio will have selected the function app that you created in the previous step. Click Finish to create a publish profile to deploy your function project to the newly created function app. If you had any existing function apps, you could have deployed your function app over there by selecting it in this step. See Figure 14-11.

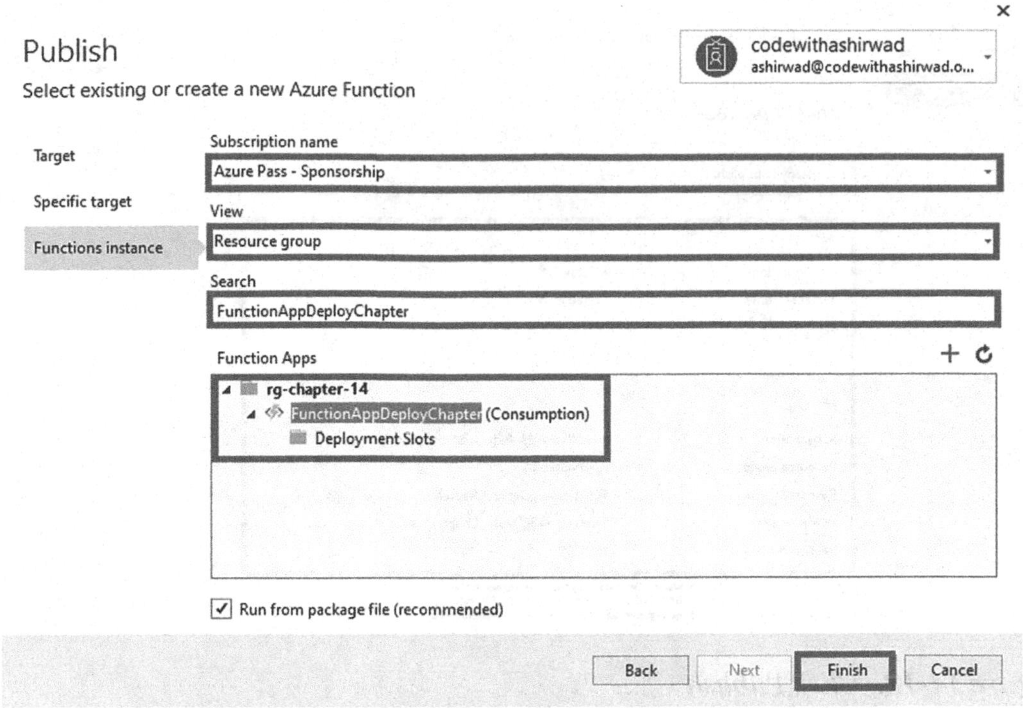

Figure 14-11. *Click Finish*

You need to click Publish to start the deployment process. In the settings section of the Publish pane, you can see the configurations of your function app, including the function app URL, resource group, and function app name. See Figure 14-12.

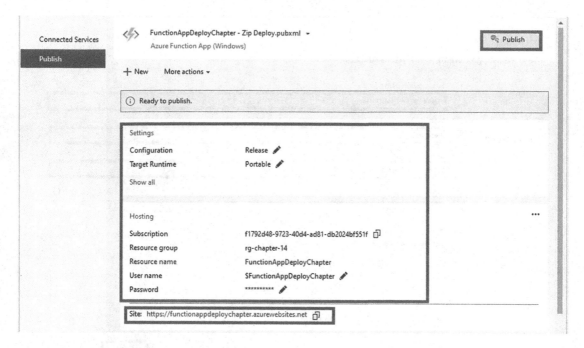

Figure 14-12. *Click Publish*

You can see the progress of your deployment in the Output window, as shown in Figure 14-13.

Figure 14-13. *View the Output window*

To test your function that you deployed using Visual Studio, you will have to go to the Azure portal. Then go to the function app that you had created in Visual Studio and click Functions in the sidebar menu, as highlighted in Figure 14-14. Here you will see the list of all the functions deployed in this function app. Let's click Function1.

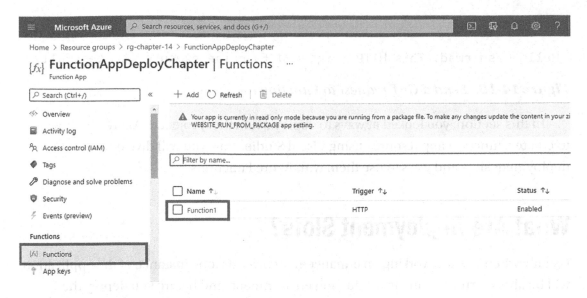

Figure 14-14. *Click Function1*

You need to click the Get Function Url button to get the URL of Function1. Copy the URL shown in the dialog. See Figure 14-15.

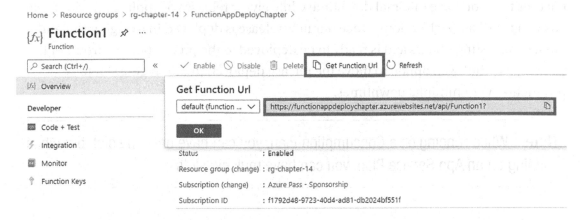

Figure 14-15. *Get the URL of Function1*

To test whether our function works well or not, open a web browser and paste the function URL copied from the previous step along with a query string of `name=ashirwad`. Now press Enter to send a request to the function. You should get a result similar to Figure 14-16.

`Hello, ashirwad. This HTTP triggered function executed successfully.`

Figure 14-16. Send a GET request to Function1

In this section, you looked at ways to deploy a function project to Azure and how to create a function app resource using Visual Studio. Now you will dive deeper into deployment slots and ways to use them with Azure Functions.

What Are Deployment Slots?

Usually when you are working on enhancement projects, one instance of the application will be already running in the production environment, and before you deploy the applications along with the enhancement to a production environment, you will usually perform multiple tests to confirm your release is issue-free. With slots, you can deploy a new instance of our application to perform sanity tests.

Deployment slots provide a mechanism to perform blue-green deployments. This ensures that you have minimal downtime while giving releases of application along with ensuring easy fallback options. Once our new release is deployed in a staging slot and passes the testing phases and is ready to be deployed to the production environment, you can use the swap option to move the release deployed in the staging slot to production with minimal downtimes.

Note   While running on a Consumption Plan, you can have only one slot, but while running on an App Service Plan, you can have multiple slots.

Deploy an Azure Function to Deployment Slots

To create a slot, go to the function app. Click Deployment Slots in the Deployment section in the sidebar menu. Now click + Add Slot to create a new slot. See Figure 14-17.

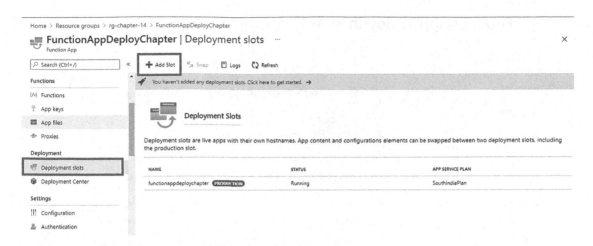

Figure 14-17. *Click Add Slot*

You will see a new screen to enter a slot name. Once you enter the slot name, you need to click Add to create a new slot for your function app. See Figure 14-18.

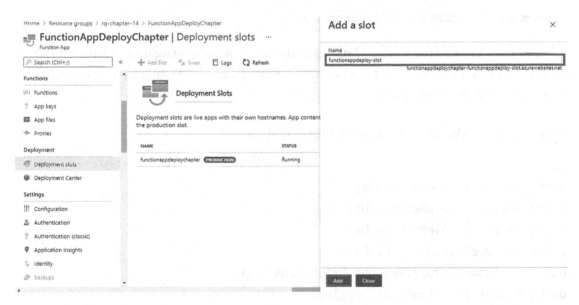

Figure 14-18. *Click Add*

A slot will be created for your function app along with its status, as shown in Figure 14-19. The slot in which the production workload is running will have a tag and production slot associated with its name.

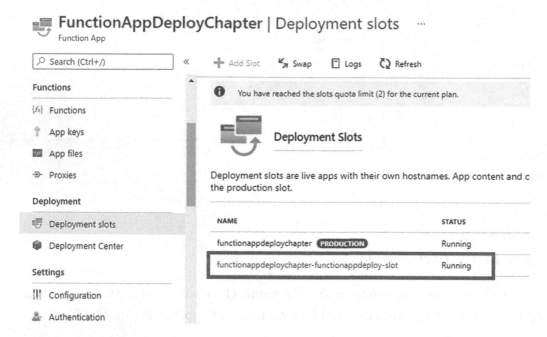

Figure 14-19.   View the deployment slots

You have created the slots, so let's open the function project again in Visual Studio to deploy a modified version of the function app to it. Refer to Listing 14-1 to view the modified version of Function1.

Listing 14-1. Modified Version of Function1.cs

```
using System.IO;
using System.Threading.Tasks;
using Microsoft.AspNetCore.Http;
using Microsoft.AspNetCore.Mvc;
using Microsoft.Azure.WebJobs;
using Microsoft.Azure.WebJobs.Extensions.Http;
using Microsoft.Extensions.Logging;
using Newtonsoft.Json;

namespace FunctionAppDeploy
{
    public static class Function1
    {
        [FunctionName("Function1")]
```

```
public static async Task<IActionResult> Run(
    [HttpTrigger(AuthorizationLevel.Anonymous, "get", "post", Route
    = null)] HttpRequest req, ILogger log)
{

    log.LogInformation("C# HTTP trigger function processed a
    request.");
    string name = req.Query["name"];
    string requestBody = await new StreamReader(req.Body).
    ReadToEndAsync();
    dynamic data = JsonConvert.DeserializeObject(requestBody);
    name = name ?? data?.name;
    string responseMessage = string.IsNullOrEmpty(name);
        ? "This HTTP triggered function executed successfully. Pass
        a name in the query string or in the request body for a
        personalized response."
        : $"Hello, {name}.";
    return new OkObjectResult(responseMessage);
    }
  }
}
```

The response returned from Function1 when you pass name=ashirwad as a query string will be "Hello Ashirwad" instead of "Hello Ashirwad." This HTTP-triggered function executed successfully.

To deploy this modified version of Function1.cs to your slot that you have created in the Azure portal, right-click the FunctionAppDeploy project and click Publish. See Figure 14-20.

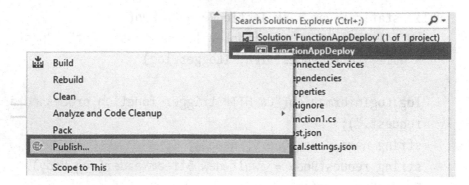

Figure 14-20. *Click Publish*

Click + New to create a new publish profile to deploy the FunctionAppDeploy project to the newly created slot. See Figure 14-21.

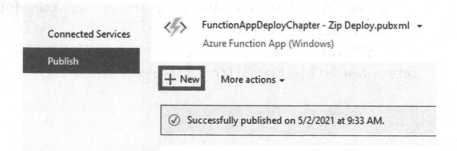

Figure 14-21. *Create a new publish profile*

Select Azure as the target in the Publish dialog and click Next. See Figure 14-22.

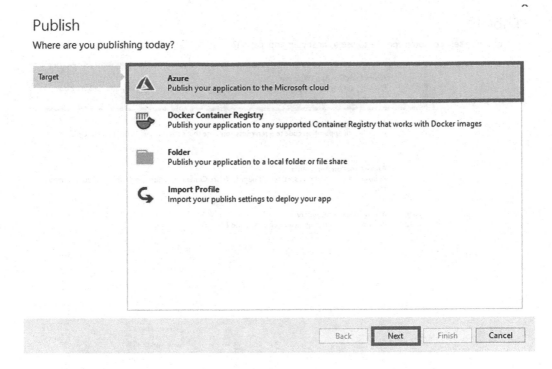

Figure 14-22. *Select Azure as the target*

Select Azure Functions App (Windows) as the specific target and click Next, as shown in Figure 14-23.

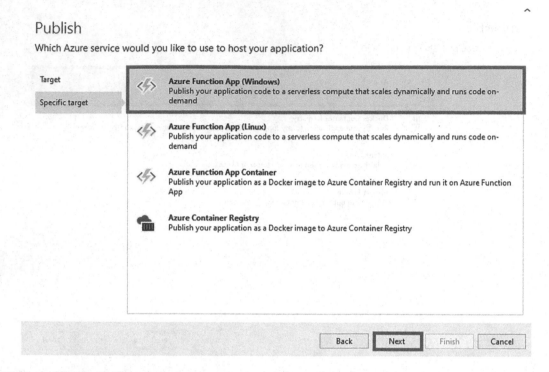

Figure 14-23. *Select Azure Function App (Windows) as the specific target*

Select the subscription, select View as the resource group, and select the newly created deployment slot in your function app. Click Finish. See Figure 14-24.

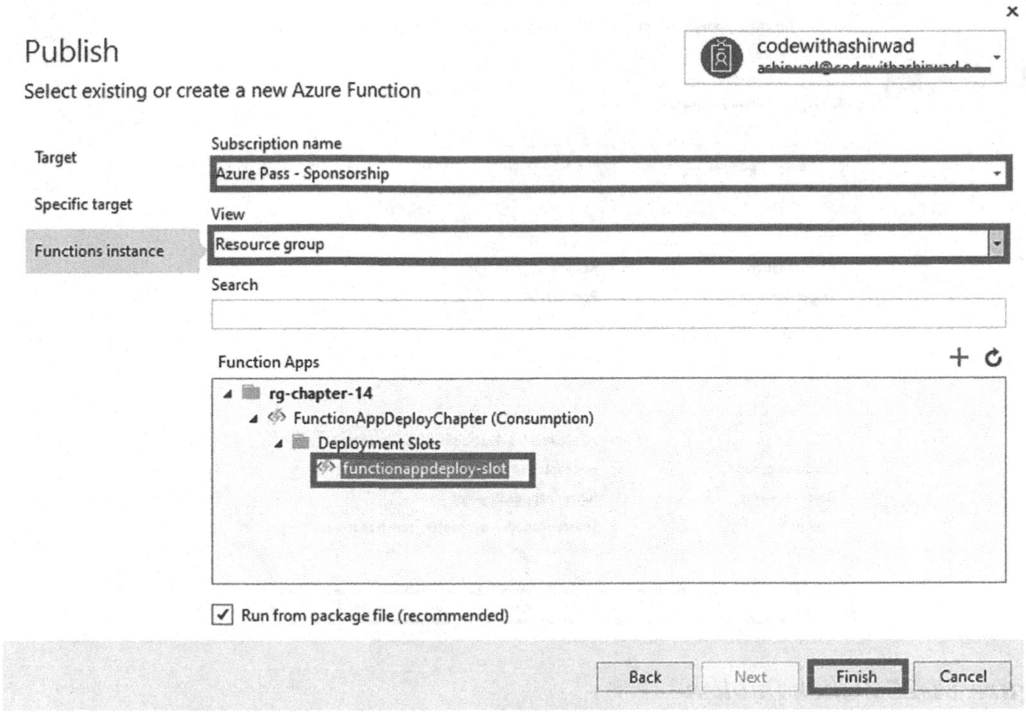

Figure 14-24. *Select the deployment slot*

Visual Studio will create a publish profile depending on the configurations you have selected. Let's click Publish to start the deployment process of the function project to the slot. See Figure 14-25.

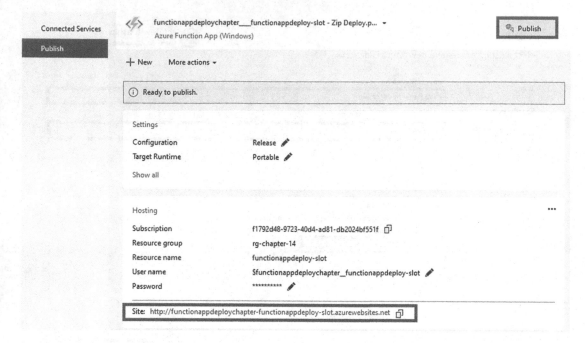

Figure 14-25. *Click Publish*

You can see the status of the deployment process from the Output window. See Figure 14-26.

Figure 14-26. *View the deployment progress in the Output window*

After the deployment is successful, let's go to the Azure portal and then click the slots by going to the deployment center of the function app. See Figure 14-27.

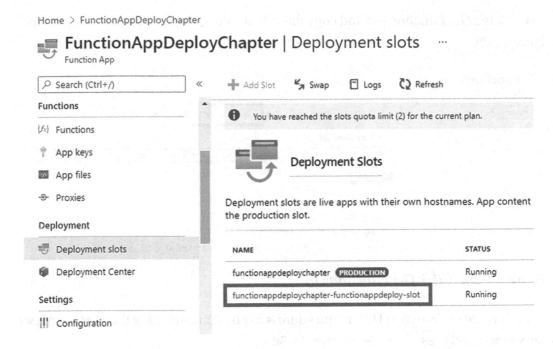

Figure 14-27. *Click the deployment slot*

Go to the Functions section in the sidebar of the function app and click Function1. See Figure 14-28.

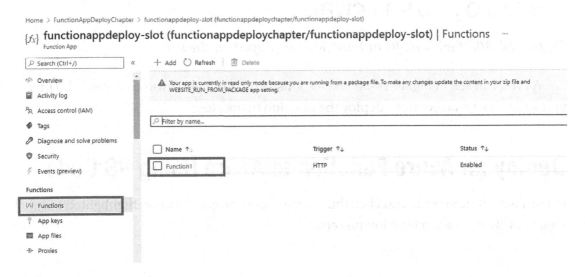

Figure 14-28. *Click Function1*

Click the Get Function Url and copy the URL to send a request to the function. See Figure 14-29.

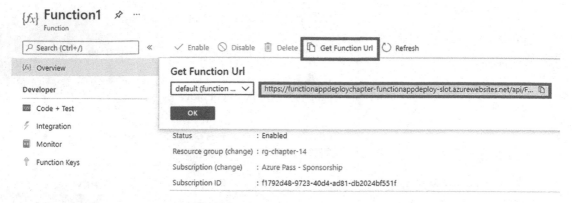

Figure 14-29. Click Get Function Url

Let's paste the function URL in the address bar by concatenating the `name=ashirwad` query string and press Enter. See Figure 14-30.

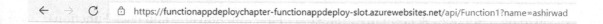

Hello, ashirwad.

Figure 14-30. Response from Function1 deployed on the slot

As you can see in Figure 14-30, the response from Function1 was as expected. Thus, you were able to successfully deploy the function in the slot.

Deploy an Azure Function to Azure Using VS Code

Open Visual Studio Code and click the "Create a new project" icon as highlighted in Figure 14-31 to create a function project.

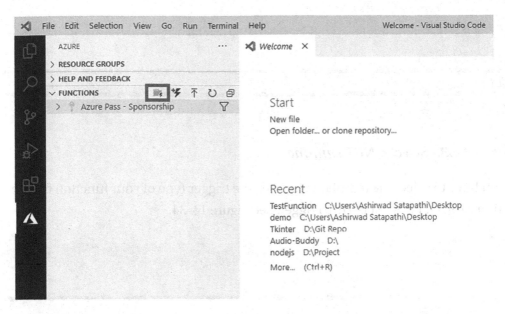

Figure 14-31. *Create a new function project*

You have to select the language in which you will be writing the functions. Let's select C# in this window. See Figure 14-32.

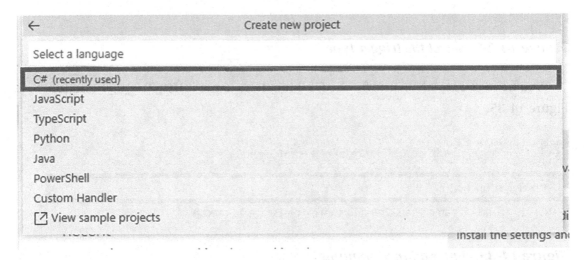

Figure 14-32. *Select the programming language*

You will have to select the .NET runtime for the function project. Let's select .NET Core 3 LTS. See Figure 14-33.

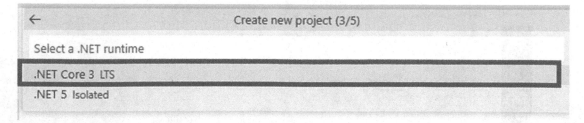

Figure 14-33. *Select a NET runtime*

You have to select the template type, i.e., the trigger type of your function for the function project. Let's select HttpTrigger. See Figure 14-34.

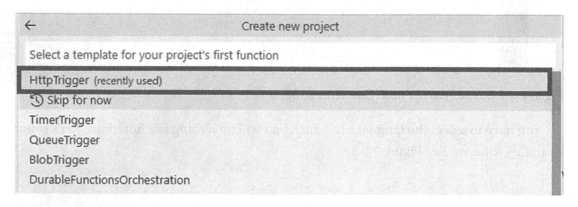

Figure 14-34. *Select the trigger type*

You need to enter the name for the function. Let's name it **HttpTriggerFunction**. See Figure 14-35.

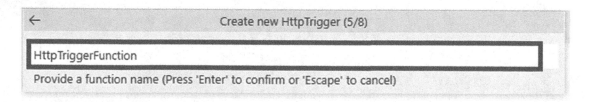

Figure 14-35. *Enter a function name*

You need to enter a namespace for the function project. Let's keep it as Company. Function. See Figure 14-36.

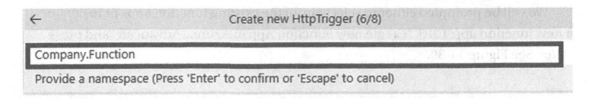

Figure 14-36. *Enter the namespace for the project*

You need to select the authorization level for the function. Use Anonymous. See Figure 14-37.

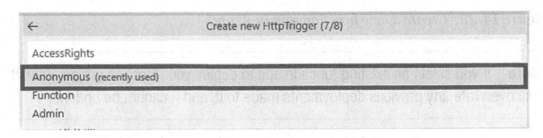

Figure 14-37. *Select the authorization level of the function*

As you can see, a local function project was created by VS Code with an HTTP-triggered function named HttpTriggerFunction. This function contains boilerplate code similar to that shown in Listing 14-1. To deploy this function to Azure, click the Deploy to Function App icon, as highlighted in Figure 14-38.

```
∨ FUNCTIONS                    ▣  ⚡ ↑  ↻  ⊡    13
  >  🔑 Azure Pass - Sponsorship        Deploy to Function App...
  ∨  ▣ Local Project FunctionProject
    ∨  ≡ Functions Read-only                    16
      ⓘ Run build task to update this list...   17
      ƒ HttpTriggerFunction HTTP                 18
                                                 19
                                                 20
                                                 21
```

Figure 14-38. *Click the Deploy to Function App icon*

We will be prompted either to select any of the existing function apps or to create a new function app. Click "Create new Function App in Azure...Advanced" and press Enter. See Figure 14-39.

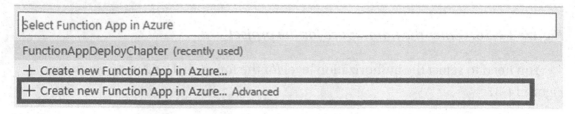

```
Select Function App in Azure
FunctionAppDeployChapter  (recently used)
+  Create new Function App in Azure...
+  Create new Function App in Azure...  Advanced
```

Figure 14-39. *Create a new function app in Azure*

Note   If you select an existing function app to deploy your function project, then it will overwrite any previous deployments made to it, and it cannot be undone.

You will have to enter the function app name. Let's enter **Chapter14FunctionApp** as the function app name and press Enter. See Figure 14-40.

```
Create new Function App in Azure (1/7)

Chapter14FunctionApp

Enter a globally unique name for the new function app. (Press 'Enter' to confirm or 'Escape' to
cancel)
```

Figure 14-40. *Enter the function app name*

You will be prompted to select the runtime stack for the function app. Since you selected .NET Core 3.1 as the runtime for the function project while creating it, let's select the same setting here. See Figure 14-41.

```
←           Create new Function App in Azure (2/7)

Select a runtime stack.

.NET Core 3.1
.NET 5 (non-LTS)
```

Figure 14-41. *Select the runtime stack*

You will have to select the OS for the function app. Select Windows. See Figure 14-42.

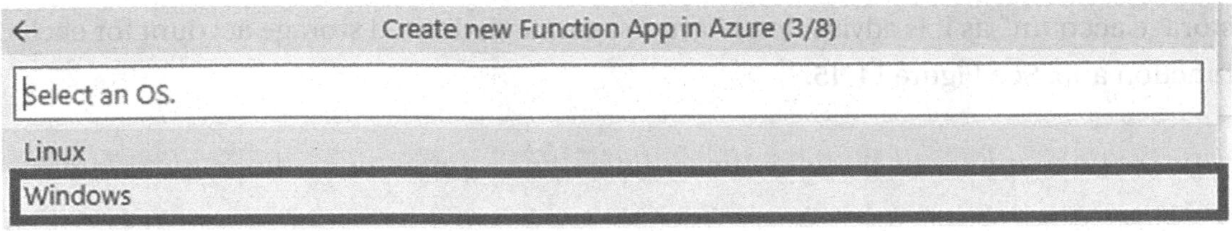

Figure 14-42. *Select Windows as the OS*

You will be prompted to select the hosting plan. Let's select the Consumption hosting plan. See Figure 14-43.

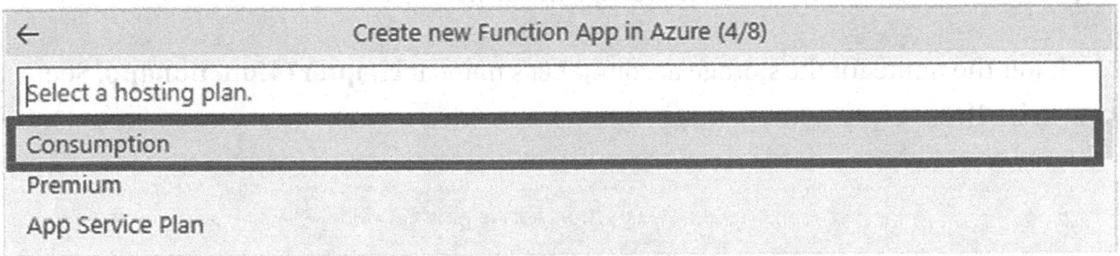

Figure 14-43. *Select the hosting plan*

Now, you will have to select the resource group inside of which your function app and other associated resources will be created. Let's select rg-chapter-14 as the resource group. See Figure 14-44.

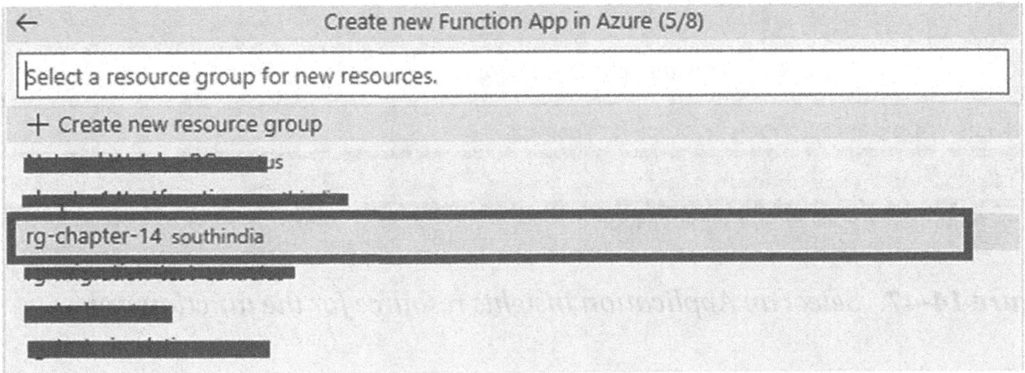

Figure 14-44. *Select the resource group*

You will be prompted to select from any of the existing storage accounts or create a new storage account that will be used by the function app. Let's select a "Create new storage account" as it is advisable to have a separate dedicated storage account for each function app. See Figure 14-45.

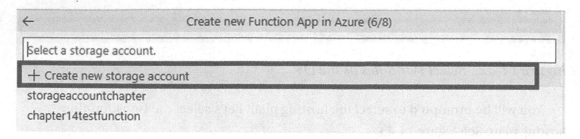

Figure 14-45. *Click "Create new storage account"*

Enter the name for the storage account. Let's name it **chapter14functionapp**. See Figure 14-46.

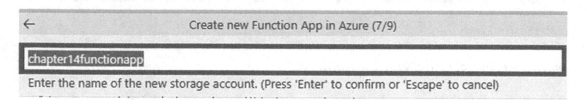

Figure 14-46. *Enter the name for the storage account*

You will be prompted to either create a new Application Insights resource or skip for now for your function app. Let's click "Skip for now." See Figure 14-47.

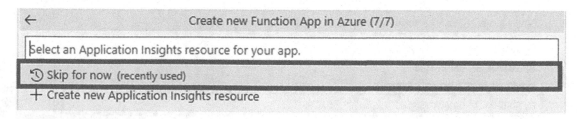

Figure 14-47. *Select an Application Insights resource for the function app*

Now you will have to select the region in which all the resources associated with the function app will be created. Let's select South India here and press Enter. See Figure 14-48.

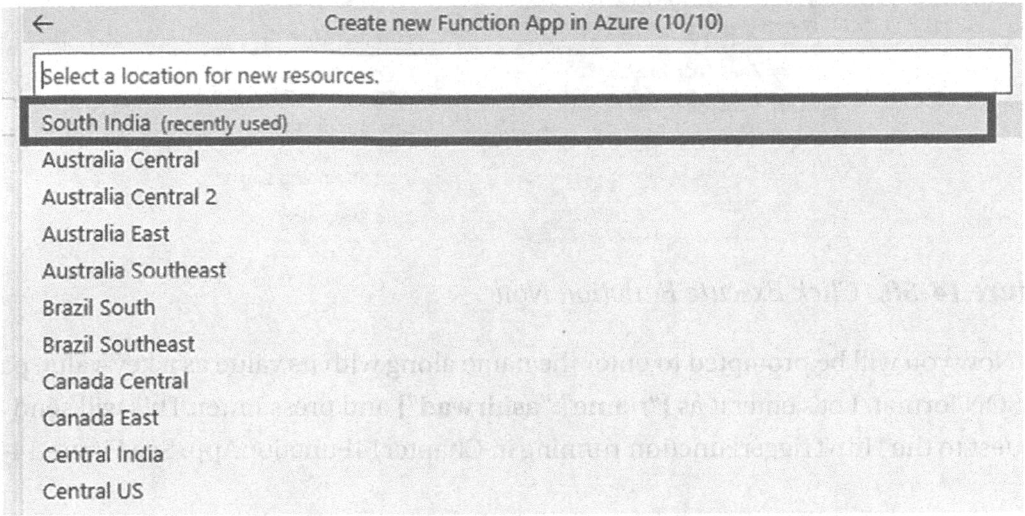

Figure 14-48. *Select the region/location*

The deployment process of your function app will be going on now in the background. You can view the progress in the Output window. Once the deployment has completed successfully, you will see a notification dialog at the bottom screen of VS Code similar to the one shown in Figure 14-49. You can also see any errors in the function app deployment in notification dialog and Output window.

Figure 14-49. *Deployment status of the function app*

Instead of going to the function app in the Azure portal to get the function URL, let's right-click the HttpTriggerFunction present inside the function app in which you had created and deployed your function project and click Execute Function Now to send a request to your function running in Azure. See Figure 14-50.

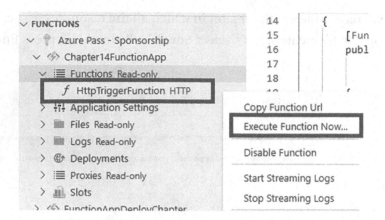

Figure 14-50. *Click Execute Function Now*

Now you will be prompted to enter the name along with its value as a key-value pair in JSON format. Let's enter it as **{"name":"ashirwad"}** and press Enter. This will send a request to the HttpTriggerFunction running in Chapter14FunctionApp. See Figure 14-51.

Figure 14-51. *Pass the name and its value as a key-value pair*

You will get back the response from the function in a notification dialog at the bottom of the VS Code window. This function gave back the response "Hello, Ashirwad." So, this HTTP-triggered function executed successfully as expected. See Figure 14-52.

Figure 14-52. *Response from HttpTriggerFunction*

Summary

In this chapter, you explored ways to deploy function projects using different IDEs. We also discussed slots and ways to create a deployment slot in the Azure portal and deploy a function project there.

The following are the key takeaways from the chapter:

- You can deploy an Azure function project using IDEs like Visual Studio, VS Code, etc.

- Deployment slots help you run multiple versions of your applications.

- Every slot has its own instance and can be swapped with the application running in the production slot.

- Slots are helpful in performing blue-green deployments with ease.

Deploying Your Azure Functions Using a CI/CD Pipeline with Azure DevOps

While a software application is being developed and deployed, you use multiple processes before the final application is completed and deployed. This often includes phases such as requirements gathering, system design, development, testing, and deployment irrespective of the SDLC models followed. These processes used to be quite time-consuming, with the development and operations teams not being in sync. With the demanding business scenarios of current times, you need a shorter time to market to release newer features of your products to serve your end customers.

To meet the demand for faster delivery of applications and features, organizations have embraced DevOps principles and practices to increase their team's efficiency by overcoming the hurdles associated with following traditional SDLC models. Often the development and operations teams are isolated from each other in a traditional setup, which makes it difficult to move or roll back features to different environments. By incorporating DevOps practices such as agile planning, continuous integration (CI), continuous delivery (CD), and monitoring, you try to ensure seamless collaboration and communication among the developer, operations, QA, and security teams to deliver and ship products quickly with robust rollback mechanisms to meet customer demands and reduce cost.

© Ashirwad Satapathi and Abhishek Mishra 2021
A. Satapathi and A. Mishra, *Hands-on Azure Functions with C#*, https://doi.org/10.1007/978-1-4842-7122-3_15

In previous chapters, you explored ways to build solutions and ways to deploy them to Azure with different IDEs. The focus in this chapter will be to explore ways to deploy your function project to Azure using CI/CD pipelines with Azure DevOps. This can also be done using GitHub actions.

Structure of the Chapter

This chapter will explore the following topics:

- What Azure DevOps is

- Creating a build pipeline and enabling continuous integration using Azure Pipelines

- Creating a release pipeline and enabling continuous deployment using Azure Pipelines

Objectives

After studying this chapter, you will able to do the following:

- Work with GitHub repositories in Azure DevOps

- Build CI/CD pipelines to deploy function projects using Azure

What Is Azure DevOps?

A typical application lifecycle contains multiple phases such as planning, development, delivery, and operations. DevOps teams use various tools to help them with each of the phases. For example, some organizations use tools like Jira from Atlassian to collaborate and plan sprints, perform issue tracking, and add feature requests, but they use a different set of tools like Jenkins or GitHub for delivery. With Azure DevOps, Microsoft provides a suite of services in a unified platform to help your DevOps teams in all the phases of the application lifecycle.

Azure DevOps provides the following services to help teams to increase the efficiency of teams in all the phases of the application lifecycle:

- *Azure Repos*: With Azure Repos, teams can keep track of changes in their code base and provide an efficient way to keep a history of their development. It is a version control system provided by Azure DevOps where you can create multiple private repositories and collaborate to add features or resolve bugs/issues.

- *Azure Boards*: With Azure Boards, teams can collaborate, plan, track, and monitor tasks, feature requests, and issues related to the projects. It provides native support for Scrum and Kanban. You can create a dashboard to visually monitor the progress of your project.

- *Azure Pipelines*: With Azure Pipelines, teams can practice continuous integration and continuous delivery to build and ship products developed by various languages to different target environments. It helps in creating the build packages and performing unit tests along with other tasks such as vulnerability assessment using tasks from third-party vendors from the marketplace.

- *Azure Test Plans*: With Azure Test Plans, teams can perform various kinds of testing such as exploratory, manual, or user acceptance tests in a browser. Azure Test Plans provides the QA teams with all the resources required to perform testing with end-to-end traceability within the browser.

- *Azure Artifacts*: With Azure Artifacts, teams can create and share NPM, NuGet, or Maven packages feeds with the rest of teams from public and private sources. It is a package management solution offered as a service in Azure DevOps.

Note   Maven is a Java project management software that helps you build, package, version, and run Java applications with ease. You can add the external packages that you will refer to in your Java project using a Maven project configuration file, and Maven will include those packages while building the application.

Before diving deeper into this chapter, you will need to provision a function app in Azure where you will be deploying your function project and then commit your function project to a repository. I have created a function app named funcchapter15 that does not contain any functions for the time being. I will show how to use Azure Pipelines to deploy the function present in your function project to this function app later in the chapter. See Figure 15-1.

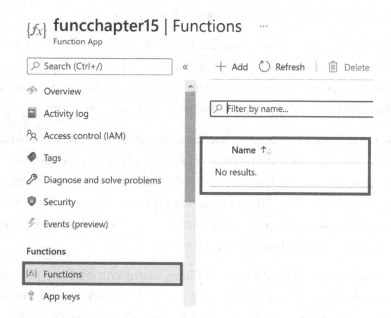

Figure 15-1. *Create a function app*

Though Azure DevOps provides you with a service to create a private repository, we will be using GitHub for this chapter. I have created a repository in GitHub called `Chapter15FunctionApp`. You can find the source code at `https://github.com/AshirwadSatapathi/Chapter15FunctionApp`.

This repository contains a function project with an HTTP-triggered function that returns a personalized message along with the value passed for the query string `name` or for the value of `name` sent in the request body. You can clone this repository or use your own repository to follow along with this chapter.

Now that you have created a function app and a repository, you are ready to create your CI/CD pipelines.

Create a Project in Azure DevOps

Go to https://dev.azure.com and click Sign In to log on to your Azure DevOps account.

Note   If you are signing up for the first time, you will be prompted to enter an organization name and select the region where you want it to be hosted.

To create a project, go to the organization where you want to create the project and click "+ New project." See Figure 15-2.

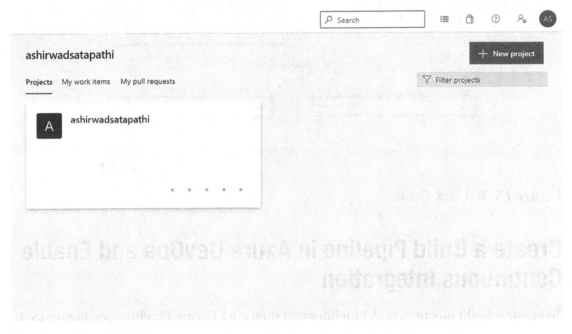

Figure 15-2. *Click "+ New project"*

You will be prompted to enter the project details on a new screen. Enter the project name and description, select Private for the visibility, and then select Git as the version control system. Then set "Work item process" to the process you follow in your organization. For example, if your organization follows Scrum, then select Scrum here. After filling in all the required information, click Create to create the project. See Figure 15-3. This will create the project and redirect you to the project screen.

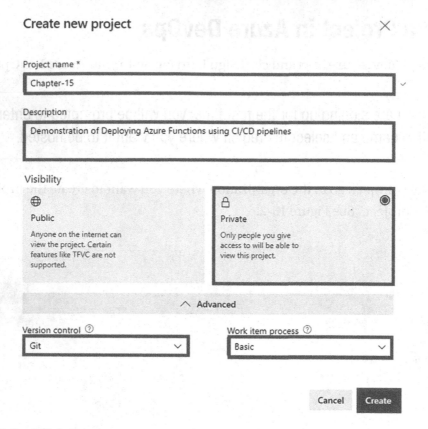

Figure 15-3. Click Create

Create a Build Pipeline in Azure DevOps and Enable Continuous Integration

To create a build pipeline, click Pipelines and then click Create Pipeline. See Figure 15-4.

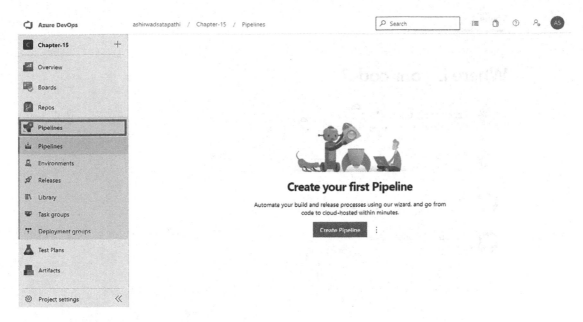

Figure 15-4. *Click Create Pipeline*

The simplest way to create a pipeline in Azure DevOps is by using the classic editor. You can also use YAML scripts to create a build and deployment pipeline. For now, click "Use the classic editor," as shown in Figure 15-5.

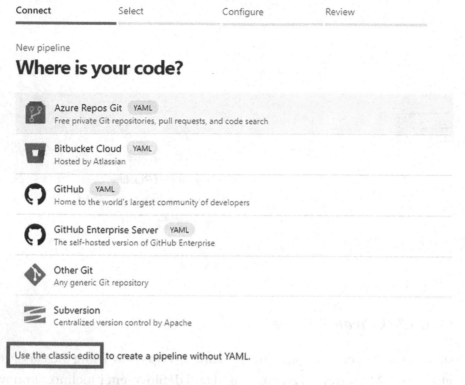

Figure 15-5. Click "Use the classic editor"

Select GitHub as the source. This will prompt you to create a connection to allow access to the pipeline to your GitHub repositories. You can create a connection by either authorizing using OAuth or using the GitHub personal access token. You will be creating the connection by clicking "Authorize using OAuth." This will prompt you to log in using your GitHub credentials and give the connection the required permissions. See Figure 15-6.

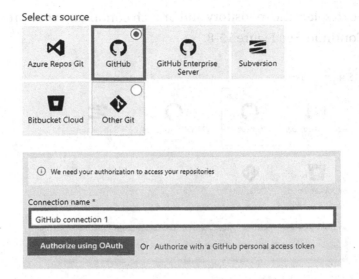

Figure 15-6. *Click "Authorize using OAuth"*

Click Authorize AzurePipelines to allow permissions to the pipeline and create a connection. See Figure 15-7.

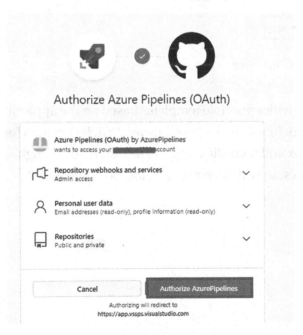

Figure 15-7. *Click Authorize AzurePipelines*

You will have to select the repository and branch containing your project files. Once selected, click Continue. See Figure 15-8.

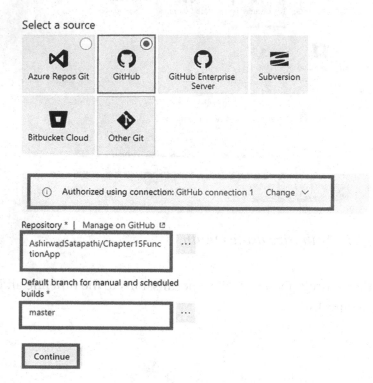

Figure 15-8. *Click Continue*

Azure DevOps provides multiple templates based on the application. Since your application is an Azure function developed using .NET, let's search for *azure functions for .NET* in the search box and then click Apply in the template, as highlighted in Figure 15-9. Alternatively, you can start with an empty job, too. See Figure 15-9.

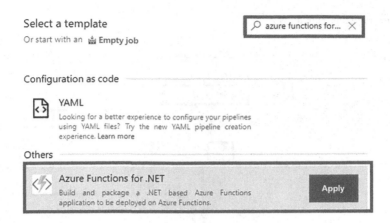

Figure 15-9. *Select the template and click Apply*

Azure DevOps will generate a build pipeline with the prepopulated tasks required to build your function project in the agent job. These are the minimum set of tasks required to build your function project.

Note   You can add further tasks from the Azure Marketplace offered by third-party vendors like WhiteSource to perform vulnerability assessment in the build pipeline and review the vulnerabilities reports after the build pipeline has executed. You can find more information at `www.whitesourcesoftware.com/resources/`.

You can configure the agent job by adding tasks or changing the agent specification to a Mac or Ubuntu instead of vs2017-win2016. Let's click Save to save the build pipeline. If you want to execute the build pipeline, you can manually start it by clicking Save & Queue after making the required changes or just click Queue to start the build process if you haven't made any changes. See Figure 15-10.

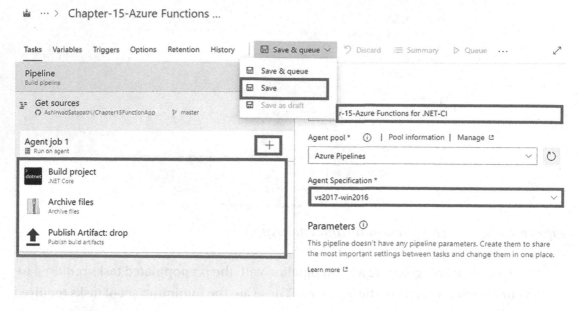

Figure 15-10. *Click Save*

You may have noticed that you do not have a test task here in the pipeline. Ideally it should be added to run all the unit and integration tests present in the project's solutions, but since you did not have any unit tests written for this solution, you have not added it in the pipeline. With this, you have created the build pipeline for your Azure Functions project that can be triggered manually. But it does not make sense to manually start the build process for most of the project. It would be ideal to have a mechanism to automatically start the build process every time code was committed to your repository. You can achieve that by enabling continuous integration for your build pipeline.

To enable continuous integration, click the Triggers tab and then select the checkbox "Enable continuous integration." Also, select Include as the type and define the branch specification as Master. You choose Master in the branch specification since you want to start the build process every time a change is made in the master branch. If you wanted to initiate the build process whenever a change was made in some other branch, then you would define that here. To save the changes, you have to enable continuous continuation and initiate the build process. Click Save & Queue. See Figure 15-11.

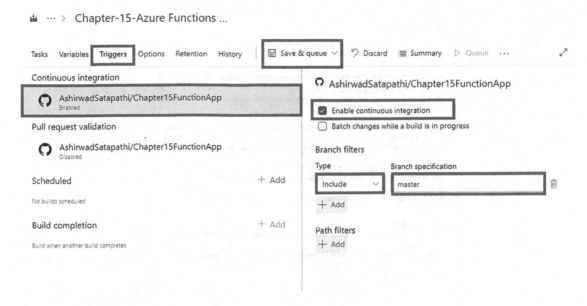

Figure 15-11. *Enable continuous integration*

You will see a dialog to enter some information and make any changes to existing configurations before starting the build process. You can add a comment here, but it is completely optional. After entering the required information or changing any of the configuration details as required, click "Save and run" to start the build process. See Figure 15-12.

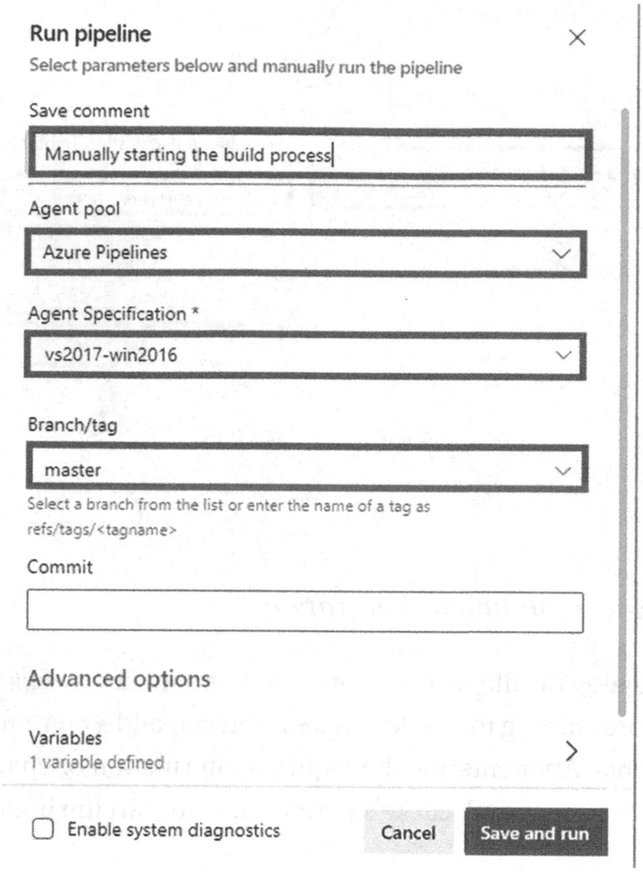

Figure 15-12. *Click "Save and run"*

The build pipeline will be in the queue for some time and should start as soon as a build agent is available. To review each of the tasks of the build and look at the logs associated with each task, click "Agent job 1." See Figure 15-13.

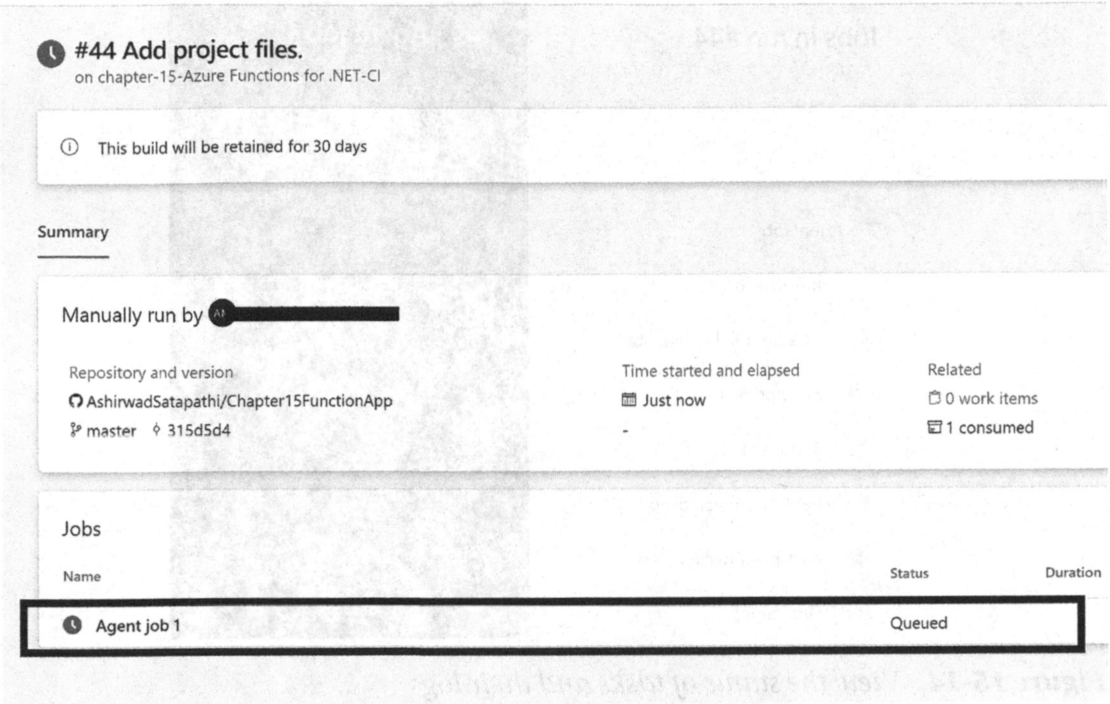

🕐 **#44 Add project files.**
on chapter-15-Azure Functions for .NET-CI

ⓘ   This build will be retained for 30 days

Summary

Manually run by

Repository and version	Time started and elapsed	Related
○ AshirwadSatapathi/Chapter15FunctionApp	📅 Just now	🗂 0 work items
⑂ master ◇ 315d5d4	-	📇 1 consumed

Jobs

Name	Status	Duration
🕐 Agent job 1	Queued	

Figure 15-13.   Click "Agent job 1"

On this screen, you can view the status of each task as well as look at the logs associated with each of the them by clicking them. Once all the tasks have completed successfully, you will see a green check mark for all of them. See Figure 15-14.

Figure 15-14. *View the status of tasks and their logs*

In this section, you created a build pipeline and enabled continuous integrations. Now every time a change happens in your repository, the build process will be initiated without any human intervention, thus automating the build process. But you have only generated the build package and published the build artifact. You need to deploy the build package to your function app.

Create a Release Pipeline in Azure DevOps and Enable Continuous Delivery

To deploy the function project by using the build package generated by the build pipeline, you need to create a release pipeline.

To create a release pipeline, go to Pipelines, click Releases and then click "New pipeline." See Figure 15-15.

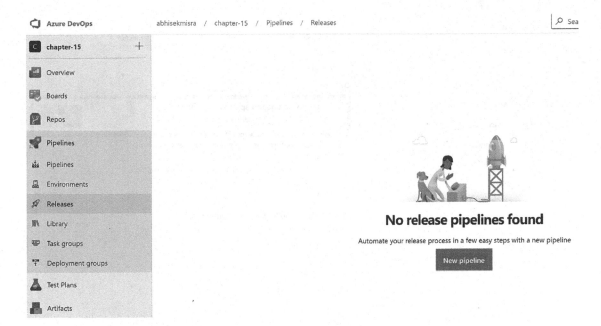

Figure 15-15. *Create a new release pipeline*

You will be prompted to select the template type. Since you want to deploy a function project, search for *function*, select "Deploy a function app to Azure functions," and click Apply. This will populate a set of tasks required to deploy out of the box. See Figure 15-16.

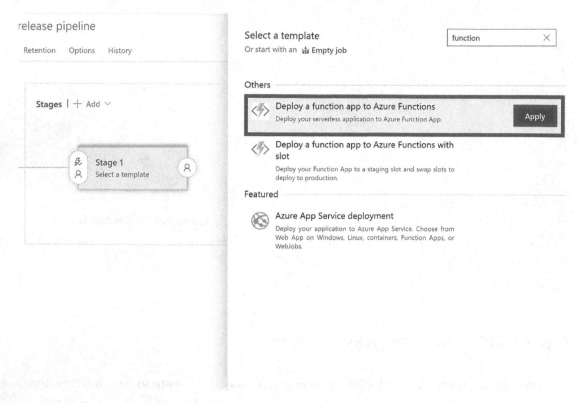

Figure 15-16. *Select a template*

You have to give this stage a name. Since you have only one function app in this case, let's name it **Production**. Depending on the solution, there can be multiple stages in a release pipeline. See Figure 15-17.

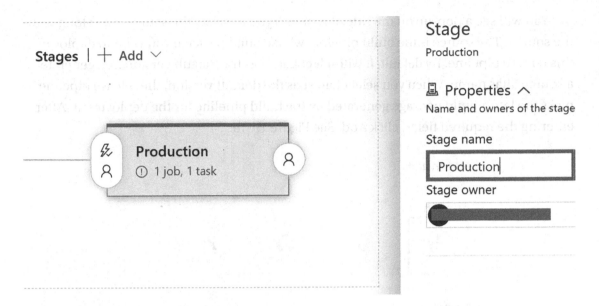

Figure 15-17. *Enter a name for the stage*

As you have already selected the template type as well as named the stage, let's add the artifact. Click + Add or "+ Add an artifact" to do so. There can be multiple artifacts in a release pipeline. See Figure 15-18.

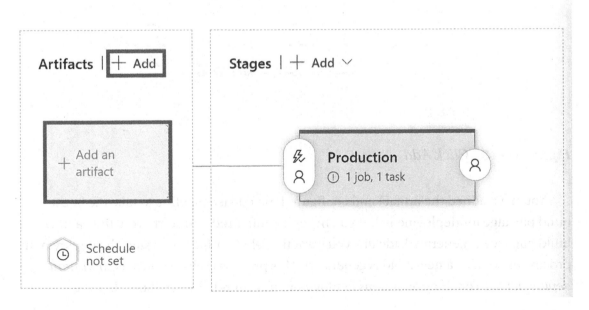

Figure 15-18. *Add an artifact to the release pipeline*

You will see a pop-up on the side; it requests you to select the source type along with the source. The source is the build pipeline whose build package you want to deploy in this release pipeline. By default, it will select Latest as the default version and generate a source alias name. When you select Latest as the default version, the release pipeline picks the latest build package generated by the build pipeline for the deployment. After entering the required fields, click Add. See Figure 15-19.

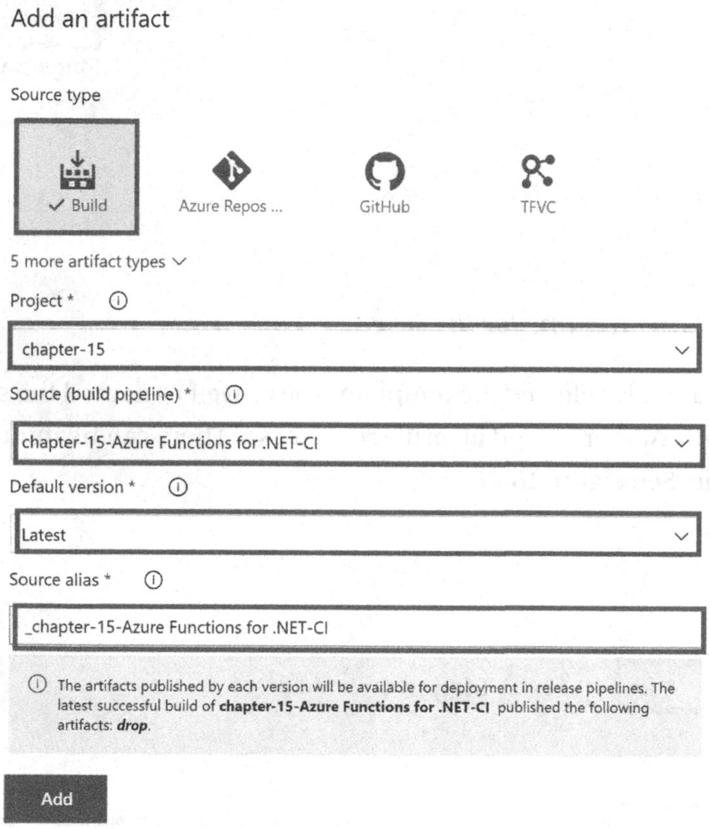

Add an artifact

Source type

5 more artifact types ∨

Project *   ⓘ

chapter-15

Source (build pipeline) *   ⓘ

chapter-15-Azure Functions for .NET-CI

Default version *   ⓘ

Latest

Source alias *   ⓘ

_chapter-15-Azure Functions for .NET-CI

ⓘ The artifacts published by each version will be available for deployment in release pipelines. The latest successful build of **chapter-15-Azure Functions for .NET-CI** published the following artifacts: *drop*.

Add

Figure 15-19. Click Add

You have added the artifact and configured the release pipeline to take the latest build package for deployment, but you haven't configured it to start every time a new build package is generated. Ideally, you want the release pipeline to start the deployment process as soon as a new build is generated. This process is also known as *continuous deployment.* To enable continuous deployment in your release pipeline, click the thunderbolt icon highlighted in Figure 15-20. Now you will see a pop-up on the side. You need to toggle the Enabled button to set the continuous deployment trigger to on. This will enable continuous integration support in your release pipeline. See Figure 15-20.

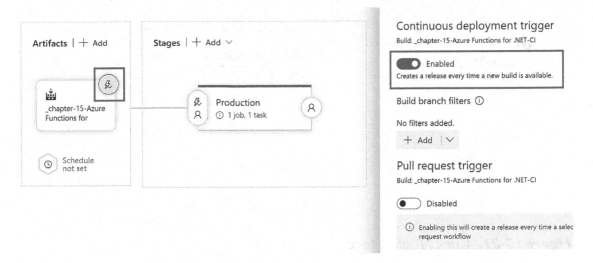

Figure 15-20. *Enable a continuous deployment trigger*

Note   In addition to providing a mechanism to add continuous deployments, Azure DevOps provides a way to have predeployment conditions such as setting predeployment approval for each stage for certain users. This is a useful feature.

You have added the artifact, selected the template for the stage, and configured continuous deployment for the release pipeline, but you haven't yet configured the agent job and task. To do so, click "1 job, 1 task," as highlighted in Figure 15-21.

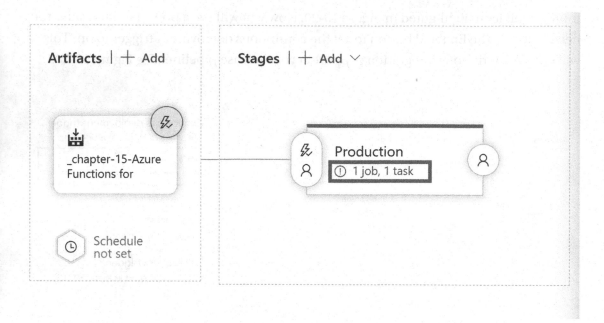

Figure 15-21. Click "1 job, 1 task"

When you have selected the template as "Deploy a function app to Azure functions," it will add the Deploy Azure Function App task to your agent, but you will have to configure the parameters. You need to select the Azure subscription and authorize the release pipeline to access all the resources present in the subscription. Now you need to select Function App on Windows for the app type and select funcchapter15 as the app service name, which is the function app you created at the beginning of this chapter. After filling in the required fields, click Save to save the changes made. See Figure 15-22.

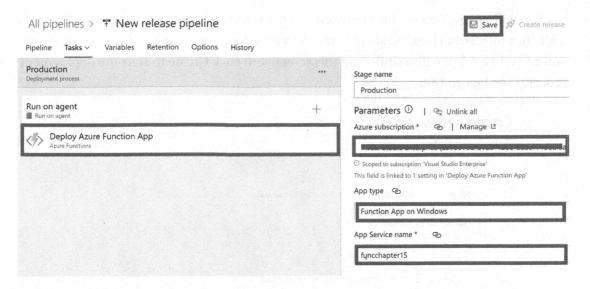

Figure 15-22. *Configure the task and save the changes*

Click "Create release" to start the deployment process. See Figure 15-23.

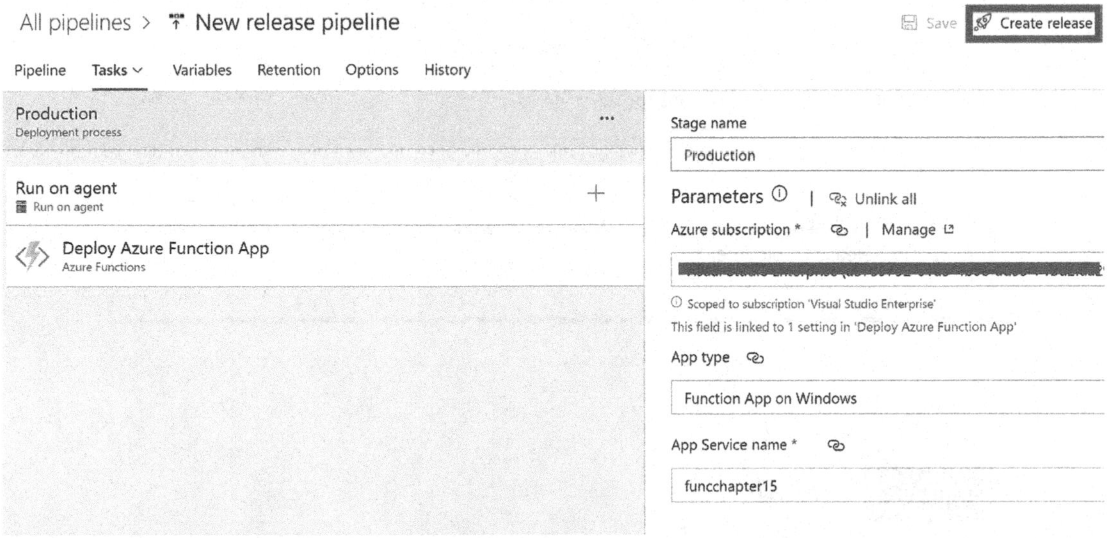

Figure 15-23. *Click "Create release"*

You will be prompted with a new screen where you will see the details associated with your release such as the stage name as well as the source alias name of the artifact. You can add a release description on this screen and click Create to start the deployment process. See Figure 15-24.

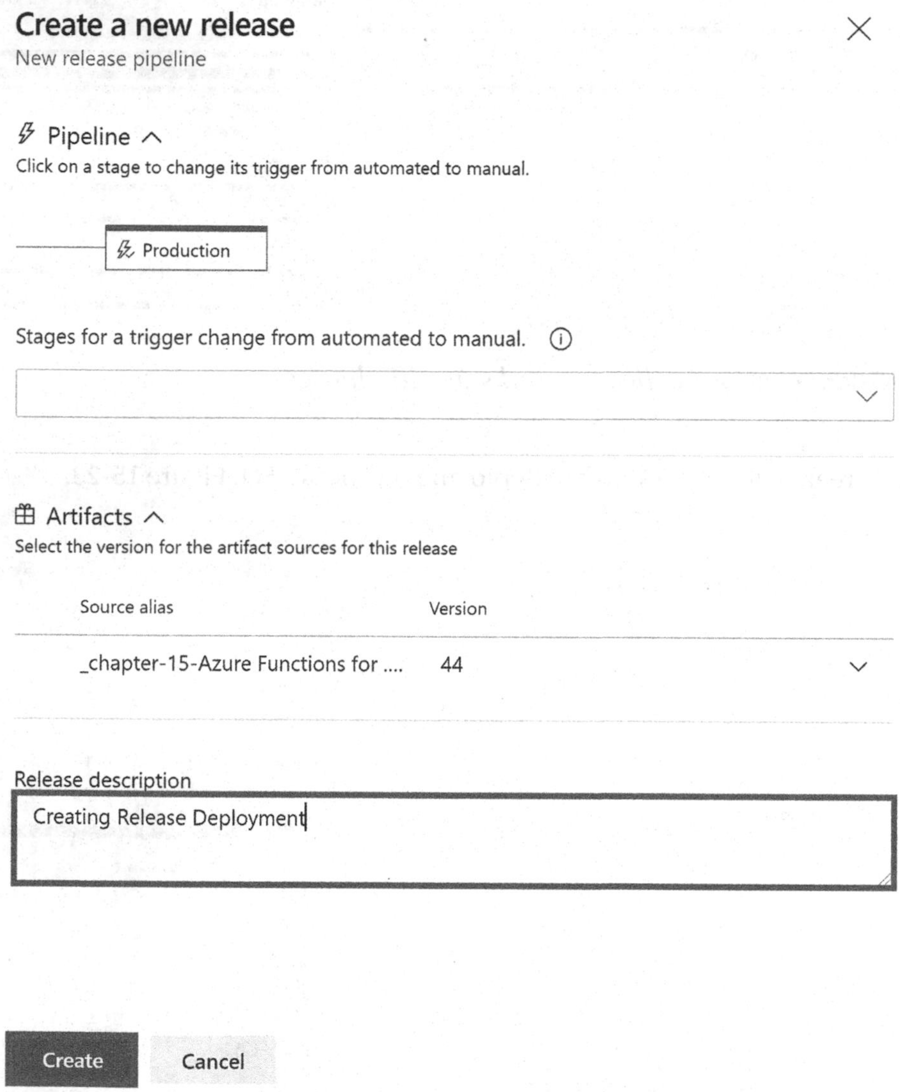

Create a new release   ✕
New release pipeline

⚡ Pipeline ∧
Click on a stage to change its trigger from automated to manual.

⎯⎯⎯⎯⎯⎯⎯⎯⎯⎯┌──────────────────┐
          │ ⚡ Production   │
          └──────────────────┘

Stages for a trigger change from automated to manual.   ⓘ

┌──┐
│   ⌄ │
└──┘

⊞ Artifacts ∧
Select the version for the artifact sources for this release

Source alias	Version
_chapter-15-Azure Functions for	44	⌄

Release description
┌──┐
│ Creating Release Deployment   │
│   │
│   │
└──┘

┌────────────┐
│   Create   │   Cancel
└────────────┘

Figure 15-24. *Click Create to start the deployment process*

To view the deployment status, click Release-1, as highlighted in Figure 15-25.

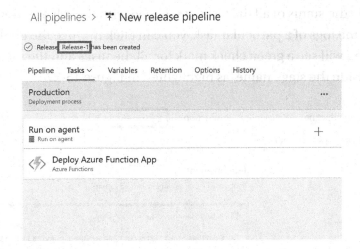

Figure 15-25. *Click Release-1*

On this screen, you can view the deployment status of the stage. To view the status of the tasks and their logs, you need to click Logs, as highlighted in Figure 15-26.

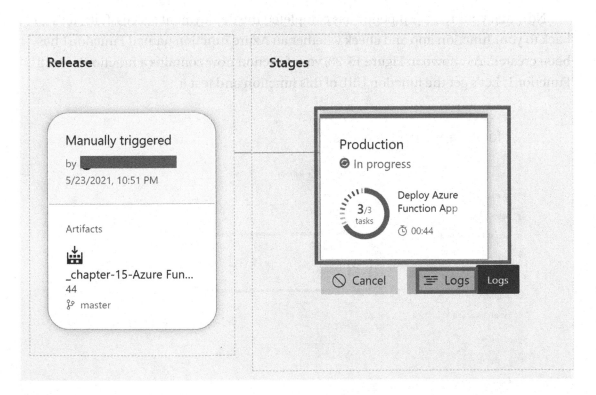

Figure 15-26. *Click Logs*

You can view the status of all the tasks associated with the release pipeline on this screen. To view the logs of a particular task, you can click it. Once the deployment is completed, you will see a green check mark for all the tasks and the message "Succeeded" beside the stage name, as highlighted in Figure 15-27.

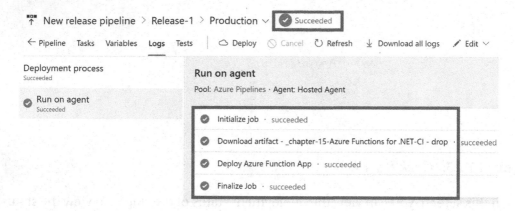

Figure 15-27.   View the deployment status

Now that your release pipeline has completed the deployment successfully, let's go back to your function app and check whether an Azure function named Function1 has been created. As shown in Figure 15-28, your function now contains a function named Function1. Let's get the function URL of this function and test it.

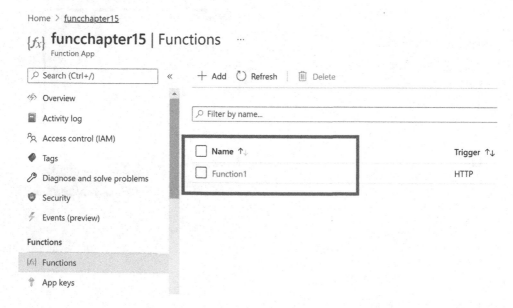

Figure 15-28.   Check the functions present in the function app

Open the web browser and paste the function URL along with the query string ?name=ashirwad to test the function. As shown in the response, your function was successfully deployed to the function app and is running as expected. See Figure 15-29.

Figure 15-29. *Response returned from the function*

Summary

In this chapter, you learned about Azure DevOps and the suite of services it offers briefly. You explored ways to create a build and release pipeline including creating a build package of your function project in the GitHub repository. You also learned how to deploy it to an existing function app. In addition, we discussed ways to build and release pipelines with continuous integration and continuous delivery/deployment. The objective of this chapter was to explore ways to deploy functions using CI/CD pipelines using Azure DevOps, but don't think that just using Azure DevOps means you are following DevOps. As Donovan Brown says, DevOps is the union of people, process, and products to enable the continuous delivery of value to your end users. Azure DevOps is simply a DevOps tool that helps in different phases of the application development cycle, and using any tool doesn't mean you are practicing DevOps.

In the next chapter, you will explore ways to deploy and run your function apps in containers.

CHAPTER 16

Running Azure Functions in Containers

Containers are a popular hosting choice for many applications because they are based on modern architecture principles. You can package your application and all its hosting dependencies in a container and run the container on the target platform. This makes your deployments portable. You can build a strategy to reuse a container across multiple environments with ease by externalizing the environment-based configurations. You can save a lot of time setting up the hosting environment for your application using a container approach. Using Kubernetes-based Event-Driven Autoscaling (KEDA), you can run your Azure functions as containers in an Azure Kubernetes Service (AKS) cluster.

In the previous chapter, you learned how to implement continuous integration (CI) and continuous deployment (CD) using Azure Pipelines for Azure Functions. In this chapter, you will learn how to containerize an Azure function and run it in AKS using KEDA.

Structure of the Chapter

In this chapter, you will explore the following aspects of Azure Functions and KEDA:

- Getting started with containers and AKS

- What serverless Kubernetes and KEDA in Azure are

- Containerizing Azure functions and pushing them to an Azure container registry

- Deploying the containerized Azure function in AKS using KEDA

© Ashirwad Satapathi and Abhishek Mishra 2021
A. Satapathi and A. Mishra, *Hands-on Azure Functions with C#*, https://doi.org/10.1007/978-1-4842-7122-3_16

Objectives

After studying this chapter, you will be able to do the following:

- Understand AKS and containers

- Containerize and run Azure functions in AKS using KEDA

Getting Started with Containers and AKS

You may choose to host your application on a physical server or on a virtual machine in the target environment. In either case, you will spend a considerable amount of effort installing and configuring the hosting environment for the application. Once the hosting environment is up and running, you again will spend a good amount of effort setting up your application and its dependencies. You will repeat the same set of steps when you need to host the application in another environment. Containers can be an excellent and intelligent hosting mechanism here. You can build your code, package the hosting environment and application, and package all the dependencies in a container. You need to run the container in the target environment without setting up the hosting environment for the application. This hosting approach saves a lot of time and effort and is quite popular among developers.

Containers are highly portable. You can build the application container image and keep it in a container registry. A container registry is a collection of container images. In the target environment, you need to pull the container image from the container registry and execute the container image as a container. Once the container starts up, you can access the environment. You may choose to externalize the configuration settings for your application and set them up depending on the target environment.

Containers are an operating system–level virtualization. In the target environment where the container runs, you need to install a container engine. Docker is an example of a container engine. The other popular examples of container engines available are Containerd, CRI-O, and Mesos. The container engine virtualizes the underlying operating system and runs the containers as operating system–level threads. Containers do not need an operating system (OS) of their own, because they run on top of the operating system that gets virtualized by the container engine. In virtual machines (VMs), the underlying hardware infrastructure is virtualized by virtualization software like Hyper-V, and the virtual machines run on top of the virtualized environment.

The virtual machines must have an operating system of their own, and hence the virtual machines are heavier than containers.

In a production scenario, your application will comprise loosely coupled components or services, and you may choose to host each of these services in a container. For example, say your application has a user interface component, a business layer component, and a data access component. You have designed these components to be loosely coupled. Your application will have three containers hosting each of these components. For complex applications, you may have more components or services, so the number of containers will be higher. You need to manage each of these containers so that they are highly available, scale independently, are fault-tolerant, and should be able to communicate among themselves securely. You need a solution to orchestrate these containers and manage them on your behalf. Container orchestrator solutions like Docker Swarm or Kubernetes can help here. Kubernetes is an open source container orchestrator solution developed by Google. It consists of a master node, called Control Plane, and child nodes where your application containers run inside pods. You plan the number of pods needed to run your container, the container images that the containers will use, and other such details and then instruct the Control Plane node to schedule and execute the application containers in the child nodes. The Control Plane node runs these containers inside the pods in the nodes based on your plan. The pods can run a single container in most cases and can also run multiple containers in complex scenarios. The Control Plane node makes sure that the containers running inside the pods are highly available and are fault tolerant.

You can plan a set of pods running identical containers in a replica set. A replica set is a group of identical pods. Each of the pods in the replica set is called a *replica*. You can define the number of pods running identical containers or replicas in the node. If one replica goes down or crashes, the Control Plane node spins up another replica. It makes sure that the number of pods running identical containers or replicas is always maintained in the replica set. This mechanism guarantees high availability and makes your application fault tolerant from an infrastructure perspective. These identical pods can scale independently based on the incoming requests. You can also scale the nodes.

Setting up a Kubernetes cluster is cumbersome and needs much effort. Once the cluster is set up, you need to keep the Control Plane node operational and manage all infrastructure aspects for the Control Plane node. It takes a reasonable amount of time to create a Kubernetes cluster. Azure provides a managed Kubernetes solution called Azure Kubernetes Service. AKS abstracts the underlying infrastructure for the Control

Plane and manages all the infrastructure and operational aspects on your behalf. You need to manage the nodes where the application will run. The nodes are usually virtual machines in the case of AKS. You do not have any control over the Control Plane, and the underlying Azure infrastructure entirely manages it. In the case of AKS, you can create a managed Kubernetes cluster in minutes.

Note   Containers are operating system–level virtualizations and are lightweight. You can package your application along with the hosting environment and run it in the target environment. Kubernetes orchestrates and manages the application containers. Kubernetes consists of the master node called Control Plane that controls the child nodes running the application container. AKS is a managed Kubernetes offering on Azure and abstracts the Control Plane from you.

What Is Serverless Kubernetes and KEDA in Azure?

AKS uses virtual machines as nodes and runs the application containers inside pods in the virtual machines. It provides an excellent scaling mechanism where additional virtual machines get added when the number of incoming requests increases, and the extra virtual machines get decommissioned when the number of incoming requests decreases. However, it takes some time for the virtual machines to spin up and be ready to serve the requests. The incoming traffic surge does not get addressed immediately. Hence, there is a delay in managing the additional incoming requests. You can use serverless nodes where Azure container instances are used as nodes instead of virtual machines to handle such scenarios. Azure container instances can spin up very fast and instantly start serving the additional incoming requests without adding any delays. Your nodes can scale rapidly and add many additional nodes in no time when Azure container instances are used as nodes. These serverless nodes use the virtual Kubelet technology and use Azure container instances as nodes in the Kubernetes cluster. Azure container instances are much cheaper than virtual machines, and you save a lot of money when you use serverless nodes.

You can containerize the Azure functions and run them in the AKS cluster using KEDA. This mechanism brings a true serverless experience to the AKS. These containerized functions can run both on virtual machines and on Azure container instances–based nodes. The Azure Functions runtime executes the application code for the functions, and the scaling is taken care of by the KEDA component. The KEDA component does the job of the Azure function scale controller.

Note   Virtual Kubelet helps you run your containerized application on Azure container instances in the AKS cluster. KEDA helps you run your containerized Azure functions on the AKS cluster.

Containerize Azure Functions and Push Them to the Azure Container Registry

Now let's containerize an Azure function and push it to the Azure container registry. Once you have the Azure function container image in the Azure container registry, you can run it in the AKS cluster.

As a prerequisite, you should have the following installed on your local system. You can read the official documentation for these tools available on their websites if you need more information.

- Azure CLI

- Azure Functions Core Tools

- Kubectl

- Docker Desktop

Let's create an Azure container registry where you can push the containerized function image. Go to the Azure portal and click "Create a resource." See Figure 16-1.

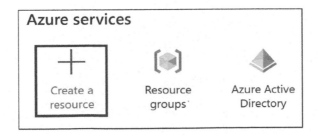

Figure 16-1. *Click "Create a resource"*

Click the Containers tab and then click Containers Registry. See Figure 16-2.

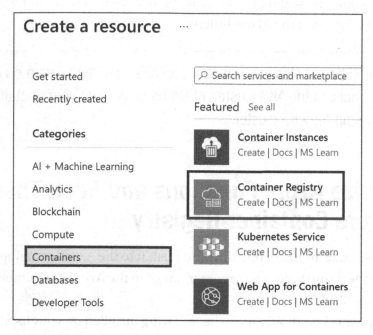

Figure 16-2. *Click Container Registry*

Provide the subscription details, resource group, name, location, and pricing tier for the Azure container registry. Click "Review + create." See Figure 16-3.

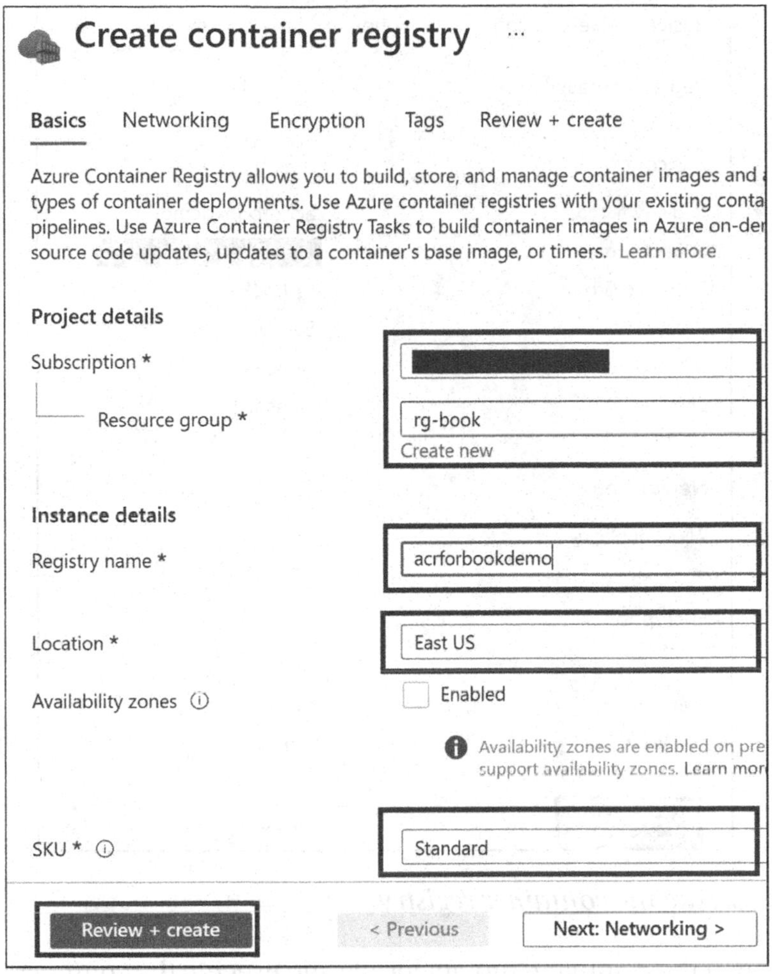

Figure 16-3. *Provide the basic details for the container registry*

Click Create. This action will spin up the Azure container registry. See Figure 16-4.

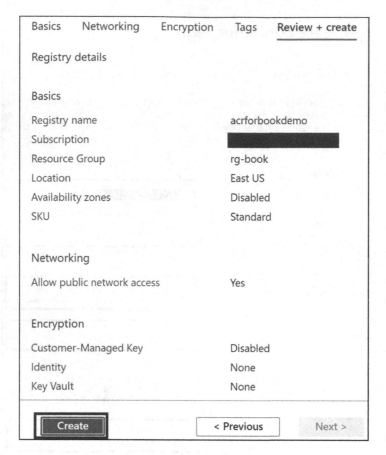

Figure 16-4. *Create the container registry*

Now let's open the command prompt locally and execute the command in Listing 16-1 to initialize the creation of a .NET Core–based Azure Functions App Service that can run in a Docker container.

Listing 16-1. Create Function App Service

```
func init . --docker
```

You will be prompted to select a worker runtime environment for the Azure function. Select dotnet.

Execute the command shown in Listing 16-2 to create an HTTP-triggered function in the Azure Functions service. Select "Http trigger" when prompted to select the trigger template for the Azure function. Provide the name of the function when prompted.

Listing 16-2. Create an HTTP-Triggered Function

```
func new
```

When the command in Listing 16-2 completes successfully, the HTTP-triggered Azure function gets generated. Now let's containerize the default Azure function that was generated without modifying any code. Execute the command in Listing 16-3. You are creating a container image named keda_func with the image tag as latest.

Listing 16-3. Build the Container Image for the Azure Function

```
docker build -t keda_func:latest .
```

Now let's run the container image you created locally using the command in Listing 16-4. The container will run on port 8080. The docker run command executes the container image. The --publish option specifies that port 8080 of the local system, where you are running the docker run command, gets mapped to port 80 of the executing container. The --detach option specifies that the container image runs in the background, and the --name option specifies the name of the executing container.

Listing 16-4. Run the Container Image for the Azure Function Locally

```
docker run --publish 8080:80 --detach --name keda_func keda_func:latest
```

Let's browse the function app running inside the container using the following URL:

```
http://localhost:8080/
```

See Figure 16-5.

Figure 16-5. *Azure function running inside the container*

Now let's push the containerized Azure function to the Azure container registry. You need the admin credentials for the Azure container registry. Go to the Azure container registry you created in the Azure portal. Click the "Access keys" tab. Enable the admin user and copy the username and the password. See Figure 16-6.

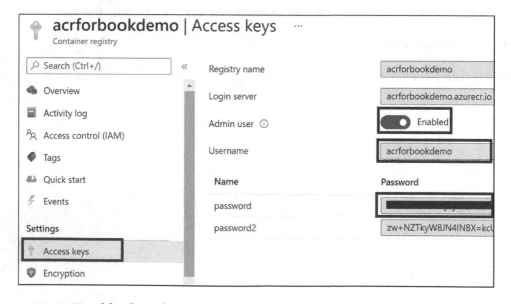

Figure 16-6. *Enable the admin user for the Azure container registry*

Now let's execute the Docker command in Listing 16-5 and provide the admin credentials for the Azure container registry when prompted. Replace {ACR} with the name of the Azure container registry in the command.

Listing 16-5. Authenticate with the Azure Container Registry

```
docker login {ACR}.azurecr.io
```

Execute the command in Listing 16-6 to tag the container image to the Azure container registry. Replace {ACR} with the name of the Azure container registry. The keda_func value is the name of the container image you created earlier for the Azure function app.

Listing 16-6. Tag the Azure Function Container Image with the Azure Container Registry

```
docker tag keda_func:latest {ACR}.azurecr.io/keda_func:latest
```

Now let's push the container image to the Azure container registry using the command in Listing 16-7. Replace {ACR} with the name of the Azure container registry.

Listing 16-7. Push the Container Image to the Azure Container Registry

```
docker push {ACR}.azurecr.io/keda_func:latest
```

Go back to the Azure container registry in the Azure portal. Click the Repositories tab, and you will see the Azure function container image there. See Figure 16-7.

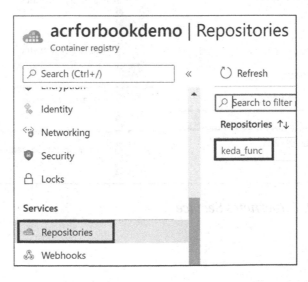

Figure 16-7. *Azure function container image in the Azure container registry*

Deploy the Containerized Azure Functions in AKS Using KEDA

Now let's create an AKS instance and run the containerized Azure function on it. Go to the Azure portal and click "Create a resource." See Figure 16-8.

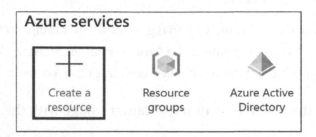

Figure 16-8. *Create a new resource*

Click the Containers tab and then click Kubernetes Service. See Figure 16-9.

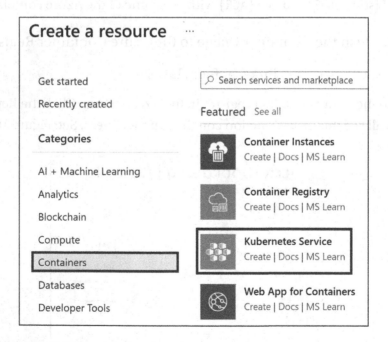

Figure 16-9. *Click Kubernetes Service*

Provide the subscription, resource group, name, location, and other necessary basic details for the Azure Kubernetes Service instance. Provide 1 as the number of nodes. See Figure 16-10.

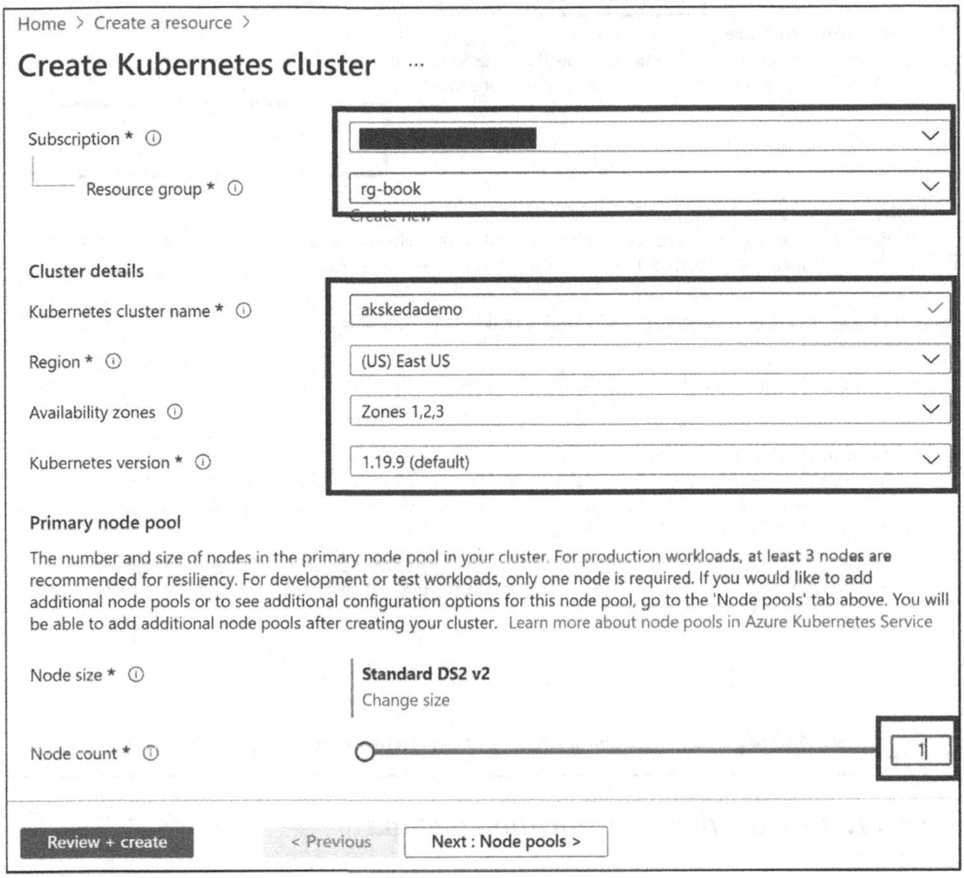

Figure 16-10. *Provide the basic details to AKS*

Go to the Authentication tab and select "System-assigned managed identity" as the authentication method. You need to integrate the Azure container registry that you created earlier with AKS. You can do this integration in the portal if you select "System-assigned managed identity" as the authentication method. See Figure 16-11.

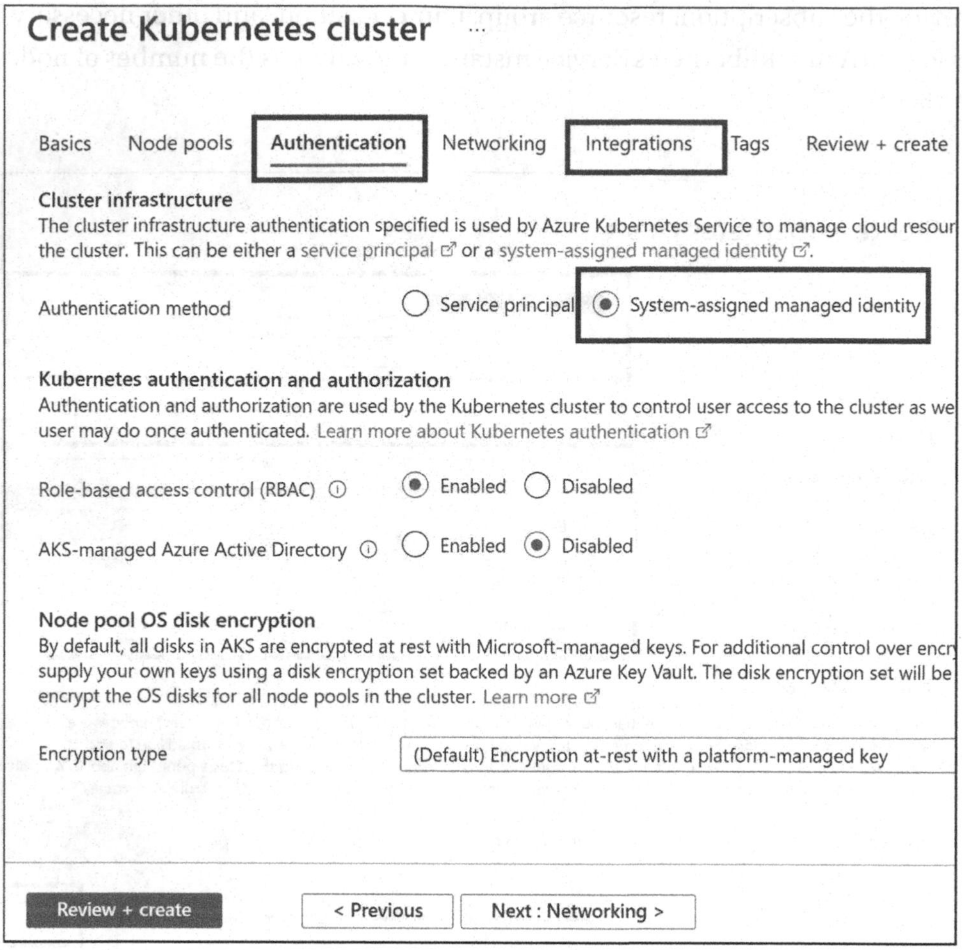

Create Kubernetes cluster   ···

Basics   Node pools   **Authentication**   Networking   Integrations   Tags   Review + create

Cluster infrastructure
The cluster infrastructure authentication specified is used by Azure Kubernetes Service to manage cloud resour
the cluster. This can be either a service principal ☐ or a system-assigned managed identity ☐.

Authentication method   ○ Service principal   ● System-assigned managed identity

Kubernetes authentication and authorization
Authentication and authorization are used by the Kubernetes cluster to control user access to the cluster as we
user may do once authenticated. Learn more about Kubernetes authentication ☐

Role-based access control (RBAC) ⓘ   ● Enabled   ○ Disabled

AKS-managed Azure Active Directory ⓘ   ○ Enabled   ● Disabled

Node pool OS disk encryption
By default, all disks in AKS are encrypted at rest with Microsoft-managed keys. For additional control over encr
supply your own keys using a disk encryption set backed by an Azure Key Vault. The disk encryption set will be
encrypt the OS disks for all node pools in the cluster. Learn more ☐

Encryption type   (Default) Encryption at-rest with a platform-managed key

| Review + create | | < Previous | Next : Networking > |

Figure 16-11. *Provide the authentication method*

Go to the Integrations tab and select the Azure container registry created earlier.
Click "Review + create." See Figure 16-12.

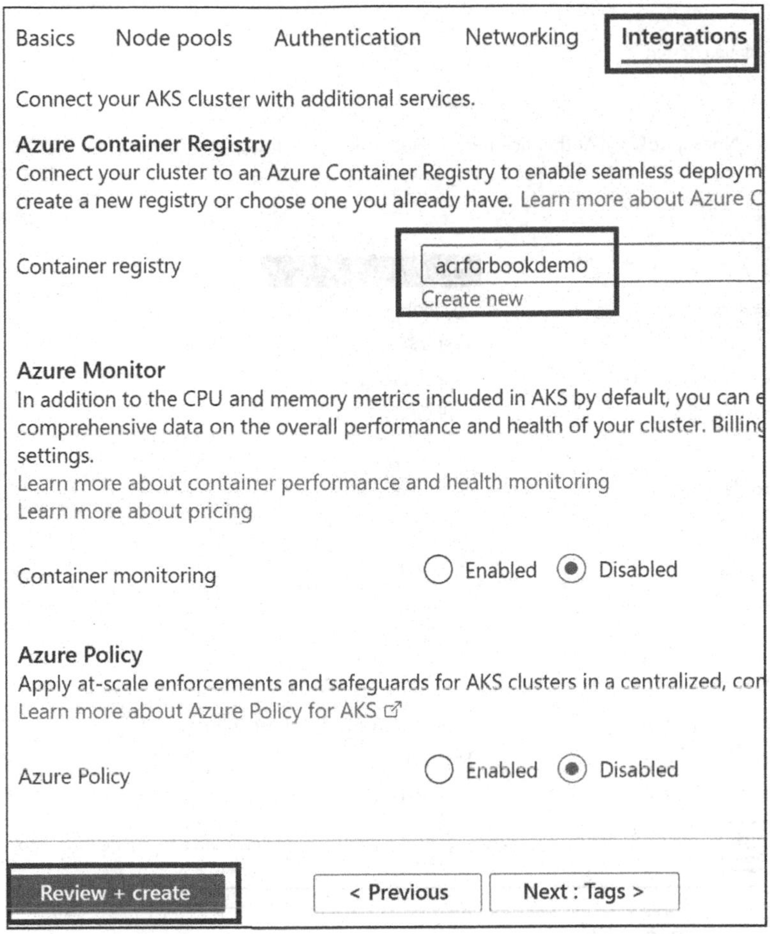

Basics   Node pools   Authentication   Networking   Integrations

Connect your AKS cluster with additional services.

Azure Container Registry
Connect your cluster to an Azure Container Registry to enable seamless deploym
create a new registry or choose one you already have. Learn more about Azure C

Container registry   acrforbookdemo
                        Create new

Azure Monitor
In addition to the CPU and memory metrics included in AKS by default, you can e
comprehensive data on the overall performance and health of your cluster. Billinç
settings.
Learn more about container performance and health monitoring
Learn more about pricing

Container monitoring   ○ Enabled ⦿ Disabled

Azure Policy
Apply at-scale enforcements and safeguards for AKS clusters in a centralized, cor
Learn more about Azure Policy for AKS ⌕

Azure Policy   ○ Enabled ⦿ Disabled

[Review + create]   [< Previous] [Next : Tags >]

Figure 16-12. *Select the Azure container registry*

Click Create. This action will spin up AKS. See Figure 16-13.

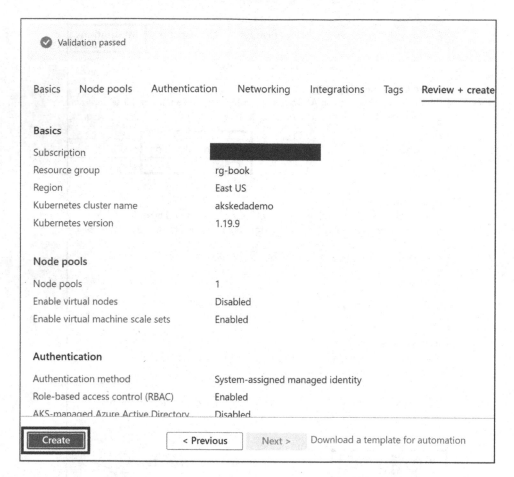

Figure 16-13. *Create AKS*

Once the Azure Kubernetes Service instance gets created, go to the command prompt on your local system and log in to Azure. Provide your Azure credentials when prompted. See Listing 16-8.

Listing 16-8. Log In to the Azure Kubernetes Service Instance

```
az login
```

Execute the command in Listing 16-9 to authenticate with the Azure Kubernetes Service instance that you created. Replace {AKS Name} with the name of the Azure Kubernetes Service instance that you created, and replace {Resource Group} with the name of the Azure Kubernetes Service resource group.

Listing 16-9. Authenticate with Azure Kubernetes Service

```
az aks get-credentials --resource-group "{Resource Group}" --name
"{AKS Name}"
```

Execute the command in Listing 16-10 to generate the deployment YAML file that you will use to deploy the containerized Azure function to Azure Kubernetes Service. Replace {ACR} with the name of the Azure container registry where you pushed the container image earlier.

Listing 16-10. Generate the Kubernetes Deployment YAML File

```
func kubernetes deploy --name "kedafunc" --image-name "{ACR}.azurecr.io/
keda_func:latest" --dry-run > deploy.yaml
```

A `deploy.yaml` file will get generated that you can apply to the Kubernetes cluster using the command in Listing 16-11.

Listing 16-11. Apply the Generated YAML to the Kubernetes Cluster

```
kubectl apply -f deployfunc.yaml
```

You can verify if the pod hosting the Azure function container is up and running using the command in Listing 16-12. See Figure 16-14.

Listing 16-12. Verify Whether the Pod Is Running

```
kubectl get pods
```

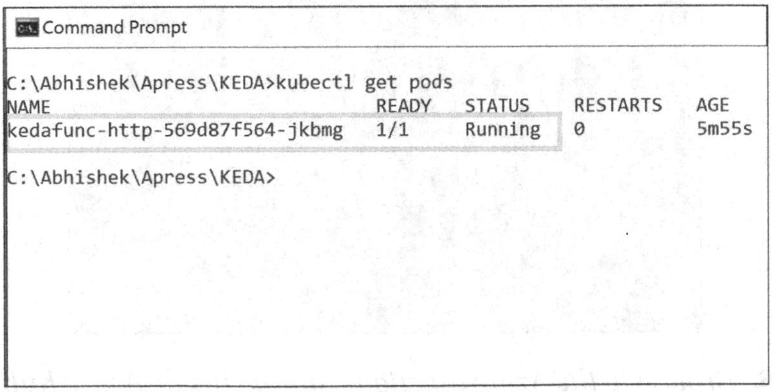

Figure 16-14. *Verify whether the pod is running*

Now let's execute the command in Listing 16-13 to get the external IP address that you can use to browse to the Azure function running inside Azure Kubernetes Service. See Figure 16-15.

Listing 16-13. Get the External IP

```
kubectl get services
```

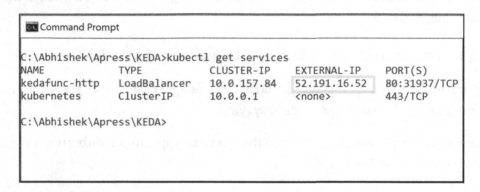

Figure 16-15. *Get the external IP*

Browse to the external IP address. See Figure 16-16.

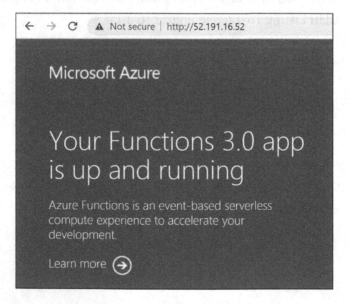

Figure 16-16. *Browse to the Azure function running inside Azure Kubernetes Service*

Summary

In this chapter, you learned how to containerize an Azure function and run it in the Azure Kubernetes Service cluster using KEDA. You explored what containers and Kubernetes are and how they provide modernized hosting support. You learned how to create an Azure container registry, push the containerized Azure function image to the Azure container registry, and run the image in the Azure Kubernetes cluster.

The following are the key takeaways from this chapter:

- You can containerize your application and hosting dependencies and run your application in the target environment.

- Containers are operating system–level virtualization and are lightweight compared to virtual machines.

- Kubernetes orchestrates the containers and manages them.

- You can run the containerized application in the Kubernetes cluster nodes that can be virtual machines or Azure container instances.

- Serverless nodes are Azure container instances that run the application containers.

- KEDA helps you run containerized Azure functions in the Azure Kubernetes Service cluster.

In the next chapter, you will explore how to add cognitive capabilities to Azure Functions.

CHAPTER 17

Adding Cognitive Capabilities to Your Azure Functions

Artificial intelligence has become an important part of modern application development. It has made its mark in every domain one can think of. Almost every app that comes onto the market has an intelligent solution inside it. Apps from simple chat applications to virtual assistants have cognitive capabilities.

In previous chapters, we discussed ways to develop and deploy Azure functions. You explored different bindings and triggers of Azure functions by building applications to solve various use cases. With the knowledge gathered in the previous chapters, you are well equipped to build serverless solutions using Azure functions. In this chapter, you will add one more skill to your arsenal by adding cognitive capabilities to your Azure functions to build intelligent serverless solutions.

You will be leveraging the power of Azure Cognitive Services to build intelligent serverless solutions with Azure Functions. In this chapter, you will learn ways to add cognitive capabilities to your functions with the help of .NET SDKs for Azure Cognitive Services.

Structure of the Chapter

This chapter will explore the following aspects of HTTP triggers and Azure SQL:

- Getting started with Azure Cognitive Services
- Getting started with Azure Text Analytics

421

© Ashirwad Satapathi and Abhishek Mishra 2021
A. Satapathi and A. Mishra, *Hands-on Azure Functions with C#*, https://doi.org/10.1007/978-1-4842-7122-3_17

- Creating a serverless application to analyze feedback using sentiment analysis

- Creating a language-based document classifier serverless solution

Objective

After studying this chapter, you will be able to do the following:

- Create intelligent serverless solutions using the Azure Functions service

- Interact with Azure Cognitive Services from Azure Functions

Getting Started with Azure Cognitive Services

Building intelligent solutions from scratch by leveraging the power of artificial intelligence can require highly skilled employees who have specific expertise, which can be quite expensive. Microsoft Azure provides a set of services in Azure Cognitive Services to help you write all algorithms from scratch to add cognitive capabilities to your applications to make them intelligent.

With the help of Azure Cognitive Services, you will make an API call to the appropriate service to embed the desired cognitive capability into your applications. Azure Cognitive Services can also be consumed using the available SDKs.

Azure Cognitive Services offer five main categories of services to help with cognitive tasks.

- *Decision*: With the help of the services in this category, you can enable your application to make smart decisions. Services such as Anomaly Detector, Content Moderator, and Personalizer fall into this category.

- *Language*: With the help of the services in this category, you can power your applications to gather and extract insights from unstructured textual data. Services such as Text Analytics, Immersive Reader, Translator, Language Understanding, and the QnA Maker API all fall into this category.

- *Search*: With the help of the services in this category, you can enable your applications to look out for web pages, images, and news over the Internet. Bing web search falls into this category.

- *Speech*: With the help of the services in this category, you can enable your application to have speech capabilities. Services such as Speech to Text, Text to Speech, Speech Translation, and Speaker Recognition fall into this category.

- *Vision*: With the help of the services in this category, you can process and analyze image- and video-based content. Services such as Computer Vision, Custom Vision, Face, Form Recognizer, and Video Indexer fall into this category.

Azure Cognitive Services helps organizations and developers embrace AI with ease to build intelligent solutions. It provides developers and organizations with the ability to build intelligent solutions in a short time for less money than it would cost otherwise. In this chapter, you will build two intelligent solutions using Azure Cognitive Services and Azure Functions. In the first solution, you will build a serverless API to process, analyze, and predict the sentiment of the feedback. Later, you will create a serverless solution for documents depending on the language they are written in using Azure Text Analytics.

Getting Started with Azure Text Analytics

In a world where almost 6,000 tweets are being tweeted every second, you know that text analytics is an important area of focus. For beginners, text analysis is the process of gathering insights from textual data to make well-informed decisions. For firms, such textual data from various social media sites can help them understand their customers and gather insights to make well-informed decisions by analyzing and processing such data.

Although there are well-established algorithms like naïve Bayes, support vector machines (SVMs), and linear discriminant analysis (LDA) that have been developed over the years in the field of natural language processing (NLP), extensive experience is required to build such algorithms from scratch. Azure Text Analytics allows you to perform text analytics on unstructured data without requiring you to have expertise in the field or worry about which algorithm to use to get the task done.

You can perform the following tasks with the help of the Azure Text Analytics API or the SDKs:

- *Sentiment analysis*: With sentiment analysis, you can find out insights about a person's impression or opinion on a topic or brand from text. Text Analytics classifies text as positive, negative, neutral, or mixed and gives a confidence score.

- *Key phrase extraction*: With key phrase extraction, you can identify the essence of the content or the talking point from the text.

- *Language detection*: With language detection, you can identify the language text was written in. It returns a language code along with the confidence score.

- *Named entity recognition*: With named entity recognition, you can find and identity entities from text. Entities can be a place, organization, or person.

To build a serverless API to perform feedback analysis, you will use the sentiment analysis feature of Azure Text Analytics. To use Azure Text Analytics, you will have to create a Text Analytics resource in Azure and get the API key along with the URL endpoint. In the next section, you will create an Azure Text Analytics service in the Azure portal.

Create an Azure Text Analytics Resource in the Azure Portal

Go to the Azure portal, search for *Cognitive Services* in the search box, and click it. See Figure 17-1.

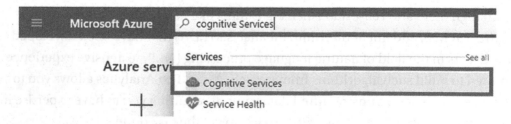

Figure 17-1. *Search for Cognitive Services*

Now Click Create, as highlighted in Figure 17-2. This will pop up a side screen that will redirect you to the Marketplace.

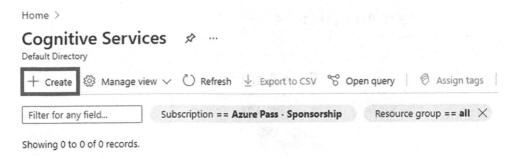

Figure 17-2. *Click Create to go to the Marketplace*

Type **Text Analytics** in the search box and press Enter. Now, select the Text Analytics service offered by Microsoft. See Figure 17-3.

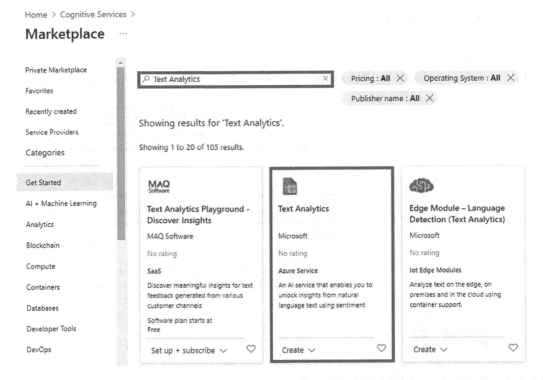

Figure 17-3. *Search for the Text Analytics service in the Marketplace*

Click Create, as shown in Figure 17-4, to create the Text Analytics service.

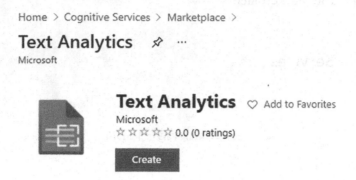

Figure 17-4. *Create the Text Analytics service*

Fill in all the required information. Click "Review + create." See Figure 17-5.

Home > Cognitive Services > Marketplace > Text Analytics >

Create Text Analytics   ...

Project details

Select the subscription to manage deployed resources and costs. Use resource groups like folders to organize and manage all your resources.

Subscription * ⓘ

> Azure Pass - Sponsorship (45abecfd-0e97-4b63-b8e9-9e6863ae01bc) ⌄

└── Resource group * ⓘ

> (New) rg-ch-17 ⌄
> Create new

Instance details

Region * ⓘ

> Central India ⌄

Name * ⓘ

> ta-ch-17

Pricing tier * ⓘ

> Free F0 (5K Transactions per 30 days) ⌄

View full pricing details

| Review + create | < Previous | Next : Virtual network > |

Figure 17-5. *Click "Review + create"*

Note Since you are just learning ways to use the Text Analytics service in your functions, you will be using the free F0 tier in this chapter. With the F0 tier, you can make 5,000 calls each month. But it is advisable to go for a standard plan if you want to use the Text Analytics service for a production-grade application.

Now a validation check will take place on the values you entered in the previous screen. If the validation is successful, you can click Create to create the Text Analytics resource in Azure. See Figure 17-6.

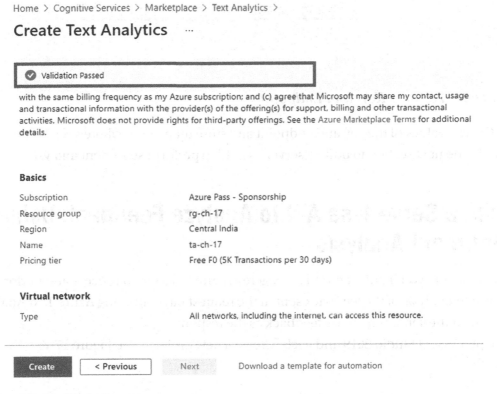

Home > Cognitive Services > Marketplace > Text Analytics >

Create Text Analytics ...

✓ Validation Passed

with the same billing frequency as my Azure subscription; and (c) agree that Microsoft may share my contact, usage and transactional information with the provider(s) of the offering(s) for support, billing and other transactional activities. Microsoft does not provide rights for third-party offerings. See the Azure Marketplace Terms for additional details.

Basics

Subscription	Azure Pass - Sponsorship
Resource group	rg-ch-17
Region	Central India
Name	ta-ch-17
Pricing tier	Free F0 (5K Transactions per 30 days)

Virtual network

Type	All networks, including the internet, can access this resource.

Create | < Previous | Next | Download a template for automation

Figure 17-6. Click Create

After the resource has been created, go to the resource and click Keys and Endpoint in the sidebar of the screen. See Figure 17-7.

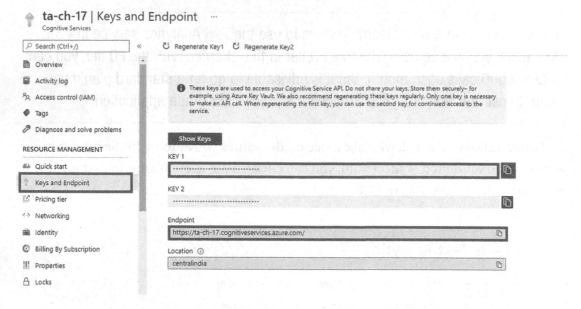

Figure 17-7. Go to Keys and Endpoint

Get the values of the key and endpoint and store them somewhere safe. You will use them in the next section to build a serverless API to perform sentiment analysis.

Build a Serverless API to Analyze Feedback Using Sentiment Analysis

In this section, you'll build an HTTP-triggered Azure function to process and perform sentiment analysis of the feedback sent in the request payload using Azure Text Analytics and return the sentiment of the feedback as the response to the user.

Open Visual Studio 2019 and click "Create a new project." See Figure 17-8.

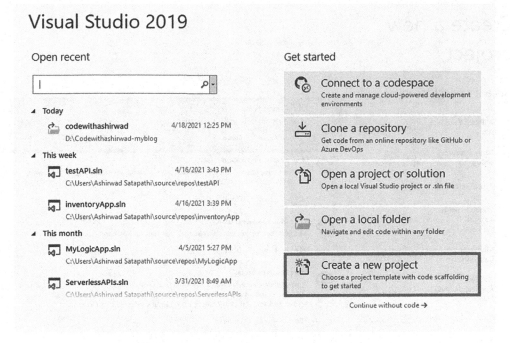

Figure 17-8. *Create a new project in Visual Studio*

Select Azure Functions for the project template and click Next. See Figure 17-9.

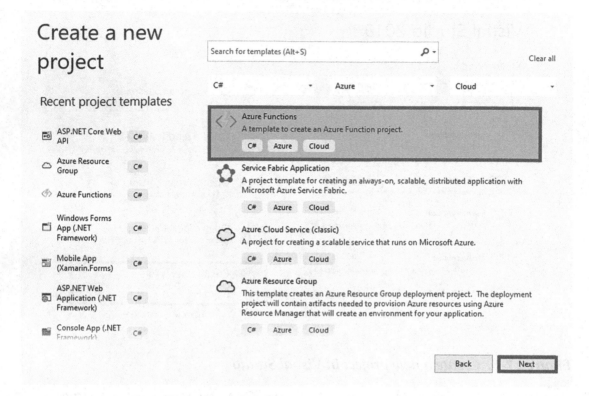

Figure 17-9. *Select Azure Functions as the project template*

Fill in the project name, location, and solution name and click Next. See Figure 17-10.

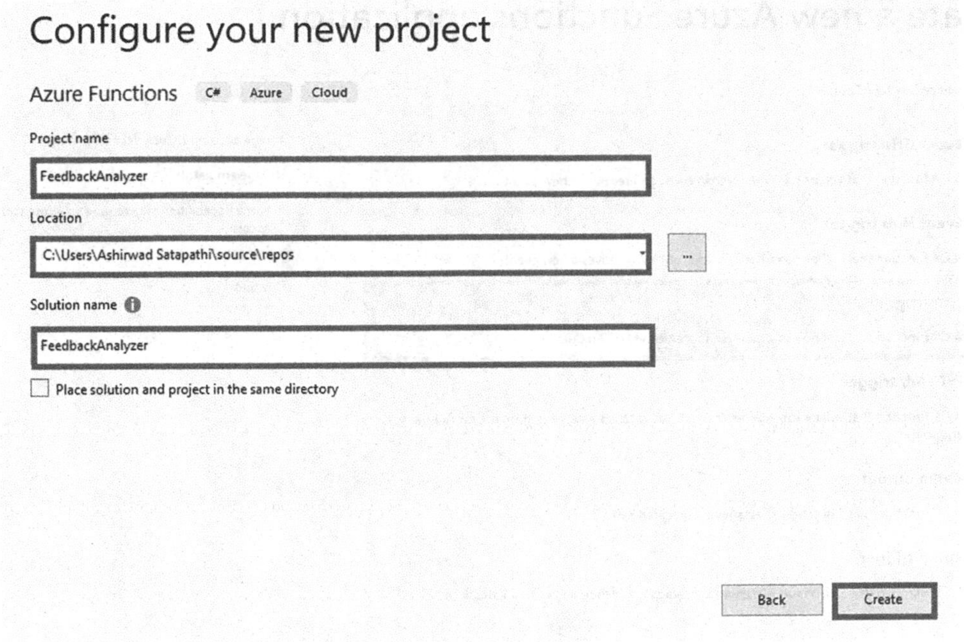

Configure your new project

Azure Functions   C#   Azure   Cloud

Project name

FeedbackAnalyzer

Location

C:\Users\Ashirwad Satapathi\source\repos

Solution name ⓘ

FeedbackAnalyzer

☐ Place solution and project in the same directory

Back   Create

Figure 17-10. *Fill in the project details*

Select "Http trigger" as the trigger type, leave the other default values, and then click Create. See Figure 17-11.

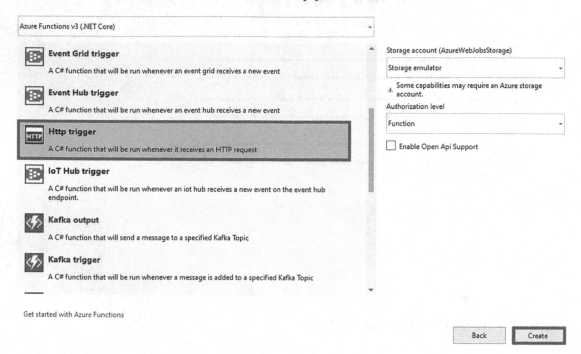

Figure 17-11. *Select "Http trigger" and Azure Functions V3*

Now, Visual Studio will generate an HTTP-triggered function. Let's open the Package Manager Console and type in the command shown in Listing 17-1 to install the Azure Text Analytics SDK. Alternatively, you can install this SDK using the NuGet package manager.

Listing 17-1. Install Azure Text Analytics

```
Install-Package Azure.AI.TextAnalytics -Version 5.0.0
```

Once you have installed the SDK, open the `local.setttings.json` file and add the API key and endpoint of the Text Analytics service as a key-value pair, as shown in Listing 17-2.

Listing 17-2. Add API Key and Endpoint to local.settings.json

```
{
    "IsEncrypted": false,
    "Values": {
      "AzureWebJobsStorage": "UseDevelopmentStorage=true",
```

```
    "FUNCTIONS_WORKER_RUNTIME": "dotnet",
    "api-key": "Enter your API Key",
    "endpoint": "Enter your Endpoint"
  }
}
```

Note Storing function secrets or sensitive information in the `local.settings.json` file or hard-coding such information in a variable is not advisable. We recommend using a key vault to store function secrets.

As you add the API key and URL endpoint and install the Azure Text Analytics SDK, let's create a Plain Old CLR Object (POCO) class named `Payload.cs`. This class will represent the data model of the request payload by deserializing it to later get the feedback sentiment and send the model in the response to the user by updating the `feedbackSentiment` property of the model. See Listing 17-3.

Listing 17-3. Create a POCO Model Called Payload.cs

```
public class Payload
    {
        public string feedback { get; set; }
        public string feedbackSentiment { get; set; }
    }
```

Now that you have created the POCO model and updated the `local.settings.json` file by adding the values of your API key and endpoint as key-value pairs, let's start building the feedback analyzer function. First, you will deserialize the content sent from the user, in the request body, and store it in a variable. Then, you will have to create an object called `client` of the `TextAnalyticsClient` type to use the Azure Text Analytics SDK along with passing the endpoint and API key as parameters. Once we have created the object, let's make a call to the `AnalyzeSentiment` method of the client object by passing the feedback sent in the request payload. The `AnalyzeSentiment` method returns a response of `DocumentSentiment` with different properties such as `sentiment`, `confidence`, and `warning` to name a few. In this case you are using the `Sentiment` property and will assign the value of this sentiment property of the response returned by the AnalyzeSentiment method to the feedbackSentiment property of your POCO model. Finally, you will send an OK response along with the POCO model back to the client. If there are any exceptions, a BadRequest response is returned to the client. See Listing 17-4.

Listing 17-4. Get the Feedback Sentiment

```
using System;
using System.IO;
using System.Threading.Tasks;
using Azure;
using Azure.AI.TextAnalytics;
using Microsoft.AspNetCore.Http;
using Microsoft.AspNetCore.Mvc;
using Microsoft.Azure.WebJobs;
using Microsoft.Azure.WebJobs.Extensions.Http;
using Microsoft.Extensions.Logging;
using Newtonsoft.Json;

namespace FeedbackAnalyzer
{
    public static class FeedbackAnalyzer
    {
        private static readonly AzureKeyCredential credentials = new
        AzureKeyCredential(Environment.GetEnvironmentVariable("api-key"));
        private static readonly Uri endpoint = new Uri(Environment.GetEnvir
        onmentVariable("endpoint"));
        private static TextAnalyticsClient client = new
        TextAnalyticsClient(endpoint, credentials);

        [FunctionName("FeedbackAnalyzer")]
        public static async Task<IActionResult> Run(
            [HttpTrigger(AuthorizationLevel.Function, "get", "post",
            Route = null)] HttpRequest req,
            ILogger log)
```

```
{
    try
    {
        string requestBody = await new StreamReader(req.Body).
        ReadToEndAsync();
        var data = JsonConvert.DeserializeObject<Payload>(requestB
        ody);
        data.feedbackSentiment = client.AnalyzeSentiment(data.
        feedback).Value.Sentiment.ToString();
        return new OkObjectResult(data);
    }
    catch (Exception ex) {
        return new BadRequestObjectResult(ex.Message);
    }
}
}
}
```

Note   We created a static client object of type `TextAnalyticsClient`, as this allows us to reuse the client object in different function invocations, instead of creating a new object for every invocation.

Test the FeedbackAnalyzer Function Using Postman

Let's run the function project and start the Azure Functions Core Tools to test your Feedback Analyzer function and copy the function endpoint. See Figure 17-12.

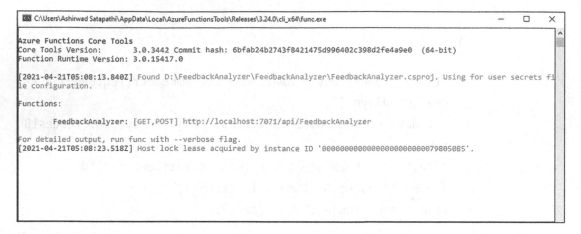

Figure 17-12. *Get the URL endpoint of the FeedbackAnalyzer function*

You will be using Postman to test the FeedbackAnalyzer API by using the URL endpoint of the function. Let's open Postman, one of leading collaboration platforms for API development. Create a new collection and add a request to it to test the HTTP-triggered Azure function you created in the previous section. Pass the value of the feedback in the request body and click Send to invoke the FeedbackAnalyzer function and get the response. See Figure 17-13.

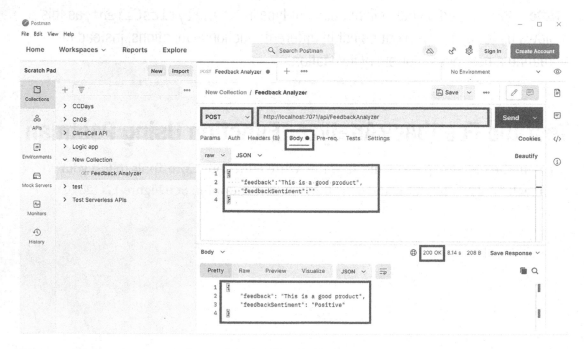

Figure 17-13. *Response from the FeedbackAnalyzer API*

As shown in Figure 17-14, you get an OK response from the FeedbackAnalyzer API along with the feedback and feedback sentiment in the response body.

Build a Language-Based Document Classifier Serverless Solution

In this section, you'll further use the language detection feature of Azure Text Analytics to classify documents based on their language in a Blob container on a scheduled basis with the help of a timer-triggered function. Your solution will process all the documents present in one container called `source` every 24 hours and classify the documents in terms of the language they are written in; it will also store them in a separate container called `destination` and delete the classified Blobs from the source container.

Open Visual Studio 2019 and click "Create a new project." See Figure 17-14.

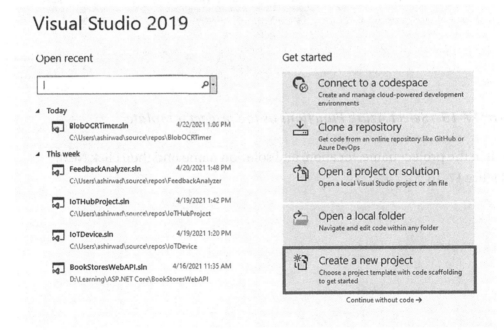

Figure 17-14. *Create a new project*

Select Azure Functions as the project template and click Next. See Figure 17-15.

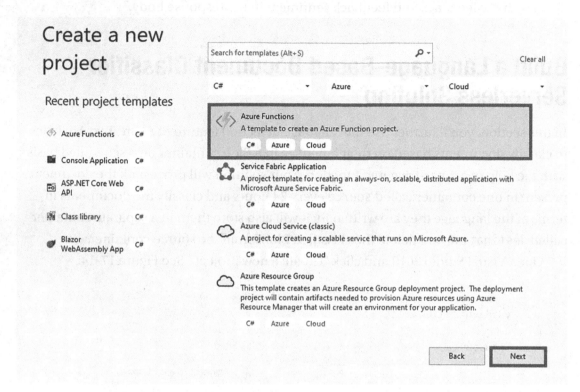

Figure 17-15. *Select Azure Functions as the project template*

Fill in the project name, location, and solution name and then click Next. See Figure 17-16.

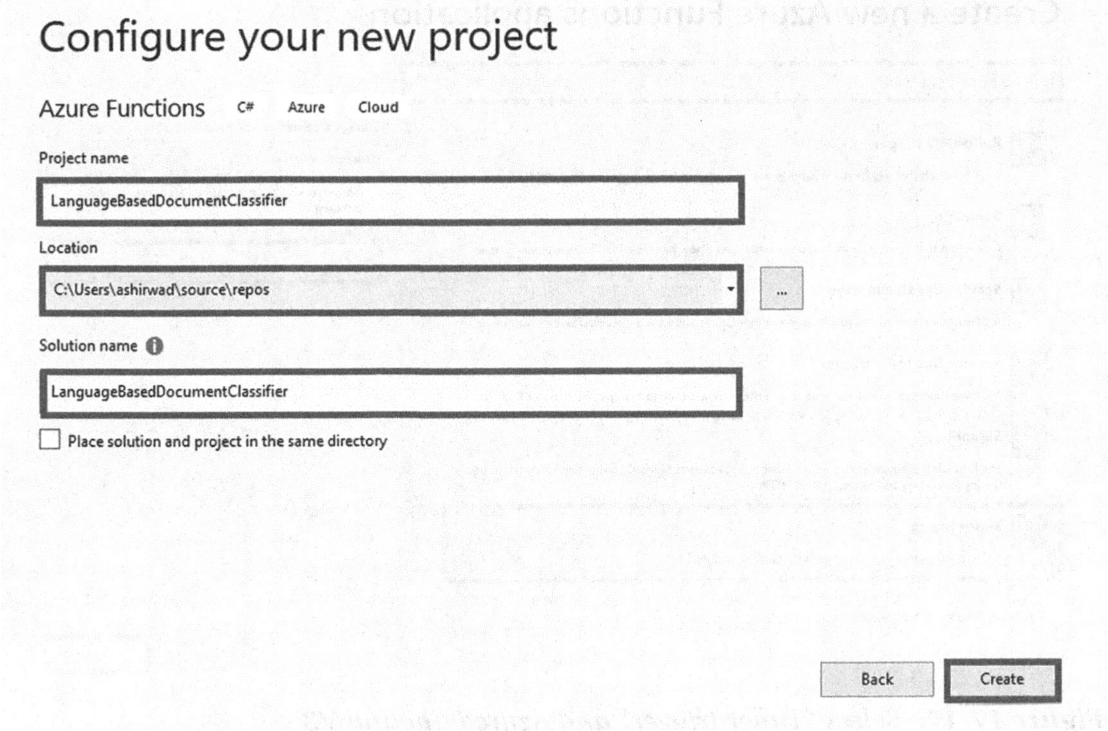

Configure your new project

Azure Functions   C#   Azure   Cloud

Project name

LanguageBasedDocumentClassifier

Location

C:\Users\ashirwad\source\repos

Solution name ⓘ

LanguageBasedDocumentClassifier

☐ Place solution and project in the same directory

Back   Create

Figure 17-16. Fill in the project details

Select "Timer trigger" as the trigger type, leave the other defaults as they are, and click Create. See Figure 17-17.

Create a new Azure Functions application

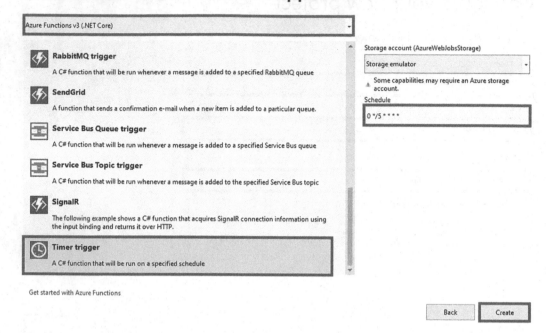

Figure 17-17. Select "Timer trigger" and Azure Function V3

Visual Studio will generate a timer-triggered function named function1. Let's remove it and add a new timer-triggered function named DocumentClassifier. Let's open the Package Manager console and type in the command shown in Listing 17-1 and Listing 17-5 to install the Azure Text Analytics SDK and the Azure Blob Storage SDK. Alternatively, you can install it using the NuGet package manager.

Listing 17-5. Install Azure Blob Storage

```
Install-Package Microsoft.Azure.Storage.Blob -Version 12.8.1
```

Once you have installed these packages, open the local.settings.json file of your project and add the key and endpoint from the Text Analytics resource you created earlier in this chapter. Now, let's create a storage account in Azure and create two Blob containers called source and destination for the project.

All your files will initially be uploaded in the source Blob container, and then your function will classify the documents on the basis of the language they are written in and store them in the destination container. Once you create the storage account and the Blob container, let's go to "Access keys" in the side menu of your storage account screen in the Azure portal and get the connection string. See Figure 17-18.

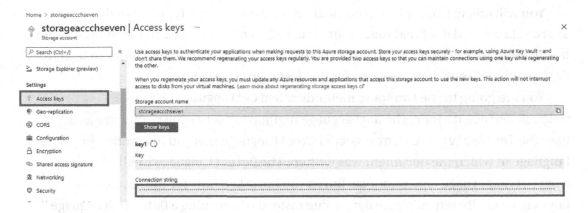

Figure 17-18. *Get the storage account's connection string*

You need to store this connection string in your `local.settings.json` file as a key-value pair. Refer to Listing 17-6 for the `local.settings.json` file after adding all the key-value pairs required for your project.

Listing 17-6. Add API Key, Endpoint, and Connection String at local.settings. json

```
{
    "IsEncrypted": false,
  "Values": {
    "AzureWebJobsStorage": "UseDevelopmentStorage=true",
    "FUNCTIONS_WORKER_RUNTIME": "dotnet",
    "key": "Enter your API key",
    "endpoint": "Enter your endpoint",
    "connectionString": "Enter your storage account connection string"
  }
}
```

Now that you have updated the `local.settings.json` file of your project, let's start working on your `DocumentClassifier` function. You will have to update the cron expression of your function to 0 0 10 * * *. This tells your function to run every day at 10 a.m. After you modify the cron expression, let's create static objects of the `TextAnalyticsClient` and `BlobContainerClient` types. You will be using the `TextAnalyticsClient` type to perform language detection on the content of the documents uploaded in your source Blob container.

You will create two static objects of `BlobContainerClient` types, namely, `sourceClient` and `destinationClient`. `sourceClient` references all the Blobs present inside the source container and gives you the ability to modify all the Blobs in it, and `destinationClient` does the same for the destination container.

You are going to use two static methods called `GetLanguage` and `UploadBlobToContainer`. The `GetLanguage` method takes a string parameter and uses the `TextAnalyticsClient` object's `DetectLanguage` method to identify the language in which the document was written. The `DetectLanguage` method returns a `DetectedLanguage` type response. But as you are asked only for the name of the language, you are returning the `name` value instead of returning a `DetectedLanguage` object from your `GetLanguage` method.

The `UploadBlobToContainer` method takes three parameters, of types `stream`, `string`, and `BlobContainerClient`. The `UploadBlobToContainer` methods use the `BlobContainerClient` object passed as a parameter to upload files to the container referenced by the object with the help of the `UploadBlob` method. The name of the Blob is the value passed in the parameter named `blobName`, and the Blob content is the value passed in the parameter named `blobData`. It wraps the `UploadBlob` method inside a `try-catch` block to handle exceptions. If there's an exception, the `UploadBlobToContainer` will return false, and if it hasn't run into any exception, then it will return true.

We have discussed the methods we are using in the function, so now let's discuss the code used in the Run method of your function. First, we are iterating through all the Blobs present inside the source container by using the `GetBlobs` method of the `sourceClient` object. Then we get the Blob data with the help of the `GetBlobClient` method and make a method call to the `GetLanguage` method by passing the value of the content of the Blob as a parameter. Assign the value returned from the `GetLanguage` method to a variable called `detectedLanguage`.

After finding out the language in which the document is written, you make a call to the `UploadBlobToContainer` method by passing the `destinationClient` object, an interpolated string, and the content of the current Blob item. You pass an interpolated string to build a string of the format `{Language Name}/{Blob Name}`. This will ensure that your Blob is visible in a folder-like format in the Storage Explorer where each folder will be the name of the language and will contain all the files written in that specific language. You have the Blob name in this format by default; Blob storage does not support folders or subdirectories, but you can logically group them by using the / after the folder or subfolder name as per your requirements.

The UploadBlobToContainer returns a Boolean response after executing. If it returns true, then you will delete the file from the source container as it has already been classified and uploaded in the destination container along with logging the status of the Blob classification. If the UploadBlobToContainer was unable to upload the file, then it will return false as a response, and you will only log the information about the Blob not being classified and upload it to the destination container and not delete this particular Blob item. Refer to Listing 17-7 for the entire code of the DocumentClassifier function.

Listing 17-7. Document Classifier Function

```
using System;
using System.IO;
using Azure;
using Azure.AI.TextAnalytics;
using Azure.Storage.Blobs;
using Azure.Storage.Blobs.Models;
using Microsoft.Azure.WebJobs;
using Microsoft.Azure.WebJobs.Host;
using Microsoft.Extensions.Logging;

namespace LanguageBasedDocumentClassifier
{
    public static class DocumentClassifier
    {
        private static readonly AzureKeyCredential credentials = new
        AzureKeyCredential(Environment.GetEnvironmentVariable("key"));
        private static readonly Uri endpoint = new Uri(Environment.GetEnvir
        onmentVariable("endpoint"));
        private static TextAnalyticsClient client = new
        TextAnalyticsClient(endpoint, credentials);
        private static BlobContainerClient sourceClient = new
        BlobContainerClient(Environment.GetEnvironmentVariable("connectionS
        tring"),"source");
        private static BlobContainerClient destinationClient = new
        BlobContainerClient(Environment.GetEnvironmentVariable("connectionS
        tring"), "destination");
        [FunctionName("DocumentClassifier")]
```

```
public static void Run([TimerTrigger("0 0 10 * * *")]TimerInfo
myTimer, ILogger log)
{
    foreach (BlobItem blobItem in sourceClient.GetBlobs()) {
        BlobClient blob = sourceClient.GetBlobClient(blobItem.
        Name);
        StreamReader data = new StreamReader(blob.Download().Value.
        Content);
        string detectedLanguage = GetLanguage(data.ReadToEnd());
        bool IsUploaded = UploadBlobToContainer(destinationClie
        nt, $"{detectedLanguage}/{blobItem.Name}", blob.Download().
        Value.Content);
        if (IsUploaded)
        {
            sourceClient.DeleteBlobIfExists(blobItem.Name);
            log.LogInformation($"{blobItem.Name} is classified");
        }
        else
        {
            log.LogInformation($"Failed to classify {blobItem.
            Name}");
        }

    }
}
public static string GetLanguage(string content)
{
    return client.DetectLanguage(content).Value.Name;
}
public static bool UploadBlobToContainer(BlobContainerClient
containerClient,string blobName,Stream blobData) {
    bool flag = true;
    try
    {
        containerClient.UploadBlob(blobName,blobData);
    }
```

```
                catch (Exception ex) {
                    flag = false;
                }
                return flag;
            }
        }
    }
```

Test the Language-Based Document Classifier Function

To test the document classifier function, you have to run the function, but before doing that, let's look at the files present in the source and destination container. As shown in Figure 17-19, the source container contains four text files. All the text files are written in different languages.

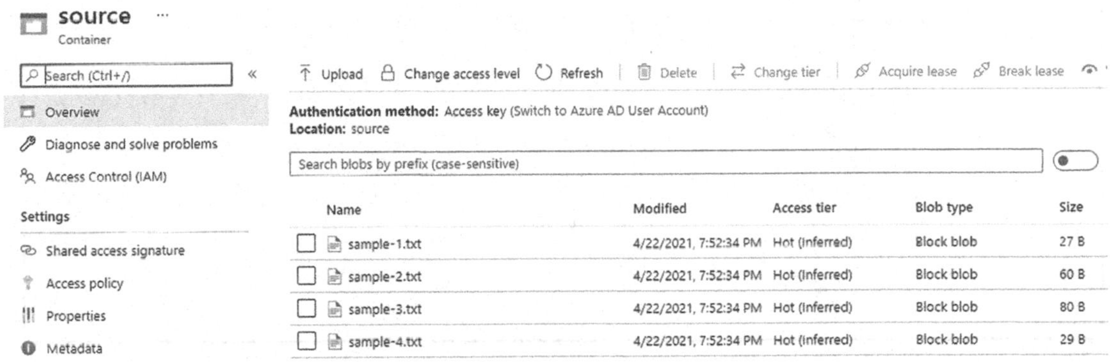
source
Container
Search (Ctrl+/)
Overview
Diagnose and solve problems
Access Control (IAM)
Settings
Shared access signature
Access policy
Properties
Metadata
Upload
Change access level
Refresh
Delete
Change tier
Acquire lease
Break lease
Authentication method: Access key (Switch to Azure AD User Account)
Location: source
Search blobs by prefix (case-sensitive)
Name
Modified
Access tier
Blob type
Size
sample-1.txt 4/22/2021, 7:52:34 PM Hot (Inferred) Block blob 27 B
sample-2.txt 4/22/2021, 7:52:34 PM Hot (Inferred) Block blob 60 B
sample-3.txt 4/22/2021, 7:52:34 PM Hot (Inferred) Block blob 80 B
sample-4.txt 4/22/2021, 7:52:34 PM Hot (Inferred) Block blob 29 B

***Figure 17-19.** Files present in source container*

Now let's take a look at the files present in the destination container, as shown in Figure 17-20. As of now, the destination container is empty and has no files uploaded into it. Once you run your `DocumentClassifier` function, it will populate this container.

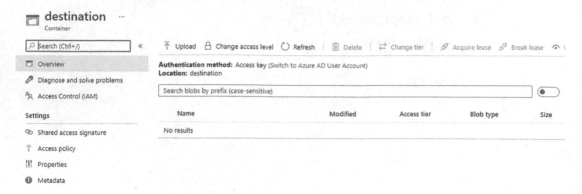

Figure 17-20. Files present in the destination container

As you have seen all the files present in both of the containers, let's run your DocumentClassifier function and check the containers again. See Figure 17-21.

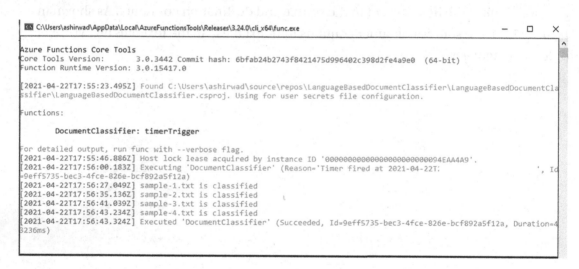

Figure 17-21. Logs of the DocumentClassifier function

The DocumentClassifier function was able to classify the documents by the language in which they were written and upload them to the destination container successfully, as shown in the logs of your Azure Functions Core Tools.

Let's go to the destination container again to verify this. Now the destination container contains four folders, namely, English, Hindi, Oriya, and Afrikaans, as can be shown in Figure 17-22. All these folders contain the files that were written in the same language as that their folder name.

destination ...
Container

Search (Ctrl+/) «   ↑ Upload   🔒 Change access level   ↻ Refresh | 🗑 Delete | ⇄ Change tier |

- 🗂 Overview
- 🔧 Diagnose and solve problems
- 🧑 Access Control (IAM)

Authentication method: Access key (Switch to Azure AD User Account)
Location: destination

Search blobs by prefix (case-sensitive)

Settings

- ☁ Shared access signature
- 🔑 Access policy
- ⫼ Properties
- ⓘ Metadata

Name	Modified	Access tier
☐ 📁 Afrikaans		
☐ 📁 English		
☐ 📁 Hindi		
☐ 📁 Oriya		

Figure 17-22. Destination container after function execution

The function had one more functionality: to remove the files that were already classified and uploaded to the destination container. Since your `DocumentClassifier` function was able to classify and upload all the files successfully, your source container should be empty now. You can verify that by going back to the `source` container, as shown in Figure 17-23.

source ...
Container

Search (Ctrl+/) «   ↑ Upload   🔒 Change access level   ↻ Refresh | 🗑 Delete | ⇄ Change tier | ⌐

- 🗂 Overview
- 🔧 Diagnose and solve problems
- 🧑 Access Control (IAM)

Authentication method: Access key (Switch to Azure AD User Account)
Location: source

Search blobs by prefix (case-sensitive)

Settings

- ☁ Shared access signature
- 🔑 Access policy
- ⫼ Properties
- ⓘ Metadata

Name	Modified	Access tier
No results		

Figure 17-23. The source container after function execution

Summary

In this chapter, you learned about ways to create intelligent serverless solutions with the help of Azure Functions and Azure Cognitive Services by building a feedback analyzer app and a document classifier app. While building both serverless solutions, you learned how to integrate the cognitive capabilities into your solution by leveraging the power of Azure Text Analytics.

The following are the key takeaways from this chapter.

- Azure Cognitive Services provides REST endpoints and client-side libraries to add cognitive capabilities in your applications.

- You can access the Azure Text Analytics service in the Azure portal.

- You can perform tasks such as language detection, sentiment analysis, and named entity recognition tasks using Azure Text Analytics.

- You can integrate cognitive capabilities into an Azure function by using the SDKs of Azure Cognitive Services.

CHAPTER 18

Introduction to Azure Durable Functions

You may have a scenario where the application logic is broken into smaller chunks, and each chunk of code is hosted in an Azure function. The application consists of a couple of Azure functions that interact with each other and exchange data and state for business processing. You may have to execute the functions in a specific order like a workflow. You need to orchestrate these Azure functions and make sure that the functions maintain their data and state. Azure functions are by default stateless. They will not be able to handle such scenarios. You need to use the service Azure Durable Functions, which will help you to make these functions stateful and build a workflow.

You learned how to create intelligent serverless applications using Azure Cognitive Services and Azure Functions in the previous chapter. In this chapter, you will learn how to build and orchestrate stateful workflows using Azure Durable Functions.

Structure of the Chapter

In this chapter, you will explore the following aspects of Azure Durable Functions:

- Getting started with Azure Durable Functions

- Benefits of Azure Durable Functions

- Application patterns

- Implementing functions with Azure Durable Functions

© Ashirwad Satapathi and Abhishek Mishra 2021
A. Satapathi and A. Mishra, *Hands-on Azure Functions with C#*, https://doi.org/10.1007/978-1-4842-7122-3_18

Objectives

After studying this chapter, you will be able to do the following:

- Use Azure Durable Functions and its patterns
- Build a durable function

Getting Started with Azure Durable Functions

Say you work for an e-learning company where students will complete an online course and you need to issue a certificate based on their course completion status and if they have paid the course fees in full. To make this scenario work, you need to design a workflow that will perform the following steps:

1. Check whether the student has completed each of the modules in the course.

2. Check whether the student has paid the course fees. If not, trigger a notification to the student to pay the fees.

3. Check whether the student has passed the exam for the course.

4. Issue a certificate for the student to download if the student has completed all the modules, paid the course fees, and passed the exam.

Sending data from one workflow step to another is crucial for workflow-based applications. You need to make each step of the workflow stateful. You can achieve this scenario using Azure Durable Functions. The Azure Durable Functions extension helps you build stateful workflows using Azure functions. It makes the Azure functions stateful. You can build durable functions using C#, F#, and Node.js.

Durable functions comprise the following components:

- Client function
- Orchestrator function
- Activity function

The Activity function performs the actual business logic and acts as a step in the workflow. The Orchestrator function invokes the Activity function and orchestrates them as a workflow and then goes to sleep. The Activity function executes the business functionality, and once it completes, it notifies the Orchestrator function to wake up. The Orchestrator function wakes up, invokes the next Activity function, and then goes to sleep again until it gets a completion status from the Activity function. The Client function invokes the Orchestrator function. The end user or the consuming application of the workflow invokes the Client function.

Azure Durable Functions maintains and manages its states using Table Storage and Queue Storage. When the Orchestrator function completes execution, it pushes its context data and state to Azure Table Storage. The Orchestrator function and the Activity function exchange data among themselves using Azure Queue Storage. See Figure 18-1.

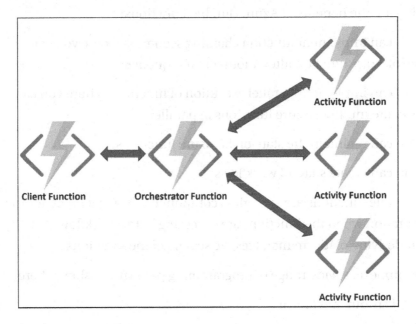

Figure 18-1. *Azure Durable Functions components*

> **Note**   The Azure Durable Functions service helps you build serverless workflows. You can also build serverless workflows using Azure Logic Apps. The Azure Durable Functions workflow is well suited for developers as you need to implement the workflows using code. You do not need to be a coder to implement Azure Logic Apps workflows. Azure Logic Apps come with a higher monetary cost compared to Azure Functions. Workflows can be developed using the Logic App Designer user interface with simple drag-and-drop and configurations.

Benefits of Azure Durable Functions

The following are the benefits of Azure Durable Functions:

- You can implement function chaining scenarios where you can invoke one function after another in a sequence.

- You can implement parallel execution of functions where you can execute multiple Azure functions in parallel.

- You can maintain the state of the Azure functions.

- You can create stateful workflows.

- Durable functions are serverless components. You get billed for the duration when the functions are executing in the workflow. The underlying platform manages the scaling of the functions.

- It supports a wide range of programming patterns, as shown here:

  - Fan-out and fan-in

  - Functions chaining

  - Monitoring

  - Human interaction

  - Aggregator

  - Async HTTP APIs

Application Patterns

You can use Azure Durable Functions to build the following application patterns:

- Fan-in and fan-out

- Function chaining

- Async HTTP APIs

- Monitoring

- Human interaction

- Aggregator

Let's discuss each of these application patterns in detail.

Fan-Out and Fan-In

In this pattern, a function executes the business logic and passes the data to either a set of functions or multiple instances of a function that execute in parallel. This process is called *fan-out*. These parallel functions or instances of the function further process the data and execute the business logic. They send the processed data to another function that aggregates the data from these parallel functions or function instances and processes the aggregated data further. This phenomenon is called *fan-in*. Figure 18-2 depicts the fan-out and fan-in pattern.

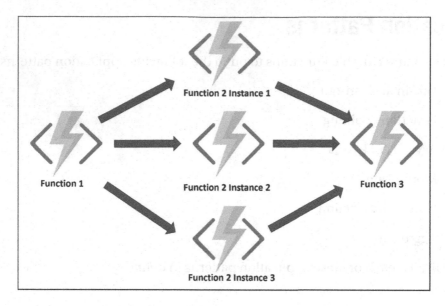

Figure 18-2. *Fan-out and fan-in pattern*

Function Chaining

In this pattern, several functions execute one after the other. The first function processes the data and sends the data for further processing to the second function. The second function processes the data further and sends the data to the third function and so on. In this pattern, we chain a set of functions, with each function in the chain performing business logic for the scenario and passing on the data and state to the next function. Figure 18-3 depicts the function chaining pattern.

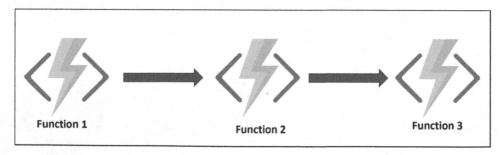

Figure 18-3. *Function chaining pattern*

Async HTTP APIs

In some scenarios, you may have a long-running activity processing the business functionality. You need to keep tracking the execution status of the long-running activity and get the processed results once the activity completes. You can build such scenarios using async HTTP APIs. A client application will trigger an HTTP-triggered orchestrator client. The HTTP orchestrator client will invoke the Orchestrator function to orchestrate the Activity functions that are executing long-running tasks. The Azure Durable Functions workflow exposes a set of REST APIs that give the processing status and results of the workflows. The client application can invoke these REST APIs to monitor the completion status of the long-running tasks and get the processed results. Figure 18-4 depicts the async HTTP APIs pattern.

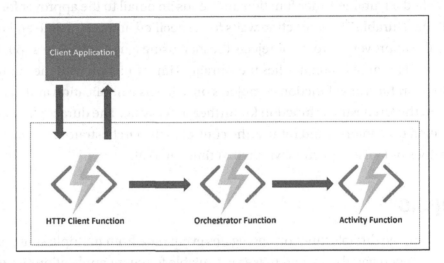

Figure 18-4. Async HTTP pattern

Monitoring

You may have scenarios where you need to monitor events or the execution status of an external process or another function. You can use long-running durable functions to continuously check the events or execution status of the external process and perform an activity when a specified condition is met. For example, you may have an Azure function that gets triggered whenever an item gets inserted in the Queue Storage. You need to generate a notification whenever the Azure function goes down or generates an exception. You can have a long-running durable function executing continuously and monitoring the exceptions generated by the Azure function or monitoring the health of the Azure function. Whenever the Azure function generates an exception or goes down, the durable function will send a notification.

Human Interaction

You may have a maker-checker scenario where a maker creates a request, and the request gets forwarded to the checker for verification and approval. For example, a loan approval system can be developed using the Azure Durable Functions workflow. A customer invokes the Orchestrator client function of the Azure Durable Functions workflow. The Orchestrator client function invokes the Orchestrator function and starts the loan approval process. The Orchestrator function calls a special type of Activity function called a Durable Timer function and sends an email to the approver for loan approval. The Durable Timer function waits for a specified amount of time and notifies whenever the approver approves or rejects the loan using a user interface application. The user interface application notifies the Durable Timer function with the approval status. The Durable Timer function completes once it gets a notification and passes on the status to the Orchestrator function for further processing. The durable function waits for a specified time interval and returns the control to the Orchestrator function if the approver does not take any action within that time interval.

Aggregator

In this pattern, the durable function aggregates event data from multiple sources, processes the aggregated data, and makes it available for client applications to query and use the data. You need to use durable entities to address such scenarios.

Implement an Azure Durable Function

Let's implement a simple Azure Durable Functions workflow using Visual Studio. The Azure Durable Functions workflow will contain an Orchestrator Client function, an Orchestrator function, and an Activity function. Open Visual Studio and click "Create a new project." See Figure 18-5.

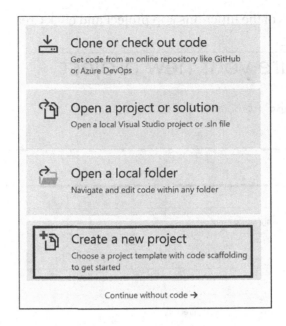

Figure 18-5. *Create a new project*

Select Azure Functions and click Next. See Figure 18-6.

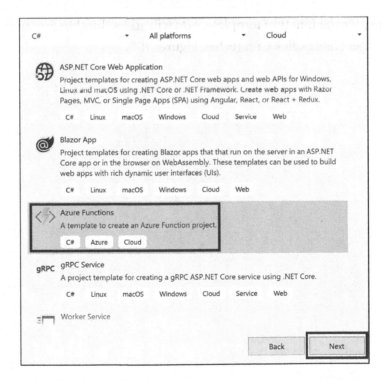

Figure 18-6. *Select the Azure Functions project type*

Provide the details of the functions app project and click Create. See Figure 18-7.

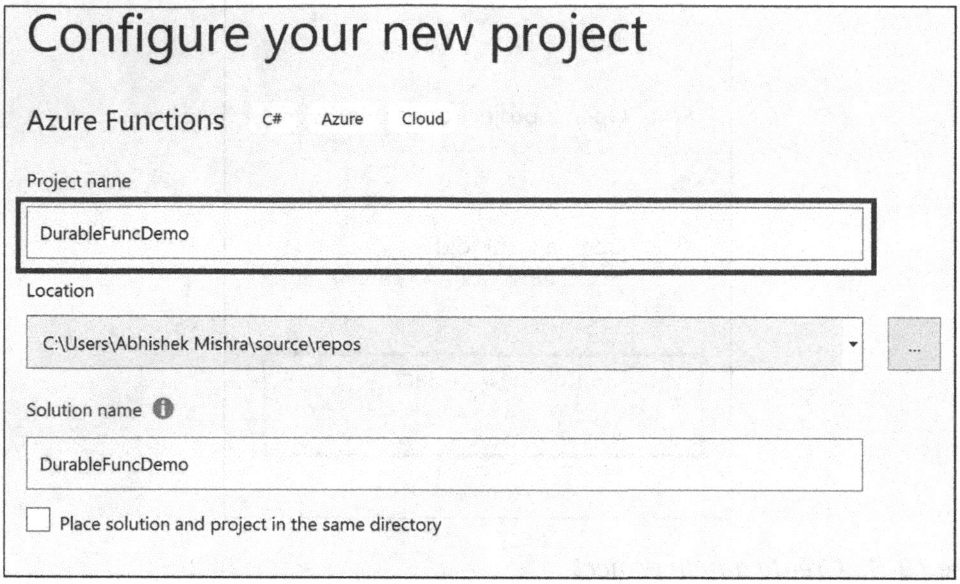

Figure 18-7. *Provide the project details*

Select Empty for the function template. You will add a durable function to the function app project later. Click Create. See Figure 18-8.

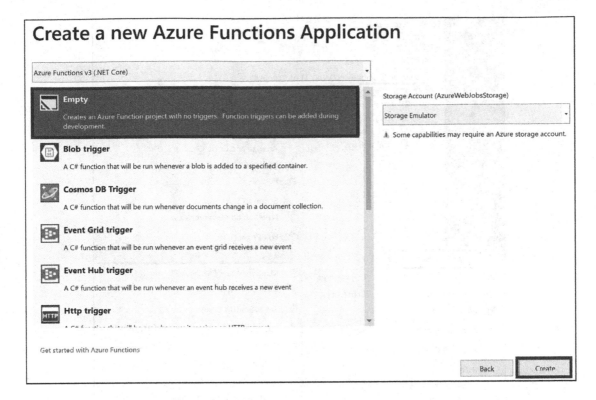

Figure 18-8. *Select Empty*

Right-click the function app project and click Add. Then click New Azure Function. See Figure 18-9.

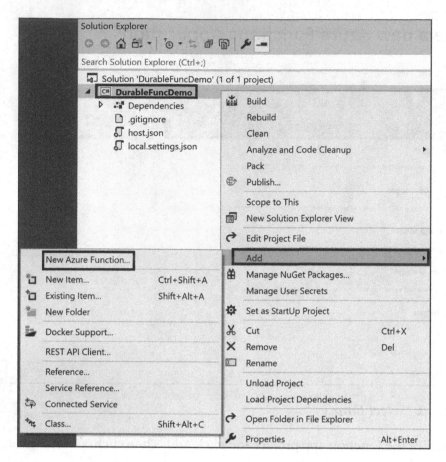

Figure 18-9. *Add a new function*

Select Azure Function, add a name, and click Add. See Figure 18-10.

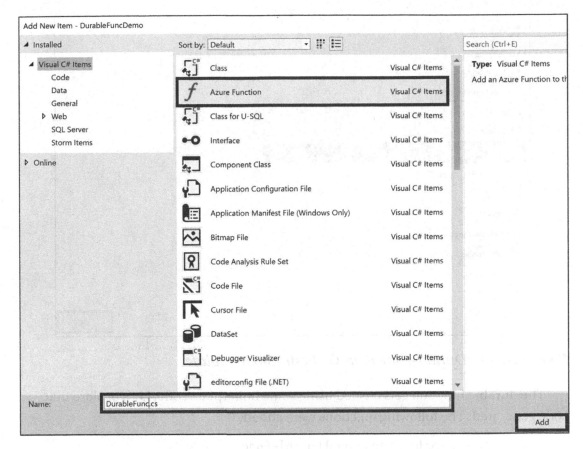

Figure 18-10. *Provide a function name*

Select Durable Functions Orchestration and click OK. See Figure 18-11.

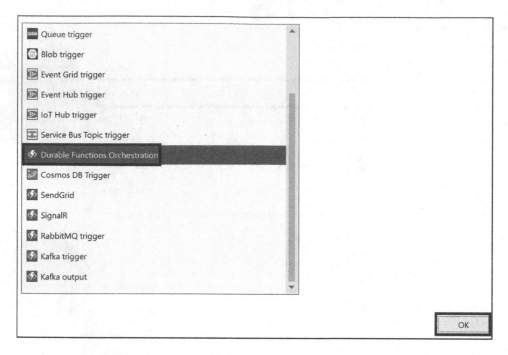

Figure 18-11. *Durable Functions Orchestration template*

The durable function gets created using some boilerplate code. Let's explore the code generated. The following functions were added:

- Orchestrator function named DurableFunc

- Activity function named DurableFunc_Hello

- Orchestrator Client function called DurableFunc_HttpStart

DurableFunc_HTTPStart is an HTTP-triggered function. You can invoke it to start the Azure Durable Functions workflow. It uses the StartNewAsync method to invoke the DurableFunc function, which is an Orchestrator function. The durable function invokes the Activity function called DurableFunc_Hello three times and passes the Tokyo, Seattle, and London parameter values. It uses the CallActivityAsync method to invoke the Activity function. The Activity function called DurableFunc_Hello prepends the word *Hello* with the parameter name and returns it to the Orchestrator function DurableFunc. The Orchestrator function DurableFunc aggregates the Activity function output and returns the output to the Client Orchestrator function called DurableFunc_HTTPStart. The Client Orchestrator function returns the output from the Orchestrator function to the caller using the CreateCheckStatusResponse method that builds the response output for the workflow.

Listing 18-1 shows the code for the durable function workflow that was generated.

Listing 18-1. Durable Function Code

```
using System.Collections.Generic;
using System.Net.Http;
using System.Threading.Tasks;
using Microsoft.Azure.WebJobs;
using Microsoft.Azure.WebJobs.Extensions.DurableTask;
using Microsoft.Azure.WebJobs.Extensions.Http;
using Microsoft.Azure.WebJobs.Host;
using Microsoft.Extensions.Logging;

namespace DurableFuncDemo
{
    public static class DurableFunc
    {
        [FunctionName("DurableFunc")]
        public static async Task<List<string>> RunOrchestrator(
            [OrchestrationTrigger] IDurableOrchestrationContext context)
        {
            var outputs = new List<string>();

            // Replace "hello" with the name of your Durable Activity
               Function.
            outputs.Add(await
            context.CallActivityAsync<string>("DurableFunc_Hello",
            "Tokyo"));
            outputs.Add(await
            context.CallActivityAsync<string>("DurableFunc_Hello",
            "Seattle"));
            outputs.Add(await
            context.CallActivityAsync<string>("DurableFunc_Hello",
            "London"));

            // returns ["Hello Tokyo!", "Hello Seattle!", "Hello London!"]
            return outputs;
        }
```

```csharp
[FunctionName("DurableFunc_Hello")]
public static string SayHello([ActivityTrigger] string name, ILogger
log)
{
    log.LogInformation($"Saying hello to {name}.");
    return $"Hello {name}!";
}

[FunctionName("DurableFunc_HttpStart")]
public static async Task<HttpResponseMessage> HttpStart(
    [HttpTrigger(AuthorizationLevel.Anonymous, "get", "post")]
    HttpRequestMessage req,
    [DurableClient] IDurableOrchestrationClient starter,
    ILogger log)
{

    // Function input comes from the request content.
    string instanceId = await starter.StartNewAsync("DurableFunc",
    null);

    log.LogInformation($"Started orchestration with ID =
    '{instanceId}'.");

    return starter.CreateCheckStatusResponse(req, instanceId);
}
}
}
```

Now let's execute the Azure Durable Functions workflow. The output will give you the URL for the Client Orchestrator function that you can use to invoke the Azure Durable Functions workflow. See Figure 18-12.

Figure 18-12. *Azure Durable Functions workflow output*

Copy the URL for `DurableFunc_HttpStart` from the function output and send a GET request to the URL using the Postman tool. Postman will return the supported URLs that you can use to interact with the workflow.

Copy the `statusQueryGetUri` URL and send a GET request to it using the Postman tool. In this chapter, you are using Postman to invoke the function URL. You can also choose to use the Swagger UI or SoapUI or any other API/REST development tool. You will get the same response as in Figure 18-13.

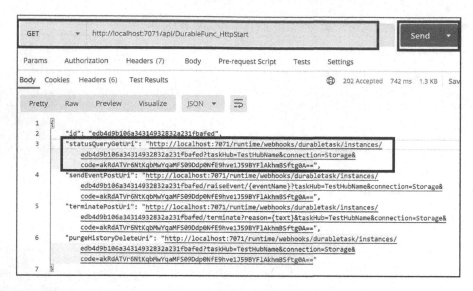

Figure 18-13. *Invoke orchestrator client URL in Postman*

You can see the output for the Azure Durable Functions workflow. See Figure 18-14.

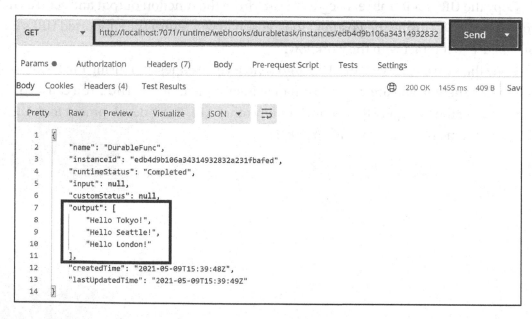

Figure 18-14. *Azure Durable Functions workflow response*

Summary

In this chapter, you learned about Azure Durable Functions. You explored the benefits of using durable functions and different programming patterns supported by them. You learned the different components of an Azure Durable Functions workflow and how it works internally. You then implemented an Azure Durable Functions workflow using Visual Studio.

The following are the key takeaways from this chapter:

- Azure Durable Functions is a serverless offering, and you get charged only when the workflow runs.

- Durable functions make Azure functions stateful.

- You can build stateful workflows using durable functions.

- An Azure durable function consists of a Client Orchestrator function, an Orchestrator function, and an Activity function.

- The Orchestrator function saves its state using Azure Table Storage and exchanges data with the Activity functions using Azure Queue Storage.

- Durable functions support a wide range of programming patterns.

  - Fan-out and fan-in

  - Function chaining

  - Monitoring

  - Human interaction

In the next chapter, you will explore how to create Azure functions with an Azure Logic Apps workflow.

CHAPTER 19

Integrating Azure Functions in a Logic Apps Workflow

In the previous chapter, we discussed building solutions using the bindings and triggers available for Azure Functions. There are quite a handful triggers and bindings available for Azure Functions, but sometimes they are not enough to build solutions to solve real-world problems. As you saw previously, you do not have any binding to perform operations with your Azure SQL Database instance; thus, you had to use the `Data.SqlClient` NuGet package. Similarly, you don't have any triggers to run when a tweet is sent or when a file is uploaded in Dropbox or when the temperature of a place changes. Does that mean you cannot perform such tasks using Azure Functions? The answer is no.

You can take multiple approaches to achieve tasks that do not have available triggers already. One approach is to create a timer-triggered function that will run every second or minute, call the REST APIs of the desired product or service, and execute the required logic whenever the business requirement is satisfied. The other approach is to create an HTTP-triggered function and configure its URL as a webhook URL. A classic example of this use case is that of GitHub WebHooks where you can configure the webhook URL as your function URL and select the events for which this webhook will send an HTTP POST request to configure the webhook URL along with the payload.

Well, these are definitely two ways to solve your issue, but are there any other ways in which you can achieve these types of tasks? Is there any other service offered by Azure to build serverless solutions to perform such operations? The answer is yes. You can use Azure Logic Apps to build serverless solutions to perform actions and solve your

© Ashirwad Satapathi and Abhishek Mishra 2021
A. Satapathi and A. Mishra, *Hands-on Azure Functions with C#*, https://doi.org/10.1007/978-1-4842-7122-3_19

business requirements. Azure Logic Apps is a low-code serverless offering by Azure that contains 200+ connectors to interact and work with different products and services. The focus of this chapter will be to learn how to build serverless solutions using Azure Logic Apps and Azure Functions.

Structure of the Chapter

This chapter will explore the following aspects of Azure Logic Apps:

- Getting started with Azure Logic Apps solutions
- Creating an Azure Logic Apps solution using the Azure portal
- Integrating an Azure function with an Azure Logic Apps solution

Objective

After studying this chapter, you will be able to do the following:

- Create an Azure Logic Apps solution using the Azure portal
- Interact with Azure functions inside a Logic Apps workflow

Getting Started with Azure Logic Apps

Azure Logic Apps is a low-code serverless offering of Microsoft Azure that enables you to build enterprise-grade workflows. A workflow can be a business process. Logic Apps is an integration platform as a service (IPaaS) offering that helps you integrate apps, services, and systems irrespective of their hosting environment. You can build logic apps using the Azure portal or with IDEs like Visual Studio or VS Code. The Azure Logic Apps service contains more than 200+ connectors from different vendors and service providers that you can use to build a workflow to solve your problems without writing any code.

Connectors act as the interface for accessing data, actions, and other events from different services, apps, or platforms. A connector is a wrapper around the REST APIs exposed by various service providers. If you don't have a connector for a product or service, you can create a custom connector provided you have the OpenAPI definition of it. Connectors can also have actions and triggers.

Actions are operations of a particular service directed by the user to be performed in the workflow. For example, you can use an action to get a list of all the files present in a folder of your Google Drive or to delete a file from your Blob storage container. Triggers in Logic Apps solutions are similar to the triggers in Azure functions. They notify your apps when an event occurs. For example, a recurrence trigger will notify your app to run at a uniform interval defined in the recurrence trigger.

The following are the advantages of Azure Logic Apps:

- Highly extensible

- Pay-per-execution billing model

- Enterprise-grade integration

- Supports versioning

- 200+ connectors

- Reusable

- Tooling support in Visual Studio and VS Code

Create an Azure Logic Apps Solution in the Azure Portal

In this section, you will create a Logic Apps solution that will act as an API, take a name from the request body, and return a response concatenating the name with *Hi*.

Go to the Azure portal. Type **Logic app** in the search box and click the result. See Figure 19-1.

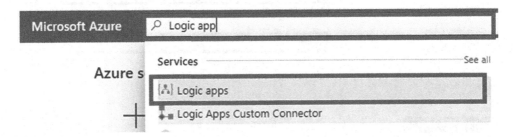

Figure 19-1. *Click "Logic apps"*

Let's click Add and then Consumption to create the Logic Apps solution. If you have any existing logic apps, you can find them on this screen. See Figure 19-2.

Figure 19-2. *Click Add and then Consumption*

You will be prompted to enter the subscription name, resource group name, and logic app name; then select the nearest region. Click "Review + create." See Figure 19-3.

Create a logic app ⋯

Project details

Select the subscription to manage deployed resources and costs. Use resource groups like folders to organize and manage all your resources.

Subscription *

Resource group *

(New) rg-chapter-19

Create new

Instance details

Logic app name *

la-apiApp

Region *

Central India

Associate with integration service
environment ⓘ

Review + create   < Previous : Basics   Next : Tags >   Download a template for automation ⓘ

Figure 19-3. *Click "Review + create"*

You will see a summary of the configuration that you entered in the previous screen. Click Create to provision the Logic Apps solution. A validation check will be done in the background before the resource provisioning begins. See Figure 19-4.

Create a logic app ···

Basics   Tags   Review + create

Basics

Subscription	Azure Pass - Sponsorship
Resource group	rg-chapter-19
Logic app name	la-apiApp
Location	Central India

Tags

Create   < Previous : Tags   Next : Review + create >   Download a template for automation ⓘ

Figure 19-4. *Click Create*

You can see the provisioning status on this screen. Once the deployment is complete, Click "Go to resource." See Figure 19-5.

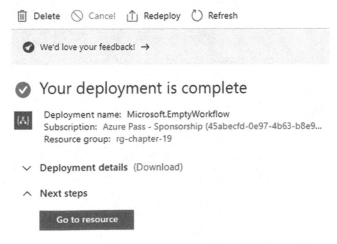

🗑 Delete   ⊘ Cancel   ⬆ Redeploy   ↻ Refresh

🧭 We'd love your feedback! →

✔ Your deployment is complete

Deployment name: Microsoft.EmptyWorkflow
Subscription: Azure Pass - Sponsorship (45abecfd-0e97-4b63-b8e9...
Resource group: rg-chapter-19

∨ Deployment details (Download)

∧ Next steps

Go to resource

Figure 19-5. *Click "Go to resource"*

On the logic app's screen, click "Logic app designer," which is present in the Development Tools section in the side menu. Here you will find multiple templates to get started. Click the "When a HTTP request is received" template as you want to build an API in this section. See Figure 19-6.

Figure 19-6. *Click "Logic app designer"*

This will create a Logic Apps workflow with a trigger of type "When a HTTP request is received." It will be accepting POST requests. Once you save the workflow, you will get the URL to send requests to your Logic Apps solution. Click "Use sample payload to generate schema" to define the request body JSON schema. See Figure 19-7.

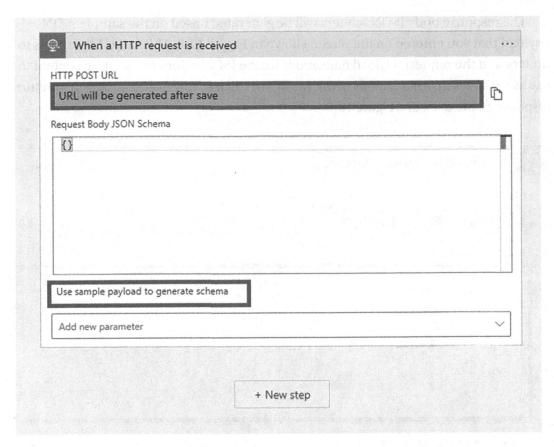

Figure 19-7. *Click "Use sample payload to generate schema"*

As you want to send a name in your request payload, let's enter **{ "name":"" }** as the sample JSON payload, as shown in Figure 19-8, and click Done. See Figure 19-8.

Enter or paste a sample JSON payload.   ✕

```
{
    "name":""
}
```

Done

Figure 19-8. *Click Done*

The response body JSON schema will be generated based on the sample JSON payload that you entered on the screen shown in Figure 19-8. This helps Logic Apps to understand the request payload data and store the JSON values as dynamic content to use as variables in other actions of the workflow. Click + New to add an action to return a response to the user. See Figure 19-9.

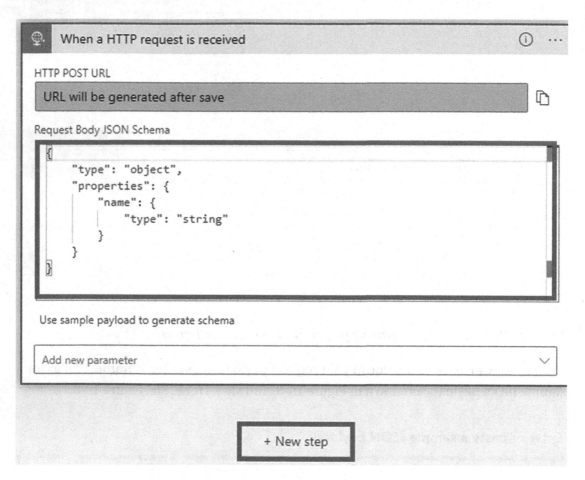

Figure 19-9. *Click "+ New step"*

You will see multiple connectors along with the related actions and triggers. Enter **response** in the search box and then click the Response Request option present in the Actions section. See Figure 19-10.

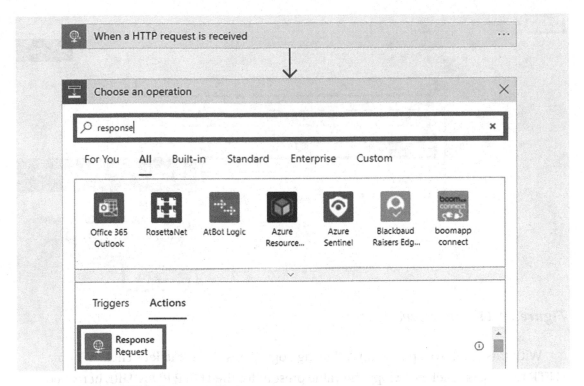

Figure 19-10. *Click Reponse Request*

This will add a response action to your workflow. Enter **200** as the status code. In the textbox for the body, enter **Hello** followed with a space, and then search for *name* in the Dynamic content menu and click it. This will send a "Hello {name}" response to the user, where the name is the value passed in the request payload by the user. After entering all the required fields, click Save. See Figure 19-11.

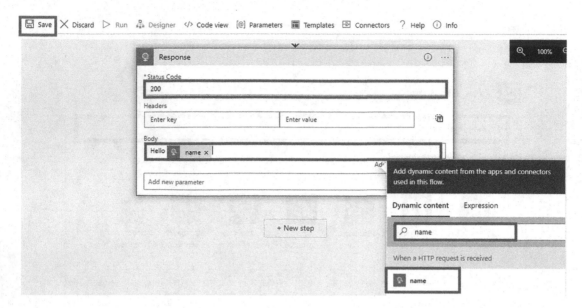

Figure 19-11. *Click Save*

With this you have created an API using Logic Apps. To test it, let's click "When a HTTP request is received." Copy the value present for the HTTP POST URL here. See Figure 19-12.

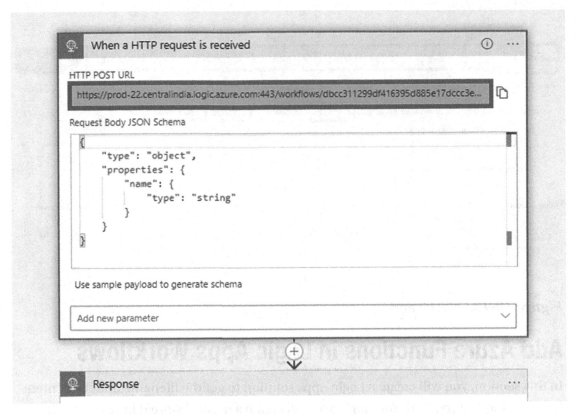

Figure 19-12. Copy the HTTP POST URL

To test the logic app, open Postman and create a request. Since your logic app will accept only POST requests, select POST as the request type and then paste the URL you earlier copied from your Logic Apps solution. In the request body, send a name along with its value in JSON format and click Send. As shown in the response body in Figure 19-13, you get the desired response from your Logic Apps solution.

Figure 19-13. *Click Send*

Add Azure Functions in Logic Apps Workflows

In this section, you will create a Logic Apps solution to get the filename and file content from the request payload. Your logic app will create a file and store it in your Google Drive after encrypting the file content with the help of an Azure function. You will be using the Caesar cipher as your encryption algorithm. At the end of this section, you will be able to work with the Google Drive connectors along with exploring ways to integrate an Azure function in your Logic Apps workflow.

Note   The Caesar cipher is an encryption algorithm that works by shifting each letter of the message by a certain number of letters based on the encryption key. For example, with the encryption key as 1, your algorithm will replace A with B, C with B, and so on.

Go to the Azure portal. Type in **function app** in the search box and click Function App. See Figure 19-14.

Microsoft Azure
function app
Services
See all
Azure s
Function App

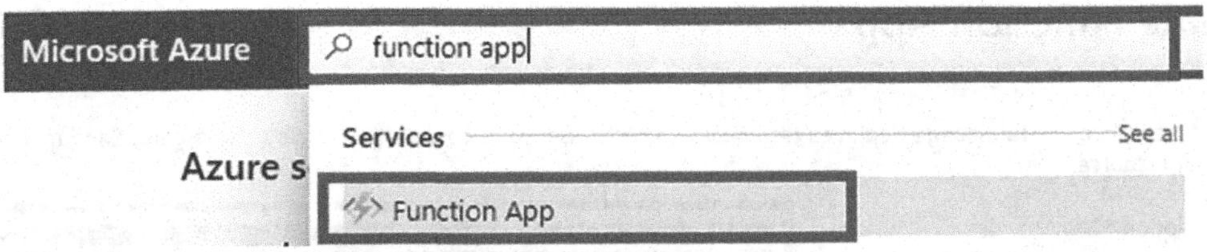

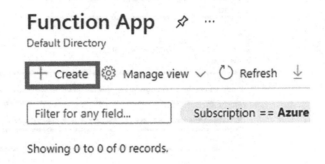

Figure 19-14. Click Function App

Click + Create to create a function app. See Figure 19-15.

Function App
Default Directory
+ Create
Manage view
Refresh
Filter for any field...
Subscription == Azure
Showing 0 to 0 of 0 records.

Figure 19-15. Click + Create

You will be prompted to enter the subscription name, resource group name, function app name, publish method, runtime stack, and version, and to select the nearest region. Click "Review + create." See Figure 19-16.

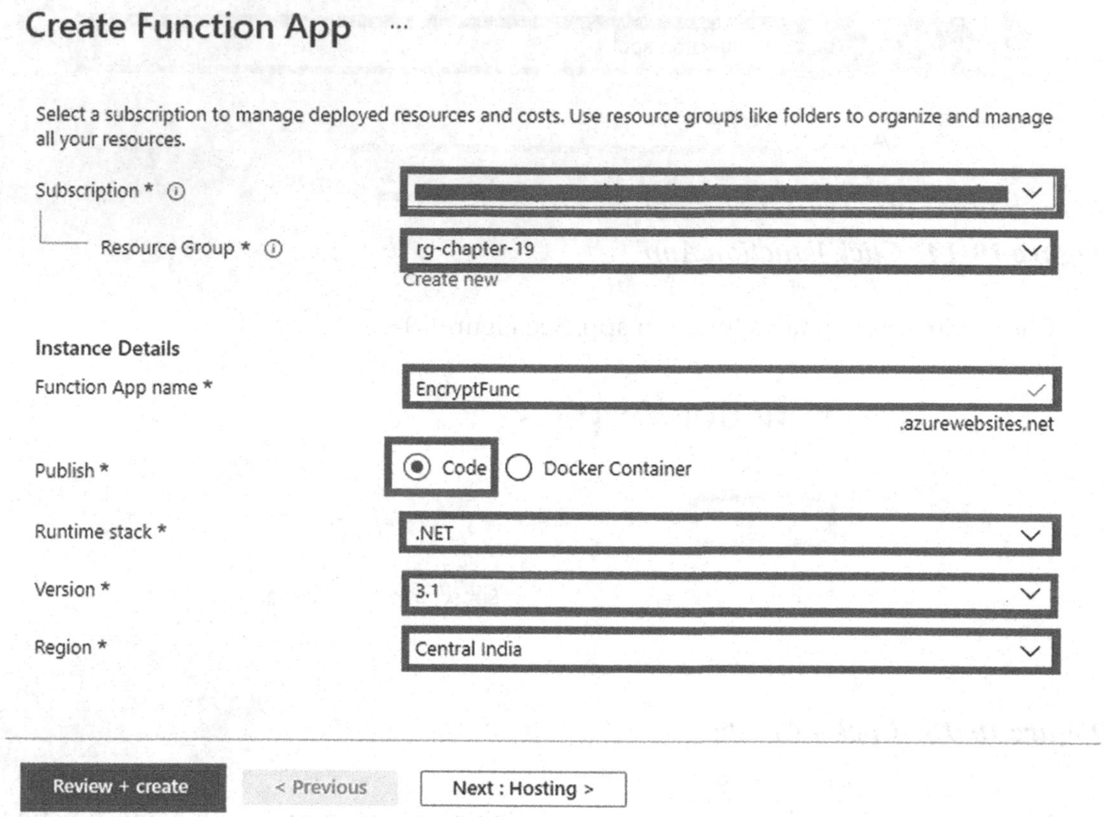

Create Function App   ...

Select a subscription to manage deployed resources and costs. Use resource groups like folders to organize and manage all your resources.

Subscription * ⓘ

Resource Group * ⓘ
rg-chapter-19
Create new

Instance Details

Function App name *
EncryptFunc
.azurewebsites.net

Publish *
◉ Code   ○ Docker Container

Runtime stack *
.NET

Version *
3.1

Region *
Central India

| Review + create | < Previous | Next : Hosting > |

Figure 19-16. Click "Review + create"

You will see a summary of the configuration that you entered in the previous screen. Click Create to provision the function app. A validation check will be done in the background before the resource provisioning begins. See Figure 19-17.

Create Function App ···

Basics   Hosting   Monitoring   Tags   **Review + create**

Summary

⚡ **Function App**
   by Microsoft

Details

Subscription	45abecfd-0e97-4b63-b8e9-9e6863ae01bc
Resource Group	rg-chapter-19
Name	EncryptFunc
Runtime stack	.NET 3.1

Hosting

Storage (New)

Storage account	storageaccountrgcha80dc

Create	< Previous	Next >	Download a template for automation

Figure 19-17. *Click Create*

You can see the provisioning status on this screen. Once the deployment is complete, click "Go to resource." See Figure 19-18.

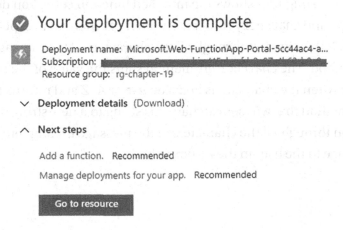

⚡ **Your deployment is complete**

Deployment name: Microsoft.Web-FunctionApp-Portal-5cc44ac4-a...
Subscription:
Resource group: rg-chapter-19

∨ **Deployment details** (Download)

∧ **Next steps**

Add a function. Recommended

Manage deployments for your app. Recommended

Go to resource

Figure 19-18. *Click "Go to resource"*

Now click Functions and then click + Add to create a function in your function app. Set the "Development environment" option to "Develop in portal" and then choose "HTTP trigger" as the template type. Then click Add. See Figure 19-19.

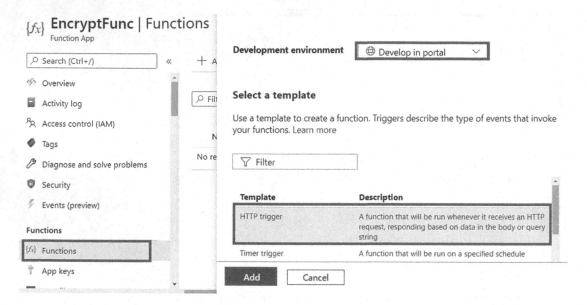

Figure 19-19. *Click Add*

This will create an Azure function named HttpTrigger1, which will contain boilerplate code to return a message along with the name passed in the query string or request body payload. You can click Code + Test to view the code of the function. Let's rewrite this function to accept a message from the request body and encrypt it using the Caesar cipher. Listing 19-1 shows the modified function code. You define two static methods, Encrypt and CharEncrypt, here. The Encrypt method accepts the message along with a key. It then iterates through all the characters of the message and calls the CharEncrypt method. The CharEncrypt method shifts the value of the character to the next ASCII value when the character is between *a–z* or *A–Z* and returns the char value to the Encrypt method that will concatenate this string to a new string named output. After the iteration through all the characters of the message is complete, it will return the encrypted message to the user in the response body.

Listing 19-1. Modified Code of the HttpTrigger1 Function

```
#r "Newtonsoft.Json"

using System.Net;
using Microsoft.AspNetCore.Mvc;
using Microsoft.Extensions.Primitives;
using Newtonsoft.Json;

public static async Task<IActionResult> Run(HttpRequest req, ILogger log)
{
    log.LogInformation("C# HTTP trigger function processed a request.");

    string requestBody = await new StreamReader(req.Body).ReadToEndAsync();
    dynamic data = JsonConvert.DeserializeObject(requestBody);
    string message = data.MessageContent;

    string responseMessage = Encrypt(message,1);

            return new OkObjectResult(responseMessage);
}
static char CharEncrypter(char ch, int key)
{
    if (!char.IsLetter(ch))
    {

        return ch;
    }
    char d = char.IsUpper(ch) ? 'A' : 'a';
    return (char) ((((ch + key) - d) % 26) + d);

}
static string Encrypt(string input, int key)
{
    string output = string.Empty;

    foreach (char ch in input)
        output += CharEncrypter(ch, key);

    return output;
}
```

Now that your function has been developed and is running, let's create your logic app.

Go to the Azure portal. Type **Logic App** in the search box and select "Logic apps" in the results. See Figure 19-20.

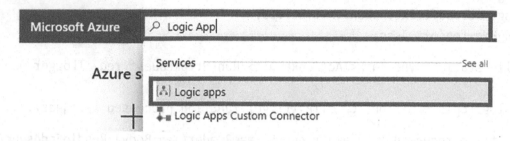

Figure 19-20. *Search for Logic Apps*

Click + Add and then click + Consumption. See Figure 19-21.

Figure 19-21. *Click Add and then Consumption*

You will be prompted to enter the subscription name, resource group name, and logic app name, and to select the nearest region. Click "Review + create." See Figure 19-22.

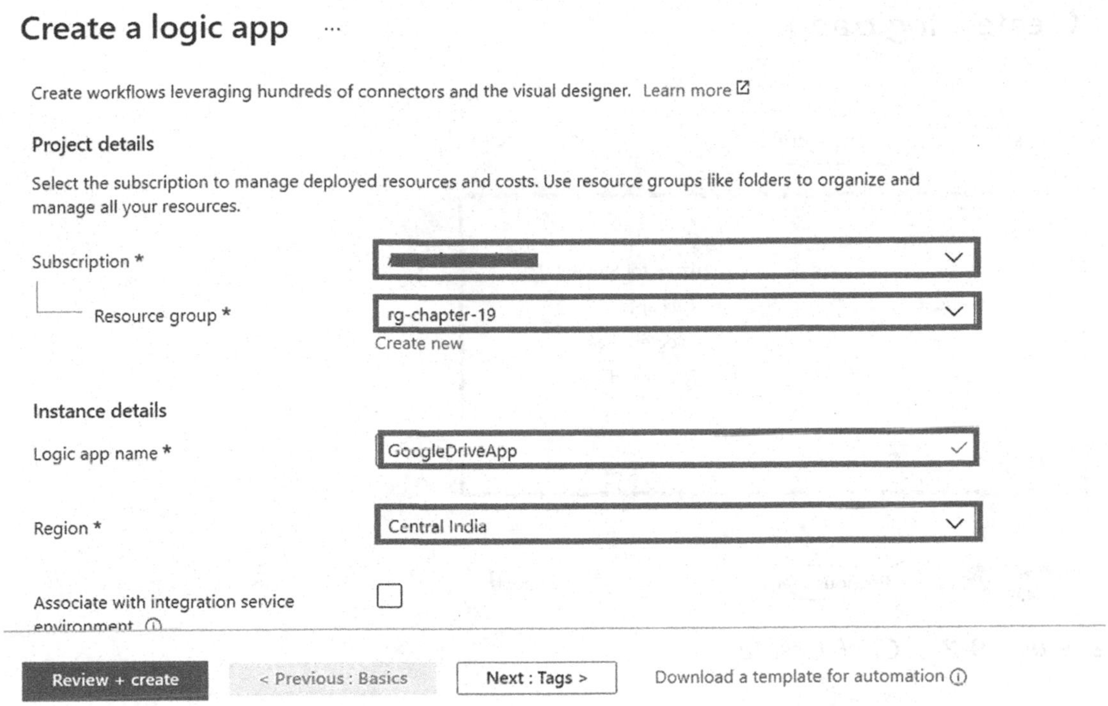

Create a logic app   ...

Create workflows leveraging hundreds of connectors and the visual designer. Learn more ☒

Project details

Select the subscription to manage deployed resources and costs. Use resource groups like folders to organize and manage all your resources.

Subscription *   [_____] ∨

└──── Resource group *   [rg-chapter-19   ] ∨
                                       Create new

Instance details

Logic app name *   [GoogleDriveApp   ] ✓

Region *   [Central India   ] ∨

Associate with integration service   ☐
environment ⓘ

[Review + create]   < Previous : Basics   [Next : Tags >]   Download a template for automation ⓘ

Figure 19-22. *Click "Review + create"*

You will see a summary of the configuration that you entered on the previous screen. Click Create to provision the Logic Apps solution. A validation check will be done in the background before the resource provisioning begins. See Figure 19-23.

Create a logic app ...

Basics   Tags   **Review + create**

Basics

Subscription   Azure for Students

Resource group   rg-chapter-19

Logic app name   GoogleDriveApp

Location   Central India

Tags

| Create | | < Previous : Tags | Next : Review + create > | Download a template for automation ⓘ |

Figure 19-23. *Click Create*

You can see the provisioning status on this screen. Once the deployment is complete, click "Go to resource." See Figure 19-24.

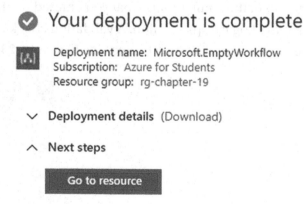

✅ Your deployment is complete

Deployment name: Microsoft.EmptyWorkflow
Subscription: Azure for Students
Resource group: rg-chapter-19

⌄ **Deployment details** (Download)

⌃ **Next steps**

Go to resource

Figure 19-24. *Click "Go to resource"*

On the logic app's screen, Click "Logic app designer," which is present in the Development Tools section of the side menu. Here you will find multiple templates to get started. Click the "When a HTTP request is received" template because you want to build an API in this section. See Figure 19-25.

488

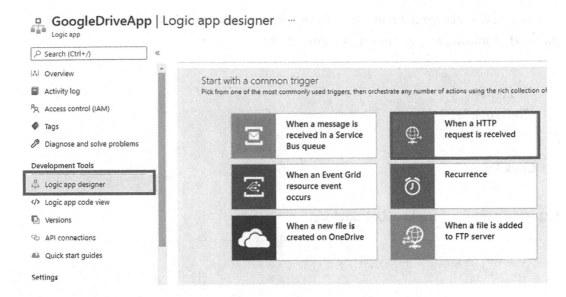

Figure 19-25. *Click "When a HTTP request is received"*

This will create a Logic Apps workflow with a trigger of type "When a HTTP request is received." It will be accepting POST requests. Once you save the workflow, you will get the URL to send requests to your Logic Apps solution. Click "Use sample payload to generate schema" to define the request body JSON schema. See Figure 19-26.

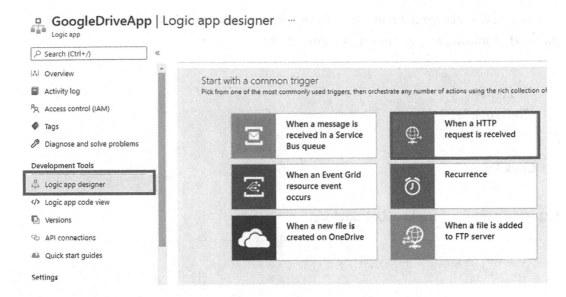

Figure 19-26. *Click "Use sample payload to generate schema"*

As you want to send a name in your request payload, let's enter the sample JSON payload as follows and as shown in Figure 19-27:

```
{

    "FileName":"",
    "Message":""
}
```

Click Done.

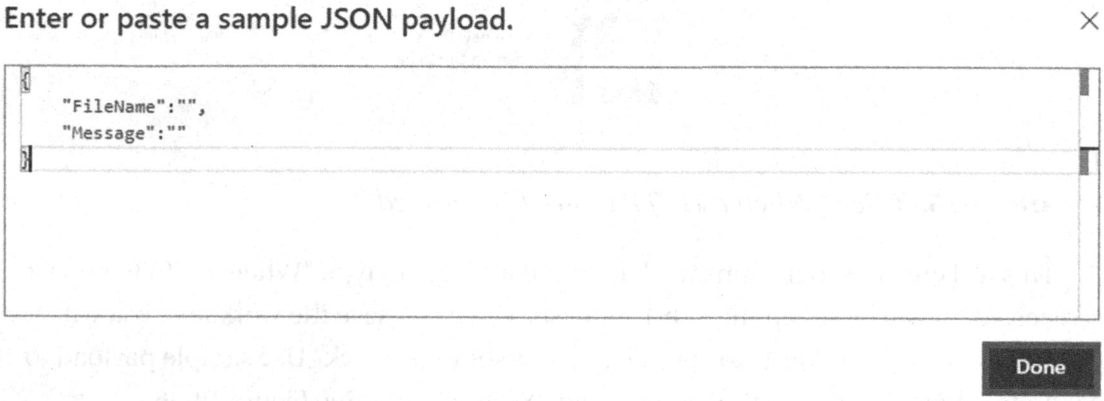

Enter or paste a sample JSON payload.   ✕

```
{
    "FileName":"",
    "Message":""
}
```

Done

Figure 19-27. *Click Done*

The response body JSON schema will be generated based on the sample JSON payload that you entered in Figure 19-27. This helps Logic Apps to understand the request payload data and store the JSON values as dynamic content to use as variables in other actions of the workflow. Click + New to add an action to call your Azure function to encrypt the message content. See Figure 19-28.

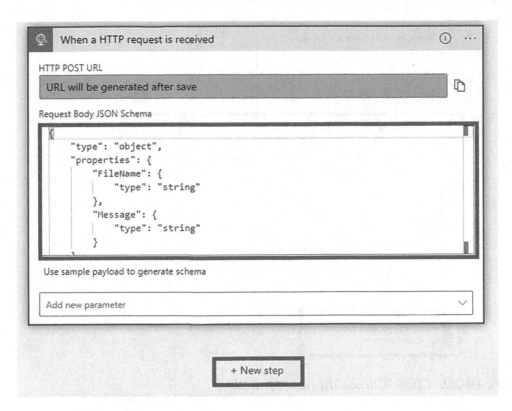

Figure 19-28. *Click "+ New step"*

You will see multiple connectors along with the related actions and triggers. Enter **Azure Function** in the search box and then click the "Choose an Azure function" option present in the actions. See Figure 19-29.

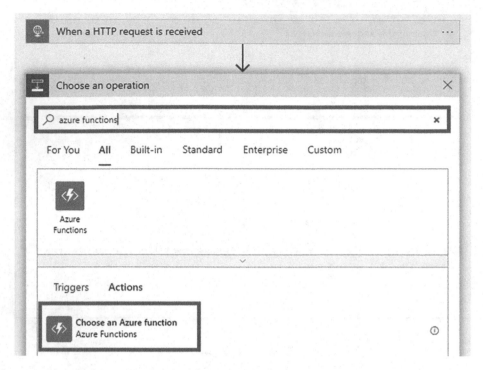

Figure 19-29. *Click "Choose an Azure function"*

Since there can be multiple function apps in your subscription, you will have to select one. Click the EncryptFunc function app. See Figure 19-30.

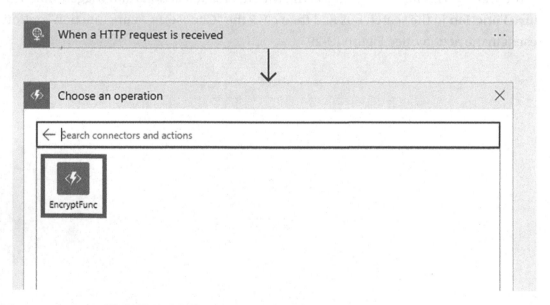

Figure 19-30. *Click EncryptFunc*

Since a function app can contain multiple functions, you will have to select the function. Let's click the HttpTrigger1 function. See Figure 19-31.

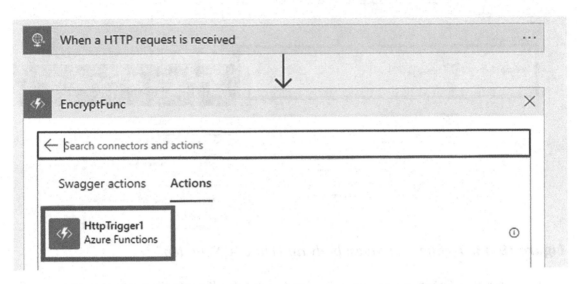

Figure 19-31. *Click HttpTrigger1*

As your function is expecting a MessageContent from the body of the request payload, you need to define MessageContent. Define a JSON payload with a key named MessageContent with the value of the message sent in the request payload of your "When a HTTP request is received" trigger. It can be found in the "Dynamic content" menu. After defining the request body, click "+ New step." Your function will take this message, encrypt it, and return the encrypted message in the request body. See Figure 19-32.

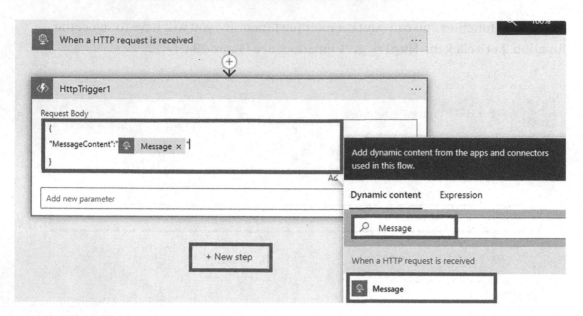

Figure 19-32. *Define the request body and click "+ New step"*

Enter **Google Drive** in the search box and select the "Create file" action to create a file in Google Drive. See Figure 19-33.

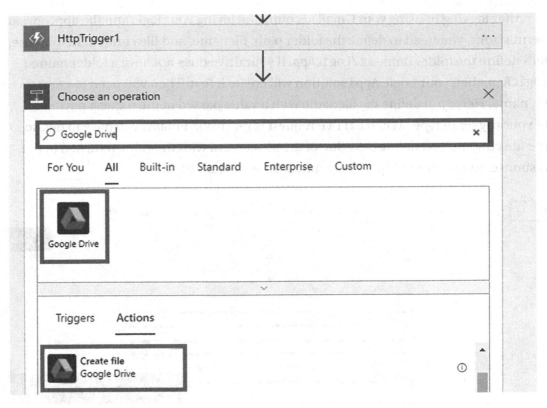

Figure 19-33. *Click "Create file"*

Now, you will have to click "Sign in" to log in using your Gmail account. This is a mandatory step to allow access to your Logic Apps solution to create files in your Google Drive. See Figure 19-34.

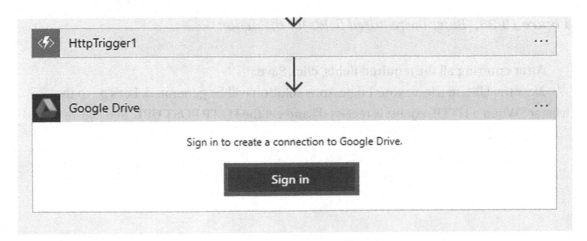

Figure 19-34. *Click "Sign in"*

After logging in using your Gmail account and giving your logic app the appropriate permissions, you need to define the folder path, filename, and file content. In this case, let's define the folder name as /LogicApp. If your drive does not have a folder named LogicApp, then your Logic Apps solution will create it first. Then you need to enter the filename. Here, you define the filename with a value passed in the request payload of your trigger of type "When a HTTP request is received." Finally, you have to define the file content. You define the value of the file content with the value returned in the response body of your HttpTrigger1 function. See Figure 19-35.

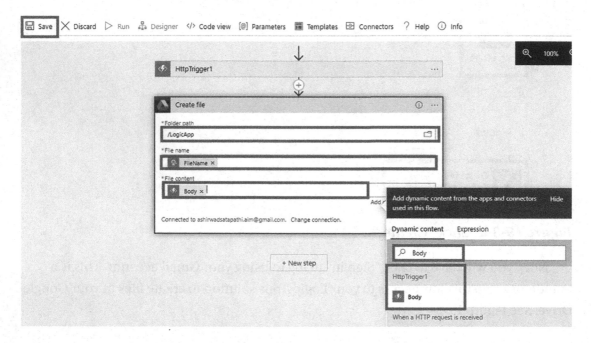

Figure 19-35. *Enter the required fields for the action*

After entering all the required fields, click Save.

Now the URL to trigger your Logic Apps solution will be generated. Let's go to the trigger "When a HTTP request is received" and get the HTTP POST URL. See Figure 19-36.

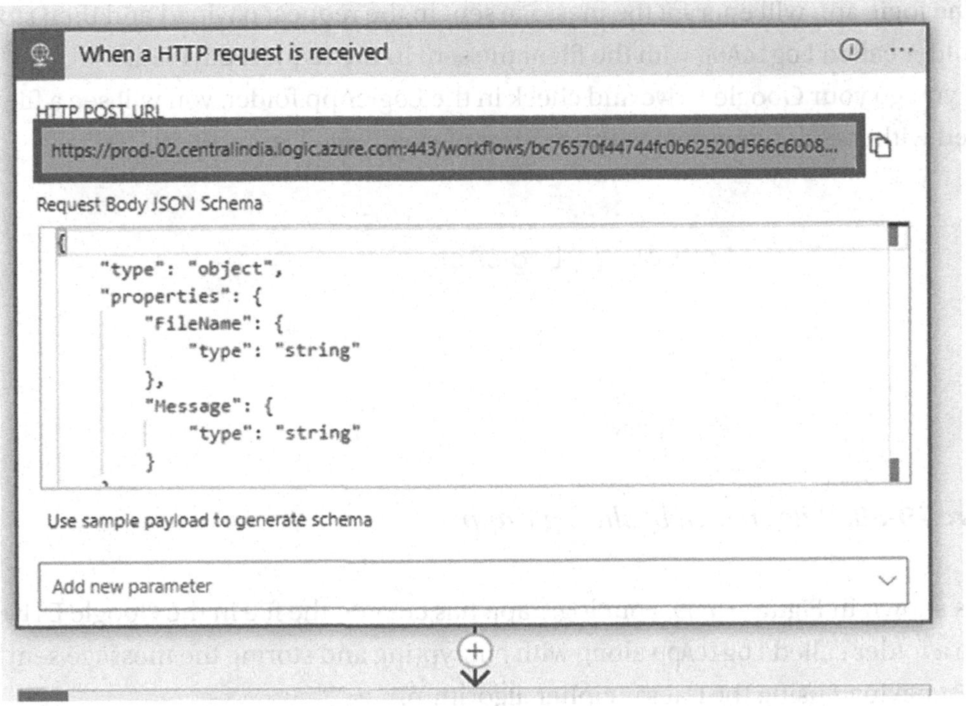

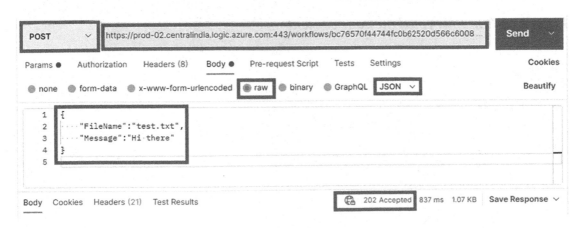

Figure 19-36. *Copy the HTTP POST URL*

To test your logic app, open Postman and add a request. Paste the HTTP POST URL that you copied from your logic app in the URL bar and define the request type as POST. In the request body, send a name along with its value in JSON format and click Send. As shown in the response body in Figure 19-37, you get the desired response from your logic app. This will trigger the logic app and start the workflow.

Figure 19-37. *Click Send*

The logic app will encrypt the message sent in the request payload and then store it in a folder called LogicApp with the filename sent in the request payload.

If you go your Google Drive and check in the LogicApp folder, you will see a file created with the filename sent in the request payload. See Figure 19-38.

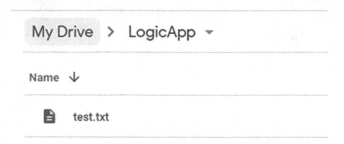

Figure 19-38. *File created by the logic app*

As shown in Figure 19-39, your logic app has created the file in the Google Drive inside a folder called LogicApp along with encrypting and storing the message sent in the request payload using the Caesar cipher algorithm.

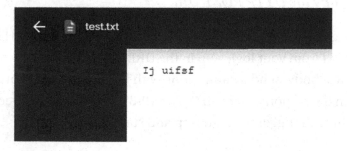

Figure 19-39. *Encrypted message content*

Summary

In this chapter, you learned about the Logic Apps service and ways to create a serverless workflow using Logic Apps in the Azure portal to solve different problems with the help of different connectors, actions, and triggers. First, you created a serverless API using the Logic Apps service app and tested it with Postman using triggers and actions. Then, you looked into ways to integrate an Azure function into a Logic Apps workflow and used the response returned from the function in other actions of your workflow. You also explored ways to use the Google Drive connectors by using the "Create file" action in your workflow to create a file with the message shared in the response of your Azure function. Logic Apps solutions are a perfect place to start building low-code serverless workflows. In the next chapter, you will look into some of the best practices followed by industry leaders while building, designing, and deploying serverless workloads.

CHAPTER 20

Best Practices and Pitfalls to Avoid

We have explored different concepts of the service called Azure Functions in detail. You have learned about the available mechanisms to build an Azure function using C# and deploy it to the Azure environment. You also explored how to create Azure DevOps pipelines for Azure functions. You created several Azure functions based on frequently used triggers and bindings and learned about many important aspects that will help you build enterprise-grade solutions using functions. By now, you have all the necessary knowledge to work with functions in production scenarios.

You learned how to integrate Azure functions with Logic Apps solutions in the previous chapter. In this chapter, you will explore the best practices that you should follow while designing and building functions.

Structure of the Chapter

In this chapter, you will explore the following design aspects for the Azure Functions service:

- Design guidelines and best practices
- Pitfalls to avoid

Objectives

After studying this chapter, you will be able to do the following:

- Design efficient serverless solutions using Azure Functions
- Understand the do's and don'ts of designing and building functions with Azure Functions

501

© Ashirwad Satapathi and Abhishek Mishra 2021
A. Satapathi and A. Mishra, *Hands-on Azure Functions with C#*, https://doi.org/10.1007/978-1-4842-7122-3_20

Design Guidelines and Best Practices

You must follow design guidelines and implement best practices while building solutions for Azure Functions. Following best practices will ensure that you build efficient, robust, fault-tolerant, highly available, and highly scalable solutions. Azure Functions is a serverless service, and you do not have any control over the underlying hosting infrastructure and how each function will scale. So, you must design the solutions based on Azure Functions to run on the underlying infrastructure in an optimized manner and scale per the business requirements. Though you do not have any control over the underlying code, you can design your solution efficiently and utilize the underlying infrastructure and the hosting environment optimally. You just have to pick a design that best suits your business requirements. For example, if you need to build a long-running task that will run on Azure Functions, it may not be a good idea to host this long-running task on a Consumption Plan. The Consumption Plan can run your task for 10 minutes after which the execution will get timed out. In other words, you cannot run any code in an Azure function for more than 10 minutes on the Consumption Plan. You also need to decide on an efficient way to manage and monitor the functions executing your application code.

Let's explore some of the best practices and design guidelines listed here that you must follow to build a solution based using the Azure Functions service:

- Decide whether to use functions or not for your scenario

- Choose the best programing language

- Choose the best hosting plan

- Pick a stateful or stateless solution

- Mitigate delay startups

- Get the right bill fitting your budget

- Handle long-running code

- Facilitate integration and communication among other Azure and external services

- Identify and manage the bottlenecks

- Make your solution fault tolerant

- Secure the APIs developed using Azure Functions

- Facilitate efficient monitoring and debug failures

- Incorporate DevOps practices and bring in an infrastructure-as-code (IaC) approach

- Bring in a defensive programming approach

Decide to Use Functions or Not for Your Scenario

In an ideal scenario, functions are serverless offerings. You do not have any control over the underlying infrastructure or the hosting environment. You do not even have any control over the scaling aspects; the underlying infrastructure scales as and when the application needs. So, you must validate whether your code can run in a serverless offering or not.

You may have scenarios where you need greater control over the hosting environment or need to install some additional software to support the execution of your code. In such scenarios, you cannot execute your code on Azure Functions. You do not have an option to manipulate the underlying hosting environment or install any software on the underlying infrastructure in the case of Azure Functions. You may have two options here. You can either look for a platform-as-a-service (PaaS) offering for the additional software that you need and consume the software from that PaaS-based software or choose to host your application on an infrastructure-as-a-service (IaaS) virtual machine. For example, say you have developed a .NET Core API that uses Apache Kafka. On the on-premises server, you can install Apache Kafka and host the .NET Core API project. If you are planning to host the API on Azure Functions, you should use Azure Service Bus, an alternative PaaS service for Apache Kafka on Azure, and then host the .NET Core API on Azure Functions. Alternatively, you can use virtual machine and install both the components together on the virtual machine.

In the same .NET Core API and Apache Kafka example, the API code in the .NET Core API project might run for a longer duration. Azure functions are best suited to run code for a short duration. In such scenarios, you should consider hosting your code on Azure WebApp and using the Azure Service Bus instead of Apache Kafka. Alternatively, you can choose to use Azure virtual machines. In the case of pure serverless functions, you use the Consumption Plan. However, you can use a Dedicated Plan that is the same as the App Service Plan, because using the Dedicated Plan is almost the same as using Azure WebApp.

503

Using a PaaS solution gives you greater control over the scaling aspects. You can define your autoscale rules or even choose to scale manually. If you need greater control over the scaling aspects, prefer hosting your code on Azure WebApp instead of Azure Functions.

Note   To sum up, if you need greater control over the hosting environment, then host your code on virtual machines. If you can find an alternate PaaS service for the code dependency, then go for Azure WebApp. You get greater control over the scaling aspects in the case of Azure Web App and virtual machines.

Choose the Correct Programing Language

The choice of programming language for your application is highly crucial. You can use various programming languages such as C#, Java, Python, TypeScript, PowerShell, and many more to implement an Azure function. However, before choosing a programming language, validate if that programming language can easily handle all the requirements for the scenario. There can be a scenario where a supported programming language covers part of the requirements, and another programming language supports the rest. For example, the application to be hosted on the function app needs to interact with a third-party application that does not expose REST endpoints. Instead, the third-party application supports using a Java package to connect to the application. In this case, you need to identify all the necessary code that interacts with this third-party application and then break the application code into multiple chunks. The chunks using the Java package to interact will use functions based on the Java programming language, and all the other chunks can use C#-based functions. In such cases, think of splitting the requirements across multiple Azure functions based on different supported programming languages.

One more challenge we face while migrating the workloads to the cloud is a developer's existing skills. You may find that some developers do not have the right skills to build the code using the programming language you have chosen for an Azure function. In such scenarios, you may choose to cross-train your developers with the necessary skills needed for the selected programming language, or you can check whether your function can be implemented with workarounds using the developer's existing skills.

Choice of Hosting Plan

Selecting the right hosting plan for the Azure function is an important design aspect. If you plan to build a pure serverless scenario, you can choose to use the Consumption Plan. The following are the characteristics of a Consumption Plan:

- Pay only when the Azure function executes

- Runs for a short time interval

- No control over underlying infrastructure or hosting environment

- No control over how the Azure function scales

If you have code that runs for a short time interval, you may choose to use the Consumption Plan. The underlying infrastructure will manage all the scaling aspects for your Azure function. If the incoming load increases, the underlying infrastructure adds new instances for the Azure function and balances the load. When the load decreases, the additional instances get decommissioned automatically. You cannot control how the functions scale and the number of instances that get removed and added as part of scaling. You pay for all the function instances that get added. However, you get billed only for the time interval when your code runs. If you have a function that runs for a short time interval and you do not need to control the Azure function's scaling aspects, you should choose the Consumption Plan.

The function does its work and goes to sleep once the execution completes. When you need to execute the function for the next time, it is not instantaneous. It wakes up from the sleep state once it gets triggered and starts executing. So, there is always a delay in serving the request when the function awakes from the sleep state. This delay in serving the request is referred to as the *cold-start* phenomenon. However, once the function is active, you will not face the cold-start phenomenon as long as the function does not go into the sleep state. To avoid this cold-start problem, you can use the Premium Plan. The Premium Plan guarantees that at least a single instance is always available to serve your incoming requests. You also get some level of control over the compute requirements by choosing one of the tiers supported by the Premium Plan.

You may have a requirement where the Azure function runs for a longer duration. For example, if you already have an App Service Plan, you can share it with an Azure function hosting the long-running code. In such a case, you can use a Dedicated Plan or an App Service Plan. However, Dedicated Plans are not true serverless functions and are the same as App Service Plans. You can define the autoscale settings and get complete control over how the function scales.

Note   To sum up, if you have a true serverless scenario and your code runs for a short duration, then choose the Consumption Plan. To avoid cold-start issues, you can either use the Premium Plan or use the Dedicated Plan. You can also use the Dedicated Plan if you have long-running code and you need greater control over how the function scales.

Pick a Stateful or Stateless Solution

You need to evaluate the customer scenario and decide whether you need to pass the execution state from one function to another. For example, say you are building a shopping cart application. You have a function that validates the customer order and passes on the payment status to the following function that processes the order if the payment is complete. In this scenario, you need to pass data from the first function to another. You may have a more complex scenario where you need to build multiple functions, and each function executes like a workflow. For example, you may have two functions processing data, and these two functions will send the data to a third function that will aggregate the data and process it further. You need to build a stateful solution for all such scenarios. You can orchestrate stateful functions workflows using Azure Durable Functions. We should use the Azure Durable Functions service for all such scenarios where you can facilitate exchanging data and state among functions.

You may have simple scenarios such as executing code based on a schedule or building an Azure function set that performs CRUD operations and gives you the data results when invoked using an HTTP trigger. In such scenarios, you can use Azure Functions instead of Azure Durable Functions as you are not interested in maintaining and exchanging data among the functions.

Note   You can also build workflow using Azure Logic Apps. For the stateful scenarios discussed, you can use Logic Apps instead of Durable Functions. However, Durable Functions is best suited for programmers. Programmers can customize the implementation to a larger extent using Durable Functions.

Mitigate Delay Startups

Azure functions execute when triggered. Once they complete execution, they go into an idle state and finally into a sleep state. Azure functions wake up and start executing only when they are triggered. However, the functions do not start executing instantaneously when triggered. They take some time to wake up from the sleep state and get warmed up before they can start processing the request. As mentioned, this phenomenon is referred to as the *cold-start* phenomenon. If you are building a real-time application, then the function needs to be active at all times. It must execute as soon as it gets invoked. You must have at least a warmed-up instance that can start execution as soon the function gets triggered. For all such scenarios, you cannot use Azure functions running on a Consumption Plan. You may choose to design an alternative solution using Azure WebApp or some other service that will take care of the real-time needs of the application. Alternatively, you can choose to run your Azure functions on a Premium Plan. The Premium Plan ensures that at least one of the instances is always up and ready to serve an incoming request.

For example, say you are building an Internet of Things (IoT) application that monitors the temperature of a room. If the temperature goes beyond a particular limit, the IoT application needs to invoke an Azure function that can instantly generate a notification or a warning. You cannot run this Azure function on the Consumption Plan as you may encounter a delay in starting up the Azure function when triggered, and this will delay the generation of the notification. If the notification gets delayed, then there can be severe consequences for the apparatus and systems in the room being monitored. To address such scenarios, you should use a Premium Plan or look for an alternative PaaS service to generate notifications for the system on demand.

Get the Correct Bill to Fit Your Budget

Cost planning is an essential aspect while designing a cloud-based solution for your application. In Azure Functions, you do not have control over the scaling aspects of the hosted application. New instances get added on the fly when the incoming load increases, and you get billed for all the instances that get added. However, you get billed for the period when the function executes on that instance. You may have a scenario when your application needs to scale exponentially during peak hours. In such scenarios, new instances get added on the fly to handle the incoming traffic, and your cost spirals exponentially. You may not have factored in the exponential scaling while designing the Azure function. In such scenarios, you must consider all the scaling scenarios and deduce the actual cost incurred for the Azure function. You may also choose options to control the degree of scaling and plan the number of instances the Azure function can scale so that the cost incurred for the Azure function is well within the limit.

Handle Long-Running Code

Azure functions are best suited to host code that executes for a shorter duration. However, you may have scenarios where you need to run your code for a longer duration. You should consider breaking the code into smaller chunks and running each of these functions in an Azure function in such a scenario. You may have a scenario where you need to run a long-running application. For example, you need to run a polling application that executes for a longer time interval. You may have challenges when splitting such applications into smaller chunks. You can choose to run the Azure function on a Dedicated Plan that allows code to run for a longer time interval to address such scenarios. Alternatively, you can choose to run the Azure function on a web job as a background process or WebApp.

Note   You can break the long-running code into smaller chunks and run each of these smaller chunks in an Azure function. In some scenarios where you cannot break down the code into smaller units, you can host the code on an Azure function running on the Dedicated Plan.

Facilitate Integration and Communication Among Other Azure and External Services

You may need to integrate Azure functions with other Azure services or external services. For example, the Azure function needs to pick the data from the Apache Kafka queue and process it. In all such scenarios, check whether there is an existing binding available to interact with the service. If there are no existing bindings available, try to build a custom binding to help you interface with other services and exchange data. Bindings help you interact with other services declaratively, and you do not need to write much code to get this working. However, suppose you see that you do not have an existing binding that supports your scenario, and it is not easy to implement a custom binding for that scenario. In that case, you can choose to implement custom code in the Azure function or build an external component that can facilitate communication with the external service.

You need to make sure you can communicate with other Azure services and the external component securely. Make sure you bring in the best security practices to make sure that your implementation is secured, reliable, and fault tolerant as much as possible. The security practices can include configuring cross-origin resource sharing (CORS) for your function access, monitoring the incoming request header and the body parameters, filtering out the unwanted or malicious requests, validating the authentication and authorization for the function app, and more.

Identify and Manage the Bottlenecks

Azure functions are serverless components, and the underlying infrastructure takes care of all the scaling needs. The functions can scale to a considerable amount automatically to manage the incoming loads. However, the Azure functions may interface with other PaaS-based or IaaS-based services that can scale within a particular limit. For example, you have an Azure function running on the Consumption Plan. The Azure function inserts data into an Azure SQL Database instance. During peak hours, a large number of concurrent requests hit the Azure function, and the function scales to a large number of instances to handle the incoming traffic. Each of these function instances may hit the Azure SQL Database instance at the same time. Azure SQL Database may not be able to scale to that extent and handle the incoming traffic. This action will result in a performance bottleneck for the Azure SQL Database instance. Even though the Azure function can scale and handle the incoming load, the SQL Database instance cannot scale to that extent. Your solution as a whole incurs performance bottlenecks. You must identify all such scenarios and implement strategies to handle them. You may need to control the degree of concurrency for the Azure functions using queuing mechanisms. You can add the items to be processed in a queue and then send a finite number of items to the Azure function for processing to avoid spinning out a large number of instances while scaling out to manage the incoming load.

Make Your Solution Fault Tolerant

You must make your solution fault tolerant. If the Azure functions fail to process the request, you must have mechanisms to process the request again. You should have a robust retry mechanism in place. The retry count should be a finite number and easily configurable for the solution. For example, if the function fails to process a request, it should send the failed requests to a queue and accumulate all the failed requests. After a specific time interval, it should pick up items for the failed queue one by one and process the request.

You may have a scenario where the Azure function picks up an item from the queue and processes the item. The Azure function may encounter an issue where the function will pick up the item but cannot process it due to the unavailability of another dependent service. This action will result in the function picking up the items from the queue and not processing them. You end up losing all the items in the queue, and none of the items is processed. In all such scenarios, you must have a circuit breaker pattern implemented. If the function fails to process the item in the queue, it should not pick the next item in the queue. It should not pick any item until the depending service is up and the items can get processed. Also, it should add the failed item in another queue to retry processing it later.

Note   The function app can invoke other services either running in the Azure environment or running outside Azure in the on-premises environment or other clouds. These services may fail to process the requests, and the function app will keep invoking these services again and again even if these services are failing. The circuit breaker pattern will help in monitoring these service calls. After a reasonable number of continuous failures, it will instruct the function app not to call these services as if you are breaking the circuit.

There can be many scenarios where we need to have a fault-tolerant mechanism in place. It is highly essential to incorporate fault-tolerant mechanisms so that the Azure function can efficiently execute the business functionality.

Secure the APIs Developed Using Azure Functions

You build APIs using HTTP-triggered Azure functions. These APIs may perform a wide range of actions that can be either simple CRUD operations or complex business logic processing. You must secure these APIs to prevent unauthorized access. The best way to secure them is by integrating the HTTP-triggered Azure functions with the Azure API Management service or an alternate third-party service similar to this. All your requests for these functions will get routed through the API Management service. You can configure and manage the request and response parameters in the header and the body, configure CORS settings, decide on whom to allow and whom not to allow, and do many such activities using the API Management service. You can even integrate the API Management service with Azure Active Directory and perform OAuth-based authentication.

Facilitate Efficient Monitoring and Debug Failures

You must ensure that you integrate Application Insights or any other alternative monitoring and logging third-party solution with Azure Functions. Logs and metrics help you to debug applications. In the case of Azure Functions, you do not have access to the underlying code hosting infrastructure. So, you must log all information and failures to figure out the root cause and use the logs for audit activities.

Application Insights provides an efficient mechanism to capture logs and metrics. You get rich visualizations of the metrics and logs that help you analyze your application, hosting infrastructure, and hosting environment with ease.

Incorporate DevOps Practices and Bring in an IaC Approach

You should avoid working with Azure functions in the portal and build automation to create, deploy, and manage Azure functions. You can create automation scripts that will help you automate your interaction with an Azure function. Automation reduces manual errors, and you will benefit in the long run. For example, say you need to replicate hundreds of Azure functions in the production environment of your customer. It will take a lot of time if you are creating these Azure functions using the portal. You may be prone to make mistakes as this process is repetitive and manual. To address such scenarios efficiently, you should build automation that will help you create Azure functions fast and with zero errors.

You can use the Azure CLI, Azure PowerShell, and IaC offerings like Terraform or Chef to build automation for your Azure functions. You can also use ARM templates to build the automation solution. Using Azure DevOps, you can build the IaC pipeline to spin up the Azure functions, continuous integration to build and package the function code, and a continuous deployment pipeline to deploy the package to the Azure functions.

DevOps-mature organizations prefer using automation solutions for creating and managing cloud resources and infrastructure. You can generate logs for your IaC activities to analyze and audit in the future.

Bring in a Defensive Programming Approach

Applications can run into exceptions at runtime. You should follow a defensive approach while processing the business functionality during runtime exceptions and failures. For example, say your function is processing a couple of images uploaded in Blob Storage. After processing 30 images, an exception occurs, and the function tries to process the images again starting from the first image. As a good practice, the function should not process the first 30 images as they have been already processed, and it should try to process the images starting from the 31st image. In the defensive programming approach, the function should resume processing precisely from where it left off when the exception occurred. Alternatively, you can insert the failed records in a dead-letter queue or a poison queue and try processing the records in the poison or dead-letter queue instead of processing all the records.

Pitfalls to Avoid

The following are some of the pitfalls you must avoid while designing applications using the Azure Functions service:

- Sharing functions in a single function app service

- Processing the input data one piece at a time

- Hosting the production and development functions in the same function app service

- Sharing storage accounts across function app services

Sharing Functions in a Single Function App Service

Do not keep all your functions in a single function app service. If you have too many functions in an app service, your function app may not get enough compute resources to scale and perform optimally. Analyze the resource compute requirements carefully and then plan the number of functions you can host in a function app service. You can logically group the Azure functions based on performance or scaling aspects of the business functionality they are performing.

Processing the Input Data One Piece at a Time

Do not keep processing the input data one by one. You make a round-trip, and the function keeps itself busy every time you get input data. The worst is when you are getting the input data as part of the triggers. The functions need to be triggered again and again. Try to get the input data in batches and process the data in batches. This action will increase the performance.

Hosting the Production and Development Functions in the Same Function App Service

Do not use the same function app service to host production and development functions. Keep the function app services separate for different scenarios. A function app service runs on a hosting plan. The hosting plan defines the underlying infrastructure and the computing needs for the function app service. If you are using the same hosting plan across multiple function apps, the underlying infrastructure will be shared, impacting the function app's performance. A function app running in a development environment may need less computing power than a function app running in an actual production environment. So, you need a lower hosting plan in the development environment as compared to the production environment. Hence, it is advisable to have a separate function app service running on a hosting plan of its own as per the computing needs. Try to leverage deployment slots as much as possible. You may plan to have a deployment slot for the staging environment and a slot for the production environment. You can promote new code changes to the staging slot, test the code in the staging slot, and once all your test passes, swap the code in the staging slot with the code in the production slot. The new code changes will go to the production slot, and the old code running in the production slot earlier will be there in the staging slot. This swap mechanism will ensure that the old production code is intact in the staging slot and can be rolled back into the production slot if needed.

Sharing Storage Accounts Across Function App Services

You must associate a storage account with a function app service while creating it. Do not share storage accounts across function app services that are hosting functions. Sharing storage accounts will bring down the performance of Azure functions, and in some scenarios each of the functions may generate a high volume of storage transactions.

Summary

In this chapter, you learned how to design a solution using Azure functions efficiently. You explored best practices to follow while designing a solution using Azure functions. You also explored the pitfalls that you must avoid while building solutions for Azure functions. The better you plan the Azure functions, the more likely you will build a highly performant and robust solution using Azure Functions.

The following are the key takeaways from this chapter:

- You must follow best practices to build performant and robust Azure functions.

- The best practices include selecting the right hosting plan, using the correct programming language to fit your scenario, planning the cost for your Azure function solutions, incorporating retry mechanisms in the case of failures, and many more.

- You must avoid pitfalls such as sharing a function app service with a large number of functions, sharing storage accounts, not processing data in batches, and keeping different function app services for production and development scenarios.

We have come to the end of this book. In this book, you learned how to design, build, deploy, manage, and follow best practices while designing functions for the Azure Functions service. You learned advanced concepts such as how to use durable functions and run functions on Azure Kubernetes Service in detail. By now, you should understand all the necessary concepts needed to build a production-grade Azure function.

Index

A

Active directory
    authentication/authorization (*see*
        Authentication/authorization)
    automation, 290
    features, 290
    identity management, 290
    objective, 290
    structure, 289
Application insights/monitor
    diagnostics (*see* Auto-diagnose issues)
    logging
        creation, 238
        enable option, 236–237
        function app, 235, 238–239
        get function URL, 242
        Http trigger, 240
        logs, 243–244
        monitoring tab, 235–236
        resource, 234, 242–243
        run.csx file, 241
        testing code, 241
        transaction search tab, 243
    objectives, 234
    structure, 233
Application programming interface (API)
    Cosmos DB, 203–232
    key permission, 84

management service (*see* Management
    service)
    serverless, 165–201
    table staorage binding, 125–146
Artificial intelligence (AI), 422
Authentication/authorization
    app creation, 295
    assigned roles tab, 305
    authentication tab, 299
    authorization (function code), 309–312
    credentials, 301–302
    definition, 291
    function app, 292, 295–296
    Function.proj file, 308
    get function Url, 298
    grant admin consent/permissions, 304
    Http trigger, 297
    identity provider, 299
    Microsoft identity provider, 300–301
    permissions tab, 303–304
    process, 292
    registrations, 303
    resource, 292
    review creation, 293–294
    roles, 291
    service editor, 307
    template ID, 306
    testing code, 298
    users tab, 305

517

W, X, Y, Z

Printed in the United States
by Baker & Taylor Publisher Services